"Hernán Gómez Bruera looks inside the PT and its social networks to understand how state power has transformed the party's reform agenda. His book provides a unique and highly insightful account of the ways in which parties with origins in social movements adapt to—and are transformed by—the exercise of political power in formal governing institutions."
—Kenneth M. Roberts, *Cornell University*

"Gómez Bruera provides a very smart, comprehensive, and nuanced account of the PT's rise to power and how it has been transformed by power. Poised between its roots in Brazil's social movements and the imperatives of governing in a fragmented polity, the PT's trajectory is a fascinating and revealing case study in the possibilities and limits of transformative politics."
—Patrick Heller, *Brown University*

Lula, the Workers' Party and the Governability Dilemma in Brazil

While scholars, activists and pundits from around the world have heralded the Lula years as a breakthrough for poverty reduction and the forthcoming emergence of Brazil as a dynamic economic superpower, many of their counterparts in the country as well as a number of Brazilianists elsewhere have expressed great disappointment.

Tracing back the trajectory of Brazilian Workers' Party (Partido dos Trabalhadores—PT), Hernán F. Gómez Bruera explores how holding national executive public office contributed decisively to a pragmatic shift away from the party's radical redistributive and participatory platform, earning the approbation of international audiences and criticisms of domestic progressives. The author explains why a unique party, which originally promoted a radical progressive agenda of socio-economic redistribution and participatory democracy, eventually adopted an orthodox economic policy, formed legislative alliances with conservative parties, altered its relationship with social movements and relegated the participatory agenda to the sidelines.

Touching on multiple dimensions, from economic policy and land reform to social policy, this book offers a distinct explanation as to why progressive parties of mass-based origin shift to the center over time and alter their relationships with their allies in civil society. Written in a clear and accessible style and featuring an enormous wealth of firsthand accounts from party leaders at all levels and within different factions, Gómez Bruera offers much needed new insights into why progressive parties alter their discourses and strategies when they occupy executive public office.

Hernán F. Gómez Bruera has a PhD from the Institute of Development Studies, at the University of Sussex, with an academic interest on Latin American and Brazilian politics, progressive parties, participatory democracy and social movements. His first two books are *Desde el Sur* (Altamira, Buenos Aires) and *Conversaciones sobre el Hambre: Brasil y el derecho a la alimentación* (CEDRSSA, México). He has worked as a consultant for international organizations, as a political analyst and as a freelance journalist.

Routledge Studies in Latin American Politics

1 **Research and International Trade Policy Negotiations**
Knowledge and Power in Latin America
Edited by Mercedes Botto

2 **The United Nations in Latin America**
Aiding Development
Francis Adams

3 **Fear and Crime in Latin America**
Redefining State-Society Relations
Lucía Dammert

4 **Populism in Venezuela**
Ryan K. Brading

5 **Civil Society and Participatory Governance**
Municipal Councils and Social Housing Programs in Brazil
Maureen M. Donaghy

6 **Representation and Effectiveness in Latin American Democracies**
Congress, Judiciary and Civil Society
Edited by Moira B. MacKinnon and Ludovico Feoli

7 **Lula, the Workers' Party and the Governability Dilemma in Brazil**
Hernán F. Gómez Bruera

Lula, the Workers' Party and the Governability Dilemma in Brazil

Hernán F. Gómez Bruera

NEW YORK AND LONDON

First published 2013
by Routledge
711 Third Avenue, New York, NY 10017

Simultaneously published in the UK
by Routledge
2 Park Square, Milton Park, Abingdon, Oxfordshire OX14 4RN

First issued in paperback 2015

Routledge is an imprint of the Taylor & Francis Group, an informa business

© 2013 Taylor & Francis

The right of Hernán F. Gómez Bruera to be identified as author of this work has been asserted by him in accordance with sections 77 and 78 of the Copyright, Designs and Patents Act 1988.

All rights reserved. No part of this book may be reprinted or reproduced or utilised in any form or by any electronic, mechanical, or other means, now known or hereafter invented, including photocopying and recording, or in any information storage or retrieval system, without permission in writing from the publishers.

Trademark Notice: Product or corporate names may be trademarks or registered trademarks, and are used only for identification and explanation without intent to infringe.

Library of Congress Cataloging-in-Publication Data
Gómez Bruera, Hernán F.
 Lula, the workers' party and the governability dilemma in Brazil / Hernán F. Gómez Bruera.
  pages cm. — (Routledge studies in Latin American politics)
 1. Brazil—Politics and government. 2. Lula, 1945– 3. Partido dos Trabalhadores (Brazil) 4. Brazil—Economic conditions. 5. Brazil—Social conditions. 6. Brazil—Foreign relations. I. Title.
 F2538.3.G67 2013
 981—dc23
 2012046635

ISBN 13: 978-1-138-92638-7 (pbk)
ISBN 13: 978-0-415-83432-2 (hbk)

Typeset in Sabon
by Apex CoVantage, LLC

We have to keep in mind that the only way to get into office and achieve the structural reforms we want is by having a minimum base in the popular movement. If we win the elections and forget the movement by thinking that only our [political] alliances will allow us to make reforms, we might be able to rule for four years, but we will not be able to carry out those reforms that gave us important victories in some cities.

> Luiz Inácio Lula da Silva during a meeting with party and social leaders in 1995.

In 2002, what was the meaning of governability for us? Governability meant having a majority in Congress, maintaining our social and historical base of support and broadening it towards other sectors, particularly the business sector, while also making sure that the economic crisis would not deepen. If the economic crisis had deepened, Lula would not have lasted even one year in power.

> Author's interview with José Dirceu, Minister for the Civil House of the Presidency, January 2009.

Contents

Acknowledgements		xi
Acronyms		xv
	Introduction	1
1	The Challenge of Governability for Progressive Parties	13

PART I
Before The Lula Administration

2	The Formative Phase of the PT and Its Socio-Political Field	27
3	Moving towards the State: The Reconfiguration of the PT Field	42
4	Social and Elite-Centred Strategies at Work: The PT in Sub-National Executive Office	60

PART II
The Lula Years

5	Political Governability under Lula: The Elite-Centred Strategy in Ascendancy	85
6	From the "Lula Monster" to an Icon of the "Responsible Left"	105
7	Participation without Counter-Hegemony	117

8	Securing Social Governability: Dealing with Allies in Civil Society	136
9	Accomplishments within the Balance of Forces	153

Final Remarks   165
Notes   175
References   205
Newspapers and Magazines   229
Appendix I: Statistical Information on Interviewees   233
Appendix II: Biographies of Interviewees   235
Appendix III: Answers to Semi-Structured Questions   251
Index   257

Acknowledgements

I first travelled to Brazil in November 2002, shortly after Lula won the second round of the presidential election, and I went back several times between 2003 and 2004, while I was working for the Food and Agriculture Organisation of the United Nations. As part of my work I had the opportunity to interview a number of social leaders and government officials and to witness some of the attempts of the new government to bring innovations in the social policy arena. It was a time of great hope and expectation in which I developed an interest on both the Workers' Party, whose electoral triumph had great impact on the Left in Latin America, and on civil society in Brazil, which was expected to play a key role in one of Lula's most important policies at the time—the Zero Hunger programme.

Things looked different in 2005, however, when I went back to Brazil to find the country wrapped in the midst of a major corruption scandal. Among several progressive leaders with which I had contact, hope had been taken over by disillusion. This research, which I initiated in Autumn 2007, started as an attempt to understand what happened with Lula, the PT and its relationship with civil society, as much as to reflect on its meaning for left-of-centre parties in Latin America, which have also been of my interest as a political analyst and as a former journalist. This book is a revised version of my PhD thesis "The Governability Dilemma: *Progressive Politics under Lula and the Brazilian Workers' Party*", presented at the Institute of Development Studies (IDS), in the University of Sussex.

I am indebted to my friend Gustavo Gordillo, who was very supportive at one of the most difficult periods of my life, for spurring in me the interest in Brazil and its progressive politics, over 10 years ago. Together we published *Conversaciones sobre el Hambre: Brasil y el derecho a la alimentación* [*Conversations about Hunger: Brazil and the Right to Food*], a book in which we reflected on the crucial moment in Brazilian history, gathering a number of interviews with social leaders and politicians. For stimulating me to study the PT, I am thankful to Professor Zander Navarro, with whom I elaborated my first research project on this subject, and who supervised my work at IDS during the first stages of my PhD. I am also thankful to Zander for his support while conducting fieldwork in Brazil.

Acknowledgements

This book owes everything to Professor Peter Houtzager, my main supervisor in IDS, who helped me to structure my thinking from the earliest days until recently. Peter commented on my writing in great detail and challenged me far beyond what I had perceived as my limit. During long hours in the cafes of Brighton and London, we discussed the different chapters of this study, sometimes even specific paragraphs. Needless to say what a great intellect he is, and despite all the extreme suffering that he caused me during the past five years, I can say that he is also a good human being. I am also thankful to Professor Alexander Shankland, who co-supervised my work during the final stages. Early on, while I was doing fieldwork, I had the opportunity to work with Alex on other research projects, which gave me the possibility to travel from North to South Brazil, learn from his knowledge of the country, its civil society and its participatory instruments. Alex provided very useful inputs to this investigation.

I am thankful to the Participation and Governance teams at IDS, especially to its team leaders, John Gaventa and Fiona Wilson, who gave useful comments to my work and offered their support. I am also grateful to Andrés Mejía and to several students with whom I shared ideas and friendship during these years, such as Linnet Taylor, Shandana Mohmand, Sofía Donoso, Suchi Pande, Ricardo Santos, Teresa Armijos, Beatriz Pérez Orto, Luciana Lupo and Julia Pacheco Nanana.

I would like to thank Professor Kenneth Roberts, with whom I discussed my work in 2010 during the time I spent as a visiting researcher in the Department of Government at Cornell University. I am also grateful to Professor Sidney Tarrow, from whom I also received useful suggestions, as much as to Professor Gustavo Flores Macías. I also would like to thank other scholars at Cornell and in the United States who gave advice on parts of my work, such as John French, from Duke University; Michael Coppedge, from the Kellogg Institute and PhD students Janice Gallagher, from Cornell; Brian Palmer Rubin, from Berkeley; Genaro Lozano, from the New School. Fiona Macaulay, from Bradford University, and Marc Berenson, from IDS, gave useful comments to my PhD thesis which were also very helpful when writing this book.

I am grateful to each and every person who shared with me their time, opinions and reflections, either formally or informally, during fieldwork. The good disposition of PT members gave this work an empirical richness that it would not have otherwise. I am especially thankful to those interviewees who trusted me and were particularly open, as much as to those who granted me access to their colleagues. Among others, I express my gratitude to Clara Ant, Ricardo Berzoini, Glauco Piai, Tarson Núñez, Valter Pomar, Clarice dos Santos and Maria Pedroso. I am also thankful to the party's think tank, the *Fundaçao Perseu Abramo*, and especially to Carlos Menegozzo, who kindly and diligently provided access to the valuable archives of this institution.

During the time I spent in Brazil I was able to discuss my work with and receive great support from a number of scholars. I am specially thankful to Oswaldo Amaral, who offered me support from the start; Raquel Meneguello and Walter Belik, from the University of Campinas; Alvaro Comin and Vera Schattan, from CEBRAP; Glauco Arbix, André Singer and Wager Romão, from the University of São Paulo; José Ribeiro, from the Federal University of São Carlos and Emília Prestes, from the Federal University of Paraíba.

Many Brazilians helped me to make my life happy and easier while doing research. In particular, I am indebted with the very generous Carlos Morales, Margaret Baroni and Julia Baroni, who opened their house in Brasília before even knowing me, and who contributed to my work in all possible ways. I am also thankful to Penny McKeon, Keith Guy Hjortshoj, Lizzie Johnson, Mir Rueda, Yvonne Gater and Alfonso Martínez for their assistance and solidarity.

During these years, I was able to present different parts of my work in a number of workshops and seminars. I am grateful to Fiona Wilson, for her invitation to participate in the workshop "Citizenship and Governance at the Margins of the State: Latin America between Post-Conflict to Neo-populism", organised by the Graduate School of International Development Studies, at Roskilde University in Denmark. In this workshop I discussed my research project and receive useful comments from Evelina Dagnino and Jenny Pierce, to whom I am also thankful. I also express my gratitude to Timothy Power and Oswaldo Amaral, for inviting me to present my work in the workshop "The PT from Lula to Dilma: Explaining Change", organised by the Brazilian Studies Centre at the University of Oxford. I would like to thank the participants of this seminar for stimulating discussions that were relevant to this book.

Funding for this research was possible with a four-year scholarship awarded by Mexico's National Council on Science and Technology and a one-year complementary scholarship from the Mexican Ministry of Education. A contribution to cover fieldwork expenses derived from a travel grant of the Society for Latin American Studies, based in London.

Last but not least, I am grateful to Riccardo D'Emidio, for an unquantifiable number of reasons that would take another entire book to enumerate.

Acronyms

ABC (or ABCD)	Santo André, São Bernardo do Campo, São Caetano and Diadema (the industrial suburbs of São Paulo)
ABONG	*Associação Brasileira de Organizações não governamentais*—Brazilian Association of Nongovernmental Organisations
AE	*Articulação de Esquerda*—Left Articulation
ANC	African National Congress
ARENA	*Aliança de Renovação Nacional*—Alliance for National Renewal
CAT	*Central Autônoma dos Trabalhadores*—Central of Autonomous Workers
CDES	*Conselho de Desenvolvimento Econômico e Social*—Council on Economic and Social Development
CEB	*Comunidades Eclesiais de Base*—Ecclesiastical Base Communities
CGT	*Central Geral dos Trabalhadores*—General Central of Workers
CGTB	*Confederação Geral dos Trabalhadores*—General Confederation of Workers
CLT	*Consolidação das Leis do Trabalho*—Consolidation of the Labour Laws
CM	*Campo Majoritário*—Majority Camp
CMP	*Central de Movimentos Populares*—Center for Popular Movements
CNA	*Confederação Nacional de Agricultura*—National Confederation of Agriculture
CNB	*Construindo um Novo Brasil*—Building a New Brazil
CNC	*Confederação Nacional do Comércio*—National Trade Confederation
CNF	*Confederação Nacional das Instituições Financeiras*—National Confederation of Financial Institutions

CNI	*Confederação Nacional da Indústria*—National Confederation of Industry
CNT	*Confederação Nacional dos Transportes*—National Confederation of Transport
CNTI	*Confederação Nacional dos Trabalhadores da Indústria*—National Confederation of Industrial Workers
CO	*Causa Operária*—Labour Cause
CONTAG	*Confederação Nacional de Trabalhadores na Agricultura*—National Confederation of Agricultural Workers
CPERGS	*Centro dos Professores do Estado do Rio Grande do Sul*, Teachers' Union of the State of Rio Grande do Sul
CS	*Convergência Socialista*—Socialist Convergence
CUT	*Central Única dos Trabalhadores*—Central Workers' Union
DIAP	*Departamento Intersindical de Assesoria Parlamentar*—Union Board for Parliamentary Advice
DIEESE	*Departamento Intersindical de Estatística e Estudos Sócioeconômicos*—Union Board for Statistical and Socio-Economic Studies
DS	*Democracia Socialista*—Socialist Democracy
FAT	*Fundo de Amparo ao Trabalhador*—Workers' Assistance Fund
FEDERASUL	*Federação das Asociações Empresariais do Rio Grande do Sul*—Federation of Business Associations of Rio Grande do Sul
FIESP	*Federação das Industrias do Estado de São Paulo*—Federation of Industries of the State of São Paulo
FNT	*Forum National de Trabalho*—National Labour Forum
FS	*Forza Socialista*—Socialist Strength
FUNCEF	*Fundação dos Economiários Federais*—the pension fund of the (state bank) Caixa Económica Federal
IBGE	*Instituto Brasileiro de Geografía e Estatística*—Brazilian Institute for Geography and Statistics
ICMS	*Imposto sobre Circulação de Mercadorias e Serviços*—Tax over the Circulation of Goods and Services
IPEA	*Instituto de Pesquisa Econômica Aplicada*—Institute for Applied Economic Research
IPTU	*Imposto sobre a Propriedade Predial e Territorial Urbana*—Property Tax on Urban Land and Homeownership
MAS	*Movimento al Socialismo*—Movement to Socialism
MDB	*Movimento Democrático Brasileiro*—Brazilian Democratic Movement

MDF	*Movimento de Defensa do Favelado*—Slums-Dwellers' Defence Movement	
MP	*Mensagem ao Partido*—Message to the Party	
MST	*Movimento dos Trabalhadores Rurais sem Terra*—Landless Rural Workers' Movement	
NGO	Nongovernment Organisation	
PAC	*Programa de Aceleração do Crecimento*—Growth Acceleration Programme	
PB	*Orçamento participativo*—Participatory Budget	
PCB	*Partido Comunista Brasileiro*—Brazilian Communist Party	
PCdoB	*Partido Comunista do Brasil*—Communist Party of Brazil	
PDS	*Partido Democrático Social*—Democratic Social Party	
PDT	*Partido Democrático Trabalhista*—Workers' Democratic Party	
PFL	*Partido da Frente Liberal*—Liberal Front Party	
PHS	*Partido Humanista da Solidaridade*—Party of Humanist Solidarity	
PL	*Partido Liberal*—Liberal Party	
PMDB	*Partido do Movimento Democrático Brasileiro*—Party of the Brazilian Democratic Movement	
PMN	*Partido da Mobilização Nacional*—National Mobilisation Party	
PP	*Partido Popular*—Popular Party	
PPB	*Partido Progresista Brasileiro*—Brazilian Progressive Party	
PPS	*Partido Popular Socialista*—Socialist Popular Party	
PR	*Partido da República*—Party of the Republic	
PRB	*Partido Republicano Brasileiro*—Brazilian Republican Party	
PRONA	*Partido de Reedificação da Ordem Nacional*—Party for the Reconstruction of National Order	
PRONAF	*Programa Nacional de Fortalecimento da Agricultura Familiar*—National Programme for the Invigoration of Family Agriculture	
PRONERA	*Programa Nacional de Educação e Reforma Agraria*—National Programme for Education and Land Reform	
PRP	*Partido Republicano Progressista*—Republican Progressive Party	
PRS	*Partido Revolucionario Socialista*—Revolutionary Socialist Party	
PSB	*Partido Socialista Brasileiro*—Brazilian Socialist Party	
PSC	Partido *Social Cristão*—Christian Social Party	

PSDB	*Partido da Social democracia Brasileira*—Brazilian Social Democratic Party
PSOL	*Partido Socialismo e Liberdade*—Socialism and Freedom Party
PT	*Partido dos Trabalhadores*—Workers' Party
PTB	*Partido Trabalhista Brasileiro*—Brazilian Labour Party
PTLM	*PT de Luta e de Massas*—PT Mass and Struggle
PV	*Partido Verde*—Green Party
SDS	*Social Democracia Sindical*—Social-Democratic Union Confederation
TCM	*Tribunal de Contas Municipal*—Municipal Audit Office
TCU	*Tribunal de Contas da União*—National Audit Office
UNE	*União Nacional dos Estudantes*—National Students' Organisation
UNICAMP	*Universidade de Campinas*—University of Campinas
UNMP	*União Nacional de Moradia Popular*—National Movement for Popular Housing
USP	*Universidade de São Paulo*—University of Sao Paulo

Introduction

This book reflects on the challenges and dilemmas that progressive parties of mass-based origin face when they exercise state power, by looking at the governing experience of the Brazilian Workers' Party (PT). By mainly concentrating on what many consider a watershed government in Brazil, the Lula administration (2003–2006/2007–2010), this study explores how holding national executive public office contributed decisively to a pragmatic shift away from the party's radical redistributive and participatory platform, earning the approbation of international audiences and criticisms of domestic progressives. The work explores why a unique party, which originally promoted a radical progressive agenda of socio-economic redistribution and participatory democracy, eventually adopted an orthodox economic policy, formed legislative alliances with conservative parties, altered its relationship with social movements and relegated the participatory agenda to the sidelines.

While scholars, activists and pundits from around the world have heralded the Lula years as a breakthrough for poverty reduction and the forthcoming emergence of Brazil as a dynamic economic superpower,[1] many of their counterparts in the country as well as a number of Brazilianists elsewhere have expressed great disappointment.[2] It is undeniable that during the Lula administration Brazil experienced the highest reduction of poverty in its history,[3] which benefited more than 20 million people, and even reduced income inequality, as measured by the Gini coefficient.[4] In a favourable economic context, some 12 million jobs were created in the formal economy; 12.6 million families became beneficiaries of an ambitious cash transfer programme, *Bolsa Família* (Family Grant); the minimum wage doubled in real terms[5] and the purchasing power of the Brazilian population reached the highest levels since 1979 (Loualt 2011:3). Nevertheless, if rather than comparing the Lula administration to previous governments in Brazil or others in the region we consider both the distinctive elements of the progressive agenda that the PT had promoted since the early 1980s and the way it was advanced in its sub-national administrations, a different picture emerges.

Given its trajectory, the PT in the national government seemed determined to make a dramatic impact in state-society relationships. For several years, the party was considered by scholars to be an inspiration for progressive politics in Latin America and the world.[6] Due to its capacity to provide institutional expression to social movement dynamics (Heller 2001) and to promote broad-based participatory mechanisms as part of its strategy to favour socio-economic redistribution—a model rhetorically known as the "PT way of governing"[7]—the party was considered as a "true political laboratory" for progressive politics (Stolowicz 2004:186). Because of its distinctive features, such as the party's solid base in labour and social movements and its programmatic profile, the PT was seen as an "anomaly" (Keck 1992:158) as well as an "exceptional political enterprise" (Sader and Silverstein 1991:3). Among other scholars, Nylen (1997a:7) claimed that the PT was not "the typical Brazilian populist party of elites cutting deals among themselves while making grand promises to an inert mass of client-supporters". Instead, scholars saw the PT as a party constructed "from the bottom up" (Nylen 1997a:7) and firmly rooted in civil society.[8]

The major developments during the Lula government, however, were "a far cry" from both the kinds of structural reforms and policies the PT pursued while in opposition (Hunter 2007:17) and the policies that the party promoted in its sub-national governments (Baiocchi and Checa 2007). From the first years of its existence, the party advocated socio-economic redistribution by changing economic and social policies "in favour of the less privileged" (Keck 1992:3) while implementing deep structural reforms based on the premise of a "significant redistribution of property or income away from the rich to the poor" (Hunter and Power 2007:17). Even in the 2002 presidential campaign, despite the fact that Lula toned down the party's radical discourse significantly, his electoral manifesto spoke about the need to carry out structural reforms, including fiscal and agrarian reforms aimed at making the tax system more progressive and egalitarian[9] and accelerating the land reform process.[10] Once in office, however, the PT continued the orthodox economic policy put in place by the Cardoso administration and even favoured an unprecedented accumulation of capital by the financial sector, according to some interpretations.[11] Rather than structural redistributive reforms, the Lula government promoted compensatory policies, while neither a fiscal reform nor an ambitious land reform took place.[12]

It is when examining the most distinctive elements of the PT agenda, however, that one realises the extent to which the Lula administration embarked on a very different political path, away from the party's main goals and strategies. This agenda used to rely heavily on strengthening civil society (Sader and Silverstein 1991:106), as well as on promoting a notion of radical democracy that was central to the party identity. As scholars have argued, the Lula administration failed to promote meaningful and broad-based participatory mechanisms comparable to those implemented at the sub-national level, leaving aside the so-called PT way of governing.[13] The social achievements seen under Lula happened not only without threatening "privileged interests" (Hunter 2010:175) and the existing order, but also without significant levels of social mobilisation (Singer 2009:84). Along these lines, Perry

Anderson (2011:4) wrote in a recent article that if Roosevelt's social reforms in the 1930s were "introduced under pressure from below, no comparable forms of collective action either sustained or challenged Lula".

Like other progressive parties of mass-based origin, the PT confronted several challenges in public office, which constitute the main concern of this book. Progressive parties are expected to favour socio-economic redistribution and respond to the demands of their social bases, and like many other parties in public office, will probably seek to keep social mobilisation and contestation against the administration at low or manageable levels.[14] But progressive parties also have to confront what Lievesley (2006:6) calls in a rather general way "the exigencies of government". In office, these parties need to balance the interests of a wide range of groups and actors—some of which are particularly influential in state institutions and are likely to oppose redistributive reforms or policies that affect their interests—such as large business groups, foreign investors, local oligarchies or conservative parties.

While some of these groups have an ability to disinvest[15] or to trigger capital flight,[16] others have sufficient power to generate political gridlock[17] or even cause a state of crisis and instability that might put at risk the capacity of any party to stay in power.[18] In particular, the PT faced great constraints in dealing with a political and socio-economic environment dominated by conservative elites, and an economy largely vulnerable to the movements of the international capital, as well as a highly fragmented political system that has created major obstacles for parties in the executive to achieve legislative majorities.[19] Because of this system the PT had the weakest representation in the legislative branch among all the other contemporary left-of-centre leaders in Latin America.

Neither the literature on political parties nor the existing academic works on the transformation of the PT[20] provide a framework to explain how progressive parties of mass-based origin are affected by the need to reconcile conflicting interests while creating the necessary conditions to govern. Rather than focusing on these issues, most of the party literature centres on the reasons why parties change. The most influential scholars on parties, from Anthony Downs (1965) to Otto Kirchheimer (1966) to Adam Przeworski (1980) and Przeworski and Sprague (1986), have focused on the influence of electoral politics in party transformations. Less attention has been placed on the way in which parties govern and how such an experience shapes their own goals and strategies as political parties. In order to fill this gap the main contribution of this study is to introduce the notion of governability, present in Latin American political debates,[21] within the party literature as a means to analyse the constraints and opportunities that parties face in public office.

This study explores why progressive mass-based parties such as the PT have modified their agendas and changed their relationships with allies in civil society[22] as a result of their experiences in executive public office. It is my argument in this book that the Brazilian Workers' Party altered its discourse and strategy not only because of electoral motivations, as most of the literature on political parties and the PT suggests, but also because it confronted what I call the governability dilemma for progressive parties. That is, the need to balance conflicting interests between social allies seeking socio-economic redistribution and concrete gains, and those of dominant strategic actors (mainly opposition parties, business elites and the financial establishment) who may act as veto players and whose power is often critical to pass legislation and create conditions to govern.

I suggest that the governability approach can be used to look systematically at the difficulties which progressive parties face in public office and their scope for advancing their policies and reforms. This notion of governability is crucial for the present study because it sheds light on the adoption, transformation or rejection of certain policies and strategies, as well as on the way in which the PT in the national executive interacted with its own social allies—another area that I examine in this book. I contend that the governability dilemma is an important reason why progressive parties have difficulties in keeping programmatic goals and maintaining their identities when they enter executive office.

It was not the first time the PT had faced this dilemma when it occupied national executive public office in 2002. At the sub-national level, the party had already accumulated a rich governability experience, which I also examine in this work. This experience is particularly interesting because through a commitment to civil society and participatory democracy a number of PT administrations provided alternatives to the historic problems of governability faced by parties of mass-based origin when entering public office. Indeed, the PT set out a governability model, which I call *social counter-hegemonic*, which differed from the *elite-centred governability strategies* put in place by most political parties in Brazil and Latin America. In the social counter-hegemonic strategy implemented by many PT administrations (though not all of them), civil society was a core part of the governability strategy and its inputs were seen as a way to solve governing problems. Participation and mobilisation were not only ideological preferences; they were also part of a strategy to alter the balance of forces within state institutions in which the elites often enjoy comparative advantages.

It is the contention of this book that one of the most important transformations in the trajectory of the PT in public office was the switch from a *social counter-hegemonic* governability strategy, influential in several cities governed by the party, to an *elite-centred* strategy that tends to accept the existing distribution of power and institutional arrangements and seeks to accommodate the dominant strategic actors. Such a strategy was already seen in some PT local governments, particularly towards the late 1990s, but it became predominant in the national sphere. How did the Lula administration accommodate the interests of the most relevant groups and actors to secure governability? What were the implications of adopting an elite-centred strategy? Why was the PT at the national level—in particular Lula and his inner circle—reluctant to engage in social counter-hegemonic strategies such as those put in place at the sub-national level? These are some of the main questions addressed in this work and which, I believe, can shed light on the challenges, obstacles and possibilities of progressive parties in government both in Brazil and Latin America.

A CONTRIBUTION TO THE LITERATURE ON PARTY–MOVEMENT RELATIONSHIPS

A second contribution of this study is to elaborate a new interpretation of the changes that occur in party–civil society relations when progressive parties of mass-based origin gain state power. The literature on both social movements and political parties persistently argues that parties and social movements are able to maintain closer ties when they are in opposition than when they are in office.[23] Different authors have found, for instance, that when social democratic parties in Europe entered government they loosened their ties with their traditional associates, the trade unions.[24] In the PT case, several observers have claimed that the party "lost touch" with its social base (Nylen 2000:143), and moved away from or abandoned its allies in civil society.[25]

I argue that what mainly changed in the PT was not the distance between the party and civil society organisations, but the way in which the party engaged with these organisations due to the increasing involvement of both the PT and many of its social allies with state institutions. My contribution to the literature on party–civil society relationships, therefore, is to conceive these relationships not only in terms of *distance, proximity* or *strength*, but also in terms of the *nature* of their relationship and the way in which it changes when a party enters government. Most work on political parties does not capture the complex and multiple relationships that can be established with civil society organisations. It is my view that the relationships parties in government establish or maintain with civil society need to be understood as part of a larger political game to preserve political, social and economic governability.

In order to show how the relationships between the PT and civil society organisations have changed, I draw on the literature of party linkages,[26] which has mainly been used to characterise relationships with interest groups. I will explore how some of the programmatic linkages that bound together this party and its allies in civil society were partly supplanted by reward-based linkages in the form of state subsidies and jobs in the state apparatus. I will also show that inter-personal linkages between the party and social leaders, which have existed since the party's creation, bringing together the PT and its allies in civil society, are still influential. These relations illustrate that the party maintained close and long-lasting relations with its allies in civil society, even after it entered public office.

Conceptually, this work is different from other studies on parties because it does not look at the party as a narrowly defined unit of analysis. In order to capture the complex and changing nature of relations between the PT and some of the most important civil society organisations in Brazil who have identified themselves with the party, I introduce the notion of the *party socio-political field* (or *party field*),[27] a term which allows us to look beyond the formal boundaries of party and civil society organisations. The party field is a network of social and political actors that act beyond their formal organisations, independent from their membership to the party or to a specific group in civil society. Such actors often move back and forth between civil and political society, and their activities are not restricted to their formal organisations. The notion of a party field captures a whole web of informal relations between the party and social leaders which takes place beyond institutional mechanisms. It covers a large network of cadres, leaders and social activists who are strongly identified with the party, even if they lack any formal affiliation.

RESEARCH STRATEGY

In a narrow perspective of political power, some attributes of governability have been measured through rates of legislative success, which give an indication of the capacity of a government to pass legislation in Congress. In the broader perspective on governability adopted in this book, however, governability cannot be empirically tested with specific measurements. To the extent that governability is understood as "getting things done" and avoiding the paralysis that can result from political, economic or social instability, it can be seen as an *outcome*. Yet the main interest of this work is to look at governability as a *process*, that is, at how governability can ultimately be achieved. In this study governability is explored in a qualitative fashion by looking at political dynamics, by identifying the presence or absence of episodes of crisis, and by mapping relationships or observing the types of alliances made among strategic actors. Because many dimensions of governability are highly subjective, the perceptions and interpretations of political actors are a critical part of the analysis of governability undertaken in this book. These perceptions and interpretations are an important part of the evidence on which this work draws in identifying whether or not governability has been achieved.

This book draws mainly on 140 interviews conducted between 2008 and 2010 with actors in the PT and its socio-political field. Political parties are not unitary actors or monolithic units. Understanding how and why they choose certain governability strategies requires a research design that can distinguish between different groups and subsystems which coexist within them.[28] Such a disaggregation is particularly necessary in the PT case, recognised since its origins by the significant internal divisions among its members, which stem from the plurality of their ideological backgrounds.[29] If one wishes to understand why one set of ideas and policies became dominant over another, it is necessary to look at different influential groups within the party. In particular, it is important to consider the role played by Lula's faction and his own inner circle in public office, which became increasingly autonomous from the party structure even before reaching the national executive.[30]

In order to capture the complexity of the PT and its field, the transformations over time and the changing perspectives and strategies to construct governability, I disaggregate the party internally along three dimensions—(1) the party organisation and the party in government; (2) the major factions; and (3) sub-national and national. I also broaden the focus and explore the party's socio-political field by looking at four organisations which have maintained close relationships with the PT and its administrations since the formative years of the party. In relation to the first dimension, this study makes a clear distinction, following Katz and Mair (1993:549) between party leaders *in public office* and party leaders *in central office* or in the party bureaucracy. The "party in public office" (Katz and Mair 1993:549) is dominated by party leaders who have won either legislative or executive elections, or who become appointed as high-level government officials. The "party in central office", in contrast, includes two (often overlapping) groups of cadres: the national executive committee (or committees), and the central staff or secretariat. It is typically made up of party bureaucrats, many of whom make their political careers within the party hierarchy, rather than within the political system (Katz and Mair 1993:600).

In this study I mainly focus on the party in public office, because this is where the governability dilemmas are mainly present. Among the total 140 interviews conducted, 63.5 percent of them were with leaders who had some kind of experience in public office (for further details see Appendix I and II). My focus was particularly on those leaders who occupied executive branch positions at the highest levels and were more directly aware of the constraints of being in government. At the national level, I relied on key interviews with 10 ministers, 18 state secretaries and 13 presidential advisors, 6 of which worked directly for Lula; I questioned them about a wide range of issues, mainly about the way in which they perceived the governability dilemma before they enter the national executive and during their time in office. At the sub-national level, I interviewed 7 former mayors and 27 secretaries who were mainly asked about the different types of governability strategies put in place. It was also useful to interview staff members at lower levels, who were often more willing to offer straightforward answers, or technocrats with no party affiliation but influential in national government, particularly in the Ministry of Finance or the Ministry of Planning.

In relation to the second dimension, this work observes the differences among the most representative intra-party groups or factions on a Right-Left continuum. This is not only important in order to consider the ideologically plural make-up of the PT, but also to show the diverse views on governability that largely stem from the fact that moderate factions have been more exposed to executive public office than those situated in the party

Left.[31] The party factions are important because they were also strategic actors in the efforts of the PT administrations to establish governability. The party has more than 10 factions, but I have focused on three which have dominated the party apparatus: *Campo Majoritário* (Majority Camp, CM), the moderate faction led by Lula and trade union leaders which was relabelled in 2005 as *Construindo um Novo Brasil* (Building a New Brazil, CNB); *Democracia Socialista* (Socialist Democracy, DS), which also in 2005 formed the *Mensagem ao Partido* (Message to the Party, MP); and *Articulação de Esquerda* (Left Articulation, AE). At least 83 of all my interviewees (59 percent) were identified with one of these factions. Because Lula's faction, CNB, was the hegemonic group in the Lula administration, I interviewed 48 of its members.[32]

In relation to the third dimension, this study contrasts the governability strategies on which the PT relied at the sub-national and national levels, and how these strategies changed over time. The PT city governments varied in the governability strategies they adopted. I selected cases that highlight contrasts between administrations that sought to rely on mobilisation to advance social counter-hegemonic strategies (Diadema, 1982–1985; São Paulo capital city, 1989–1992); others that combined mobilisation with more institutionalised participatory mechanisms (Porto Alegre 1989–2005); and others that prioritised the accommodating of dominant strategic actors in an elite-centred fashion (São Paulo capital city 2000–2004). The experiences that I look at are mainly in the states of São Paulo and Rio Grande do Sul, which are key socio-political bases for the PT as a whole. Many in the party's national leadership drew crucial lessons about the challenges of governability from these experiences. A large number of leaders who participated in these governments also occupied key positions during the Lula administration and are very influential in the PT bureaucracy. Among my interviewees, at least 55 leaders were associated with the party in the state of São Paulo and 33 with the party in Rio Grande do Sul. Interviewing them was particularly useful in order to trace a clear story of the PT from the sub-national to the national level.

In order to understand the evolution of the party's social field, I interviewed 30 leaders from across four large civil society organisations, which allow for variation in discourses and strategies, from moderate to more radical rhetoric; as well as in the representation of labour unions, and urban and rural organisations. Above all, I gathered testimonies from social leaders from these organisations who have maintained close relationships with the PT since the party's foundation. I mainly interviewed leaders or activists who have also been PT members or have maintained close relationships with the party. I selected four organisations in the PT field. At one end of the spectrum I interviewed leaders from the *Central Única dos Trabalhadores* (Central Workers' Union, CUT), the largest labour peak organisation in the country, which was born out of the same process that led to the PT's creation. At the other end, I interviewed members of the *Movimento dos Trabalhadores Rurais sem Terra* (Landless Rural Workers' Movement, MST), a very visible organisation in Brazil and one of the main governability challenges in the relationship with civil society. I also spoke to members of the *Confederação Nacional dos Trabalhadores na Agricultura* (National Confederation of Agricultural Workers, CONTAG), which represents the rural trade unions, and also to the Housing Movement in São Paulo, one of the most influential civil society organisations in the city.

The concrete experience of the leaders interviewed for this study largely shaped my understanding of the PT trajectory in public office and the way in which some of its most influential figures understood and responded to the challenge of governability. My interviews were semi-structured but included a number of structured questions in order to be able to compare quantitatively across members of different factions, and the national and sub-national dimension, as well as groups within the party field. Among the issues about which I asked all the interviewees was their position on policy arenas that posed challenges for governability, such as land reform or economic policy; the extent to which they supported counter-hegemonic governability strategies and their assessment of the Lula administration in areas that are key for my study, such as social participation (for questionnaires and main answers see Appendix III). The interviews are not a random sample, but these structured questions nonetheless still reveal important differences across particular groups. Most semi-structured interviews were recorded, with exceptional cases,[33] and were analysed using Nvivo 8.0 software for qualitative analysis.

This investigation draws on a vast literature review of published and unpublished studies on the PT, its party administrations at the sub-national level or its relationships with specific social allies. Many of these issues are covered in master's and PhD theses in Brazil, which are not available in English. In order to offer evidence on issues such as policy preferences or relationships with social allies, I have relied on a number of surveys conducted by the party's main think tank, the *Fundação Perseu Abramo*, among party delegates during successive party conferences or congresses—considered in the literature as representative decision-making bodies of middle level party elites[34]—and other survey studies, including those conducted by independent scholars.

I conducted archival research and analysis of newspapers in particular, to triangulate interviews and to cover specific periods for which there is no living memory. The archive of the *Fundação Perseu Abramo* provided a large number of party documents and publications from the 1980s and 1990s, which I mainly used in order to map discursive changes and shifting approaches to civil society organisations. PT documents were used with particular care and preferably in combination with other methods. Many students of the party have relied heavily on these sources to trace the PT's programmatic transformations, on the weak assumption that they mirror the party ideology. This can be misleading because the PT, as Singer (2010:108) notes, never revised its historical positions and it certainly did not experience an ideological purge as the SPD did in Germany in 1959, when it officially abandoned Marxism and its nationalisation programme in Godesberg, or as the British Labour Party did, when it excluded its famous Clause 4, under Tony Blair. As Singer (2010:108) highlights, even in 2007 the Third PT National Congress still defended "the social property of the means of production". Early on, when conducting fieldwork, I found that PT documents do not always reflect the majority views, ideas and values and they are written in a language that is hardly ever the one that party leaders use when addressing the electorate.[35]

CHAPTER OUTLINE

This book is organised into nine chapters. Leaving the first chapter aside, in which I offer a theoretical framework, it is divided in two main parts, the first one (Chapters 2 to 4) looking at the PT, both in opposition and in government, prior to Lula's arrival in power; the second part (Chapters 5 to 9) studying the PT in national government during the Lula years.

Chapter 1 develops the first theoretical approach of governability in the literature on political parties. It focuses on the sources and consequences of the governability dilemma for such parties and contrasts this approach to other explanations of party change. The chapter distinguishes between the two main governability strategies, the elite-centred and the social counter-hegemonic and defines three main dimensions of governability—political, economic and social. It also shows how the relationships between parties and civil society organisations are shaped by a rationale of governability.

I dedicate Part I (Chapters 2–4) to looking at the transformations in the PT prior to the Lula administration. This part is important because despite the fact that changes in the party became more visible after the party assumed power at the national government, many of them started to take place years before and were the result of a gradual process. I look at these changes by relying heavily on secondary sources, and also by adding new empirical evidence to complement existing explanations, thereby bringing in elements that have been neglected, challenging certain views or making reinterpretations whenever necessary.

In Chapter 2, I look at the formative phase of the PT, by characterising the party as the byproduct of a heterogeneous socio-political field. I explore some of the characteristics that made the PT a useful instrument for progressive politics, showing how this party was different from most of its Brazilian and Latin American counterparts. Three distinctive elements of the PT identity are highlighted—the belief in participatory democracy, the hope for a transformative role of civil society and the strong interpersonal linkages between party and social leaders.

Chapter 3 recounts some of the earliest changes that the PT and its allies in civil society experienced in the years that followed its creation as party and social leaders started to occupy municipal governments. The chapter challenges the widely held assumption among Brazilian and Brazilianist scholars that the PT abandoned social movements. Instead, I argue that the PT socio-political field went through a number of systemic changes, which generated deep changes not only within the party but also among its societal allies. These changes lay important foundations for the future transformation of the party at the national level.

Chapter 4 examines some of the most relevant experiences of the PT in municipal administrations and the political lessons that party leaders learned from them. I show how the PT at the sub-national level balanced the interests of different groups and actors within and outside the field. The chapter focuses on the different strategies deployed by PT administrations to solve the governability dilemma at the sub-national level, showing how a number of municipal governments relied heavily on social mobilisation and participatory democracy as part of a social counter-hegemonic strategy to alter the balance of power in their benefit.

The second part of this book (Chapters 5–9) mainly analyses the different dimensions of governability—political, economic and social—and the switch from the social counter-hegemonic to the elite-centred strategy. It is in this second part that I examine the experience of the party in national executive public office and I make my strongest empirical contributions.

Chapter 5 analyses the *political challenge of governability*. It explains how the PT, despite the fact that it lacked a majority in Congress, created conditions to govern by managing to pass most of its initiatives and avoiding political gridlock. I show how the elite-centred strategy became increasingly influential at the national level and eventually predominant. In this chapter I explain the reasons why the most influential leaders, mainly within Lula's inner circle, were reluctant to engage in a counter-hegemonic governability strategy based on social mobilisation.

Chapter 6 studies the reasons why the PT adopted a conservative economic policy at the national level. Here I challenge the view, common among a number of Brazilian intellectuals and leftist activists, that the PT experienced an ideological shift to neoliberalism. Rather, I argue that the adoption of an orthodox economic policy was part of a strategy to accommodate the interests of the financial establishment—therefore to secure economic governability. The strategy proved successful: Considered as a "monster" by many in the financial sector during his campaign, Lula eventually came to be regarded as an icon of the "responsible left".

Chapter 7 explains how and why social participation, a key element of the PT identity, lost momentum when the party governed at the national level. I argue that, in spite of initial efforts undertaken during the first year, the Lula administration put the participatory agenda to the sidelines as a result of electoral motivations and the need to accommodate the interests of dominant political and economic elites. Here I trace the paradigmatic change by which the PT, after first casting aside its political commitment to democratise the national budget through participatory budgeting, surrendered to a technocratic rationale guiding its most important infrastructure program.

Chapter 8 studies how the Lula government managed to keep social contestation and disruptive practices at low or manageable levels as part of a strategy to secure social governability. I argue that this dimension of governability was achieved by engaging a number of civil society organisations in negotiations processes, by distributing a great number of jobs to their leaders, by allocating them massive state resources, as well as by relying on the strong leadership exercised by Lula within both the PT and its socio-political field.

Chapter 9 looks at three policy outcomes achieved under Lula: land reform, the trade union reform and the increase in the minimum wage. I argue that the PT in government was willing to deliver to its social allies and honour some of its pledges. I show, however, that the capacity of the administration to deliver on its campaign pledges largely depended on the balance of forces in each and every policy area, and the capacity of certain strategic actors such as large landowners, the financial establishment or opposition parties to act as "veto players".

In the conclusion to this book I examine the recent experience of the PT and the Lula administration, reflect on the challenge of governability for progressive parties and make some contrasts with other left-wing or left-of-centre parties in Latin America, such as Evo Morales in Bolivia or Hugo Chávez in Venezuela, widely regarded as confrontational in their approach towards the dominant elites.

1 The Challenge of Governability for Progressive Parties

This study brings the notion of governability to the party literature in order to examine the challenges and constraints that progressive parties face when they occupy executive public office. These challenges and constraints, I argue, are perceived and interpreted by party leaders in government and influence their responses. In this chapter I set out the case for incorporating the notion of governability into the study of political parties and explain the framework that I will use in this book. Unlike the most common views on governability, often focused on politico-institutional aspects, I broaden the lens by incorporating two important dimensions, the economic and social, both closely interrelated with the political dimension. I emphasise that governability can be both an analytical tool and a specific strategy that results from certain ideas and values. Hence, I use governability analytically to examine the way in which the PT accommodated the interests of key actors. I also look at governability as a strategy based on two different perspectives vis-à-vis such actors: the elite-centred and the social counter-hegemonic.

In the first section I set out the case for incorporating the notion of governability into the study of party politics. In the second section I explain how I rely on the strategic actors' approach in order to use governability as an analytic tool. As part of this section, I distinguish between the two main governability strategies, the elite-centred and the social counter-hegemonic, and define the three main dimensions of governability—political, economic and social. In the third section, I show how the relationships between parties and civil society organisations are also shaped by logics of governability. Drawing on the literature on party linkages, this section develops a typology to characterise the relationships between parties and actors in the field, explaining how different forms of engagement may act as instruments to secure governability.

BRINGING A GOVERNABILITY APPROACH TO THE PARTY LITERATURE

The literature on political parties does not provide a framework to analyse the obstacles, opportunities and challenges that parties face in executive public office. Experience shows, however, that progressive parties (or even political parties in general) are not always capable of advancing their agendas once in office. This is not only due to the commitments they make in order to win elections, as most of the literature emphasises,[1] but also because they are forced to make a compromise with a wide range of groups and actors once they assume public office. However committed to certain issues political actors may be, it is widely accepted that their motivation is not enough to promote change. Very often, governing parties in liberal democracies cannot fulfil their entire platform either because they lack formal institutional power to pass and enforce legislation and implement public policies, or because they need to accommodate the interest of groups in society with sufficient capacity to undermine stability, spread violence or affect the country's economic performance.

Scholars have shown that parties find several constraints in the political systems.[2] The need to form parliamentary alliances is one of the reasons that has limited the potential of social democratic policies in Western Europe (Padgett and Paterson 1991:127). In the mid-1940s, for instance, the fact that labour parties in Britain and Norway were able to form majority governments was key to the implementation of their economic programmes in government. In Britain, the overwhelming parliamentary majority of the Attlee government allowed the administration to create a sizeable economic sector owned and administered by the state. This was not possible at the time in countries in which social democratic parties formed coalition governments (Padgett and Paterson 1991:127). But these are only two reasons among many others. In this book I argue that a more systematic approach is needed to study the nature of the constraints and the types of challenges that parties face in government.

The notion of governability, which has been part of Latin American political debates over the last three decades,[3] is a useful tool for looking at the possibilities for progressive parties in government, provided that one differentiates its discursive and normative aspects, which influence the adoption of certain governability strategies, from the analytical use of the term. The notion of governability in Latin America has spread beyond academic circles and become part of a political language used by the media, commentators and politicians alike. These discourses associate governability with a wide range of different issues from institutional capacity, to social stability, public order and lack of conflicts, to the ability of any government to perform its basic functions, and to design and implement public policies in a way that is simultaneously effective, efficient and legitimate.[4]

Giving a precise definition of governability is not an easy task because many of its attributes and conditions vary depending on the political, geographic or historical contexts. Moreover, governability can be a problematic term because it has a strong normative dimension. Attributes commonly associated with governability, such as stability, efficiency or legitimacy, can be highly subjective. For a progressive political agenda, in particular, the language of governability is troubling because it is ideologically conservative in its origin and in some of its motivations.[5] Often, governability has been used to justify small government, to limit the scope of citizen participation (see Huntington, Crozier, and Watanuki 1975), to promote hierarchical views of power based on a *raison d'État*, or even to defend the permanence of certain political regimes (Dos Santos 1991:293). In a study on the post-democratic transition in Chile, for instance, Cecilia Baeza-Rodríguez (2008) found that the discourse on governability was used to validate top-down and technocratic visions of power. In her view, such a discourse limited political disagreement, stigmatised public disorder and subordinated grass-roots activity by creating an idea of political consensus that can only be reached through agreements among the elites.

Due to its ambiguities, strong ideological connotations and the broadness of the term, some analysts have suggested abandoning governability altogether and have renounced using it as an analytical category.[6] Others, however, consider that governability, although a valuable term, should be treated as a "general principle" or a "notion" rather than a concept with a clear definition and a rigid characterisation (Curzio 1998:189–90). This is the approach that I ultimately prefer. In this work, governability is broadly understood as the capacity of a party in government to "get things done". In polities with a significant history of political, economic and social instability such as Brazil, this not only means the capacity to pursue a positive agenda but also the ability to avoid the negative consequences that may come from instability in any of these three spheres. Hence, governability in this study is also understood as the capacity to avoid episodes of crisis that can put at risk the ability of a government to last over time.

Political governability exists when a party in public office is not only able to find support for its major policy initiatives and reforms, but also to overcome legislative gridlocks, judicial investigations or any type of institutional crisis. Economic governability consists of a government's faculty to gain the confidence of the most relevant economic actors and thereby avoid capital flight, speculative attacks, financial turbulence or any other phenomena capable of affecting the main macro-economic variables. Finally, social governability is found when a government is perceived as legitimate by its civil society interlocutors, when there is social peace, and when social unrest, contestation, disruption and conflict stay at low or manageable levels. Looking at governability is important for this study because it sheds light on the adoption, transformation or abandoning of certain policies and strategies, as well as on the way the party in government interacted with its own social allies.

An Analytical Tool: The Strategic Actors

Scholars consider that a reasonable degree of governability is reached when the interests of different groups are adequately represented in proportion to their power (Coppedge 2001:214) in a way that presupposes a certain social legitimacy (Camou 2001:10). Along these lines, a crisis of governability (or a situation of ungovernability) might occur when key players do not receive a guarantee that their interests will be respected or when such actors have deep disagreements that preclude them from negotiating stable formulas to solve their problems.[7] Whatever strategy is adopted, without certain agreements being reached among the elites, political conflict and instability is almost inevitable.

Coppedge (2001:215) uses the term *strategic actors* for groups that enjoy sufficient power to influence political processes and undermine governability in a particular country. These actors are strategic because they control at least one important power resource, which can range from the power to influence ideas and propagate information, to control over capital and "the means of production", as well as being able to distribute public jobs, affect public order or even generate social unrest and violence. Among the strategic actors, Coppedge identifies in Latin America the media, powerful economic groups, trade union confederations and the military (Coppedge 2001:216). However, strategic actors change over time and across geographic settings, and therefore so do the conditions for achieving governability. In economic terms, an analogy of the role of strategic actors can be found in theories of structural dependence of the state on capital.[8] Such theories argue that, under capitalism, all governments must respect and protect the essential claims of those who own the productive wealth of society. This is because capitalists' ability to disinvest fundamentally conditions policy choices in democratic capitalist systems.

Historical accounts of social democratic and labour parties in Western Europe have explored how the balance of forces among strategic actors and the need to accommodate their interests, both in the political and economic sphere, have set conditions as to what is possible and shaped progressive agendas. On the political sphere, for instance, Padgett and Paterson (1991:Ch.4) explain how in the second half of the 20th century the position of the labour and social democratic parties vis-à-vis other political parties in parliament produced different outcomes. Whereas majority labour party governments, in countries such as Britain and Norway, allowed the implementation of ambitious nationalisation programmes after the Second World War, coalition governments in which socialists or social democrats lacked a clear majority took more moderate economic decisions. In the economic sphere, the same authors show, the balance between capital and labour also played an important role. In places where the interests of large enterprises were more consolidated, and their allied parties were strongly represented in government, "capital was able to set the terms of government intervention and veto any radical social programs" (Padgett and Paterson 1991:143). In contrast, in countries where trade unions were stronger and better represented, more radical socio-economic transformations became possible.

I distinguish between two types of strategic actors which the PT had to deal with in public office: dominant strategic actors and strategic actors in the party's socio-political field. *Dominant strategic actors* are actors with supremacy over other social groups and more influence over the state as a whole. Under the Lula administration, these actors were mainly large business groups, the financial establishment; landowners, rural producers and their allies in formal representative institutions, as well as conservative political parties, particularly strong in the Brazilian political landscape. I call the second group *strategic actors in the party's socio-political field*, which are mainly civil society organisations such as CUT and the MST, and intraparty groups or factions. The need to accommodate the interests of these types of actors has shaped the PT administrations at both the sub-national and national levels.

Analyses emphasising the role of strategic actors and how they have shaped the agendas of progressive parties in Latin America are few. Notwithstanding, accommodating the interests of these actors has been part of the fundamental dilemma that these parties face in government in order to avoid capital flight, political gridlocks or episodes of crisis and instability; promote economic growth, and at the same time meet expectations of socioeconomic redistribution; respond to their social allies and keep mobilisation and contestation at low or manageable levels. My work focuses on strategic actors to understand some of the challenges that the PT faced in sub-national and national executive public office and the extent to which the need to accommodate their interests forced programmatic transformations, changed the nature of the relationships between the PT and its social allies in office and altered the PT participatory agenda.

Two Governability Strategies

The approach of governability used in this study assumes that the adoption of a certain strategy to achieve governability is not only the response to a set of "objective" constraints that force parties to adopt certain courses of action, but also the byproduct of a set of ideas and values. Unlike the structural or institutional approaches, this work goes beyond the assessment of constraints such as the electoral laws or the political system. Rather, it pays attention to ideational aspects and the way in which political actors perceive their constraints. My study not only focuses on events, but also on people's interpretations of those events and how such interpretations shape their responses. The underlying assumption is that people interpret their governability choices and respond to them based on imperfect information. These types of approaches, which emphasise ideational aspects, have been used in the literature on social democratic parties in Western Europe. Fox Piven (1991:17) argues, for instance, how labour parties construct "interpretations" about what is "within the realm of the politically possible" and Sheri Berman (1998:33) explains how ideas shaped the policies that social democratic parties formulated during the interwar years. In her view, such ideas affected the way political actors "perceive the constraints and opportunities provided by their environment" (Berman 1998:33).

The elite-centred and the social counter-hegemonic governability strategies are two of the main ones present in Latin America and used by progressive parties such as the PT.[9] The elite-centred strategy, which accepts the existing distribution of power and institutional arrangements as given, seeks an accommodation with dominant strategic actors and emphasises the need to make agreements with them in a way that is usually top-down. Civil society is not necessarily excluded and even mechanisms for citizens' participation might be welcomed. However, these mechanisms do not play a central role because citizens participate mainly as electors. The most conservative visions of governability, represented by Huntington and colleagues (1975), tend to consider that excessive participation can make societies ungovernable. These views are troubling for progressive politics because they adopt the state reason acritically, neglect a major role for civil society and embrace a narrow perspective of democracy that is limited to its formal representative dimension.

Elite-centred strategies often embrace views of "elitist democracy" (Nylen 2003)[10] in which certain groups, particularly the economic elites, have more material advantages and greater influence within formal representative institutions than the popular sectors. Nylen (2003:4–5) argues that in "elitist democracies" the "powerful" and "well connected" are more able to use the "institutions and procedures" of representative democracy in their benefit, while the political relevance of citizens is reduced to "the periodic casting of votes". In "democratic elitism", voters do not set the political agendas, do not make political decisions and do not choose policies (Avritzer 2002). Only their leaders are capable of aggregating interests and decide which of those interests are to become potentially salient (Gaventa 2006). These views are an obstacle to progressive politics because they ultimately embrace the idea that democracy needs to narrow the scope of participation in order to be preserved, and are therefore inclined to restrict the role of mobilisation and participation.

Frequently, elite-centred strategists engage in technocratic approaches, which are presented as the best way to "get things done". The technocratic view is the "unbounded faith" in science and "the ability of experts" (Heller 2001:135–6). Technocrats believe that the common good can be objectively identified, based on scientific knowledge (Leach, Scoones and Wynne 2005), and because their power is unquestioned, participation loses value. Technocratic approaches are frequently used by elite-centred strategists to promote policies that result in the benefit of dominant strategic actors, such as the financial establishment. Writing on Mexico's neoliberal elites, for instance, Centeno (1997, in Heller 2001:135) described how technocracy became a "state elite committed to the imposition of a single, exclusive policy paradigm based on the application of instrumental rational techniques". In certain technocratic views, some economic policies which follow the concerns of the international financial sector and the principles of the Washington Consensus are perceived as key to the "good functioning" of the economy and the state.

In contrast to the elite-centred perspective, with its emphasis on elite bargains and the common adoption of technocratic approaches, social counter-hegemonic governability strategies rely heavily on citizens and civil society to mobilise extra-institutional support.[11] The defenders of these types of strategies tend to be ideologically committed to participation and seek to engage civil society organisations or common citizens in decision-making processes. Progressive parties deploy counter-hegemonic governability strategies to alter the balance of forces in their favour and to overcome their weaknesses in state institutions. In order to achieve this objective they can promote proactive forms of mobilisation to build political support for certain reforms or policies that dominant strategic actors are likely to oppose (such as those favouring socio-economic redistribution) or they may engage in reactive forms of mobilisation, by which they instigate collective action and seek support among social allies in order to defend themselves against dominant strategic actors, avoid political crisis or secure their own survival. Progressive parties can also promote broad-based participatory strategies that rely on more institutionalised mechanisms used to build alternative sources of democratic legitimacy.[12]

At the sub-national executive level, the PT deployed the different governability strategies referred above. The social counter-hegemonic governability strategy put in place by several administrations was not counter-hegemonic in the Gramscian sense of seeking an overthrow of the "dominant bloc" or promoting an assault on the privilege sectors. As I study in Chapter 4, most PT leaders did not seek to confront strategic actors directly, but to creatively neutralise their influence in state institutions through mobilisation and broad-based participation. Chapters 5 and 7 will show how such a strategy lost momentum when the PT entered the national executive.

Three Dimensions of Governability

Governability is a multidimensional concept with a number of mutually reinforcing synergies. Authors have generally distinguished political, economic and social dimensions of governability.[13] In this study, I mainly associate *political governability* with the way in which the interests of parties or lobby groups representing specific interests in the legislative branch are accommodated in order to avoid legislative gridlocks, secure support for government initiatives or maintain the stability of elected governments (their ability to last over time), by avoiding, for instance, judiciary investigations that could result in the impeachment of elected officials. The political dimension of governability (see Chapters 4 and 5) is emphasised in this study not only because it represented a major challenge for the PT since its election to local public office, but also because it affected other dimensions. In Latin America, the most common view holds that governability exists when the executives are able to build cross-party legislative coalitions to pass key legislation.[14] In Brazil, due to the nature of the electoral system, and the many obstacles that it creates for parties in the executive to form parliamentary majorities, *governabilidade* in the country's political jargon is usually synonymous with legislative support for the executive and the absence of political gridlock (more in Chapter 5). *Economic governability* is a general notion used to explain the role of "the markets" in a capitalist economy and the restrictions they might impose on democratic governments, in line with the aforementioned structural dependence of the state on capital. As an analytical tool, economic governability, studied in Chapter 6, mostly focuses on the way in which a party in office accommodates the interests of powerful economic actors with sufficient power resources to destabilise the economy, such as large business groups or the financial sector. Finally, *social governability* focuses on the process by which a party in government creates conditions to keep conflict with civil society organisations at low or manageable levels, promote social peace and secure a minimum sense of public order. In this study I mostly look at some of the strategies by which the PT in government sought to reduce contestation, appeased sources of opposition, upheld its legitimacy and avoided social unrest. In doing so, party administrations needed to fulfil electoral promises and accommodate the interests of various social groups, many of them its own allies (see Chapters 4, 8 and 9).

This book presents evidence of the different ways in which the Lula administration was able to secure political, economic and social governability by accommodating the interests of adversaries as well as allies. In a highly fragmented Congress, the PT in the national executive managed to secure political governability by forming alliances with several parties, including conservative and opportunistic forces; by distributing among them cabinet positions and other jobs in the state apparatus, as well as by keeping potential sources of conflict and instability such as land reform off the table. In the context of a highly indebted economy and the uncertainty generated among the financial markets by the prospect of a left-wing government, the PT managed to secure economic governability through a pragmatic response: It accommodated the interests of the financial establishment in a way that resulted in the continuity (and initially in the reinforcement) of the neoliberal economic policy implemented during the Cardoso administration. Finally, the PT in the presidency managed to secure social governability by engaging a number of civil society organisations in negotiations processes, by distributing a great number of jobs to their leaders, by allocating them massive state resources, as well as by relying on the strong leadership exercised by Lula.

The political, economic and social dimensions of governability are interrelated. In the same way as an economic crisis might cause political and social unrest, conflicts involving civil society organisations might pose challenges for political stability. In Bolivia, for instance, as in other Andean countries, several presidents have been thrown out of power by street mobilisation despite having a majority in Congress (Hochstetler 2006). In these countries, the political dimension of governability has a strong social component. In the context in which Lula assumed public office in 2003, as

Campello and Zucco (2008:6) observe, "no social movement represented a 'threat' to the political system". Yet I argue that the capacity of civil society organisations such as the MST to promote disruption could affect the relationship between the PT and dominant strategic actors.

PARTIES AND CIVIL SOCIETY: A RELATIONSHIP SHAPED BY GOVERNABILITY

The relationships parties in government establish with civil society organisations, my secondary aim in this book, are understood here as part of a larger political game to preserve political, social and economic governability. I argue, in particular, that the need to accommodate dominant strategic actors shapes the way in which progressive parties interact with their allies in civil society, the extent to which they promote mobilisation strategies and, no less important, their capacity to deliver. By making concessions to certain strategic actors, such as powerful economic groups, parties might compromise long-lasting commitments and promises made to their social allies.

A concern with stability affects the way in which parties in government relate to civil society organisations. This occurred, for instance, in countries that experienced democratic transitions, such as Spain, South Africa and Chile, where left-of-centre parties deliberately encouraged demobilisation once they entered executive public office.[15] Roberts (1998:141) shows how the Chilean Socialist Party, which promoted mass mobilisation during the final years of the Pinochet era, downplayed mobilisation once in government for the sake of "elite-negotiated" social and political pacts established to "mitigate the fears of conservative sectors". Concerns with stability have also been present in other contexts. Before the debt crisis, they shaped the type of alliance social democratic or labour-based parties forged with the unions, based on the fact that the latter offered "industrial peace" in return for certain economic policies and concrete benefits (Astudillo 2001:291).

The literature on social movements tells us that governments seek to limit the potentially disruptive effects of mobilisations through different mechanisms. Meyer (2007:126) explains how most governments try to make social movement activity more "routinized and predictable". While some of them might suppress mobilisation by means of repression, many others try to integrate socially mobilised groups into established political channels or create institutions that give them access to the state and help process their demands, as it occurred in Brazil during the years of the postdemocratic transition (Hipsher 1998:162–7; see Chapter 3). The types of linkages parties establish with civil society organisations, as I argue in this work, can act as instruments to secure social governability.

I look at three types of party linkages—programmatic, reward-based, and interpersonal. The list is obviously not exhaustive and it only reflects ideal types, which in the real world are mixed and blurred. In developing these linkages I emphasise the party side of the relationship (the main focus of my research) and their implications for progressive parties. This does not mean, however, that civil society organisations are passive actors.

Programmatic Linkages

Parties in public office can achieve governability by sharing and promoting the agenda of their social allies. Programmatic linkages can be conducive to governability in at least two different ways: one is by fulfilling demands from civil society organisations and, as a result, avoiding or decreasing social contestation. Another is by forming social alliances that can be used to overcome the weaknesses that parties might face vis-à-vis dominant strategic actors (as in social counter-hegemonic governability strategies). In the literature, programmatic linkages exist when parties appeal for support on the basis of ideological platforms or policies that they commit themselves to pursue in office (Kitschelt 2000:845–3). Roberts (1998:18) argues that programmatic linkages are important to progressive politics because they help parties and civil society organisations to complement each other in positive ways, "encourage collective rather than individualistic solutions" and "politicize inequalities". In social democratic and labour parties, programmatic linkages used to be the basis of a close relationship between parties and trade unions, based on the perception of shared values and policies that political parties promised to pursue once in office (Haugsgjerd 2010:Ch.3–4).

Reward-Based Linkages

Scholars have defined reward-based linkages as those formed when parties exchange specific favours with groups in civil society calculating the potential votes that they can obtain from specific groups (Haugsgjerd 2010:Ch.4–5). But these benefits, I argue, can also be distributed based on the political support they can receive once in office. Reward-based linkages are useful for parties because they allow them not only to maximise votes, but also to secure social governability. Parties often rely on these types of linkages, in order to "appease potential sources of opposition", develop "a sense of legitimacy" or gain an "aura of respectability" within civil society (Selznick 1966:13,161,250). Reward-based linkages can take a wide variety of forms; the two most relevant for this study are the distribution of jobs and the provision of state subsidies to specific groups. One of the problems noticed by authors in relation to reward-based linkages is that instead of promoting "universal" or "general aims" they are usually "particularistic" and "direct", as they provide benefits to specific groups or individuals, easily identifiable, and "engage in a contract-like exchange relationship" with them (Müller 2007:251). Scholars regard these linkages as potential obstacles to progressive politics because their discretionary logic promotes a "detachment from the broader programmatic interests of the poor" (Roberts in progress) or because they act as "mechanisms of class control" that "depoliticize social inequalities" (Kitschelt, Mansfeldova and Markowski 1999:49).

Interpersonal Linkages[16]

Interpersonal linkages can either take place in the context of programmatic or reward-based linkages. These types of linkages, which I use in this study as a key element to illustrate the notion of a party's socio-political field, establish an unmediated and informal interaction between party and social leaders based on their personal ties. When a party occupies public office, social leaders might be brought to government to mediate the relationships between the party and its allies in civil society and, often, to limit their potentially disruptive effects. By activating interpersonal ties, organisations in civil society can become beneficiaries of policy implementation and dispute budgetary resources, but also obtain political favours to speed up decisions or bypass institutional mechanisms. Interpersonal linkages can also be used to promote mobilisation processes based on common programmatic motivations. Working through interpersonal linkages is not inherently harmful to progressive objectives, even if it often implies changes in the strategies that civil society organisations adopt. These linkages might relate leaders with a common history and shared values and can help to promote common programmatic goals. However, they can be problematic when they are used to obtain direct and particularistic benefits, typically reward-based. Furthermore, interpersonal linkages might divert political energy away from formal spaces of state-society interaction and weaken participatory institutions.

Part I
Before the Lula administration

2 The Formative Phase of the PT and Its Socio-Political Field

The emergence and formative years of the PT attracted enormous scholarly attention and great enthusiasm among progressive intellectuals worldwide.[1] For a number of reasons, ranging from its internal cohesion and discipline (Mainwaring 1995:375) to its "solid base in labor and social movements" (Keck 1992:3) to the fact that its creation represented a "break with the old left tradition" and so-called real socialism (Sader and Silverstein 1991:15–6), scholars presented the PT as an "anomaly" (Keck 1992:3); an "exceptional political enterprise" (Sader and Silverstein 1991:3), a "sui generis" political phenomenon (Lima 2005:44) or even as a "a new day in Brazilian politics" (Miguel 2006:123). Several features made the PT different from most parties in Brazil and Latin America, and even from social democratic or labour-based parties in Western Europe. In this chapter I focus on those aspects that made the party unique in its approach towards civil society.

My intention in the following lines is not to provide a full account of the elements that gave the PT a distinctive character and why it acquired them. It is mainly to highlight the particulars of the PT's formation and the programmatic linkages established with social allies. In particular, I emphasise three features that were present in the years of the PT's foundation and left indelible marks on its identity—the use of mobilisation strategies, the strong interpersonal linkages established between party and social leaders and the participatory ideology. Margaret Keck (1992), who authored the most influential book on the formative years of the party, situated its emergence in the context of Brazil's democratic transition. Keck (1992:4) persuasively argued that in order to understand this period of party formation it is necessary to examine the dynamics of this transition. In this chapter I rely heavily on her approach, but I also broaden the lens by looking at the progressive socio-political field from which the PT emerged in the late 1970s, during the final years of the military dictatorship. I also show how this historical context shaped the development of the entire field.

This chapter is composed of five sections. In the first section I describe the main features that made the PT unique and characterise it using existing typologies for political parties. In the second section I study the creation of the progressive socio-political field from which the PT emerged, under three umbrella groups—the "new unionism", the progressive Church and the organised Left. In the third section I study the formation of the party and show how the positions and strategies of the entire field were shaped by the characteristics of Brazil's democratic transition. A fourth section explores the way in which the PT related to civil society organisations in the field. Finally, I concentrate on the three elements of the PT identity—mobilisation, interpersonal linkages and participation—and show how they managed to survive over the years, even when the party occupied executive public office.

THE PECULIARITIES OF THE PT

The PT was born as a socialist party, created to channel the demands of a wide range of popular civil society organisations, and led by an emerging labour movement, to articulate their concerns into a larger political project. Since its formation during the final years of a long military dictatorship (1964–1985), the party was conceived as the political instrument of a wide variety of segments in civil society which opposed the existing political regime and sought to project themselves into politics.[2] One of the main objectives in the PT was to challenge the way in which the Brazilian state, "corporatist in structure" and "clientelistic in its practices" (Hipsher 1998:170), had historically approached both civil society organisations and citizens' participation in public affairs. The PT rejected the practices of tutelage, subordination and manipulation used by traditional parties in Latin America and Brazil, and wanted to challenge such practices by creating an organisation genuinely interested in civil society and its input, and capable of developing more programmatic and participatory relationships between its different groups.[3]

Formally created in February 1980, the PT represented a major change in the history of the Brazilian Left.[4] In the legal political spectrum, the Left had traditionally been occupied by populist organisations such as the *Partido Trabalhista Brasileiro* (Brazilian Labour Party, PTB), created by Getúlio Vargas,[5] the *Partido Democrático Trabalhista* (Workers' Democratic Party, PDT) of Leonel Brizola, or by the *Partido Comunista Brasileiro* (Brazilian Communist Party, PCB), only legal for a short period in the mid-1940s. These parties had not emerged "from below" and lacked a strong base in the "working class" (Keck 1992:3). In contrast, the PT was arguably constructed "from the bottom up" (Nylen 1997a:9), bringing to the political arena "the accent and syntax of the popular classes" (Miguel 2006:123). The innovative character of the party started from the characteristics of its membership, which mainly stemmed from social organisations, rather than from those with previous political party experience.[6] According to Keck (1992:3), "never before had a party [in Brazil] emerged from below, with a strong working class base and a substantial proportion of its leadership drawn from the labour movement".

For these reasons, some scholars have characterised the PT as the first mass-based party in Brazilian history.[7] Indeed, the PT had some of the elements of Duverger's (1959) mass party type. These elements were not only present in the way in which the party was created, with an "extra parliamentary origin" rooted in social organisations (Meneguello 1989:33), but also in the characteristics it developed during its first decade, being a policy-seeking and a highly programmatic party, with a mass membership organised at the local and national levels, and mobilised not only for electoral campaigns, but also in between electoral periods.[8] However, the way in which the organisation was created differed in some respects from the type of mass-based parties that emerged in Western Europe during the 19th century. The PT was more than "just another a labor party" (Guidry 2003:83) because its initial support base went far beyond industrial labour or one specific segment of the working class. The party not only incorporated in its first years various categories of workers outside industrial labour, such as bank clerks, teachers or civil servants, but also Church-based organisations, traditional left-wing parties and a wide variety of segments of civil society that did not necessarily identify themselves with a class perspective, such as feminist groups, gay movements, Afro-Brazilians, human rights advocates or environmentalists.[9]

The PT was also different from a number of labour-based parties in that it was not constituted as the political arm of one sector of the labour movement, neither was it formed by the trade unions as organisations (Keck 1992:7). Partly as an attempt to avoid compromising "union autonomy" and be more democratic and participatory than other left-wing parties, a "formal separation" between the party and the unions was maintained from the start, while no mechanisms for the collective membership of unions was established (Keck 1992:69,184,185).[10] The party did not affiliate associations that would automatically incorporate new members, as did many other labour-based parties. Those who joined the PT did so "as individuals", rather than as representatives of their own organisations (Keck 1992:68).[11] This was in part because the PT sought a different approach towards civil society organisations than previous progressive parties in Brazil had done. Labour leaders who participated in the PT's formation were critical of the history of "subordination" that had characterised the relationships between the labour movements and political parties (Keck 1992:184).

The PT was different from most populist labour-based parties in Latin America, in which the linkage with trade unions normally resulted in attempts to deradicalise and manipulate, whilst social organisations were used as electoral "shock troops" that could mobilise votes and provide large-scale demonstrations of public support (Collier and Handlin 2009:84). The PT did not want to be like the PCB, which tried to convert the trade union movement into an "appendix of the party", nor to turn social groups into its "power transmission belt" (Lima 2005:49). Furthermore, the new party of the Brazilian Left did not want to resemble the PTB, created by Vargas in 1945 to mobilise union support and control the working class "from above" (Collier and Collier 1991:370). The relationship with the labour movement had to be different. "If anything, the party should be subordinate to the labor movement" and represent union-identified goals in the political arena (Keck 1992:185), but it should never be the other way around.

Beyond its mass-based type elements, I argue that in its first decade the PT also shared characteristics of what scholars have more recently attributed to "movement parties".[12] Indeed, the PT was "the mouthpiece of a range of social movements" (Poguntke 2001:7) with one foot in electoral and parliamentary activities and another foot in grassroots movements and social organisations (Frankland 1995:32). The PT's political project itself "was informed by the discourses and practices of the popular movement webs by which the party was traversed and with which the party itself was thoroughly imbricated" (Alvarez 1997:100). Like the Green Party in Germany, the new party of the Brazilian Left was also "a 'promoter' of new themes and issues" in which "parliamentary representation" was not necessarily considered the main goal (Poguntke 2001:5).

The strong commitment towards participation, which has been found in certain movement parties[13] and characterised the PT and its administrations early on, made it different from other mass-based parties, such as social democratic or communist parties (Guidry 2003). These parties, as Sirianni (1983:119) tells us, made "little progress in elaborating a conception of democracy that could go beyond parliamentarism and statism". The way in which the PT addressed redistributive issues through participatory means, so distinctive of the "PT way of governing", differs from the experience of mass-based parties during the Welfare State years, when redistribution was very often conducted in a more centralised or bureaucratic fashion.[14]

A PROGRESSIVE SOCIO-POLITICAL FIELD: THREE UMBRELLA GROUPS

In this study I characterise the formative process of the PT as the byproduct of a progressive socio-political field created during the second half of the 1970s, in which the discourses and practices of the three main umbrella groups converged—the "new unionism", the organised Left and the progressive Church.[15] The "new unionism", which mainly led the formation of the PT, was a mass movement created from previously established trade unions, which became radicalised and turned into a key social and political actor (Sader and Silverstein 1991:23). It was very influential in the automobile sector in the periphery of São Paulo, and its leaders demanded union independence from the state and employers, and challenged the Brazilian state corporatist trade unions inherited from the Vargas era[16] to support, among other things, the organisation of the unions at the factory level and the participation by the rank and file, both of which had been legally restricted (Keck 1992). The great strikes that took place between 1977 and 1978 made the "new unionism" the strongest social movement, and its activity eventually

The Formative Phase of the PT and Its Socio-Political Field   31

converged with different mobilisations demanding, among other things, land, housing, health care and transport.

The "new unionism" was led by a group called the *autênticos* (the "authentic"), in which the most influential figure was Luiz Inázio Lula da Silva (Lula), leader of the Metalworkers' Union of São Bernardo and Diadema. As the leader of the strongest and most important social movement at the time, Lula incarnated better than anyone the political identity of this progressive field and became a strong leader. It is worth mentioning, despite the digression, that the type of leadership he came to exercise in the PT field was not another form of *personalismo*, so recurrent in Latin American politics (Mainwaring 1995), in which parties derive their popular support from the glorification of a single leader and his exceptional capabilities. Lula became a strong figure in the PT field, but he did not represent a "redemptive myth" usually associated to classic populist leaders such as Vargas, Perón or Cárdenas himself.

The progressive sector of the Catholic Church was the second umbrella group in the progressive field that formed the PT. Strongly inspired by Liberation Theology, this sector of the Church, which was "the only progressive force in the countryside of national scope" during the military dictatorship (Houtzager 2001:23), helped to bring together a wide range of civil society organisation and to mobilise significant numbers of people, especially in rural areas (Houtzager 2000:70). As part of the "preferential option for the poor", proclaimed by the Church after the Medellin Conference in 1968, the progressive Church sponsored the formation of several opposition movements and promoted a new type of "mobilisation from 'below' "—known as *basismo*—that led to the formation of pastoral commissions and *Comunidades Eclesiais de Base* (Ecclesiastical Base Communities, CEBs) (Lehmann 1990:xii).[17] Popular education initiatives, literacy programmes and the sponsoring of combative trade unions across the country were some of its initiatives.

The work of Houtzager (2000:62–3) has shown how the progressive Church assumed the role of an "institutional host" of several organisations, providing, among other things, organisational resources, ideological frameworks and, no less important, financial resources. The Church was in a "unique position" to secure resources from abroad, which came in the form of international cooperation projects that were used to support movements directly and indirectly (Houtzager 2000:71; see also Lehmann 1990:xii). The role of the Church was essential to the PT's pluralistic character because it helped the party to acquire a "strong presence in a number of rural areas" and become a mass-based socialist party that "united workers from the city and the countryside" (Houtzager 2000:76). This capacity to mobilise the rural world is another distinctive feature of the PT, not present in the formation of most labour-based or social democratic parties elsewhere.

The third umbrella group, the organised Left, was a vast and very diverse congregation of Marxists, Trotskyites, Maoists and other small organisations spread in small groups around the country, which also included social democrats and ex-militants of 1960s guerrilla groups (Sader 1998:167–78). Some of these groups were already organised into political parties or had formed political parties in the past, but many others were clandestine organisations that were seeking for legal recognition so as to leave behind their often sectarian and marginal character (Sader 1998).

It was not an easy task to reconcile the views of the different components of the organised Left that joined the new party, some of them representatives of the "old Left", with the "new unionism" and Church-based organisations. Partly because of this, when the PT was eventually formed it did not formulate a narrow definition of socialism (Martins 1997),[18] and it allowed different groups in the party to form factions, which were represented at the different levels of the party apparatus. In order to consolidate the party leadership and counteract the influence of the organised Left, which brought into the party its own internal discipline and solid ideological repertoires, the trade unionist wing (with Lula as the head), Catholic activists and several intellectuals formed the *Articulaçao dos 113* (Articulation of the 113) in 1983 (Ozaí 1998:88),[19] which became hegemonic within the party apparatus in the following years (Keck 1992:114), forming what Panebianco (1988:38) calls the party's "dominant coalition".

THE PT FORMATION IN HISTORICAL CONTEXT

The formation of the progressive socio-political field that led to the creation of the PT and its evolution in the following years can only be understood in its historical context; that is, as part of the larger dynamics of a democratic transition characterised as conservative and particularly long.[20] The transition timidly started in 1973, when the military authorities initiated a gradual liberalisation, the *abertura* (opening up), and formally ended in 1985 with the first indirect election of a civilian president. According to many interpretations, however, the Brazilian transition only culminated in 1989, when the first direct presidential election in three decades took place. Before that, presidents were elected by an Electoral College that was subject to political manipulation (Skidmore 1989:28). The different forms of collective action that emerged in the 1970s, prior to the establishment of the PT, took place after President Geisel (1974–1979) had gradually restored several civil and political rights (including free speech and free association), but maintained control of the political system with the intention of remaining in power at least until 1991 (Keck 1992:27). In that scenario, civil society became the main space for resistance against the military authorities and one of the main arenas in which several progressive leaders chose to act (Keck 1992:21).

In 1979, a new military president, General Figueiredo (1978–1985), decided to open up the party system by allowing the creation of new political parties.[21] This gave progressive leaders in the field an opportunity to become active in institutional politics. By creating a party, however, they did not intend to leave their organisations or left-wing mobilisation activities. Their intention was to diversify their strategies between civil and political society. For several years, the PT field maintained social mobilisation and remained sceptical of formal representative institutions. The reason for this, according to Keck (1992:33), was precisely the "prolonged period of uncertainty over the timing of the military's exit from power". In this scenario, the "main sphere of opportunity" for the PT during the greater part of the 1980s lay "outside, rather than within political institutions" (Keck 1992:252). Nevertheless, there is another reason which Keck mentions briefly and it has great importance: Many leaders in the PT field were opposed to a conservative transition entirely negotiated by political elites; they challenged the idea, dominant among politicians opposed to the military authorities (and the realm of political science), that the transition should take place in stages, building first a democratic regime and only afterwards discussing the democratisation of the state or other substantive issues (Keck 1992:34–5). PT leaders wanted to transcend the democratic elitism that I referred to in the previous chapter, in order to promote their radical conceptions of democracy and to alter state-society relationships. For them, the transition was not only about promoting formal representative democracy. In the transition they also saw an opportunity to promote participatory democracy and build political institutions in which they could express their own voices and promote their own interests.

At least until the mid-1980s, as Keck (1992:187–9) explains, the PT clearly prioritised social mobilisation over participation in institutional settings. In her view, this was mainly because the cycle of protest was still at its peak, the transition had not yet been consolidated and the benefits of participating in democratic institutions were still not entirely visible. For several years, many leaders in the PT field acted simultaneously in the party and in the labour movement or alternated from one to the other (Keck 1993:168). As Keck (1993:24) explains, social movements did not vanish after the creation of the PT, and many of them, particularly urban and rural landless movements, became even "more militant" during the 1980s. The energies of the PT socio-political field were mainly focused on civil society and were not dissipated when the party was created. Moreover, two of the most important organisations in the field were created after the PT had been formally established: the first was the Central Workers' Union (CUT), in 1983, and then came the Landless Rural Workers' Movement (MST) in 1985, also sponsored under the umbrella of the progressive Church. In the following years CUT became the largest labour peak organisation in the country and the MST one of the most visible farmer movements in Latin America.[22] In 1984, the PT participated with CUT, the Church and other organisations in the direct elections campaign, which aimed to elect a new president by direct universal suffrage. The demonstrations occurred in many cities, most notably in Rio de Janeiro, where the number of participants exceeded 1 million (Keck 1992:220). One year later, the PT helped to organise public rallies that successfully sought to establish a Constituent Assembly.

Authors have argued that the party's position towards institutional politics and representative democracy was somewhat ambiguous during this period.[23] The party was critical of formal representative institutions, but it participated in elections and occupied spaces in those institutions from 1982 onwards, when the military regime allowed direct local elections for the first time since 1965. The use of institutional spaces, however, was often conceived instrumentally, or justified in PT documents as part of a strategy to support "the organisation and mobilisation of workers for the sake of people's power" (Compans 1993:83). In its 1982 electoral manifesto, where for the first time the party positioned itself for electoral competition, it explained that participating in the ballots was in order to "back social struggles", "accumulate strength", and publicise its "programme of transformations", as much as to "conquer wider spaces" for its organisations (Compans 1993:79).

When the PT occupied its first institutional spaces, however, it did not prioritise them. Rather, it used them to mobilise people. In Diadema, a small city on the outskirts of São Paulo where the party first rose to power (1983–1985),[24] the city's Director of Planning, Amir Khair, declared in his early days in office that the government's priority was to "organise the people" for political objectives (Assis 1992:137). At the federal level, despite having a small parliamentary group the PT introduced very few legislative proposals and mostly used Congress as a political tribune from which it could deliver speeches and make public denunciations (Keck 1992:217). The party not only had little interest in political institutions, it also distrusted formal representative democracy. Such a position was still present in December 1985 when Lula declared during an interview, several months after the military regime had handed the presidency to a civilian government elected by Electoral College:

> I am trying to show that representative democracy is false. We want to fulfil the rules of the game, but we do not regard parliament as an end in itself, but only as a means. We will try to use it [representative democracy] as much as we can, but if we realize that we don't achieve power through those means, I will personally assume the responsibility of telling the working class that we will have to pursue other strategies. (García 2000:71–2)

The ambiguity of the PT's stance towards formal institutions was still present during the Constitutional Assembly, which eventually took place in 1987 after intense pressure from opposition parties and civil society organisations. Although the party played an important role in the drafting documents and obtained important victories in the constitutional debates,[25] it refused to endorse the final document on the grounds that the party supported "socialism" and rejected "the bourgeois constitution order" that the new Constitution would endorse (Sader and Silverstein 1991:19). The position of the PT was not simply rhetorical. Those PT deputies who decided to vote in favour of the new Constitution were expelled from the party and only readmitted years later. The slow pace of the democratic transition, in which leaders of the PT field were still not seeing clear advantages, shaped many of the radical discourses and strategies that were adopted by a great number of them. In the next chapter I will show how these positions changed in the years that followed, when these actors perceived clear benefits in taking part in state institutions, but also when they were able to advance some of their views on participatory democracy.

INITIAL APPROACH TOWARDS CIVIL SOCIETY

Civil society organisations became from the outset a symbol of the PT identity and a defining feature of the party ideology. Since the beginning, leaders insisted that the PT was not born "ready-made" and that its programme arose "from the political practice of its social bases" and of "the workers".[26] For this reason, the lack of a precise definition of socialism made sense: The idea was that the party ideology would derive from what Bianchi and Braga (2005:106) call "empirical class action". The aim was to promote social transformation by people themselves through grassroots participation.[27] Considered by progressive leading intellectuals at the time and many people in the field as "entities not contaminated by the vices of ordinary politics" (Gohn 1991:282), civil society organisations were central to accomplishing the party's main goals.

Inspired by the "schools of citizenship" that characterised the Ecclesiastical Base Communities, many leaders in the PT considered that the party had a pedagogical role and believed that their social network could "provide the means of educating workers for alternative forms of democratic participation" (Davies 1997:164). These forms of education would eventually liberate the poor from pervasive clientelistic practices and persuade them of the need for radical transformation. As the main contact point with the poor sectors of the population, many leaders in the PT thought that their social allies would give the party a reliable base and allow them to attract massive support among the public. PT leaders were aware that their main constituency relied on the interests of organised groups, but many leaders also hoped that these groups would enable the party to build support in poor regions where clientelistic practices were widespread (Hunter 2010:28–9). In such a context, winning office was not as important as having a pedagogical instrument that could spread its "message" to the poor (Hunter 2010:28).

For several years the PT was seen in the entire field as a complement to the activity of civil society organisations. During the 1980s, the party became "the main sounding board for popular struggles" (Sauer 2008:10), which gave a political dimension to sector-specific and local demands; and translated their concerns into political issues. Among the many links it forged, the PT became an important ally of rural trade unions (Houtzager 2000, 2001) and landless workers around the country (Branford 2010). The party assisted the landless by publicising violence committed against them (Sader and Silverstein 1991:59), promoting common goals and participating in joint mobilisations (Branford 2010:409–415). In many regions MST activists campaigned in elections or ran as PT candidates. Despite the lack of official ties, the relationships between the party and the movement were close from the outset, being largely shaped by interpersonal linkages among its leaders. Alexandre Rangel, who was an activist in both the PT and the MST, recalls that he saw "no contradiction" in belonging to both organisations simply because "they walked together" (08/04/09). During the 1980s, he argues, "there were no divisions between the party, the social movements, the Church and the unions" as "we all belonged to the same groups" and "we regarded the party as the tool of the movements" (Rangel 08/04/09).[28] Clarice dos Santos, who also developed her career in the MST and the PT, recalls that before conducting a land occupation the movement always consulted party leaders informally, either to decide on the best timing or on the best way of doing it (07/05/09). Very often, party leaders gave the movement protection against repression. David Stival, a former party president in the state of Rio Grande do Sul who was strongly linked to the MST, recalls that when the military dictatorship was still in power, the movement camped within the State Assembly, supported by PT deputies, who offered them protection (Stival 17/12/08).

The ties between the PT and CUT were even more solid. The contribution of the party to the creation of the *central* was "decisive" (García 2008:98). The *autênticos*, the sector of the labour movement which led the formation of the PT, also sponsored its formation in 1983 (García 2008:98). CUT expanded its membership vigorously and by 1985, 15 million workers and 1,250 unions were affiliated to it (Keck 1992:177). Although CUT was formally independent from political parties, its position was always identified with that of the PT (García 2008:98). The strategies of both organisations were often formulated together in informal settings among leaders. Very often, strike decisions, with their economic and political implications, were debated within the party in the same way as political decisions adopted by the party directorate were discussed by the most influential union leaders within both CUT and the PT (Moroni 07/10/08). The relationships between the PT and CUT were always complex and not easy to define. Keck (1992:184) argues that the PT always had difficulty in making a "clear separation" between "union questions" and party issues. Labour leaders, in practice, continuously attempted to act on two different fronts. According to other observers, PT and CUT maintained an "umbilical relationship" (Lima 2005:178) that was "permanent" and "fluid" (García 2008:109). Although CUT included some unions whose leaders were not involved in the party or who belonged to other parties, its decision-making structures were "unquestionably dominated" by unionists who were also PT members (Keck 1992:178).[29]

The PT maintained strong programmatic linkages with its social allies in the field, based on complementary goals and agendas. From the outset, the party incorporated the demands of specific social sectors in its programmes (Moraes 2004:144–64). The party became a defender of the right to land and embraced comprehensive land reform as a top priority (Sader and Silverstein 1991:59), giving a sense of purpose to its relationship with the landless movements. In 1989, when Lula first ran for president, he established a comprehensive agrarian reform as the main priority of his future government. In his own words, land reform was seen "as necessary as the air we breathe" (Campello 2012:24). The candidate framed land reform in a confrontational fashion in which landowners were regarded as "enemies" that needed to be "defeated" (Mendes 2004:17–21), using a language that was not very different from the discourse of the MST. During the election, Lula spoke about the "sacred character" of the right to land and justified the occupation of large properties (Mendes 2004:17–21), which was very controversial in the media.[30] Likewise, the PT championed the expansion of workers' rights and supported a trade union reform that would be capable of altering the Brazilian corporatist relationships, as CUT demanded. On several fronts, programmatic linkages were possible because, in the words of Roberts (2002:18), the party adopted positions that were "reasonably consistent", "coherent", and "differentiated from its competitors in the political system".

Until 1989, the discourse of both Lula and the PT was easily compatible with the positions of its allies in civil society and the groups that these organisations sought to represent. In the rhetoric that Lula used in his first presidential campaign there were clear allies and adversaries, as Campello (2012:21) found in a study of Lula's political discourse. As she observed, the most recurrent terms with which he identified allies and "friends" in 1989 were "steel workers", "clerks", "public workers", "labor leaders", "public servants" or workers in general. Conversely, the enemy was represented by the terms "bankers", "oligopolies", "sugar mill owners", "traditional oligarchies", "the privileged", "the powerful", "the rich" or "the political class". All of these groups carried a negative connotation in Lula's speech (Campello 2012:21).

LONG-LASTING FEATURES OF THE PT "GENETIC MODEL"

In his classic work on political parties, Angelo Panebianco (1988:xiii) argues that the way in which a political organisation is created, "the crucial political choices made by its founding fathers" and the relationships established with certain groups in society become legacies that place parties on historical trajectories that are difficult to leave. Among the several aspects of the PT "genetic model", to borrow from Panebianco's notion, I highlight three of them—the continued use of mobilisation strategies, the strong interpersonal linkages between party and social leaders and the belief in participatory democracy. These elements, I argue, shaped the PT field for several years, even after the mid-1980s when the arena of political contestation gradually shifted to state institutions and party leaders were increasingly elected for public office.

The continued use of mobilisation strategies, the first element, was particularly important during the PT's first decade. Keck (1992) argues that by the late 1980s the party still retained many characteristics of a social movement. The reasons for this "political anomaly", she contends, resided in the relations between the PT and the character of the Brazilian democratic transition (Keck 1992:251) examined earlier. Despite changes in the political scene and the fact that in 1985 the party won its first state capital, Fortaleza (in the northeastern state of Ceará), and doubled its representation in Congress,[31] it maintained its mobilisation strategies. When the organisation participated in the Constitutional Assembly in 1987, for instance, it put in place a strategy that, as Keck (1992) explains, combined the mobilisation of its social base with negotiations among political parties in institutional settings. The PT formed a coalition that opened the process of popular initiatives to a wide variety of organisations in the field, thereby producing 122 amendments and gathering more than 12 million signatories (Keck 1992:224–5). The party only started to work more seriously in state institutions from 1988, when it elected 36 municipalities, including three state capitals (São Paulo, Porto Alegre and Victoria), six middle-sized industrial cities in Minas Gerais and many small towns throughout the country.[32] However, in many of these cities, as Chapter 4 will show, mobilisation strategies were combined with institutionalised participatory mechanisms.

Mobilisation also played an important role during the 1989 presidential election, when Lula ran for president the first time, with the support of almost 2 million volunteers, who participated all over the country in decentralised local committees (Ribeiro 2008:112). Unexpectedly, Lula moved ahead in the second round when he received 31 million votes (16.5 percent of the total), an achievement that, according to some interpretations, would not have been possible without the mobilisation of the party's social allies (Sader and Silverstein 1991:142). The PT field mobilised once again in August and September 1992, when millions of people marched in the streets of the large Brazilian cities calling for impeachment of the first president to actually be directly elected, Fernando Collor (1990–1992). This campaign, which went beyond the field, was successful at pushing the National Congress to vote for Collor's removal from office later that year (Hochstetler 1997:8).

The strong interpersonal linkage between party and social leaders was the other indelible mark. Notwithstanding the rhetorical emphasis on the "autonomy of social movements" present in the PT field and among some Brazilian intellectuals at the time, this concept does not necessarily express the nature of the relationship in practice. The different segments in the field were formally separate, but strongly interdependent in practice. At least between 1980 and 1985, no distinction between movement and party activity existed (Keck 1992:Ch.7) and activists were even allowed to wear two hats (Branford and Kucinski 1995:49).[33] The PT field established a relationship of this type with groups in civil society so that many social activists could pursue common goals and strategies with the PT, and even identify themselves as *petistas* (PT members), without necessarily having to be formally affiliated. Benedito Barbosa, a leader of the Housing Movement in São Paulo who has always maintained a close relationship with the party, said during our interview: "The PT was in our heart, so it was not necessary to sign an affiliation sheet. We were so closely identified . . ." (02/12/08).

After the second half of the 1980s, however, the PT experienced a process of institutionalisation through which, following Huntington's (1968) notion of this term, the organisation acquired salience and became a political project in and of itself. A number of leaders started to make their political careers within the party, where they found incentives to become professional politicians and to dedicate themselves more to party activities. Leaders could not easily jump back and forth between the party and civil society organisations, as they did in the initial years, particularly between the PT and the unions (Keck 1992:Ch.7). Most cadres started to define their own political priorities and the majority made a choice to make their careers either within the party or in a civil society organisation. And yet, party and social leaders maintained a fluid relationship that was based on interpersonal linkages between leaders who had a common history and shared similar purposes. In Chapter 3 I show how these linkages bound together the party and its allies in civil society in sub-national executive public office, while in Chapter 8 I explain how these types of linkages were also very influential during the Lula administration, despite the fact that they became more reward-based than programmatic.

The strong belief in participatory democracy, developed by the party in its very early years, became another indelible mark of the PT field.[34] This belief went very far. During the PT foundation ceremony in 1980, the document *Guidelines for the Drafting of an Electoral Manifesto* stated that: "the PT position in those issues that most interest the people should be adopted through a deliberation process in which the grassroots of society, not just the party, should be listened to" (Compans 1993:73). The view that this document espoused was highly unusual for a political party: "*The PT should not have anything that resembles a government programme for the time when the party gets into power*" (Compans 1993:73, my emphasis). A discourse of civil society autonomy and the antistate approach that was so dominant during the late 1970s nurtured what Compans (1993:115) labelled a "myth of popular self representation" by which many leaders believed that the formulation of alternative redistributive policies could arise from the direct participation of the masses in policy-making processes.[35]

This view was incorporated by the new party of the Brazilian Left, partly as a consequence of a distrust of formal institutions dominated by traditional elites, and partly as a strong critique of their clientelistic methods. Nylen (1995:29), who studied the first PT participatory experiences in municipal governments, wrote that many leaders in the party regarded popular participation as "a collective action strategy necessary [not only] for the political emancipation of repressed classes or groups, but also as the vehicle for an individual's psychological emancipation". He went on to note that some activists perceived "empowerment through participation" as "a profoundly life-altering experience, akin in many respects to a religious conversion" (Nylen 1995:29).

The first government experience in Diadema embodied the heightened belief of some party leaders in participation. In 1982, when the PT ran in elections for the first time, the candidates refused to write a government programme, arguing that the future administration would rule with "the people" (Compans 1993:74). According to Assis (1992:96), who wrote the only book on this period, the party in the city only had a set of "radical principles in favour of popular control and redistribution", but lacked concrete policy plans. Before the elections, all PT candidates running for posts in the city signed a "Letter of Commitments", registered with a public notary, in which they declared that those elected would give up any decision-making power and transfer it to "grassroots municipal councils" which would be "de facto rulers and representatives" (Assis 1992:98). The commitment to participation was restated by the elected mayor, Gilson Menezes, a toolmaker trade union leader, when he reaffirmed in his early days in office that "everything" would be discussed in councils that would have the power to make binding decisions. As a mayor, he would only act as an "articulator" to "solve urgent matters", while the city would be "managed through a collective" in its day-to-day running (Assis 1992:96).

In the following years, the participatory strategies that the party put in place were more pragmatic and down to earth (Abers 1996), but participation remained a powerful idea that inspired many future PT administrations, even during Lula's term. The PT at the sub-national level, as the introduction to this book mentions, would later be praised for creating a government model which combined "inversion of priorities" towards the poorest, "good governance" and the right to participation in the implementation of public policies, the so-called PT way of governing, by which the party eventually found a formula to translate into practice its participatory ideology and even reconcile the views that derived from the heterogeneous background of its members.

CONCLUSION

In this chapter I have drawn attention to some of the aspects that shaped the PT identity by briefly sketching how the party was created and developed during its first decade of existence in the context of Brazil's democratic transition. My account has not focused only on the party. I have broadened the lens by looking at its socio-political field and the way its internal components related to each other. The participatory ideology, the interpersonal linkages and the reliance on mobilisation strategies that became part of the identity of the PT field are important to understand the type of social counter-hegemonic governability strategies that the PT put in place in several subnational executive experiences and the way in which the party related to its social allies in government, issues that I develop in the next chapters.

In her study on the PT, Keck concludes correctly that by the end of the 1980s the party had not yet lost its "character as a movement", whilst its original goals and ends had remained "exceptionally strong" (Keck 1992:251). In her view, the reasons for this "anomaly" resided in the relationship between the PT and the "extremely gradual" and "ambiguous" character of the Brazilian democratic transition (Keck 1992:251). The dynamics of this transition were such, she contends, "that its main sphere of opportunity lay outside, rather than within political institutions" (Keck 1992:252). More than 10 years later, when Samuels (2004:1021) wrote about the transformations of the PT, he reached very different conclusions, reflecting with accuracy the transformations that the party had undergone. In his view, the party did not resemble a social movement anymore and its main sphere of opportunities was no longer external to political institutions, but was situated within them. Indeed, as the democratic transition "consolidated", the Brazilian state became more inclusive and brought new opportunities and challenges for the PT and its socio-political field. In the next chapter I will show how both the PT and its allies in civil society increased their presence in political institutions and I will consider some of its implications.

3 Moving towards the State
The Reconfiguration of the PT Field

Before setting out to explore how the PT confronted the challenge of governability it is necessary to understand how the party and its socio-political field changed in the years of the postdemocratic transition and throughout the 1990s. During those years, the PT field experienced a reconfiguration in its goals and strategies, which affected the way in which its different components—the party on the one hand and its social allies on the other—related to each other and approached the state. The literature on the transformation of the PT has mainly analysed the changes in the party as a result of the electoral competition[1] and, to a lesser extent, due to its increasing control of public office,[2] particularly the executive office at the sub-national level. In this chapter I show how these changes not only affected the party but also the dynamics of its socio-political field.

The democratic transition in Brazil and its consolidation, I will argue, had a considerable impact on how the most influential leaders in the PT field rationalised what was politically possible. Because political institutions became more inclusive, the state turned into a critical platform from which social and political leaders in the field sought to promote their views and interests. On the one hand, the dominant coalition in the party became more pragmatic. It incorporated strategies of incremental social change and adopted a more coherent electoral route to power, which resulted in the endorsement of the rules and dynamics of formal representative democracy. On the other hand, several civil society organisations, such as CUT or the Housing Movement (although not others such as the MST), adopted more moderate practices, increasingly engaged in processes of negotiations with the state and deployed strategies that were less confrontational and disruptive.

In analysing the reconfiguration of the PT field, this chapter confirms part of what is theorised in the literature on political parties and party–civil society relationships, but it also differs from this literature in important aspects. The PT trajectory does confirm, as Kirchheimer (1966:193) points out, that when parties adopt "catch-all" electoral strategies (hence seeking to attract a maximum of voters beyond their original constituencies), they "modulate [their] relations with interest-groups in such a way so as not to discourage potential voters who identify themselves with other interests". During the

1990s, as I will show, the PT dominant coalition, seeking to appeal to a broader electorate, adopted some discourses and strategies that were different from its social allies. Such differences, as I will show, were particularly visible in the case of organisations such as the MST, which maintained disruptive practices and an antisystemic rhetoric, but it also affected other organisations in the field, such as the Housing Movement in São Paulo.

The PT trajectory does not confirm, however, the assumption that parties and civil society organisations move away from each other when the former switch from opposition to government.[3] In particular, classic authors on party transformations have argued that when these organisations adopt electoral strategies and increasingly hold public office, their relationships with social allies become weaker and more intermittent.[4] In the PT case, this assumption is present in the work of Ribeiro (2008), who assumes that because the PT became a large and competitive party machine, and because it approached the state and became dependent on its resources, it moved away from civil society.

That is not the case, I contend, because both the party and its social allies made a movement towards the state and still maintain close relationships. What happened, however, was that when the PT occupied public office, party leaders and social activists related in a different way, now that the party in government was in a position to deliver jobs and public goods. As I will show, some of the programmatic linkages that brought together the party and its allies in civil society became weakened, while reward-based linkages acquired more importance. Unlike other authors who have written about the PT,[5] in this chapter I will show that the party did not move away or abandon its social allies. In contrast with such views, I will argue that some legacies of the PT "genetic model" have given cohesion to the PT field until recent years: in particular, the fact that civil society organisations are part of the PT identity, and the strong interpersonal linkages between leaders in the political and social sphere, whose memberships overlap.

This chapter has five sections. Section 1 explores the opportunities and challenges that the democratic transition brought to both the party and its social allies. Section 2 will show how the increasing adoption of electoral strategies created a programmatic and discursive hiatus between the PT and some organisations in the field. Section 3 shows how reward-based linkages largely shaped the relationship within the field in public office. Section 4 will provide evidence that the PT has not abandoned its social allies. Finally, Section 5 will explain how some legacies of the PT "genetic model" have been the basis of an ongoing relationship between the party and its allies in civil society.

THE POSTDEMOCRATIC TRANSITION AND THE 1990S: OPPORTUNITIES AND CHALLENGES

The democratic transition gave the PT the opportunity at a very early stage to participate in elections and occupy legislative and executive public office.

In the 1982 municipal elections, before control of the national executive passed into civilian hands, the party won, almost unexpectedly, the cities of Diadema, in the state of São Paulo, and Santa Quitéria do Maranhão, in the northeastern state of Maranhão. In 1985, it won its first state capital, Fortaleza, in the northeastern state of Ceará, and only eight years after its foundation, the party had 36 mayors, thus including six middle-sized industrial cities in Minas Gerais and three state capitals: Porto Alegre, Victoria and São Paulo capital city, the main centre of economic power in Brazil. This early presence in formal representative institutions made the PT very different from social democratic or labour-based parties in Western Europe, many of them legally excluded from participating in elections or unsure for quite some time about participating in such institutions.[6]

The benefits of the PT's early political development became evident when the party won the first important state capitals and, later on, when Lula passed to the second round of the presidential election in 1989 (and eventually ended up losing by a 6-percentage-points margin). At this stage, the rewards of electoral politics started to speak for themselves. During the 1990s, the presence of the party in sub-national executive public office continued to expand. In 1992, 54 city halls were already in the hands of the PT, and the party won new important state capitals like Belo Horizonte, Rio Branco and Goiânia. In 1996, the PT acquired 115 municipalities, including Belém, and in 2000 the party had impressive results when it won 187 city halls, governing 18 percent of Brazil's population (Baiocchi 2003a:13). Already by the late 1980s, a number of party leaders had realised that the transition was delivering concrete results and that they could profit from representative democratic institutions. Perhaps, after all, representative democracy was not as biased towards the elites as they had initially thought. The moderate sector led by Lula's faction, which formed the party's dominant coalition, started to prioritise the institutional arena more clearly by acting inside the political system, and gradually ceased to promote mass mobilisation strategies. Such strategies, however, did not disappear from the field: They still had an echo among the leftist factions—though sometimes more in rhetoric than in practice—and among certain social organisations such as the MST.

In any case, the PT ventured into electoral politics with many of its social allies, either by actively engaging them in political campaigns to win votes for the PT, or by promoting social leaders as candidates. It was not only trade union leaders, who were constantly incorporated by the party in large numbers, who ran for office. To a lesser extent, leaders from the urban or landless movements did so as well. In Rio Grande do Sul, one of the party's most important enclaves, MST members elected city councillors, congressional representatives at the state and national level and even some mayors.[7] One of the elected leaders was Adão Pretto, one of the founders of the Landless Movement who also became one of the first PT congressional representatives in Rio Grande do Sul, and three times was a National

Congress Representative. Pretto became famous for saying that he had "one foot in Parliament and another foot in the streets" (02/12/08). Several activists from other organisations, such as feminist movements and promoters of gender issues, also ran for office as PT candidates.[8] Eventually, many social activists were hired by PT governments as aides, parliamentary advisors or civil servants.

The democratic transition not only brought social leaders the opportunity to engage in electoral politics, but also gave them greater access to the state. During the 1990s, several civil society organisations in Brazil increasingly came to pursue their goals through negotiations with the state. Many of them promoted their agendas through political parties (Baldez 2003), with a preference for the PT, and they began to work in partnership with government institutions and agencies.[9] In particular, a new form of institutionalised participation integrated civil society into decision-making processes (Hipsher 1998:155), thereby creating "a permanent form of interaction" between civil society and the state (Avritzer 2009:9).

The input of the PT field in the constitutional drafting process, in which the party and its social allies actively promoted participatory democracy, resulted in the creation of several participatory institutions operating under the principles of participation and representation, such as sectoral policy councils, national conferences, city master plans or public hearings (Avritzer 2009:9). Many of these institutions brought together government officials and representatives from civil society organisations who were responsible for social oversight for discussing general policy guidelines and for expressing policy preferences[10] through a decentralised participatory system.[11] From the late 1980s and throughout the 1990s, a number of such institutions were created in areas such as healthcare, urban policy, social assistance or environmental protection (Avritzer 2009:8).

The creation of participatory institutions and the way in which the state engaged civil society during the 1990s had important consequences, because several civil society organisations in the field changed their strategies significantly, adopting less disruptive forms of collective action, such as street protests, mass demonstrations, boycotts or sit-ins, and incorporated more institutionalised strategies, which took place under certain rules and procedures. Social mobilisation did not disappear from the stage during the 1990s, but with a few exceptions—such as the MST—protest actions decreased significantly. By and large, civil society organisations came closer to the state by "lobbying it", negotiating with its authorities, "participating in its processes" and even "accepting contracts from it" (Hochstetler 1997:170). These changes were also motivated by the fact that funding civil society organisations became a common practice under the neoliberal approach adopted during the decade, both in Brazil and Latin America. As the state was leaving many of its responsibilities aside, governments transferred vast amount of resources to social organisations with which they delivered public services.

During the 1990s, several groups in the PT field turned into major recipients of state subsidies[12] and some of them eventually became highly dependent on them.[13] Even the MST benefitted from massive state resources during the 1990s.[14] Despite its anti-state discourse, its proclamations of autonomy and the fact that it maintained land occupations and other forms of disruptive action, the movement engaged itself in the delivery of public services such as technical assistance, production and education in the settlements. As Navarro (2006:161) explains, MST leaders became "mediators of government policies", such as the National Programme for the Invigoration of Family Agriculture (PRONAF), in great part aimed at the settlements. Its leaders also benefitted from a privileged access and influence within the Institute of Colonisation and Land Reform (INCRA), and from the establishment of the Ministry of Agricultural Development. In 1996, the press announced, quoting INCRA as its main source, that the MST had a US$20-million budget, in great part from governmental sources, and that with these resources it paid the salaries of 800 professional militants.[15] Navarro (2006:165) considers that the MST eventually came to derive "its main financial resources" from the state and even that the interruption of this funding "could compromise" the survival of the movement.

Within the PT, the course adopted by the democratic transition process eventually led party leaders in the dominant coalition to believe that the expectations of the late 1970s—that a major political and social transformation in society could derive from the action of a wide network of civil society organisations that would "unite and expand" throughout the country to defeat the authoritarian regime—could no longer be sustained (Cardoso 1992:291). Given the alternatives opened by the Brazilian transition for both party and social leaders, the opportunities within institutional mechanisms seemed far more feasible and became more attractive for most leaders in the moderate sector of the PT and many of its social allies. If any change was foreseeable in the near future, it would take place through the institutional channels that were opened by the democratic transition. For the moderate sector of the PT, only by winning elections could the party eventually put in place its programme of transformations. The long-term strategy of mobilising and "organising the people" was subordinated to the expansion of the party's presence in public institutions, more feasible in the short run, with the ambitious aim of winning the presidency.

By making pragmatic electoral strategies and moving towards the centre of the political spectrum as the PT did during the 1990s, the party's dominant coalition—the main promoter of these changes—was not adopting a substantially different path from that of most of its social allies. The PT not only incorporated many civil society organisations in its own electoral dynamics, but many of these organisations also adopted more pragmatic and moderate strategies. As Samuels (2004:1008) puts it, "unions and social movements have not 'stayed in place' while the PT has 'moved away to the center' ". In his view, such a claim is false, because it assumes that these organisations have "remained rooted to self-perceived status as 'outside the system' and 'confrontational'", while the party became moderate and pragmatic. In the case of CUT, the party's most powerful ally, the shift in strategies occurred even before it did in the PT. Early in the 1990s, in response to the economic recession and the neoliberal reforms, CUT's dominant sector modified its approach towards the private sector and the government, in order to avoid massive job losses.[16] Because organising strikes and mobilising workers had become increasingly difficult in such a context (Riethof 2002:40),[17] unions more affected by job losses concentrated on preserving their existing jobs rather than achieving higher salaries or expanding benefits (Samuels 2004:1006). Eventually, the *central* decided to create partnerships between workers and employers in order to overcome the negative effects of the economic crisis (Rodrigues 1994), and began to negotiate in a "'realistic fashion'" around specific issues (Galvão 2004:220). In these negotiations, CUT did not question "the essential elements of the government or bosses' proposals", and even "softened its demands to make them compatible with the vocabulary of the business sector" (Galvão 2004:239).[18]

PRIORITISING ELECTORAL POLITICS: THE PROGRAMMATIC AND DISCURSIVE HIATUS

The way in which the PT decisively embraced electoral politics after the mid-1990s and penetrated state institutions during the decade had significant consequences for the party and changed its relationship with its social allies. For several party leaders, particularly within Lula's faction, it became evident that in seeking to attain their most ambitious electoral objectives—the pursuit of executive public office—civil society organisations did not provide enough votes. This was especially the case in large cities in which majorities are needed in order to win in a run-off.[19] The alliance with civil society organisations was not dissolved, but PT leaders started to perceive that these groups were not as representative as they had expected and only embraced certain interests, which were not necessarily those of the whole of society which they had to reach.[20]

This understanding started to mature once PT leaders participated in its first sub-national executive experiences. Once in office, mayors had to govern for everyone, not just for their social bases. This was clear, for example, in Campinas, during the administration of Jacó Bittar (1989–1992), and in São Paulo, with Luiza Erundina (1989–1992), both of whom were forced to look beyond their own bases of support and become more concerned with the "public interest". Bittar, a former union leader, declared that despite the fact that he was a "trade unionist", he could not "behave like one in the mayor's office".[21] Likewise, Erundina, a former grassroots activist of the Housing Movement, eventually realised that "movements constitute a minority of the population", that they are not always capable of "representing more universal interests" and that most of them are "locally oriented, fragmented and partial" (Kowarick and Singer 1997:36). After only one year in power, Erundina declared in an interview that she was "an administrator of the public interest" and she had to govern "thinking about the majority" (Kowarick and Singer 1997:40).

Party leaders in the dominant coalition, and possibly beyond, gradually abandoned the illusion that social organisations could be their main or only contact point to communicate and liaise with the public. The PT needed to expand its alliances with other groups and widen its appeal among voters. But many party leaders also acknowledged that their social allies were not sufficient to reach the entire popular sector. In the Brazilian context, as noted in the introduction, appealing to the middle classes was not as difficult as reaching a wide sector of what I call the unorganised poor, who were more concerned, as Hunter (2010:33) explains, in "acquiring specific material benefits sooner rather than later". According to this author, during the 1990s PT leaders realised that "poverty and inequality, however egregious, did not translate readily into support for the party" (Hunter 2010:33).

André Singer (2009:87–90; 2000), a party intellectual who conducted survey studies at the time, found that these poorest voters—to whom he refers as the "sub-proletariat" (Singer 2009:90)—had many conservative characteristics. In the 1989 presidential election, the great majority of them voted for Fernando Collor, the right-wing candidate who defeated Lula (Singer 2009:86). These voters tended to favour "order", rejected instability, were particularly afraid of inflation and even showed hostility towards strikes (Singer 2009:87). A large proportion of the unorganised poor even favoured repressive practices against disruptive forms of collective action and rejected a destabilisation of "the existing order" (Singer 2009:87).[22] I found no evidence that party leaders made such an assessment during the 1990s, but it is safe to argue that exhibiting close linkages with some of the most radical social groups in the PT field could have created difficulties. This was the case, in particular, when the intention was to improve the image of PT candidates among a vast sector of the unorganised poor, and not only among the middle classes, as it occurred in the earlier decades with social democratic parties.[23]

The electoral strategy adopted by the moderate sector of the PT during the 1990s, which was reflected in the discourse and programme of both Lula and the party,[24] generated after the mid-1990s a hiatus between the strategies, discourses and programmes of the PT and those of certain organisations in the field which still embraced confrontational approaches and disruptive practices, such as the MST or even one sector of CUT which did not adopt the moderate strategies of the dominant sector. As part of their centrist strategy, moderate party leaders wanted to make it clear that they were ready and willing to work within the institutional mechanisms and to play by the rules of formal representative democracy.[25] Many of them had become increasingly uncomfortable with the actions of the Landless

Movement, which, as many party leaders say, had "difficulties in recognising the limits of the democratic process" (Berzoini 29/10/08) and the "institutional dimension" (Cardozo 04/12/08). The adoption of a moderate strategy made it inadvisable for PT leaders, especially for those more engaged in electoral strategies, to be seen to have a close relationship with an organisation that was clearly portrayed by the media as violent, and which many of them increasingly regarded as sectarian and isolated from society.[26]

In some respects, the PT and the MST took opposite trajectories during the second half of the 1990s, both ideologically and strategically. While the party's dominant coalition was more seriously embracing the electoral route to power, the movement started to engage in more confrontational tactics, going far beyond the occupation of unproductive land, where its origins lay, and it resorted to invading public buildings, laboratories of multinational companies and cargo ships with genetically modified crops, to which the MST had become radically opposed (Navarro 2006:158–9). The PT did not and could not deny its relationships with the movement, which had developed strong ties, particularly with the party's leftist factions. However, many PT leaders, particularly those running for executive public office, realised that the linkage with the MST could have negative electoral consequences and opted to manifest their differences publicly (Sader 2005). Over the years, more and more *petistas* grew critical of the movement. I asked 79 party leaders their opinions about the MST and 67 percent of them expressed some kind of criticism. Among members of Lula's faction, "Building a New Brazil" (CNB), the percentage was higher than in other factions, reaching 77 percent of them. In the centre-left faction, "Message to the Party" (MP), 60 percent of my interviewees expressed some type of criticism, whereas within Left Articulation, it was 40 percent (see Appendix III for details). Although most interviewees were careful in their words about the movement, one of the most outspoken, a city councillor in Porto Alegre who belongs to Lula's faction, said:

> 90 percent of the population in Porto Alegre hate the MST. I supported the movement when it was founded, but I don't do that anymore (. . .) They are in permanent confrontation and that affects the PT. The movement today has a leftist direction, far too radical and irresponsible. They are kids in front of human battalions. That type of struggle makes no sense today (. . .) The movement only brings us a limited number of votes and it usually affects us because it costs us the support of the middle class and other sectors that identify us with their sectarianism. (Sell 15/12/08)

During the 1998 and 2002 presidential campaigns the programmatic linkages that had shaped the relationship between the PT and the MST since the early 1980s were largely weakened. A close examination of Lula's discourse during successive electoral contests shows the way in which his position on radical redistributive policies was toned down as part of a vote-maximising strategy. In the 1998 presidential campaign the old opposition between "the elites" and "the people" that characterised Lula's and the PT's discourse was almost absent, while the "national bourgeoisie" was no longer portrayed as an enemy (Mendes 2004:61). Lula wanted to show a moderate face and replaced the old politics of confrontation with the politics of conciliation, negotiation and consensus. As a result, the discourse on land reform, which had played such an important role in the two previous presidential campaigns, was almost left aside. Lula did not, for example, use a single segment of the free television advertising time that the Brazilian electoral legislation grants to presidential candidates to discuss land reform or to criticise big landowners, as he had done in the past (Mendes 2004:68–9).

In the 2002 presidential election, Lula downplayed the old dichotomy of landowners versus the landless and his discourse on land reform eradicated any sign of confrontation. In a clear strategy to differentiate the party from the controversial occupations of the MST, largely portrayed by the media as violent actions, Lula announced that he would conduct a "peaceful land reform" implemented on unproductive lands and strictly within the constitutional framework (Mendes 2004:87–9). As a candidate, Lula clearly chose the words that he would use during the campaign. This possibly occurred after his electoral marketer, Duda Mendonça, produced a survey study showing that more than two-thirds of the voters were opposed to a violent land reform process (Moreira 2004). In 2002, every time Lula referred to land reform, he added terms such as "pacific", "organized" or "well-planned" and disconnected the terms from any reference to "social justice or income redistribution" (Campello 2012:25). Lula no longer condemned all types of large rural properties. In a remarkable difference with the MST discourse, the candidate praised the Brazilian agribusiness sector for being "modern" and "productive" (Mendes 2004:88). Although the movement supported Lula's election in 2002, its participation during the campaign was not as enthusiastic as it had been in previous contests. In the discussion of the rural programme, for instance, the movement participated only marginally[27] and many of its proposals were left aside (Teixeira 07/04/09). Many leaders of the MST concluded that in the 2002 election neither Lula nor the PT represented their demands as before.[28]

REWARD-BASED LINKAGES IN PUBLIC OFFICE

The occupation of public office altered the way in which party and social activists in the field earned their living, by becoming elected representatives, officials or employees in PT municipal administrations or legislative bodies. As Table 3.1 shows, in 1990 only 22.1 percent of the party delegates worked for the party in public office, 7.2 percent worked for the party bureaucracy and 28.3 percent for civil society organisations (Amaral 2010b:88). In the

Table 3.1 Sources of Remuneration among Party Delegates 1990–2001 (in percentages)

	1990	1991	1997	1999	2001
Public office	22.1	28.5	40	42	53.1
Central office	7.2	8.6	7	6	9.7
Civil society organisation	28.3	17.5	9	2.1	2.7
Voluntary members	40.8	40.2	31	34	25.5
Others	1.6	5.2	11	9	7.5

Source: Adapted from Amaral (2010b:89).

12 years that followed, this proportion was inversed. By 2001, 53.1 percent of the PT delegates served the party in public office (Amaral 2010b:88), 9.7 percent worked for the party in central office, while a mere 2.7 percent earned their living from a civil society organisation (Amaral 2010b:90).

From these numbers we can induce that a story of social mobility took place in the PT field. The effects of that mobility have been addressed in the party literature since Michels (1998:259) claimed that socialist parties become a "a new branch of employment" from which social leaders secured "a rise in the social scale". Frei Betto, a priest who championed the formation of the Ecclesiastical Base Communities and played a key role in the creation of the PT, put it bluntly in 1995 when he argued, bitterly and nostalgically, that popular leaders had "exchanged the slums for the cabinet offices", "the graffiti for the inaugurations" and "the buses for the official cars".[29] Thus, during the 1990s, the largest proportion of the middle-level party elites, most of them from a social movement or a trade union background, came to depend directly on the state to secure their income and became professional politicians (Ribeiro 2008). Scholars argue that this had a "moderating effect" because it brought many radical party leaders and social activists "closer to the state" and gave them "economic security".[30]

PT administrations, local and national congressmen directly appointed social leaders to public positions, often as a reward for their electoral support. An independent survey study on the political behaviour of PT national congressmen confirms the extent to which party leaders distributed jobs among these organisations, forming a relationship based on reward-based linkages. When Figueira (2005:84), who put together this survey, asked PT deputies how they recruited their staff members, 42.5 percent responded that the nomination of a civil society organisation was the first criterion, while 36 percent said that "personal relationships" (many of which included leaders or activists of social organisations) were their first choice.[31] Furthermore, 61.7 percent of the respondents acknowledged that at least one of their aides was appointed after being proposed by a specific group in civil society (Figueira 2005:84). Coincidentally or not, an equal proportion of the PT deputies (62 percent) consider that their election was strongly influenced by their linkages with a specific social organisation. This suggests that the appointment of social leaders comes as a reward for support in electoral campaigns.

The distribution of jobs among social leaders was particularly widespread in big cities with large bureaucracies that allowed mayors to recruit a considerable number of civil servants. During the Erundina administration (1989–1993), when the PT governed the city of São Paulo for the first time, some of the key names selected to participate in the administration were decided in negotiations with civil society organisations (Feltran 2007). Some trade union leaders, social activists and PT intellectuals strongly linked to civil society organisations were also appointed to public positions.[32] This gave civil society organisations an opportunity to play a considerable role in the development of government policies. The Housing Movement, at the time one of the largest and strongest organisations in the city, played a major role in policy debates (Rodrigues 12/12/08) and was directly involved in several community self-build initiatives (Carneiro 2006:76).[33]

Over the years, however, the relationship between the PT and civil society organisations acquired a more instrumental character, as the linkages between the party in public office and civil society organisations became more reward-based and less programmatic. The electoral support that many candidates running for legislative positions received from specific civil society organisations did not always involve a particular commitment to the causes that such organisations promoted. This happened, for instance, when the PT governed São Paulo for the second time, with Marta Suplicy as a mayor (2000–2004). Several Housing Movement leaders and activists who supported her campaign occupied positions in government, working directly in housing issues. However, the housing sector was not a priority according to Carneiro (2006), who did extensive research on this subject. No community self-building initiative or any new related policy was encouraged or developed and the average expenditure on the housing sector was rather low (only 2.5 percent of the city hall's budget), just slightly above that of the previous conservative government of Paulo Maluf (Carneiro 2006:90–3). This means that the fact that social leaders received jobs in government did not necessarily contribute to strengthening programmatic linkages.

The growing use of reward-based linkages had deep consequences for the organisations in the PT field. Many of them became dependent on "direct contributions" to subsistence costs and "indirect contributions" by which social activists were included on the public payroll, thereby acquiring a permanent source of income (Carneiro 2006:80). The beneficiaries of indirect contributions became *lideranças liberadas* (liberated leaders), a term used in Brazil's posttransition for those social leaders appointed for a public job with little or no formal obligation in return. The direct and indirect contributions that social leaders could derive from their allies in public office became particularly important during the 1990s because the progressive sector of the Church had diminished in importance and with the reestablishment of civilian rule it had "retreated from its role as institutional host" (Houtzager 2000:62). Hence, the financial resources that many social leaders and activists could obtain from public office through its allies in the PT (if not from other parties) became essential in order to secure their material survival.

It was also for this reason that a number of social leaders became increasingly involved in electoral campaigns, to which they dedicated an important part of their efforts. This had consequences for the way in which these leaders organised collective action. Evaniza Rodrigues, a leader of the Housing Movement in São Paulo who later worked for the Lula administration, acknowledges that, "instead of concentrating their performance at the grassroots", many activists "started to gravitate more around party cadres in public office", and invested most of their energies in the relationship with governments (12/12/08). Many PT leaders have acknowledged that organisations in the field became largely dependent on the resources that they could obtain from the party in public office or even from other parties and state institutions. The PT National Secretary for Organisation, Paulo Frateschi, clearly made the case during our interview that the strategy of many organisations today is based on the specific material benefits they can obtain from politicians—on "What can we give them?", as he put it (Frateschi 11/11/08). Likewise, a young cadre of the party in São Paulo noticed that civil society organisations "come to us mainly in order to obtain resources and specific benefits" (Rodrigues 13/11/08).[34]

Social leaders acknowledge that by participating in PT administrations, civil society organisations lost their capacity to criticise the authorities. A member of CONTAG who worked for the PT administration in Brasília argued that "when you take part in a government you lose autonomy" (Beze 03/07/09). "It happened to me when I did it", he confided. "You get trapped within the reasoning of the state, which has its own objectives and purposes" (Beze 03/07/09). For this activist, "being in a government limits your ability to criticise" because "you feel the need to support the person who appointed you to the job". When studying the performance of the Housing Movement during the Suplicy administration, Carneiro (2006:93) argues that the government used political appointments to exercise "individual pressure" in order to discourage activists from becoming involved in collective actions that could "destabilise the administration". In his view, patronage strategies as well as the allocation of public resources were largely implemented to "control", "subordinate" and "co-opt" this and other movements (Carneiro 2006:93).

In contrast to this view, I do not characterise the relationship between the party and its allies in the field in terms of co-optation, control or subordination (more in Chapter 8). As Avritzer (13/06/09) clearly put it during our interview, "the civil society organisations in the PT entourage were never as independent as they claimed to be". After the 1990s, when the party started to occupy public office, he argues, "their discourse of autonomy could no longer hold" (Avritzer 13/06/09). And yet, Avritzer (13/06/09) argues that this does not mean that the party or its administrations came to "control" civil society organisations or to politically subordinate them by appointing some of their leaders to public office, as Carneiro (2006) and others have claimed. The relationship between the party and its allies in civil society, Avritzer (13/06/09) contends, "is not one in which the PT governments say and the social movements do". Instead, he claims, "it is a relationship in which the governments and the movements talk to each other. Sometimes they cooperate with one another, sometimes they don't; sometimes they agree, sometimes they disagree".

Indeed, it would be hard to argue that subordination and control characterised the relationship between civil society organisations and PT governments when one observes that such relationships were far from harmonious. Studies on CUT and the MST show that the interaction with PT governments saw many conflicts. In cities like São Paulo or Brasília, the PT faced severe financial restrictions and could not deliver many of the demands made by CUT-affiliated trade unions.[35] Likewise, in places such as Rio Grande do Sul, the MST had many contentions with the PT administration led by Olívio Dutra (1999–2003), because it failed to settle the promised number of families on expropriated land (Ros 2007) (to be discussed in more detail in Chapter 4). If while in opposition the PT was in a more comfortable position to make radical programmatic commitments and managed to incorporate the concerns of its social allies, in government this task was far more difficult. Reward-based linkages, as I will argue in Chapters 4 and 8, were one of the strategies by which the party in public office accommodated the interests of civil society organisations in order to keep disruptive mobilisation at low or manageable levels, but it was not a strategy by which it could dominate, subordinate or control its allies in the field.

ABANDONING SOCIAL ALLIES?

As mentioned in the introduction to this chapter, not only scholars consider that the PT distanced itself from civil society organisations. Since the early 1990s, social leaders and the leftist factions in the party started to argue that by prioritising the electoral route to power, the party was leaving "social struggles" (Freire 2002:55–7) to one side.[36] Indeed, during most of the 1990s, the main discourse of the PT Left was that these "social struggles" should be prioritised before institutional politics (Freire 2002:55–7). Even until recently, the perception that the PT distanced itself from civil society organisations has been part of a revisited discourse.[37] During the interviews conducted for this study, the idea that the party moved away from its social allies was widespread among both party and social leaders, including almost three-quarter of my interviewees and all of the main leaders of the party

Left that I spoke to. I asked 85 party and social leaders whether the PT had moved away from civil society organisations: 73 percent of them answered affirmatively. All of the leaders from Left Articulation and 80 percent of the centre-left faction "Message to the Party" (MP) shared this opinion. Even within Lula's faction, "Building a New Brazil" (CNB), 55 percent of my interviewees also considered that the party had moved away from its social allies (see Appendix III for details).

Nevertheless, the evidence that I provide below, based on survey studies and my own empirical findings, suggest that the PT still maintains close relationships with social leaders and civil society organisations, it is largely influential in some of the most important groups in civil society, and party leaders in public office (both in the legislative and in the executive branch) have frequent interaction with social leaders. First, there are elements suggesting that party delegates did not leave their organisations as a result of their growing immersion in public office. Survey studies conducted during party congresses and national meetings by the main party's think tank (the *Fundação Perseu Abramo*) between 1997 and 2007, show that almost two-thirds of the middle-level elites have maintained some kind of "participation" (a participation that was not defined in specific terms in the survey), in at least one civil society organisation between 1997 and 2007.[38] As Amaral (2010b:91) suggests, middle-level elites within the party have maintained a "double activity" by which they simultaneously play a role in civil society and in public office.[39] Unlike what Ribeiro (2008) argues, despite the fact that party leaders became closer to state institutions, this did not result in them dissociating themselves from civil society.

Second, there is evidence that elected leaders have maintained constant interaction with groups in civil society. A survey study of PT congressional representatives (called *Deputados*)[40] shows that 62 percent of them acknowledged that their election was largely made possible by their linkages with a specific social movement (Figueira 2005:83). The study also found that the average PT representative in Congress dedicates half of his or her time (52 percent) to interacting with their electoral bases (Figueira 2005:114), which are mainly civil society organisations. PT congressional representatives interviewed for this study confirmed that they have an ongoing relationship with groups in civil society, receiving their leaders for all sorts of purposes on a continual basis, particularly within the Left and centre-left factions.[41] For instance, Florisvaldo Fier, a member of the PT Left, claims that he gives civil society organisations such as the MST "institutional and political support" (Fier 03/12/08). He arranges public hearings, intervenes in conflicts with the authorities, mediates in episodes of rural violence or introduces legislative proposals in the interest of such organisations.

Third, for some of the largest and most important civil society organisations in Brazil the PT is still the main reference within party politics. The sources I consulted within organisations like CUT, CONTAG and the Housing Movement confirm that the PT is, by and large, their main entry point to the political system as well as the first party to which the majority of its members are affiliated or which they vote for.[42] In the case of the MST, an important albeit indeterminate number of leaders officially left the party during the 1990s and in the early months of the Lula administration. However, the PT is still influential at the grassroots level, as some of its leaders have acknowledged (Rangel 08/04/09; Santos 07/05/09).

Last but not least, quantitative data shows that the party has continued to recruit social activists. The great majority of the party delegates who joined the PT after its formative years were still overwhelmingly from civil society or, more precisely, claimed to participate in a specific organisation when they became affiliated to the party. In 2007, the *Fundação Perseu Abramo* asked delegates who became PT members at five different moments in the PT history whether they had participated in a civil society organisation at the time they formally joined the party. As Amaral (2010b:95) reported in his work, the percentages were never below the initial threshold, remaining always above 80 percent on all five occasions (1980–1982, 81.4 percent; 1983–1989, 84.3 percent; 1990–1994, 87.0 percent; 1990–1995, 80.3 percent; 2001–2007, 82.9 percent). The numbers seem to confirm that the PT never ceased to incorporate into its structure cadres with a civil society background.

LEGACIES OF THE "GENETIC MODEL"

I argue that the relationship between the PT and its social allies cannot be understood without considering two legacies of its "genetic model", which make up the PT field: on the one hand, the extent to which the relationships with civil society organisations are part of the PT identity and, on the other, the overlapping membership of an important number of party leaders who are also social activists and maintain strong interpersonal linkages. In relation to the first legacy, Chapter 2 explains that since the party's creation, civil society organisations have constituted a symbol of political identity. Because of this, having a relationship with them gave party leaders credibility in the eyes of its supporters. Despite the discursive and programmatic gap developed during the 1990s, many leaders interviewed for this work still regard civil society organisations as a component that gives meaning to the PT's existence. Within the party Left, a number of cadres strongly identify with civil society organisations. *Deputado* Adão Pretto, the MST leader who developed his political career within the PT, regards himself as "a legislator of the social movements" (02/12/08); while *Deputado* Fier considers his own seat in Congress to be "an instrument of social movements' struggles" (03/12/08). But the importance of civil society organisations is also praised among moderate cadres, who also value groups in civil society. Glauco Piai, the Secretary for Organisation in São Paulo, strongly claims that "the day on which the party ceases to value social movements and popular mobilisations it will no longer be the PT" (05/11/08).⁴³ Paulo Frateschi, Secretary for Organisation at the national level, regards civil society organisations as the party's raison d'être, one in which history also plays a very important role: "We were born together and we grew up together", he argues, "we would be dead if we left them" (11/11/08).

The other legacy that binds the PT socio-political field is the large space for interaction between the party and civil society organisations in which membership overlaps, identities are blurred and political priorities are not always clearly established. Although most social leaders put their own organisations first, many of them simultaneously regard themselves as social activists and PT members.⁴⁴ Several social leaders do not make a clear distinction between party politics and the politics of their own organisations. Neither do they formulate such a distinction in their day-to-day political endeavours, nor in their long-term political objectives. Evaniza Rodrigues, a member of the Executive Committee of the Popular Housing Movement in São Paulo, explained: "I cannot differentiate between the party and the movement. To me they have different roles and one cannot substitute the other. A movement without a political vision will always have a very limited role" (Rodrigues 12/12/08). Another leader of the Housing Movement, Carlos Roberto de Oliveira (07/04/09), went much further:

> Some people try to separate what belongs to the movement from what belongs to the party. I don't agree with that kind of thing. I am a whole person, and so I see politics as a whole too. I defend the positions of the party and those of the social movement. Some guys say that they just belong to the movement and they don't mix that with party politics. I think they are simply lying to themselves. I am a PT activist and I defend a project for Brazil. I don't think that you are going to solve the problems of the working class by solving the housing issue. My struggle is larger. It is for the transformation of society as a whole.

Multiple identities can also be found in the intersection between the MST and the PT, in spite of the hiatus between the two organisations described earlier. A PT parliamentary advisor who was promoted by the movement to work for the PT members in Congress said "I consider myself a cadre of the movement and a cadre of the party without distinction" (Fernandes 01/04/09). Others, despite being more identified with the MST, also consider themselves party cadres. Many of them, in fact, have occupied important positions in PT administrations. A good example among my interviewees is Clarice dos Santos, who developed her political career simultaneously in the PT and the MST. Dos Santos became Director of the National Programme for Education and Land Reform at the Institute for Colonisation and Land Reform (INCRA) under the Lula government (see Chapter 8).

Strong interpersonal linkages between party and social leaders informally connect the party and civil society organisations. In many cases, cadres acting in the social and political spheres, either in public or central office, develop relationships of cooperation and mutual understanding based on common political trajectories, shared goals and values, and even on the fact that they face similar political adversaries. Because PT leaders and social activists have been "partners in the same struggles", as many of them claim, they are also "comrades" more willing to understand each other in difficult circumstances, regardless of whether social leaders are still PT-affiliated members. Interpersonal linkages, however, are not always based on shared goals and principles. In some cases, party and social leaders are no longer bound by programmatic linkages and have a rather instrumental relationship based on specific benefits that they can obtain from each other. In many sub-national PT administrations, interpersonal linkages were one of the main criteria to recruit social activists. In other cases, they became a mechanism to bypass institutional mechanisms, which were often slow and complicated, in order to obtain public goods.[45] Sometimes by activating their personal networks—by simply making a phone call, for instance—social activists could have easy access to their friends and colleagues in government in order to get things done.[46]

CONCLUSION

In this chapter I have shown how the PT socio-political field changed during the years of the postdemocratic transition and throughout the 1990s. The transition provided the PT field with unexpected opportunities that encouraged a change of strategies and discourses. The strategies of mass mobilisation that gave a sense of unlimited possibilities to promote progressive politics during the late 1970s and part of the 1980s lost ground among many groups in the field. Instead, state institutions became a privileged platform from which both the party and civil society organisations would seek to achieve their goals. Many groups in the field, as a result, adopted strategies of incremental social change and switched from a clearly antisystemic approach to one that would pursue many of its objectives within the political system. In doing so, however, the PT did not abandon civil society organisations, because both the party and its social allies generally followed similar trajectories.

In the previous pages I have offered some evidence that neither the PT nor its social allies in the field are coherent homogeneous actors. In the former case, the shift towards a moderate and pragmatic strategy was mainly promoted by Lula's faction, which controlled the party's dominant coalition. In the latter case, I have shown how despite the fact that most civil society organisations adopted more moderate practices, some of them maintained or even increased their disruptive actions. In the latter case, I have mainly relied on the conspicuous example of the MST. It is interesting to note, however, that despite the variety of strategies, the movement towards the state did affect the socio-political field as a whole. It stands out as a paradox that even the MST—one of the most radical groups in the field—became a major beneficiary of state resources, promoted candidates for Congress and even employed many of its cadres in state institutions.

This chapter has shown that the electoral strategies of the PT and its increasing occupation of public office did not result in the party's abandoning of civil society organisations. However, it did create some difficulties in maintaining programmatic linkages. In contrast, reward-based linkages became increasingly important in public office, shaping the relationship between the party and its allies in the field. As a result, the party in public office and its allies in civil society came to use each other more *tactically* and less *strategically*. In 2003, when Lula came to occupy the presidency, these types of linkages were a very common practice in the PT field and, as Chapter 8 will show, became an instrument for securing social governability.

4 Social and Elite-Centred Strategies at Work
The PT in Sub-National Executive Office

PT leaders drew a number of political lessons from their experiences in municipal governments. In this chapter I concentrate on the learning process of governability and their implications for the changing strategies of PT administrations from the early 1980s, when the party formed its first administrations, up until Lula assumed national executive public office in 2002. Most of the literature that explores PT municipal administrations focuses mainly on their participatory innovations, especially the Participatory Budget.[1] Here I use this literature and draw on additional sources to explain how many of these innovations were also an element of the PT governability strategy. It is my view in this book that the participatory strategies developed by the party at the sub-national level not only resulted from the ideological convictions of its leaders, but were also functional to a larger and more complex political game that helped a number of administrations to build political support, accommodate interests and, more important, help overcome the party's minority status in legislative assemblies.

The two main governability strategies outlined in Chapter 1, the elite-centred and the social counter-hegemonic, were present in PT governments. Counter-hegemonic strategies, which sought to rely on civil society and use mobilisation and participatory democracy as alternative sources of power, were particularly influential since the earliest PT administrations. The implementation of these strategies, however, was neither easy nor always successful. The earliest municipal governments, expecting to rely exclusively on the mobilisation of the PT social base, faced disappointment, conflicts on many fronts and political gridlock. Conversely, administrations which combined mobilisation with participatory strategies bearing certain characteristics, as observed in Porto Alegre, were able to reduce confrontation, while simultaneously managing to circumvent and neutralise political opposition in the legislative branch. In any case, the experience of the PT at the sub-national executive level was mixed. Notwithstanding the importance of social counter-hegemonic strategies, elite-centred strategies, which favour top negotiations with dominant strategic actors, also took place. As I will show, towards the late 1990s, as the party put electoral politics centre stage, the elite model became stronger in certain cities, with the notable case of

São Paulo, where conservative methods of top-down party elite agreements across partisan lines became more common.

In this chapter I look at four strategic actors that were particularly important at the local level: two within the PT socio-political field, factions and civil society organisations; and two outside that field, business groups and political parties (also referred to in this work as dominant strategic actors). In dealing with actors inside the field, from the earliest PT administrations on, distributing jobs among members of the main factions and social leaders proved useful. In dealing with actors outside the field, governability required negotiation and compromise. Given the nature of the Brazilian political system, in which the party that holds the executive hardly ever wins a majority in legislative assemblies, the relationship with political parties became one of the most serious challenges. Due to its importance, the current chapter is mostly focused on this dimension of political governability.

Two main sections make up this chapter. Section 1 explains the importance of four types of strategic actors, the consequences that they had for different administrations and the strategies used to accommodate their interests. This section goes on to make the case that parties in the legislative branch are key elements in constructing governability at the local level. Section 2 explores this issue in greater detail, by looking at the implications of the two main governability strategies adopted by the PT in government. Examples of the social counter-hegemonic strategy are the administration of Luiza Erundina in São Paulo (1989–1992) and the four consecutive PT administrations in Porto Alegre, between 1989 and 2004. Finally, I examine the administration of Marta Suplicy in São Paulo (2000–2004) as an example of an elite-centred strategy. In looking at the participatory experiences put in place by these governments I concentrate on the Participatory Budget. This was not the only participatory instrument deployed by PT administrations, but it was its most important innovation. No other participatory mechanism has been so clearly associated with the PT.

DEALING WITH STRATEGIC ACTORS: A NEW WINDOW OF OPPORTUNITY

The Constitution Brazil adopted in 1988 gave greater political, administrative and financial autonomy to sub-national governments. The new legal framework transferred significant resources to municipalities and states; conferred on them the right to institute and collect taxes and gave them wide discretion to make public expenditure decisions.[2] This process mostly affected municipalities, which became the main beneficiaries of federal transfers and almost doubled the resources under their control in the years that followed the adoption of the new Constitution.[3] With these resources, municipal governments had to organise and deliver public services such as health, transportation and basic education, as well as to cooperate with the federal and state governments in the provision of social policies. The municipal responsibilities, however, were defined in a rather general way, giving mayors (particularly in large cities where they could command more resources) a certain discretion and opportunities to innovate.

In parallel, the Constitution instituted for the first time in Brazilian history the principle of semi-direct and participatory democracy, while giving local governments the freedom to institutionalise channels of direct popular participation in public affairs.[4] Specific legal provisions for participatory mechanisms were allowed for the development of social programmes, calling for the input of institutions of participatory governance such as sectoral policy councils and national conferences organised at all three levels, as advanced in the previous chapter. Other innovative democratic experiments resulted from the participatory democracy envisaged by the 1988 Constitution, such as city master plans, public hearings and negotiation roundtables. Participatory budgeting mechanisms also drew inspiration from the new constitutional framework.[5]

The combination of decentralisation and incentives to participation that were present in the new legal framework created a window of opportunity for the PT. It gave its municipal administrations a fruitful and concrete political space in which they could prove their capacity to govern, become players within the political system and simultaneously innovate in policy-making processes. In the promotion of participatory mechanisms several PT governments made a significant step forward, going beyond the creation of sectoral policy councils, which became widespread after 1988. Unlike these bodies, which mostly represented organised citizens in specific policy arenas, the participatory budgeting introduced by the PT was a particularly innovative mechanism opened to all citizens and effective at allocating and redistributing public resources.[6] The policies of the PT at the local level aimed at the so-called inversion of priorities, a key element of what was termed the "PT way of governing", by which the party's administrations intended to favour the poor and improve the quality of social services.[7] By increasing social expenditure, improving tax collection and making it more progressive, the inversion of priorities was meant to have a redistributive effect.[8]

Despite the opportunities opened by the new legal framework, party leaders soon learnt that their own chances of success in government were limited by the balance of forces among strategic actors, which they needed to engage. PT administrations could not ignore the interests of groups with sufficient power to influence political processes, either by their willingness to cooperate or by potentially deciding to boycott the party and its initiatives in the executive branch. Chapter 1 explains that strategic actors control specific power resources that can range from the power to influence ideas or propagate information that discredits elected authorities, to creating institutional gridlocks, political instability or social unrest.

PT administrations had to deal with and accommodate the interests of a wide range of groups. Here I analyse two types of actors that were particularly relevant to generating minimum conditions for governability: on the one hand, strategic actors within the party's socio-political field, such as factions and civil society organisations. On the other hand, I look at dominant strategic actors or actors outside the field, such as business groups and political parties represented in the legislative branch. Examples drawn from different PT administrations show that the way in which PT governments accommodated the interests of these groups was essential to relative success in policy-making processes, including the participatory innovations and the attempted inversion of priorities.

Strategic Actors within the PT Field: Factions and Social Allies

Since the first PT municipal administrations, party factions proved to be a strategic actor for governability given their capacity to support the policies of the administration or to create obstacles to them. These factions could undermine the government in the eyes of public opinion by criticising PT administrations publically or even by promoting disruptive forms of collective action, especially strikes. Mayors such as Gilson Menezes in Diadema (1983–1988), Luiza Erundina in São Paulo (1989–1992), and even Vítor Buaiz as governor of Espírito Santo (1995–1998), faced high levels of conflicts with intraparty groups in control of the PT municipal and state directorates.[9] Many of these conflicts were ideological and largely attributed to the PT's plural origins, but many more took place because these administrations failed to accommodate the different factions in proportion to their representatives in PT directorates.

In Diadema in the early 1980s, for instance, the mayor was a member of Lula's moderate group, *Articulação*, the faction that formed the party's dominant coalition at the national level. In this city, however, the PT Municipal Directorate was in the hands of far leftist factions like *Convergência Socialista* (Socialist Convergence, CS), *Causa Operária* (Labour Cause, CO), and other groups on the party Left like the Trotskyite *Democracia Socialista* (Socialist Democracy, DS). Despite the fact that these groups supported Menezes's candidacy within the party, once in government the new mayor failed to reward them (Assis 1992:Ch.3). The pattern was similar in São Paulo, under the Erundina administration because her government also failed to include figures from the most influential intraparty groups in the apparatus. During her four years in government, Erundina had bitter arguments with the local party leadership, who even supported strike actions against her government (Kowarick and Singer 1997; Macaulay 1996).

Eventually, it became a standard practice in several PT administrations to reward leaders from the most representative factions with administrative positions. This first became common in the southern city of Porto Alegre, where the party governed for four consecutive terms (1989–2004), adopting a "principle of proportionality" in all decision-making structures (Abers 2000:58). Other PT administrations used similar strategies, which in practice meant that municipal departments and government secretaries were staffed with members of different factions independent of their expertise or experience (Baiocchi 2005:33). When the PT regained power in São Paulo in 2000, the lessons of proportionality had been assimilated. Suplicy and her pragmatic political strategists understood that distributing jobs among different intraparty groups was a key element to secure governability. As Suplicy said during our interview, one of the lessons that she had learnt from previous PT administrations was precisely that "governing with all factions" was necessary to avoid the internal conflicts that had previously undermined the Erundina as well as other PT administrations (09/01/09).[10]

Within the PT field, civil society organisations were another strategic actor for governability, given their capacity to affect the delivery of essential public services or to generate social unrest. Many of these organisations not only defended their own interests but also intended to obtain extra benefits once their allies came into power. One of the main sources of problems for PT governments was public sector workers, a strong union lobby that benefits from a large share of the public budget in salaries and other employment benefits in Brazil. As a general rule, once in office, the party had to act as the patron in the labour relationship, putting authorities in an uncomfortable position with its own allies (Macaulay and Burton 2003:135). In São Paulo, for instance, the Erundina administration confronted numerous strikes by, among others, the CUT-affiliated Bus Drivers Union, which in May 1992 caused a total shutdown of the public transportation system for nine days (Macaulay 1996:223).

In the southern state of Rio Grande do Sul, 90,000 members of the Teachers' Union (CPERS), one of the largest trade unions in the state, went on strike against the PT administration in 2000. Teachers demanded a 190 percent pay rise, whilst the government of Olívio Dutra, citing serious financial constraints, offered 10 percent (Goldrank and Schneider 2003:162). Whereas the previous teachers' strike against a PMDB administration in 1997 only lasted 12 days, this one extended to 32 days,[11] severely affecting the administration, the public image of the PT in the state and the attempts of the party to elect another governor in 2002.

As it occurred with intraparty groups, the distribution of jobs to social leaders also helped PT administrations contain disruptive practices. These types of strategies became widespread during the 1990s when the PT established reward-based linkages with a number of groups in civil society, as Chapter 3 shows. During the Suplicy administration, numerous social leaders from large organisations, mainly the Housing Movement, were appointed to office.[12] Unlike during Erundina's government, when the Housing Movement occupied the Secretariat of Housing several times, these forms of collective action hardly ever took place during Suplicy's tenure (Carneiro 2006). In fact, the Housing Movement did not even demonstrate outside the Secretariat of Housing, as they so frequently had done during previous administrations. According to Carneiro (2006:94), "the government and the social movement almost came to a truce" during this period.

Dominant Strategic Actors: Large Economic Groups and Political Parties

Outside the PT socio-political field, in the realm of the dominant strategic actors, the PT faced some of the greatest challenges to construct governability. In dealing with powerful economic groups in the business sector, party leaders in public office learned from their early experiences that they could not deny or ignore their interests. A certain level of compromise with economic groups was necessary to maintain private investment. After his experience as Secretary for Planning in the city of São Paulo (1989–1992), Paul Singer concluded:

> The left in the municipal executive power may and should (due to its class commitments) prioritise popular interests. However, it can only do this if it counts on the collaboration of the dominant classes, whose interest, albeit not being prioritised cannot be either denied or ignored. Both the accumulation and permanence of private investment is in the best interest of popular sectors. (Singer 1996:39)

In spite of the fact that PT administrations acknowledged the importance of promoting private investment, many of its leaders opposed what they regarded as illegitimate privileges, such as multimillion-real fiscal exceptions or concessions granted to the private sector that provided poor public services. While some administrations adopted a line of negotiation and compromise, others assumed a more confrontational strategy. Erundina, for instance, was forced to negotiate with the private sector in order to improve the provision of public services, most importantly transportation, arguably the most demanded service in the sprawling city. Her government intended to change the terms in which transport services were provided in São Paulo, where concessionaries were making large profits and provided poor services.[13]

Erundina intended to municipalise the bus companies and provide a fully subsidised service, funded by increasing the tax on urban property (IPTU) by around 600 percent overall (Macaulay 1996:218). The authorities claimed that this tax increase would have a redistributive effect because the most valuable buildings in the city were usually owned by big companies or by the wealthiest people, and these would pay the largest share of the IPTU (Singer 1996:142). Despite the support of public opinion,[14] in February 1990 the plans were rejected in the City Assembly, where according to Singer (1996:155) organisations of the private sector lobbied opposition parties against the initiative. Only in May 1991, when the government was in its third year, was a bill passed after intense negotiations with business groups and city councillors (Kowarick and Singer 1997). The Erundina administration realised that it could not ignore the interests of the concessionaries and made "major concessions" to big bus companies

(Macaulay 1996:217–9). Eventually, the government managed to increase this tax by 125 percent, far less than the original proposal.

Particularly complicated was the relationship between PT administrations and the private sector at the state level, where governments in Brazil have larger responsibilities for economic investment, services and infrastructure than their municipal counterparts (Macaulay and Burton 2003:135). In Rio Grande do Sul the relationship with multinational corporations was a major challenge. In fact, when Dutra announced his intention to renegotiate the multimillion-real fiscal incentives that previous administrations had signed with automobile manufacturers to operate in the state, Ford changed its plans to set up a new plant. Although the government made attempts to negotiate, which were successful in the case of General Motors, the lack of experience in dealing with multinational corporations resulted in the company's move to the northern state of Bahia, where a conservative government offered better conditions.[15] The opposition in the State Assembly and local business organisations bitterly criticised Dutra's government, arguing that the failure to negotiate a deal with Ford cost 200,000 jobs.

The uneasy relationship between the PT administration and powerful economic groups in Rio Grande do Sul had serious consequences in the state and also beyond. Also for this reason, the PT eventually failed to retain the state government. In the 2002 election the five most important business organisations in Rio Grande do Sul, representing industry, agriculture and trade, actively promoted a vote against the PT.[16] Paulo Feijó, president of FEDERASUL, the Federation of Business Associations of Rio Grande do Sul, even declared: "The PT hates the business sector. They want to impose socialism, which has been abolished even in Russia. If Lula wins, we will become another Venezuela or another Cuba".[17] This was not the position of the Brazilian business sector towards Lula as a whole in 2002, as I will show in the next chapters. However, the attitude that some business groups in Rio Grande do Sul took against both Lula and the PT during the election is indicative of the extent to which Dutra's government alienated a dominant strategic actor. In any case, other PT administrations established more fluid relationships with the business sector, particularly those in which members of Lula's faction, Campo Majoritário, were hegemonic. One of them was Antonio Palocci, mayor of Ribeirão Preto (1993–1996/2001–2002), a medium-sized Brazilian city in the state of São Paulo. Palocci, who later became Lula's Finance Minister, completed one of the first privatisations of the 1990s (the municipal telephone company), and was particularly known for his "market friendly" approach (more in Chapter 6).

By far the most important governability challenge for PT administrations derived from the constraints of being a minority government, as well as the need to deal with opposition parties and their representatives in municipal and state assemblies. These constraints were particularly serious because the Brazilian party system is highly fragmented due to its open-list proportional representation in the legislatures. As a result, the party that wins executive

Table 4.1 Electoral Results in Five Municipal and State Government Elections

City/state	Municipal level					State level	
	Diadema	São Paulo I	São Paulo II	Porto Alegre	Espírito Santo	Rio Grande do Sul
Year of election	1982	2000	1999	1988	1994	1997
Head	Gilson Menezes	Luiza Erundina	Marta Suplicy	Olivio Dutra	Vítor Buaiz	Olivio Dutra
Results first ballot	27.8%	29.8%	38.13%	34.00%	35.02%	46.26%
Results second ballot	–	–	58.81%	–	50.93%	50.78%
Legislative Seats obtained by PT electoral coalition	PT 6	PT ....16 PCB........1 PCdoB....1 PDT 1	PT ....16 PCdoB....3 PSB........2	PT ....9 PCB........1 PSB........1	PT ....4 PCdoB....1 PSB........1	PT ....11 PCdoB....1
Subtotal	6	19	21	11	6	12
Legislative seats obtained by other parties	PMDB.....5 PTB.........5 PSD.........1	PMDB.....9 PDS.........8 PSDB......5 PTB.........5 PFL.........4 PL 3	PSDB......8 PPB.........6 PMDB.....6 PTB.........3 PL ....3 PRONA ..2 PPS.........2 PDT ....2 PFL 2	PMDB.....5 PDS.........4 PFL ....1 PL ....1 PDT 11	PDT ....4 PFL ....2 PL ....1 PMN ......1 PMDB.....4 PSDB......4 PTB.........4 PPB.........4	PPB ......14 PMDB...10 PTB......10 PSDB......1 PFL ....1 PDT 7
Subtotal	11	34	34	22	24	43
Total number of legislative seats	17	53	55	33	30	55

Source: Developed by the author, based on *Correio do Povo* (06/10/97, 27/10/97); Couto (2003); Oliveira (2008:227); Fiorilo (2006:28); *Folha de S. Paulo* (27/10/97); Goldfrank and Schneider (2003); Macaulay and Burton (2003); Assis (1992:90–3).

office, either for president, governor or mayor, rarely achieves a majority in legislatures (Mainwaring 1999). From the municipal administration in Diadema, in the 1980s, to the government of Suplicy in São Paulo in the 2000s, to the administration of Olívio Dutra in the state of Rio Grande do Sul, the PT and its electoral coalition members, traditionally small left-of-centre parties like the Brazilian Communist Party (PCB), the Communist Party of Brazil (PCdoB), or the Brazilian Socialist Party (PSB), invariably obtained less than the required number of parliamentary seats to form a simple majority (above the 50 percent threshold). As Table 4.1 shows, even when PT candidates performed well in two electoral rounds,[18] like Suplicy or Dutra, the party and its electoral allies had minority status in the legislature.

In Erundina's São Paulo, the PT and its electoral allies only won 19 city legislature seats, while six opposition parties held 34. Eight years later, when the PT returned to office, the balance of forces was not much different. Despite the fact that Suplicy performed very well in the election, reaching one of the best results among all PT mayors elected in 2000, her electoral coalition only won 21 of 55 legislature seats, and the opposition gained a clear majority. In Dutra's Porto Alegre the situation was somewhat different because conservative parties were less dominant and the Workers' Democratic Party (PDT) often supported government initiatives. Still, the PT and its allies only held 11 seats. When Dutra became state governor 10 years later, the PT was in an even weaker position, with only 12 of 55 seats. In the next section I will analyse the different ways in which PT administrations dealt with their minority status in the legislative branch.

STRATEGIES TO SECURE GOVERNABILITY

Despite the fact that the legislative branch in Brazil is not particularly strong vis-à-vis the executive branch, without more than 50 percent of the seats in state and municipal assemblies (two-thirds in the case of constitutional amendments) mayors and governors might face great difficulties in passing legislation, approving annual budgets, creating new taxes or increasing the existing ones.[19] As in the national level, in the sub-national sphere such majorities are usually formed through legislative alliances, made either before the elections, during the elections (after the first round) or once in government (Nunes 2009:65). At the municipal level, as at all three levels, it is the exchange of favours between the executive and the legislative branches—rather than programmatic agreements—that mostly allows governments to pass their initiatives.[20] It is mainly through the distribution of jobs in government, or by means of pork-barrelling (which is sometimes more important) that executives manage to achieve legislative success at the sub-national level.[21] Scholars argue that the practices by which Brazilian political elites exchange particularistic favours for votes in the legislative branch, known as *fisiologismo* in the country's political idiom, are so deeply embedded that executives reluctant to deploy them might not only face difficulties in passing their bills, but might also have to face parliamentary or judicial investigations organised against them (Amorim 1994:18).

Several PT administrations were reluctant to engage in top-down elite agreements that are traditionally made in Brazil by exchanging votes for government jobs or monetary benefits—the typical elite-centred strategy. The PT strongly opposed these practices since its creation, particularly when they involved the formation of alliances with parties beyond the Left, and was critical of pork-barrelling.[22] In the name of opposing traditional politics, many PT leaders sought to promote social counter-hegemonic strategies by which their administrations could eventually put extra institutional pressure on representative institutions. These strategies were used to put pressure on the legislative branch by proactively mobilising its social base or by using mobilisation reactively, in order to defend PT administration from any potential parliamentary or judiciary investigations, avoid crisis and secure its own survival in power. PT leaders also promoted social counter-hegemonic strategies by means of broad-based participation (the way in which the PT sought to put pressure on representative institutions but through more institutionalised mechanisms). PT administrations combined these strategies in different ways. Erundina made attempts to promote proactive mobilisation and participation, which largely failed, but instigated defensive mobilisation with relatively better results. The PT administrations in Porto Alegre found a successful formula which combined proactive mobilisation with institutionalised broad-based participation. A third case will show, however, that not all PT administrations were committed to the counter-hegemonic strategies. Towards the late 1990s the elite-centred strategy became more influential as the PT emphasised electoral strategies and prioritised winning the 2002 presidential election. My third example, the Suplicy administration in São Paulo, will demonstrate that.

Counter-Hegemony under Erundina: The Failed Strategy[23]

The Erundina administration faced conflict on multiple fronts, within and outside the PT field, and was characterised by the reluctance of the former mayor to form alliances in the City Assembly where her party lacked a majority. This was a revelatory experience for the PT: Influential leaders learnt that party administrations could not govern in isolation; they needed to avoid the risk of legislative paralysis that could frustrate their initiatives as much as the perceptions of public opinion or their own electoral ambitions. During the Erundina administration, I argue in this section, many PT leaders perceived that the attempt to put in place a counter-hegemonic governability strategy by means of social mobilisation proved to be more difficult than originally expected.

From Erundina's first taking power, her government tried to negotiate with other parties, but came out against the formation of any type of government coalition with formal commitments (Couto 1995:6). Her cabinet, mostly dominated by PT members, intellectuals or figures associated with social movements, not only excluded representatives of other parties outside the electoral coalition, but also failed to incorporate her own allies. Even left or left-of-centre parties that supported Erundina's candidacy, such as the PCdoB or the PDT, were not awarded cabinet seats despite having supported the government in the City Assembly from the outset.[24] In fact, the PT at the time had not discussed how to deal with the legislative branch. Party leaders had a general expectation that its governments could surmount any lack of strength in legislatures and other institutional settings by counting on their social base. In concrete terms, however, they never explained how they would pass legislation without a majority in legislative assemblies, perhaps because they underestimated their importance, while at the same time overestimating the attributions of the executive branch. In São Paulo, for instance, when the PT Municipal Directorate discussed the issue before the election of Erundina in 1988, the conclusion was that "a permanent absolute majority in the chamber is not essential for the PT to develop its activities in the executive and legislative branches" (Couto 1995:202–3). Whenever important issues would require a vote in the Municipal Chamber, the party expected to promote "popular amendments" by which "social pressure will be able to force case specific alliances" that, according to the party, would help pass their initiatives (Couto 1995:202).

It was difficult, however, to put such pressure on city councillors. The administration could not take for granted the capacity of civil society organisations in the PT field to mobilise meaningful support in favour of its initiatives. Shortly after being elected, the party faced a strong reaction from opposition parties. During Erundina's term, the opposition initiated more than 100 actions against her administration in the law courts (Macaulay 1996:225), in great part because her government refused to distribute pork and undertake the bargaining typical of Brazilian politics. The most serious attack came from the Municipal Audit Office (TCM), internally dominated by conservative politicians (Macaulay 1996:225–6). The TCM rejected the city accounts on "mere technicalities" and sought to promote the mayors' impeachment (Macaulay 1996:226). This move, however, was widely interpreted as a political vendetta and was finally overturned in the Municipal Chamber, in great part because a large sector of the public opinion, including social organisations, intellectuals, artists, and even some businessmen and politicians from opposition parties, publicly endorsed the mayor.

Contrary to their expectations, mobilisation proved ineffective in neutralising the implacable opposition. By and large, social organisations were focused on their own concerns, rather than on broader political issues, and hardly ever engaged in mobilisation to endorse key government initiatives. In 1990, for instance, when Erundina tried to increase the IPTU on large industries to fund a "zero tariff" policy of free public transport in the city, the government's attempt to mobilise support had no result. The mayor's big gamble was that social movements and the population at large would act to back this redistributive measure and put pressure on the members of the Municipal Chamber. However, this was not the case (Macaulay 1996:218). In fact, as two party intellectuals later observed, the "zero tariff" proposal never spawned street demonstrations of support or any other large mobilisation in its favour. The government was unable to defeat the opposition and eventually abandoned its proposal (Kowarick and Singer 1997:38).

Mobilisation influenced a vote in the City Assembly only once in Erundina's term, when this body had to decide whether it would admit an impeachment investigation in 1991. This episode of defensive mobilisation took place on 25 September, when Erundina called for a massive demonstration outside the City Assembly. Many social organisations ranging from the CUT to the Housing Movement and the MST were present to support the mayor, both outside the chamber and within the internal galleries. Eventually, in October, the Assembly voted against the impeachment by 41 votes to 9.[25] Despite the fact that mobilisation played a role at this critical point, it was never useful to alter the votes of the legislative branch to actually support government initiatives.

Another type of social counter-hegemonic strategy, the promotion of participatory mechanisms, did not produce successful results during the Erundina administration, as different studies show.[26] Although the government attempted to create a participatory mechanism to discuss the public budget, and several assemblies and meetings to set up priorities were conducted, the process eventually generated too many expectations which the government was unable to fulfil and the meetings never attracted a significant number of participants (Compans 1993).[27] In fact, Erundina, who had strongly campaigned for participatory institutions with power to make binding decisions, limited the scope of the Participatory Budget to a simple consultative mechanism after her second year in office (Compans 1993; Pires 2006). By and large, the participatory mechanisms implemented in her administration were not strong enough and lacked the legitimacy to put pressure on city councillors, who could easily ignore the outcomes. The priorities that citizens established in these settings were significantly modified when the budget went to the City Hall for approval, "causing popular movements to claim that PT had broken its promises" (Macaulay 1996:222). The case of Porto Alegre was different, as I show in the next subsection.

The first PT government in São Paulo had some positive redistributive effects. Despite not fulfilling the original expectations, the agreements that the administration eventually negotiated with the opposition allowed a moderate increase in tax revenue, and social expenditure was much higher than in previous years, reaching 48 percent of the budget (Kowarick and Singer 1997:37), while some improvements were seen in health, education and housing. Nevertheless, in 1992, when a new municipal election took place, the PT lost the city of São Paulo and did not regain it until 2000. If electoral defeats produce deep changes in the strategies and discourses of political parties, as Panebianco (1988) holds, it is not difficult to understand why the PT in São Paulo was such a different party when governing for a second time. Surveys conducted in 1992 revealed that São Paulo electors evaluated the services of the City Hall positively, but Erundina and her party negatively, presumably "due to an anti press campaign" (Macaulay 1996:226–7). The conflicts that the first PT administration in São Paulo established with strategic actors in multiple fronts might have been one of the reasons.

Party cadres who experienced the first PT administration in São Paulo learnt that the PT could not expect to govern alone if its leaders wanted to avoid political gridlock. The most recurrent self-criticism of those who participated in the Erundina administration was the government's failure to assemble a legislative coalition. Shortly after the end of her term, the former mayor affirmed: "My biggest error as mayor was not putting together a coalition right away on the first day in government" (Couto 1995:6). During our interview, she also acknowledged: "One of the main self-criticisms that I make is over the type of relationship that my government established with the Municipal Chamber. Notwithstanding that we were a minority, we could have had a more intelligent relationship with the legislative branch" (Erundina 14/11/09), she said. José Eduardo Martins Cardozo, who was at the time Home Affairs Secretary, alleged during our interview: "We were too narrowed-minded and did not value alliances. We were naïve, messianic and too ideological" (04/12/08). Marty Suplicy, who did not participate in politics at the time, but was elected mayor of São Paulo almost one decade later opined: "I think Erundina's administration had wonderful ideas, but few of them were implemented due to the political inability of the party and the mayor herself. She was far too radical, unable to perceive that it is necessary to give in a negotiation and bargain politically. Erundina could not pass one single project in the Chamber! Not even one!" (Suplicy 09/01/09).

Participation and Mobilisation: Porto Alegre and the *PT Way of Governing*

The PT in Porto Alegre, in power for 16 years, adopted a social counter-hegemonic governability strategy that combined mobilisation of its social base with broad-based participatory mechanisms. This counter-hegemonic strategy was successful for two main reasons: first, because the PT was able to overcome its limitations within formal institutions, when it was in a minority position as with many other administrations. In doing so, instead of exchanging legislative support for government jobs or allocating budgetary resources by means of pork-barrelling, like most Brazilian parties in government, the participatory strategy put in place helped build support for a redistributive programme. Second, because the party in public office found creative ways to accommodate the interests of its organised social base and ordinary citizens—most notably the unorganised poor—and simultaneously received support from the middle classes and even some business groups. Many scholars have mentioned these elements in the vast literature that explores participatory budgets in Porto Alegre.[28] In this section, rather than writing from the point of view of participation, the emphasis is placed on governability.

Like other PT administrations, when Olívio Dutra was elected mayor of Porto Alegre in 1988, the party expected to mobilise its social base to overcome its weakness in institutional settings. As occurred with most PT governments at that time, when the party came to power, it lacked a clear participatory model in mind, and only embraced a set of ideological and general notions of participation (Navarro 2005). In tune with the PT agenda of the 1980s, the Dutra administration attempted to create "popular councils" in which "the workers" would make decisions such as budgetary allocations. Nevertheless, after the first few years in power, party leaders in public office realised that they could not count exclusively on the support of the PT's organised social base, whose competing demands would not be easily met with the limited resources of municipal governments.[29] The PT in Porto Alegre, dominated by leftist factions in alliance with moderate groups, realised that the participatory strategy needed to be more inclusive and to process different claims from a wide range of civil society organisations. By allowing widespread participation among groups with different interests, both the organised and the less organised, compromise and negotiation could take place, while the dominance of the latter could diminish (Hunter 2010:96). After intense disputes between social organisations, party leaders and neighbourhood associations, which had a longstanding associative tradition in the city, it was finally agreed that participation would not only include previously organised sectors ("the workers"), but, in contrast to São Paulo under Erundina, would also appeal to a wide range of groups and social classes, including common citizens with no prior political or social participation.[30]

The participatory budgeting process only started to work well in the last year of the first PT administration in the city, after the government was able to pass a decisive municipal fiscal reform. This reform added to the redistribution of federal resources and allowed the city of Porto Alegre to enjoy the advantages of the Brazilian decentralisation process[31] addressed in the first section of this chapter. The reform, which proved essential to the PB's success, increased the IPTU and made it more progressive. As a result, this tax over urban land and homeownership, which only amounted in 1990 to 5.8 percent of the municipal revenue, reached 13.8 percent in 1992 and around 18 percent by the late 1990s (Sousa 1998:477).[32]

The way in which this reform was achieved in the City Assembly is in itself a good example of a successful social counter-hegemonic governability strategy. Despite the PT not having a majority in Porto Alegre, both the executive and the party directorate promoted a "massive mobilisation of the popular classes" to put pressure on the rightist and centrist legislators who were initially reluctant to raise taxes (Sousa 1998:477). The tax reform was also possible because conservative parties were not as strong in the city as they were at the state level and an influential centrist party with 11 councillors, the PDT, supported this and other PT initiatives. Unlike other cities governed by the PT, where similar tax reforms proved impossible or were limited in scope, the government in Porto Alegre was able to secure sufficient resources to allocate to investment in infrastructure projects[33] and all of these resources were subject to the participatory budgeting process. This had positive effects because it made concrete impacts on people's lives and attracted further involvement in the participatory process as a whole, which only increased over the years.

Strictly speaking, the approval of the budget is a legal prerogative of the City Assembly. The mayor submits a budget proposal that the legislative is free to approve, change or even reject. However, as Boaventura de Sousa (1998:467) observed, because the executive's proposal was "sanctioned by the participatory budgeting institutions" it became "a fait accompli for the legislative body" due to the "political risk" that deputies perceived in "voting against the will of the citizens and the communities". Indeed, by the time the annual budget was sent to the Municipal Chamber for approval, city councillors did not find it easy to oppose because a strong popular pressure, mostly exercised by neighbourhood leaders, accompanied the whole process. Every year, when the budget was discussed and voted on in the city assembly, PB representatives were physically present, observing from the galleries. This had a powerful effect, even on conservative opposition parties (Hahn 2002).

PB is a particularly interesting mechanism because it did not undermine formal representative democracy, nor did it infringe the formal separation of powers between the executive and the legislative branch. It did help, however, to circumvent and "neutralize" a source of opposition in the Municipal Chamber that could be used to block its initiatives, by "stamping the budget with popular approval" (Schneider and Goldfrank 2002:14).[34] Although legislatures in Brazil have never deliberated substantially on the formulation of the budget,[35] they do influence its execution (Sousa 1998:502). Legislators do have a margin of manoeuvre to introduce modifications (or earmarks) on the budget in order to allocate specific resources that are usually addressed to their own constituencies in a clientelistic fashion. Moreover, during the budget cycle legislators tend to negotiate the liberation of those funds with the executive in exchange for supporting its initiatives—the pork-barrelling to which I referred above.

The introduction of PB in Porto Alegre changed these practices profoundly, by weakening the "old ways of doing politics" (Sousa 1998:502) and counteracting one of the main sources of power for the political elites. On the one hand, citizens came to rely on participatory institutions to satisfy their demands, rather than looking to their legislative representatives to activate clientelistic mechanisms.[36] On the other hand, once the budgetary proposal arrived in the City Assembly for approval, it had already been legitimated by a sizeable citizens' participation. In that context, approval became a simple formality (Sousa 1998:502–5). Indeed, the number of modifications (or earmarks) introduced by city councillors to the budget bill decreased significantly with PB (Hahn 2002). Ramos (2004:262–3) explains that this was in great part because legislators did not want to act against a participatory process that enjoyed great social acceptance, as they feared the electoral consequences. According to this author, who did a cross case study on participatory budgeting experiences, PB's capacity to intimidate legislators from opposition parties in Porto Alegre derived largely from the robustness of the whole process and the fact that in this city, unlike elsewhere, 100 percent of the budget allocated to investment, which increased significantly under PT governments, was discussed at PB assemblies (Ramos 2004:262–3).

PB in Porto Alegre was particularly important to a party looking for alternative solutions to secure governability, while facing electoral pressures to broaden its constituency beyond the party's social base. PT leaders in the southern state of Rio Grande do Sul, most of them particularly enthusiastic about PB, argued during our interviews that this instrument allowed the party to broaden its "dialogue" towards the middle class and other sectors in Porto Alegre and enable it to move beyond organised groups in the PT field.[37] Studies show, on the one hand, that a wide diversity of groups participated in the process, ranging from community movements to members of trade unions and even business sector representatives and, on the other hand, that an important proportion of ordinary citizens engaged.[38] Surveys show that by the late 1990s between 30 and 40 percent of participants in PB assemblies belonged to no specific organised group.[39]

This participatory instrument also helped the party reach many of the unorganised poor, as the PT had been unable to do in previous years. Survey studies show that some of the poorest citizens participated in the process with great intensity.[40] Abers (2003) found that not only did the poorest areas of the city took part in PB assemblies, but impoverished areas with little prior history of civil organisation and previously dominated by clientelistic neighbourhood politics, engaged with even greater intensity. By giving unorganised sectors a chance to participate and negotiate their demands, PB enabled the PT in Porto Alegre to gather support from a sector of the population that was difficult to mobilise electorally and did not necessarily agree with the party in the past. Interestingly, PB also became acceptable for the middle classes, many of which, without necessarily participating, looked on approvingly at a process that seemed to promote transparency, accountability and "good governance" at a time when corruption had become a major political issue in Brazil, particularly after Collor's impeachment.[41] Moreover, powerful economic groups did not oppose PB in itself. Large construction companies even supported the instrument because they directly benefited from the massive and unprecedented investment in public works seen during these years (Abers 1996:39).[42]

According to different authors, PB had a positive electoral impact in Porto Alegre.[43] In 1988 the Popular Front, the coalition of left parties led by the PT, won the mayoral election by only 34.3 percent of the vote and by 40.8 percent in 1992. After 1996, once the PB had been consolidated, it took 56 percent (Sousa 1998:464), while in 2000 Tarso Genro was elected mayor with 63.51 percent.[44] This made Porto Alegre one of the main electoral bastions of the Workers' Party.[45] The success of PB, and the promise to implement it at the state level, helped the PT to win the governor's race in Rio Grande do Sul in 1998, with Olívio Dutra as its candidate.[46] In the capital city, almost 80 percent voted for Dutra.[47] This was not only evidence of the PB's electoral success. Possibly, it was also an indication that multiple strata of society, not just the working class or organised sectors, were enthusiastic about the "PT way of governing" in Porto Alegre.

PB in Porto Alegre became an international reference point and many Brazilian cities incorporated some type of participatory budgeting mechanism. The number of cities adopting this instrument increased from 36 in 1996 to 140 in 2003, and to 170 in 2004.[48] By 2004, most PT governments had implemented participatory budgeting mechanisms (Wampler 2007), including large and important state capitals such as São Paulo, Bello Horizonte and Recife. Even other parties came to adopt the model, although none of them in the same proportion.[49] The way this instrument was implemented had different characteristics and did not always reach the same scope. Porto Alegre was one of the few cases in which the resources related to investment that were discussed in the PB process amounted to 100 percent.[50] Nevertheless in many other cities it became a legitimate and influential instrument that councillors could not ignore.[51]

São Paulo under Suplicy: Moving Towards an Elite-Centred Strategy

The governability strategy under Marty Suplicy prioritised elite alliances across party lines over popular mobilisation or participatory politics, moving the PT as a whole closer to mainstream Brazilian parties. When Suplicy was elected mayor in 2000, the PT was a very different organisation than in 1988, the year in which Erundina won the City Hall by a very small margin. In Chapter 3 I discuss how the party as a national organisation became more of a vote-seeking machine towards the late 1990s. Authors have argued that, because of electoral motivations, alliances were playing a more important role, particularly among PT members running for sub-national executive public office.[52] This emphasis on alliances, as Hunter (2010:86) explains, resulted in great part from new electoral legislation passed in 1992, which established a runoff after the first round in municipal elections. This provision, she maintains, encouraged the formation of electoral alliances with nonideological or centrist parties in order to secure victories in runoffs. Such a practice derived from the practical calculations made by party leaders. In the 1996 municipal election, the PT only won 2 of the 11 races that involved a second round. After examining the results carefully, party leaders found that by broadening their alliances they could easily have won in the second round in several cities (Hunter 2010:99).

The change of strategy was visible in the mayoral race of 2000. In the same election that made Suplicy mayor, party candidates running for capital cities such as Rio Branco (Acre) or Macapá (Amapá) incorporated support from centre-right organisations such as the Liberal Party (PL) or even the ultranationalist Party for the Reconstruction of National Order (PRONA). In São Paulo, however, the PT did not go this far during the contest. Its electoral alliance was with only two left-of-centre parties—the PCdoB and PSB. Nevertheless, in government the party eventually approached conservative parties. The case of São Paulo illustrates clearly that this shift in the alliance strategies of the PT was not motivated only by electoral concerns, as authors have emphasised. As in many other transformations experienced by the party, governability was also a powerful driving force.

After 1998, as the PT concentrated its energies more directly on winning the presidency, the enthusiasm around social counter-hegemonic governability strategies started to lose momentum among influential moderate leaders within the PT who had become dominant in São Paulo. In 1999 José Dirceu, who was president of the party from 1995 to 2002, provocatively argued that the "PT way of governing" was "outdated" (Dirceu 1999:18). Although he acknowledged the importance of its most characteristic features—participation, transparency, redistribution—he also explained that the party was facing a new challenge and PT local authorities needed to "keep in mind the national situation" and search for new allies among political parties (Dirceu 1999:23–5). Dirceu's statement formally inaugurated a new phase in the life of the PT. Indeed, by the early 2000s, when Suplicy was elected in São Paulo, moderate party leaders were convinced that PT administrations would have to pay a certain price to promote alliances and avoid gridlock.

With the 2002 presidential election in mind, the PT selected a candidate for São Paulo that could be palatable to the middle classes and the elites, mainly in order to meet the conservative profile of the *Paulista* electorate which differs from that of Porto Alegre. Strongly influenced by Lula's faction at the national level, the party opted for someone with no working-class background, almost a complete outsider: a psychologist known publicly for hosting a controversial national TV show on sexuality. Married to Eduardo Suplicy, a well-respected PT Senator, Marty Suplicy entered politics in 1994 as a congressional representative. Due to her upper-class background, she was portrayed in the media as the "PT Chanel" or the "PT Light".[53] Concerned with the presidential election, party leaders knew that the Suplicy administration would be at the centre of media attention. The Erundina experience and its permanent conflicts with dominant strategic actors and among PT factions could not be repeated.

After the election, one of the PT's main concerns was the mayor's relationship with the City Assembly. The party had 21 out of 55 seats (see Table 4.1), while the government needed at least 28 votes to pass legislation. "It was very clear to me", Suplicy acknowledged during our interview, "that without support in the chamber I could not pass one single law" (09/01/09). In order to secure that support, the PT government opted to exchange votes for patronage appointments with almost all sorts of political parties. This traditional approach to governability came to be understood in the following years as "the gathering of political support across party lines" (Ottman 2009:71). From the outset, Suplicy's main power broker, Rui Falcão, attempted to approach city councillors from other parties, intending to negotiate a plural cabinet in the form of a coalition government. Achieving this, however, was not possible because some PT city councillors, particularly on the party Left, expressed serious objections, and because the different factions demanded a large share in government portfolios. Seeking to avoid paralysing conflicts with intraparty groups, the mayor did not contradict these groups and offered cabinet seats to their main representatives. Despite these constraints, she was careful to form a government that would not be regarded as entirely *Petista* (Fiorilo 2006:105–9) and included some members from other parties or with no partisan affiliation.[54]

The Suplicy administration did not distribute cabinet seats to form a coalition government. Instead it gave out jobs at lower bureaucratic levels, and that eventually allowed the government to pass most of its initiatives. Suplicy also promoted a decentralisation process by which her government created 31 sub-municipalities to replace the old administrative structures of the city. This measure, conceived as a democratic achievement, allowed the administration to obtain votes in exchange for the newly created positions. The government negotiated the appointment of sub-mayors with seven different parties,[55] including politicians from previous administrations, some of them "ultra-conservatives" (Ottman 2009:73). Although the strategy made many PT and social leaders uncomfortable, it yielded results: The Suplicy administration passed more than 75 percent of its bills during its four-year term (Fiorilo 2006:160). The bargaining with other parties, however, involved not only appointments, but also a discretionary distribution of budgetary resources and the liberation of parliamentary earmarks to specific allies in the Municipal Chamber. The comfortable majority that the PT administration achieved in the legislative branch came at a price: The party eventually cultivated practices of patronage and pork-barrelling not unlike those to which it had long been ideologically and ethically opposed.[56]

Suplicy ruled out any possible counter-mobilisation strategy to put pressure on the legislative branch.[57] In São Paulo, the most influential leaders of the party were either opposed or sceptical of the extent to which it could be successful. José Américo, Secretary of Communications at the time, later president of the PT in the city of São Paulo, argued during our conversation that "the idea of a governability supported on social movements is completely utopian". In his view, "social movements are not strong enough to sustain a government" and "people cannot remain mobilised for ever" (11/11/08). Antonio Donato, head of sub-municipalities during the Suplicy administration, has a similar opinion: "A strategy of this type", he holds, "is only possible in revolutionary situations (. . .) Social movements are not active all the time, as was demonstrated during the Erundina administration" (12/11/08).

Participation, the other element by which a social counter-hegemonic governability strategy was promoted in some PT governments, was not prioritised by the Suplicy administration. Suplicy did create a Participatory Budget, but it never became a central part of her government.[58] PB in São Paulo did not acquire a high profile in the planning process or within the administrative structure (Pires 2006) and was made subordinate to other welfare policies (such as the minimum-income cash-transfer programme or the unified centres of education) that were more important for the administration. Studies show that these policies were successful at tackling extreme poverty in the city and promoted redistribution, but did not involve citizen participation,[59] and were managed in a rather "technocratic" fashion (Ottman 2009:70). Interestingly, PB assemblies attracted a large number of participants[60] and were enthusiastically supported by social organisations (Teixeira and Tatagiba 2005). However, no relevant public works resulted from their decisions (Carneiro 2006; Pires 2006) and, unlike in cities such as Porto Alegre, Recife or Belo Horizonte, São Paulo's PB was mostly limited to previously organised sectors, failing to reach the unorganised poor in the periphery.

By and large, the mayor and her inner circle lacked a strong commitment to participatory democracy, and some leaders were even against promoting broad-based participatory mechanisms. I found some examples among PT leaders who occupied key positions in the Suplicy administration. For instance, when I asked Arselino Tatto, a leader of one of the most influential factions of the PT in the city of São Paulo and one of Suplicy's closest political allies, his opinions on participatory democracy, he said: "That's a mess.[61] People's participation takes place through their elected governments" (12/11/08). Likewise, Donato went as far as arguing that councils or assemblies with power to make binding decisions constitute a form of "leftist populism" that is "deployed to manipulate the masses" (12/11/08).

PB in the city did not have real decision-making power. In the way officials understood participation, conclusions reached in those arenas were only suggestions exerting no power of compulsion over the government. The policy in relation to resolutions made in participatory spaces was one of "pick and choose" in which the administration would have the prerogative at all times to decide if their implementation was desirable (Carneiro 2006:100). Without the legitimacy that PB acquired in other cities, the final budgetary decisions in São Paulo were always in the hands of the city councillors (Teixeira and Tatagiba 2005) who negotiated allocations in the traditional Brazilian way of doing politics. A study conducted by the Polis Institute, which gathered the views of social activists regarding the administration, found great disappointment with PB under Suplicy. In general, activists thought that the government manipulated participatory arenas and used them to legitimise decisions previously made in closed spaces (Teixeira and Tatagiba 2005). The study concluded that although Suplicy's government established dialogue with and listened to social organisations, it failed to back up participatory mechanisms as other PT administrations had.

High-ranking officials who served in the second PT administration in São Paulo argue that the size of the city, with 10.4 million inhabitants in 2000 (more than the population in most Brazilian states), made PB implementation more difficult than in municipalities such as Porto Alegre.[62] By the time Lula became president of Brazil, moderate sectors seemed to believe that the size of the polity imposes limitations for PB.[63] Indeed, the experience of implementing PB at the state level did not go far. In 1995 the administration of Vítor Buaiz in Espírito Santo briefly made an attempt, but abandoned it within a year (Macaulay and Burton 2003), while other experiments were undertaken in Rio de Janeiro, Mato Grosso do Sul and the Federal District (Brasília).

Only in Rio Grande do Sul, under Dutra, was PB maintained for a whole government term. Despite the lack of sufficient studies on this experience, the evidence suggests that this instrument was not particularly successful. Goldfrank and Schneider (2006), the only authors who have seriously studied this experience at the state level, even consider that the PT's failure to win reelection in Rio Grande do Sul was in great part due to the unfulfilled expectations that the PB raised among the middle sectors and the popular classes. According to them, the failure to increase investment in infrastructure, particularly roads, hospitals and schools, and the raises in state-controlled taxes, among other reasons, weakened the PT's campaign and eventually "raised questions about the sustainability of participatory budgeting and about its utility in advancing partisan goals" (Goldfrank and Schneider 2006:21).[64]

One could also argue that what was possible in a capital city with 1.3 million inhabitants (Porto Alegre in the 1980s) was not easy to achieve in the wider state with a population of more than 10 million, such as Rio Grande do Sul or a city as populated as São Paulo. This might sound obvious to some observers, but it was not evident to the PT. Many party leaders in Rio Grande do Sul, particularly those placed in the party Left, considered that the PB process at the state level was a successful experience.[65] Arno Agustín, Finance Secretary in Porto Alegre and Rio Grande do Sul and later Secretary to the Treasury under the Lula administration, even argued that PB at the state level was a "great success, which demonstrated that the instrument could be implemented in the national sphere" (20/10/10). Even Lula's government programme contemplated the creation of a participatory budgeting mechanism at the national level, a story that I relate in Chapter 7.

CONCLUSION

Throughout the 1990s PT national leaders became aware of the challenges that local administrations experienced to achieve governability. Many of them increasingly understood the importance of forming legislative alliances in municipal chambers and state assemblies. However, they were unwilling to adopt practices by which mainstream Brazilian parties establish those alliances—that is, by exchanging votes for political favours and budgetary resources. At least until 1998, when Lula and the PT at the national level started to prioritise legislative alliances with centrist and conservative parties, influential leaders in central office expected that governability strategies could follow a social counter-hegemonic model, different from mainstream Brazilian politics. Under the influence of the PT "genetic model", these leaders envisaged social mobilisation and politics of participation as the main pillars of this model.

By the time Lula assumed national executive public office, the PT had not resolved its own debate on governability and it had not necessarily found a replicable successful formula for its innovative counter-hegemonic governability approach. As I have shown in this chapter, mobilising the party's social base alone proved to be insufficient to counter-balance a minority status in the legislative branch, as was clear under Erundina. Promoting broad-based participatory strategies, as in Porto Alegre, seemed to be more effective in putting pressure on the legislative branch and passing some government initiatives. This became possible, however, under specific circumstances that were not present in all cases: on one side, the political commitment to promote a strong, inclusive, legitimate and broad-based participatory process such as PB that covered all of the resources allocated to investment; on the other side, the lack of a strong conservative opposition and the existence of centre-left allies like the PDT willing to support the administration. Other factors not extensively analysed here might have played a role, such as the strong associative tradition in the city or the size of the polity.

Part II
The Lula Years

5 Political Governability under Lula
The Elite-Centred Strategy in Ascendancy

The governability dilemma contributed a great deal to the transformation of the Brazilian Workers' Party and shaped its behaviour in profound ways since the party occupied sub-national executive public office. This has been neglected in existing accounts on the transformation of the PT, even when the Lula administration is studied. Most scholars emphasise the way in which Lula altered his discourse as part of an electorally maximising strategy. In their works, they mainly pay attention to how Lula moderated his programme in his fourth attempt to become president, and professionalised his electoral strategy even further than in previous electoral contests.[1] In this chapter I argue that the changes that occurred during the electoral campaign took place because Lula and his inner circle were creating conditions to enable them eventually to govern, and so they were not only concerned with putting in place a successful electoral strategy.

Once Lula had assumed the presidency, I contend, governability became an even more important issue, which altered the discourses and strategies of the party in public and central office. PT scholars have not acknowledged this because even their accounts of the party in power emphasise electability. When Hunter examines the experience of the PT in the national executive, for instance, she regards the developments of the Lula administration as "a continuation of the same process" that the party experienced during the 1990s (Hunter 2011:307). I argue that the experience of the PT in national government was far more than simply the continuation of a process that started in previous years, and which drove the party towards moderation and pragmatism. Rather, it was a process with its own rationale and motivations.

The political dimension of governability during the Lula years is the main focus of this chapter. Scholars who study the Brazilian political system have explained how the Lula administration faced a major challenge because, despite the massive number of votes received in the 2002 presidential election, the PT was in a very weak position in the legislative branch.[2] Many scholars have explained that in the context of a hybrid political system defined as "coalition presidentialism" (Abranches 1988), Brazilian presidents need to engage in intensive negotiations with political parties in order to secure legislative majorities and avoid gridlock.[3] When analysing governability under

Lula, they have adopted a similar approach.[4] These authors, however, have failed to address the whole spectrum of governability strategies that the PT put in place at the sub-national level and that went beyond the traditional elite bargains of Brazilian politics described in previous pages.

One cannot assume *tout court*, as some of the literature on the Brazilian political system does when it looks at the Lula administration, that a party with the PT tradition was expected to construct governability in the national executive just like other Brazilian parties when they govern. Empirical evidence shows that when progressive parties are in a minority position or act in multiparty alliances they tend to make stronger appeals to their social allies in order to build broader bases of support (and they do this less when they enjoy comfortable legislative majorities).[5] During the two Lula administrations, the PT had the lowest number of congressional representatives of any other progressive party in government in Latin America at the time.[6] Scholars have not yet tried to explain why, despite such a scenario, the party in government did not seek greater support among its social allies to promote counter-hegemonic governability strategies. These types of strategies, as Chapter 1 explains, can take place through mobilisation (both in its proactive and defensive forms) and broad-based participation. In this chapter I mainly look at the first two, while participation is analysed in Chapter 7.

In the following pages I show how the PT in the national executive—Lula and his inner circle, in particular—adopted an elite-centred strategy similar to other Brazilian parties. This strategy, however, was not coherent from the beginning and it took place in three different stages. The first was during the electoral campaign, when Lula's inner circle started laying the foundations for governability should they win. By taking an anticipatory response to face the future challenges of public office, Lula's campaign team started to accommodate the interests of dominant strategic actors in an elite-centred fashion. His discourse, however, also appealed to the mobilisation of civil society in order to support the PT project. The second stage took place once he was in office, between January 2003 and June 2005, when the PT put in place a hybrid governability strategy. It was a hybrid strategy because it was neither counter-hegemonic nor elite-centred in the classic Brazilian way. Despite the fact that the party made bargains with political elites to secure congressional support, it put itself in an artificial hegemonic position in government and it did not share power with different parties in proportion to their share of congressional seats. Finally, the third stage took place after June 2005, when the initial arrangements led to a political crisis that revealed the failure of the governability strategy which had been put in place. As a consequence of this crisis, PT leaders adopted an elite-centred strategy similar to most Brazilian parties. This strategy became even stronger during the second Lula administration.

This chapter relies on party documents, with the intention of highlighting the contrasts between the official positions of the party in central office with those of Lula's inner circle, but it also relies on a number of interviews with

THE FIRST STAGE: THE PT EN ROUTE TO THE PRESIDENCY

In 2002, Lula presented an electoral manifesto that appealed for a "new social contract" between the government, business and workers to resume economic growth and promote an "alternative development model".[7] It was a social democratic programme (although PT leaders have always rejected such a label) because the future administration would respect the existing legislation and institutional mechanisms, but it would also promote deep structural reforms of a political, economic and social nature. Lula's manifesto not only included some short mid-term objectives that his administration eventually delivered with positive results, such as raising the minimum wage in real terms (Coligação Lula Presidente 2002a:25) or expanding compensatory social policies for the poor (Coligação Lula Presidente 2002a:41–4). It also included several legal reforms, most of which were never accomplished. As part of a strategy to improve income distribution, for instance, the core of the programme included a progressive income tax reform, the creation of new contributions on patrimony and inheritance; urban reform, and the acceleration of constitutionally mandated land reform. The document also encompassed labour reform to alter the corporatist system inherited from the Vargas era;[8] political reform; and even the creation of a Participatory Budget at the national level, but with adaptations (see Chapter 7).[9]

Before Lula came into office, the experience of democratically elected left-wing parties in national governments was limited in Latin America, and not always successful in securing governability. The Chilean case of Salvador Allende (1970–1973) was an important reference for the PT, as for many others in the Latin American Left. Notwithstanding the different historical circumstances, PT leaders did not want to revisit an experience of political and social instability, which ended tragically in a military coup. At least since 1989, when Lula first ran for president, the Sixth PT National Conference acknowledged the need to incorporate the lessons of "the rich experience of the Allende Government" in order to avoid "repeating any similar outcome".[10] From this experience, many in the party learned that dominant strategic actors in the political and economic sphere could cause the failure of a progressive government. They had also perceived that winning the presidency was not the same as "fully conquering political power", as PT delegates wrote in their 1989 resolution.[11] The PT field, however, did not share a single vision on how to approach these strategic actors. Some groups supported a counter-hegemonic approach, inspired by the "PT way of governing" while others were more inclined to accommodate the interests of the most influential elites.

It is not easy to draw a precise line between the two strategies, the social counter-hegemonic and the elite-centred, because they coexisted in contradictory ways among PT leaders and even within certain individuals. By and large, the social strategy was more influential in the party Left, within factions such as Left Articulation and Socialist Democracy, the latter of which formed "Message to the Party" in 2005. It was also present among party leaders with no experience in public office who had mainly developed their careers within the party bureaucracy. In addition, the social counter-hegemonic strategy had strong support among the leaders of civil society organisations such as the MST and the Housing Movement, but at this stage was less strong in CUT's dominant sector. Leaders who took part in PT municipal administrations in which participatory instruments were stronger and particularly successful, such as Porto Alegre, were also enthusiastic defenders.

The elite-centred strategy, in contrast, had more followers in the heterogeneous *Campo Majoritário* (Lula's faction, later known as "Building a New Brazil"), which formed the party's dominant coalition. Its supporters were some of the keenest office-seeking cadres, who had mostly developed their careers in sub-national executive public office, governing large and complex cities in which they became accustomed to negotiating with a wide range of groups and actors. The main defenders of this strategy were inside Lula's inner circle. Support for this strategy was also strong among PT members who became professionals in public office either as technocrats, civil servants or political advisors. Many trade union leaders from the private sector, who had engaged in negotiations with business representatives and the state during the 1990s, also tended to sympathise with the elite-centred perspective.

The influence of the supporters of a counter-hegemonic strategy was clear in the resolution that the party passed in December 2001 in its 12th National Conference. In contrast, the manifesto for election that Lula presented to the voters, mainly drafted by his inner circle or members of his faction,[12] had a stronger elite-centred approach. These two documents differed in their positions towards dominant strategic actors and the institutions under the control of these actors. On the political side, the party document was critical of a "conservative political system" in which decisions result from the "exchange of favours" conducted in a "top-down" fashion and excluding "the participation of the people".[13] In this context, the document valued the PT participatory experience, not only as part of an effort to democratise the state, but also as a deliberate strategy to "dispute hegemony"[14] in the Gramscian perspective that had influenced party documents since the late 1980s (Burgos 1994:Ch.3). Such an approach was not contemplated in Lula's campaign manifesto, in which the emphasis was placed on the promotion of inclusive negotiations and "great national agreements" in which all sectors, even large business groups, opposition parties and other dominant strategic actors, would participate.[15]

The social counter-hegemonic strategy in the PT did not seek an overthrow of the "dominant bloc", neither did it entail an attempt to suppress adversaries nor to promote "anti-institutional confrontational strategies" such as those attributed to Hugo Chávez (Valencia 2005:81) in Venezuela, and Evo Morales (Larson, Madrid et al. 2008:7), in Bolivia. As Chapter 1 explains, the PT did not propose an assault on the privileged or a serious challenge to their interests by means of a massive programme of expropriations, factory take-overs or anything of that kind. The attempt was not to confront strategic actors directly, but to neutralise their influence through radical democracy, mass mobilisation and broad-based social participation. In 1987, for instance, the PT regarded the dispute of hegemony as a process of "accumulating forces" that would combine "mass struggle" with the occupation of institutional spaces. In its First National Congress, which took place in 1991, the party had established that disputing hegemony meant "constructing an enormous social movement in favour of deep political, economic and social reforms".[16]

Social counter-hegemonic strategies had been contemplated by the PT since Lula first ran for the presidency in 1989. In the document *Guidelines for the Drafting of an Electoral Manifesto* discussed before the campaign, party delegates established that despite the limitations imposed by the dominant elites, not only was mobilisation a "key element in the balance of forces", but also all their chances of success would rely "on the perspective of promoting workers' mobilisation on a gigantic scale".[17] Influenced by these ideas, the defenders of a social counter-hegemonic strategy, knowing like everyone else that the PT would not easily achieve a majority in Congress, calculated that popular pressure would be able to modify the balance of forces and help to pass progressive reforms. This strategy was spelt out by the 12th National Conference:

> [O]nce we succeed in the first and the second round [of the presidential election in 2002] we will need to build a wide social and political base capable of putting into practice the programme of transformations defended in the elections. We have to guarantee both governability and the fulfilment of our programme (. . .) Our programmatic objectives can only be fulfilled with an intense mobilisation of society. The articulation between popular struggles and the institutions is decisive in this new historical period". (Partido dos Trabalhadores 2004:588–9)

The position that the party officially adopted in its 2001 conference was not well received by Lula's entourage. In particular, campaign strategists rejected the recurrent language of "ruptures", used in the document, and which they regarded as "associated with revolutionary or violent change" (García 10/04/09). In the opinion of a Lula advisor, the PT resolution did not address "the crucial issues that were at stake in the 2002 election" and it "blocked the relationship with the middle classes and the business sector" (Ant 26/11/08 and 03/12/08).[18] The defenders of the elite-centred perspective emphasised alliances and negotiations with both the economic *status quo* and a broader range of political parties. The Minister for Social Development, Patrus Ananias, pointed out:

> You cannot rule a country alone. You need to establish a dialogue and negotiations. In the past, great [left-wing government] experiences failed because they lacked such understanding: it happened in Chile with Salvador Allende[19] and it also happened here in Brazil with João Goulart. The government that wants to generate transformation must search for allies. The political and economic forces surrounding us do exist. We did not win a revolution . . . but even when you do, you always have to negotiate unless you want to exterminate anyone who thinks differently. . . (Ananias 16/07/09).

Lula's electoral manifesto in 2002 emphasised the need to negotiate the main reforms and policies it contemplated with a wide range of groups and actors. This approach characterised his campaign from the start. Political strategists presented Lula as an "aggregator" of multiple interests and as the "great negotiator" that the country needed in order to seat every relevant actor around a negotiation table (Miguel 2006:133). Lula approached the business sector in a way he had not done before, and reassured its representatives that their fundamental interests would not be at risk. For the first time in a PT national campaign, the party incorporated in its electoral coalition a centre-right political organisation, the Liberal Party (PL), and appointed its main leader, José Alencar, a businessman from the textile sector, as candidate to the vice presidency.[20] The general strategy proved electorally effective. Scholars have argued that key to Lula's triumph was not only the result of the professionalisation of his communication strategy, and the way in which his "unpalatable aggressive image" was replaced by a "conciliatory and docile" one,[21] but also a result of his capacity to gather support among prominent members of the traditional elite and the business class that endorsed his candidacy.[22]

Despite the importance of these elements, I argue that the transformation of Lula's discourse during the campaign was not only part of an electoral strategy. It also anticipated a governability strategy. The clearest signal of that strategy was the "Letter to the Brazilian People",[23] drafted by a small group of leaders within Lula's entourage and published in June 2002.[24] In this document Lula departed from the positions adopted by the PT in central office, influenced by the supporters of a counter-hegemonic strategy. In the context of a delicate economic situation, which I explore in more detail in the next chapter, Lula used this letter to generate trust and avoid a crisis that would jeopardise his future government. By doing so, he reassured the financial sector that their fundamental interests would not be at risk.

In retrospect, the letter can be read as a manifesto for governability, but as one constructed through agreements among strategic actors. From the very first line, the document not only spoke about the need to "pacify" the country and promote "stability", but also highlighted the interests of promoting changes based on alliances and negotiations.[25] Interestingly, the letter failed to mention what the role of civil society would be in the future Lula administration. Instead, attention was largely put on the economy. Not everyone in the PT field understood the implications of the letter. Many social leaders at the time considered that it was simply an electoral move. Only later did they perceive that both its content and its spirit were there to be followed.

THE SECOND STAGE: LEAVING COUNTER-HEGEMONIC MOBILISATION ASIDE

It was not entirely clear what type of governability strategy Lula intended to put in place when he assumed the presidency in January 2003. The uncertainty persisted because the 2002 election gave Lula a massive number of votes, revealing him to be a highly popular leader, but it left the PT in a very weak position in Congress. In the second round of the 2002 presidential election, the former metalworker received 53 million votes (61 percent of the total),[26] the highest record in a Brazilian presidential election. The position of the PT, however, was weak in both legislative chambers: It had 17.7 percent of the seats in the Lower House and 17.3 percent in the Senate. The party in government had to relate to a chamber of 513 congressional representatives, in which only 91 were *petistas*, and a Senate of 81 members where it only held 14 seats. With the parties that officially supported Lula during the first and second rounds of the presidential campaign[27] the PT had 42.7 percent of the votes in the Lower Chamber and 37 percent in the Senate (Couto and Baia 2006:10), an insufficient majority to pass legislation. Centre-right and right-wing parties controlled at least 328 seats. The strongest parties represented in the Lower House of Congress after the PT were the main three parties that supported the Cardoso administration—the Liberal Front Party (PFL), the Brazilian Social Democratic Party (PSDB) and the Party of the Brazilian Democratic Movement (PMDB) (Pereira, Power and Raile 2011:44–5).

This balance of forces made a number of party and social leaders believe that a counter-mobilisation strategy could eventually be put in place, at least in order to promote certain reforms. The idea was not to avoid negotiating with other parties in Congress, but to build social support in order to negotiate with these parties from a position of strength. Members of the party Left were the most enthusiastic supporters of such a strategy, but even some leaders within Lula's entourage sympathised with the idea.[28] Social leaders in particular wanted to see Lula and the PT "putting social movements in the streets" in order to encourage legislative reforms according to common interests.[29] Many of them favoured using the charisma and popularity of the president to instigate citizens' mass mobilisation in public campaigns.

In the party Left, leaders were particularly convinced that counter-mobilisation was a precondition to promote a progressive government.

Valter Pomar, one of the most visible figures of the faction Left Articulation (AE), defended this strategy during our interview on the grounds that "it is impossible to generate transformation only by institutional means. An external pressure and a certain subversive strategy are necessary". According to this leader, "the PT has to respect institutions, but it also has to oppose them. If we only 'respect them', as some claim, there will be no transformation" (Pomar 08/04/09). Another member of Left Articulation who requested anonymity made a similar point, but in a metaphorical way: "Lula should put pressure on Congress and then negotiate. We have to smash the windows of Parliament. When legislators have pressure upon them they get scared and vote".

The most influential party leaders in public office, however, even rejected social leaders when they suggested the use of mass mobilization in one way or another. Two members of the National Confederation of Agricultural Workers (CONTAG) confided that in private meetings with PT congressional representatives they were systematically turned down whenever they offered to engage in mobilisation strategies to promote common agendas. This occurred, for instance, when they visited the speaker of the Lower House, *Deputado* Arnildo Chinaglia, and suggested demonstrating outside Congress to support a reform of the rural pension system. The activists were said to be disillusioned when Chinaglia apparently told them: "There is no point in going and shouting outside Congress. That does not solve anything. If you think that is going to alter the votes you are simply deluded" (Borba and Cleia 03/04/08).

During the interviews conducted for this study I found that counter-hegemonic mobilisation strategies were only supported in strong terms by leaders in the party Left and social activists in the PT field. These leaders considered that putting pressure on parliament is a legitimate and desirable alternative; 80 percent of my interviewees in Left Articulation (AE) and 72 percent in "Message to the Party" (MP) endorsed this strategy. However, only 23 percent of the interviewees within Lula's faction, "Building a New Brazil", supported this approach.[30] Within this faction, a number of leaders consider that the role of the PT is no longer to promote mobilisation, but mainly to act in institutional settings within the political system. For them, the centre of political action is in government, and no longer in the streets. This was clear in an interview with the PT National Secretary for Mobilisation and a member of Lula's faction, Marinete Merss, with the statutory responsibility of promoting mobilisation campaigns. During our conversation I asked why the PT Executive Commission failed to promote mobilisation during the Lula years. She answered:

> When we arrived in government we assumed the agenda of many social movements because we were many of those movements or we were inserted within them (. . .) Today we are in the position to make public policies (. . .) Our role in society is not just to mobilise, it is to govern

Brazil (. . .) I do not feel any nostalgia for the old PT. I think being in government is wonderful. It is by implementing public policies that you can change people's lives. The party exists to achieve power. Our route is institutional (. . .) We made the PT and disputed elections to win and to conduct a democratic and popular government. This is what we are doing. I do not feel nostalgia for my time as a trade union leader when I had to struggle for 57 days because the government simply would not receive us. (Merss 10/12/08)

The main detractors of a counter-mobilisation strategy were inside the "hard nucleus" of the party in government. The first and most important reason for their scepticism—and most probably the main reason why this strategy was not implemented—was a fear of political and social instability. Many leaders were afraid that confronting formal representative institutions could have resulted in a takeover or a coup promoted by conservative sectors.[31] Alberto Cury (02/12/08), a government official responsible for the liaison between the presidential office and civil society organisations, observed: "We did not want to install a government of crisis, because the conservative sectors would have immediately acted against us. The power of the Right in this country is immense". Cury emphasises that the PT opted to "avoid a government of confrontation", and instead create one of "negotiation and compromise among different sectors for the sake of a national development project".[32] The PT Left did not observe the risks that those in the "hard nucleus" did. For the leftist leaders, counter-mobilisation was not attempted because Lula was "scared of seeing the people in the streets" (Hipólito 03/04/09). The same characterisation of Lula's "aversion to conflict", made by Perry Anderson (2011:7) in a recent article, is considered by leaders in the party Left as the reason why such a strategy was not used, and for Pomar (08/04/09), the president was "an extremely conservative and cautious guy" who "did not want any risk".

In the view of the "hard nucleus" of the party in government, however, previous Latin American experiences suggested that instigating mobilisation can be a risky bet. Party leaders argue that Lula was different from Chávez or Morales, who tried to mobilise their social bases so as to put pressure on strategic actors and formal representative institutions.[33] Unlike some members of the party Left or social activists who explicitly expressed sympathy for the strategies of these governments,[34] the defenders of an elite-centred perspective regarded them with strong suspicion. "Brazil is not a country in which a problem of governability can be solved through popular pressure", was the comment made by José Dirceu (07/01/09) in this regard. Rui Falcão, leader of one of the most influential factions in the city of São Paulo, acknowledged that mobilisation can play a role "in times of rupture, or during periods of political, social and economic crisis". However, he warned that this could be problematic because "neither Evo nor Chávez are free from eventual coups d'état attempts" (Falcão 11/12/08).

There is another reason why counter-hegemonic mobilisation might have not been attempted: Many social leaders were dubious about the strength of civil society organisations in Brazil to support it in practical terms. Even some members of Lula's inner circle (who argued during the interviews that they were not opposed in principle to a strategy of this type) considered that Brazilian "social movements" lack sufficient "strength" to put pressure on the legislative branch.[35] In the centre-left of the party, José Eduardo Martins Cardozo, PT General-Secretary during the Lula years and member of "Message to the Party", argues that it would be "naïve" to expect to be able to construct governability with civil society organisations. Martins Cardozo, who was Home Affairs Secretary under Erundina, recalls that such a strategy was attempted during that administration, but failed. In order to be successful, he argues, "social movements should have an influence that they do not have in reality" (Martins Cardozo 04/12/08). Even in the party Left, some leaders acknowledge that civil society organisations could not easily alter the balance of forces in parliament.[36] A congressional representative from Left Articulation, Iriny Lopes, argues that "social movements are not hegemonic in our society and do not articulate properly even among themselves". In her view, these organisations are not at "their peak" and would not mobilise to sustain a country of the size of Brazil" (Lopes 03/12/08).

These views suggest that, regardless of the fears of political and social stability, the odds of failing were high. A counter-hegemonic governability strategy could not rely exclusively on the potential of the PT social base to promote mass mobilisation in the form of street protests or large demonstrations. Besides, strategies of disruptive action, as Chapter 3 explains, were largely left aside during the postdemocratic transition years and could not easily be readopted. However, the PT at the sub-national level had developed other types of counter-hegemonic governability strategies, such as the promotion of broad-based participatory mechanisms. In some cases these initiatives proved useful for circumventing or neutralising legislative opposition and building an alternative democratic legitimacy. In Chapter 7 I will analyse the characteristics of Lula's participatory agenda and why it did not serve to achieve similar objectives.

A Hybrid Strategy to Deal with the Brazilian System

In the highly fragmented multiparty system (in which the election of Congress is made from an open list and on a proportional basis) it is almost impossible for any president to achieve a legislative majority, as scholars have explained.[37] In order to pass reforms, presidents are forced to form large coalitions and engage in a permanent bargaining process with other political forces. Under the Brazilian political system of "coalition presidentialism", executives are only capable of passing legislation by forming large coalitions, similarly to European prime ministers in multiparty systems. Amorim (1994:18), for example, suggests that the institutional characteristics of the Brazilian system are so decisive in orientating the formation of cabinets that any executive reluctant to negotiate ministerial jobs with other political parties might face serious difficulties, not only to pass legislation, but also to defend itself from eventual parliamentary investigations.

One of the problems of "coalition presidentialism" that other political scientists have noticed is that the formation of multipartisan cabinets in Brazil is "an insufficient strategy to guarantee legislative success" (Power 2009:27). Because the system is characterised by numerous "weakly disciplined parties" (Ames 2000:160), patronage-based agreements between national party organisations are not always enough to secure the votes of all their members in Congress. Brazilian presidents also need to engage in pork-barrelling strategies to secure support among their allies in Congress (Pereira, Power and Raile 2011:38). Because in Brazil the executive has discretionary authority to choose which individual amendments introduced by legislators in the annual budget will eventually be executed and disbursed by the government,[38] the release of budgetary resources is used as "political currency" in exchange for votes (Alston and Mueller 2006:87). In sum, both the distribution of jobs and the use of pork are important elements of what Raile, Pereira and Power (2010) define as the "executive toolbox".

The paradoxes of the Brazilian political system were there from the beginning of the democratic transition, when the military authorities sought to create a fragmented multiparty system in order to divide the opposition, as mentioned in Chapter 2. When the PT assumed national executive public office, however, party leaders experienced the constraints of this system as never before, particularly because the conditions to secure governability are far more complex at the national level. In the national executive the PT had to deal not only with more political parties, but also with powerful actors such as state governors, who are very influential in Brazilian politics. When Lula assumed the presidency in 2003, the PT only elected 4 out of 26 state governors. These actors play an important political role in national politics. It is vital for Brazilian presidents to accommodate the interests of governors when they deal with the National Congress, particularly because the governors shape the behaviour of congressional representatives, who depend on them for electoral purposes.[39]

In dealing with its minority status in the legislative branch the PT failed in its first few years to perform adequately under the most common practices of the Brazilian system of "coalition presidentialism", as a number of specialists of the Brazilian political system have argued.[40] Rather than applying the "executive toolbox", the Lula administration created a vote-buying mechanism by which the PT sought to pass key legislation (Pereira, Power and Raile 2011:47). This mechanism is what eventually resulted in a corruption scandal called the *mensalão* (big monthly payment). The *mensalão* was not a traditional corruption scheme used by government officials for personal enrichment. It was a tactic by which the PT administration sought to secure legislative support in order to pass key legislation in Congress.

Studies show that the political crisis generated by this scandal was the consequence of the initial arrangements, when Lula failed to give cabinet posts to allies and to distribute sufficient pork-barrel among them (despite the fact that his party was in a minority position in Congress).[41] Instead of negotiating a cabinet with the political elites represented in Congress, as previous Brazilian presidents had done, Lula initially appointed 16 out of 29 ministers from the PT (55 percent of all the seats) and 8 nonpartisan members (28 percent), which did not help to secure congressional support. The latter, despite being useful for accommodating some dominant strategic actors such as the business sector, did not help to directly secure congressional support (Couto and Baia 2006:12).

The PT had long considered that legislative alliances should be based on policy and programmes rather than on the nontransparent exchange of particularistic favours traditionally used in Brazilian politics, such as pork-barrelling. However, the party faced a difficult dilemma in 2003. In contrast to various sub-national executive experiences, in which alliances with left and centrist parties had allowed it to pass legislation, the PT at the national level had to widen the scope of its alliances much further, in great part because the centre of the political spectrum was occupied by the PSDB. The formation of alliances was a divisive issue within the party. On the one hand, many sectors in the party bureaucracy, especially the party Left, resisted allying with forces that could compromise their agenda or alienate their social base. On the other hand, the party in government knew that without sufficient allies in Congress its hands would be severely tied and little could be done.

In this context, the most influential party leaders in government considered two main options to secure parliamentary support: either to make an alliance with one of the largest parties represented in Congress or to make *ad hoc* alliances with small parties. Old rivalries between the PT and the PSDB (in the presidency between 1995 and 2002) made an alliance between these two parties unthinkable,[42] the first option left only the PMDB, the second-largest party represented in the lower chamber, as a potential ally. Such an alternative could have given the government a stable and more or less reliable parliamentary base of support, but it also meant putting the PT in a weaker position in the state apparatus. According to Couto and Baia (2006:33), many *petistas* believed that by making an alliance with weaker parties the PT could "preserve the hegemonic position in government". Furthermore, Lula could not offer sufficient jobs to PMDB members or to other parties because he faced pressure to accommodate PT leaders from the main factions and from his own intraparty group.[43]

Accommodating PT factions in government, I contend, was important because the Lula government did not want to repeat the "paralysing conflicts" between the party in public office and the party in central office which characterised many of the PT sub-national governments (Dirceu 07/01/09). José Dirceu, Chief of the Civil House[44] (2003–2005) and one of the most influential figures in government, explained during our interview that the relationship with the party and its different factions was regarded as one of the main elements needed to secure governability.[45] By distributing jobs among their main leaders, PT administrations had found an effective formula to avoid factional disputes and appease potential sources of opposition (see Chapter 4). Guaranteeing the support of PT factions was important to prevent opposition to Lula's economic policy. Lula was aware that the party Left opposed the strategy by which he was seeking to accommodate the interests of dominant strategic actors, particularly the business and financial sectors, which was key to securing economic governability.

In the first year in office, Dirceu and other leaders tried to form a legislative coalition with the PMDB, but Lula ruled that option out. Observers have suggested that his rejection was for ideological reasons. That is, because forming an alliance with the main party tolerated under the dictatorship, and a key ally of the Cardoso administration, was not easy to justify to PT supporters (Couto and Baia 2006:12). Furthermore, the PMDB is a political organisation known for its opportunism, its clientelistic practices and the corruptness of its leaders. The reasons, however, were not merely ideological. After all, Lula formed specific alliances with eight smaller parties in his first years in office, in which he included three conservative forces whose reputations are possibly no better than that of the PMDB, namely the Popular Party (PP), the Brazilian Republican Party (PRB) and the Brazilian Labour Party (PTB).[46] The problem was that the support of these organisations was not sufficient for constitutional amendments to be passed. The government coalition was only able to achieve 318 votes in the Lower Chamber (around 60 percent of the house), and not a majority in the Senate (Pereira, Power and Raile 2011:47). To make matters more complicated, these parties did not receive cabinet positions.

The government, having insufficient votes, decided to buy them among a group of congressional representatives. The *mensalão* scandal was eventually revealed in June 2005, when Roberto Jefferson, chairman of the PTB, accused the PT treasurer, Delúbio Soares, who was associated with José Dirceu, of paying a monthly bribe of R$30,000 (US$13,000) to several parliamentarians. When opposition parties proposed Lula's impeachment, it became crystal clear that the governability strategy which the PT administration had initially put in place had failed.

The 2005 Political Crisis: Instigating a Defensive Mobilisation

Although the "hard nucleus" of the party in government ruled out a proactive form of mobilisation, it did deploy a strategy of defensive mobilisation when the opposition threatened to impeach Lula in 2005. The defenders of an elite-centred strategy, who were initially reluctant to use mobilisation to put pressure on parliament, decided to encourage a defensive strategy at a critical point in time, when they considered that it could contribute to the survival of the PT in government. Studies on governability during the

Lula administration[47] have neglected the fact that, at this specific moment of Lula's presidency, the social allies in the PT field played an important role in putting pressure on strategic actors in the legislative branch. For a number of reasons the impeachment did not take place; one of them was the mobilisation that the party instigated against its promoters.

In 2005, in the middle of the political crisis generated by the *mensalão* scandal, the political climate in Congress became increasingly polarised. On one occasion, for instance, the president of the PFL, Jorge Bornhausen, declared in a meeting with businessmen that he was happy that these scandals had erupted because "we are going to get rid of the PT race for at least 30 years".[48] When the possibility of impeachment appeared on the horizon, Lula immediately presented it as an attempt by the Brazilian elites to overthrow his government and went to seek support from his social base.[49] In late June, more than 40 organisations, including the national leaders of CUT, MST, the National Student's Organisation (UNE), the Brazilian Association of NGOs (ABONG), gender and black movements, among others, published a statement in which they accused Brazilian elites and the mass media of "launching a campaign to demoralise both the government and the president in order to undermine his administration or to overthrow him".[50] However, in spite of the fact that they urged an investigation of the scandals and criticised certain policies of the Lula administration, especially its economic policy, the signatories expressed an emphatic position against "any attempt to destabilise the government".[51]

In the following months, many organisations issued their own public statements and organised protests. According to press sources, such protests never reached more than 10,000 participants.[52] However, trade union leaders threatened larger street demonstrations and massive strikes. José Antonio Lópes Feijóo, President of the ABC Metalworkers' Trade Union, echoed the president in asserting that the impeachment was "an attempt by the elites to attack the social conquests of the workers", while Jõao Felício, from CUT, made an unprecedented threat: "If they want to go for impeachment, the country will become uncontrollable".[53] The positions against the impeachment were clearly dominant among civil society organisations, even beyond those in the PT field. The *Folha de São Paulo* (16/08/05) interviewed 57 leaders of civil society and found that only 13 of them were in favour.

Eventually, leaders from seven different parties concluded that the necessary "political environment" to initiate an impeachment investigation did not exist, while conservative senators declared that it could generate "social instability" as well as its promoters being accused of "attempting a coup".[54] Opposition leaders from the PFL and PSDB also expressed concerns about the potential consequences of impeaching a highly popular president.[55] The impression of high government officials interviewed for this study was that because Lula had "most of the social movements on his side", the leaders of the opposition were fearful of their reactions.[56] A similar view is shared by representatives of civil society.[57] José Antonio Moroni, one of the national coordinators of the Brazilian Association of NGOs (ABONG), put it bluntly: "Lula just needed to snap his fingers for the people to go out and defend him on the streets" (Moroni 03/07/09).

It is difficult to determine how important PT social allies were in halting Lula's impeachment. The political, economic and social dimensions of governability do not exist separately from each other, as I argue in Chapter 1. Other factors played a role in alleviating political tensions and solving the crisis. The fact that the opposition was supportive of Lula's economic policy was also important. By the time the political crisis erupted, the government had gained the confidence of the financial sector, which was not particularly interested in impeaching the president. On the political side, the opposition parties that promoted the impeachment needed the support of at least two-thirds of the Lower House for their petition to be accepted, which was not easy to achieve.[58] Eventually, the *mensalão* crisis was solved in institutional settings and through negotiations between parties.[59] In April 2006, when a special joint congressional committee presented its final report, Lula was released from direct responsibility. Nevertheless, the committee clarified that 18 Lower House representatives had received illegal payments through a bribery scheme and several high-ranking government officials and members of the party in central office were accused of operating the scheme (Pereira, Power and Raile 2011:33–5). Six years later, in October 2012, the Supreme Court condemned José Dirceu, José Genoino and Delúbio Soares under charges of active corruption.[60]

The role that civil society organisations in the PT field played during the crisis shows two main things: First, that although the defenders of an elite-centred strategy were reluctant to use a proactive strategy of counter-hegemonic mobilisation, they did consider that a defensive mobilisation strategy was viable. Second, civil society organisations might have not been strong enough, or might have been incapable or even unwilling to put pressure on Congress in order to pass progressive reforms. However, PT social allies were determined to defend the field. This provides additional evidence that the PT and its social base are much closer than most observers have argued.[61] An activist of the Housing Movement put it in the clearest terms: "We could not allow the Right to destroy the dream of an entire generation" (De Oliveira 07/04/09).

THE THIRD STAGE: BRAZILIAN POLITICS AS USUAL

The PT adopted an elite-centred strategy similar to other Brazilian parties as a direct consequence of the *mensalão*. The 2005 political crisis, as I show in this final section, not only had an immediate effect on the "hard nucleus" of the party in government, but also on the party in central office, including leaders of the party Left. Lula and his inner circle understood that it was important to form a solid majority in Congress, based on stronger alliances with large parties. In order to secure that support, therefore, they decided to incorporate the same strategies by which previous Brazilian presidents had gathered congressional support, that is, by allocating more cabinet seats and other jobs in the administrative apparatus and by increasing the use of discretionary budgetary powers. Lula's Chief of Staff, Gilberto Carvalho (10/04/09), explained that by sharing power with large parties, the government could avoid being constantly blackmailed by small parties and could therefore build a more stable alliance.

In his second government, Lula appointed several ministers from other parties, but particularly from the PMDB, which became one of his most important political allies.[62] The president also made more use of pork, which increased in an unprecedented fashion. To give a simple indicator: When the PT took public office in 2003, every congressional representative was entitled to introduce amendments to the budget for up to 2 million Reals (US$583,090 at the time). The values of these amendments increased significantly after the political crisis, growing from R$3.5 million (US$1.3 million) in 2005 to R$12 million (US$7 million) by 2010. During the Cardoso years, in contrast, parliamentary amendments never reached 2 million Reals per congressional representative.[63]

Lula fully justified his elite-centred strategy and the practices it entailed, during an interview:

> No-one who wins an election in this country, regardless of whether he is the most Shiite[64] or the most conservative guy, will be able to form a government outside our political reality. Between what you want to do and what you can actually do there is a difference as big as the Atlantic Ocean (...). In the future, anyone who wins the Presidency will have to do the same kind of deals [that we do] because that's the way the Brazilian political spectrum works (...). If Jesus Christ came down here and Judas had the votes he needed, no matter which party they each came from: Jesus would have to call on Judas to form a coalition.[65]

The Lula government eventually received the support of a dozen parties and almost two-thirds of the Lower House.[66] The endorsement of key allies such as the PMDB and the PP was secured by jobs and monetary resources that its leaders obtained through pork-barrelling. However, the fact that some of the parties in the coalition endorsed the economic policy put in place by the administration facilitated the alliance with conservative parties (Simões 04/11/08). The elite-centred strategy proved "efficient": The Lula administration obtained high rates of "legislative success", achieving 76 percent during its second term in office, a record high in the history of the New Republic (Santana and Rodrigues 2009:7–8). The government coalition lacked programmatic consistency, however, and did not allow the PT to promote its progressive agenda in key areas of Lula's electoral manifesto that I mentioned earlier in this chapter.

In eight years the PT was not able to pass substantive changes to the tax system. On two occasions, in April 2003 and March 2008, the administration and the party lost initiatives proposing the creation of taxes on inheritances and private donations[67] and the establishment of a tax on great fortunes[68] that would have taxed patrimonies progressively.[69] In August 2008 the administration also failed to negotiate a political reform aimed at reducing the fragmentation of the party system, promoting party discipline, limiting the use of private money in presidential campaigns and diminishing corrupt practices (Verlaine and Queiroz 18/10/10). This reform was frustrated, because at least four PT allies (PTB, PSB, PR and PP) threatened to leave the government coalition and blocked all negotiations.[70] Pomar (30/09/08), one of the main leaders of Left Articulation, argues that the reason why this political reform did not take place was because the PT was "blackmailed" by its allies in parliament. He saw this as a paradox, because "these were the same types of parties that generated the 2005 political crisis, a crisis that had its origins in the lack of political reform".

Renato Simões, a member of the PT National Executive Committee, and a representative of the PT Left, bitterly complained about the governability strategy put in place by Lula:

> (. . .) These allies only vote for what is basic for the administration, but they do not support more important measures that have more of a social content. What we have is not a parliamentary coalition with a programme to which other parties adhere. There is only an endorsing by other parties of the functioning of the neoliberal model, rather than a political programme on which other parties are always obliged to vote according to the government orientation. (Simões 04/11/08)

In its Third National Congress in 2007, the PT officially acknowledged that the 2005 political crisis was a consequence of the party's failure to prioritise political reform.[71] Members of the party Left argue that the main mistake was "trying to govern within the existing rules without changing them".[72] A similar assessment was made by José Genoino, President of the PT until the *mensalão* scandal, when he was forced to step down:

> One of our first mistakes was to enter the system without changing the way it works. We should have promoted a greater change in the [political] system to avoid being almost completely swallowed up by that system. We should have promoted an institutional reform, altered the forms of representation, and switched [both] the electoral system and the party system. That is why we were so affected by the 2005 political crisis (. . .). Nobody became rich within the PT; no-one made a great fortune or became part of the dominant class. The PT's undertakings were part of the procedures embodied in the nature of our own political system. We should have changed all those rules from 2003 and the

PT should have put pressure for this to happen early in 2003. (Genoino 08/12/08)

Many PT leaders, however, regret the consequences of the governability strategy put in place. Congressman Fernando Ferro (02/07/09) asserted: "We became hostages of an archaic political model that we were unable to change because we were too concerned with stability and governability". In his view, "The pragmatism of governability limited our capacity to promote political struggles and generate the necessary social tensions". Even members of Lula's inner circle were frustrated with the governability strategy that they promoted because it led the party to adopt the very same practices that it had criticised from its creation. Lula's Chief of Staff, Gilberto Carvalho, made the following assessment:

> We should be self-critical about the governability strategy that we adopted. Our government could not innovate in its relationship with Congress. The *physiological* relationships[73] that characterised previous administrations survived and continued within our government. We could not eliminate the very bad practice of "give and take" which is so typical of Brazilian politics. This rationale is one by which congressional representatives vote for certain projects as long as they have access to specific benefits. Most of our allies only gave us support in exchange for something else. It was important to open the government up to these parties during the second Lula administration because this forced them to commit themselves and vote with us in Congress without becoming involved in any undesirable practices. But despite all this, the behaviour of our allies did not change completely. (Carvalho 10/04/09)

Despite all these shortcomings, the fact is that the elite-centred strategy gained more supporters within the party in central office as a result of the governing experience and the 2005 political crisis. In its Third National Congress in 2007, the PT officially endorsed an alliance with the PMDB, arguing that it was a mistake not to have had one from the start.[74] From that Congress onwards, the most important factions in the party, with the exception of Left Articulation, came to support alliances beyond left-wing parties (Amaral 2010b:181). Amaral (2010a: 165–72) found that during the course of a decade, PT factions significantly modified their position towards electoral alliances. In 2001, two important factions, Socialist Democracy and Left Articulation, as well as two small factions, which altogether received 35.4 percent of the party delegates, only supported alliances with progressive parties. By 2009, only Left Articulation and three marginal factions maintained this position, which represented a mere 13.9 percent of the delegates (Amaral 2010a: 165–72). One of the survey studies conducted in 2007 by the party's main think tank, the *Fundação Perseu Abramo*, found that 61 percent of the party delegates endorsed an alliance with the PMDB for the upcoming presidential election in 2010. Ten years earlier, in 1997, only 15 percent of the delegates had supported such an alternative (Amaral 2010c:116–7). These studies show that the governability dilemma has acted as an important driver of change in the Brazilian Workers' Party and suggests that the elite-centred perspective, initially weaker within the party in central office, did become stronger as a result of the government's experience and the 2005 political crisis.

CONCLUSION

This chapter has made the case that the governability dilemma affects the performance of parties in public office and it is a powerful reason why progressive parties alter their strategies and discourses when they occupy the executive. My work has also broadened existing debates on political governability in Brazil, by contemplating the role that civil society has (or might have) in supporting governability strategies. In the previous pages I looked at two types of social counter-hegemonic strategies: proactive and defensive mobilisation. I argued that the former did not take place under Lula, mainly because the most influential leaders in government regarded it as a source of political and social instability, but also because many other leaders considered that civil society organisations were not strong enough to alter the balance of forces in Congress. Interestingly, defensive mobilisation did play a role, as it had in previous PT government experiences. This shows that progressive parties can count on an extra institutional base of support that they might deploy to counteract the power of dominant strategic actors and secure their survival in power.

During its first two and a half years in office, the PT government resisted using the same strategies as previous Brazilian presidents to pass its initiatives in Congress. The hybrid strategy that it adopted was contradictory, damaging to its own reputation, and led to a political crisis. It was a hybrid strategy that had the worst of both worlds because it sought to accommodate the interests of the political elites, but it deployed corrupt practices as a means for being hegemonic in government (needless to say, a hegemony in which civil society played no major role). After the 2005 political crisis, the PT and many of its factions called for political reform capable of changing the rules of the game and its constraining character. After the *mensalão* crisis, such a reform could have probably gathered social support, at a time in which corruption was a sensitive issue in the public opinion. However, no significant steps were taken in such a direction. Rather than engaging actively in the promotion of a political reform, Lula and his inner circle decided to act strictly within the institutional limits, keep within the unwritten rules of the political system and incorporate the practices of other parties.

The adoption of an elite-centred governability strategy cannot be attributed to the failure of counter-mobilisation, however, because such a possibility was never really attempted. Yet in Chapter 1 I argued that social mobilisation is not the only way in which a proactive counter-hegemonic strategy can be put in place. Broad-based participation in institutionalised settings is another. In cities such as Porto Alegre, it was the combination of mobilisation within and outside the PT field, with the promotion of inclusive and robust participatory mechanisms, that made social counter-hegemonic governability strategies successful. At the national level, the party in public office did promote several participatory instruments. These initiatives will be analysed in Chapter 7. Before doing so, however, the next chapter will look at the economic policy decisions of the Lula administration, which played a central role in the strategy to secure governability.

6 From the "Lula Monster" to an Icon of the "Responsible Left"

This chapter examines how Lula's inner circle and the hard nucleus of the party in government approached the relationship with the financial establishment as part of a strategy to secure economic governability. Scholars, public intellectuals in Brazil, and even some social and political leaders in the PT field, suggest that an ideological shift towards neoliberal positions took place during the first Lula administration,[1] or even earlier, during the 2002 presidential campaign.[2] In this chapter I contend that rather than a switch to neoliberalism (which only took place among certain groups in the PT), the continuation of the macro-economic policies implemented by the Cardoso administration was a pragmatic response to accommodate the interests of the financial establishment, particularly foreign investment banks and holders of Brazilian bonds. These dominant strategic actors, with sufficient power to generate capital flight and destabilise the main macro-economic variables, were seen by the party in public office—and Lula's inner circle in particular—as essential to secure governability in its different dimensions.

Scholars who examine Lula's economic policy largely concentrate on economic and financial aspects,[3] but here I emphasise the political motivations behind the economic policy decisions adopted, as part of a strategy to secure governability. Studying economic policy decisions in this fashion poses some epistemological challenges. In Chapter 1 I argued that governability is often used to justify all sorts of regimes and policies and it is rooted in a conservative tradition. In order to avoid this problem I distinguish between governability as an analytical tool and governability as a discourse. In economic terms, the analytical dimension of governability that I use here seeks to explain the role of "the markets" in a capitalist economy and the restrictions that they impose on governments. As an analytical tool, economic governability mostly focuses on the way in which a party in government accommodates the interests of dominant strategic actors capable of influencing a country's economic performance.

This is different from the *discourses of economic governability*. In particular, international financial institutions have propagated a discourse in which certain economic policies are perceived as key to the "good functioning" of the economy and the state, such as reducing public spending to a minimum, privatising public utilities and enterprises or maintaining inflation under strict control (Tomassini 1993a). In this chapter I will show that some groups in Lula's economic team did defend some of these positions during the first Lula administration. However, there is no evidence that such groups were dominant in the PT (certainly not among my interviewees) and, in any case, their ideological shift was not the main driving force in the adoption of a conservative economic policy.

The economic policy trajectory under Lula, as with political governability, took place in three different stages, which I study in the different sections of this chapter: a first stage during the 2002 presidential election, in which the PT dealt with the anticipated reactions of the financial sector; a second stage during the first three years in power, when the new government sought to conquer the confidence of the financial markets, and a third stage between late 2005 and the end of the second term, in which the administration relaxed the most orthodox aspects of the economic policy initially put in place. In the first stage, during the campaign, Lula and his inner circle had their first real contact with a sector with which they had had little or no relationship at the sub-national level and which was sceptical of a left-wing government. In the context of a vulnerable macro-economic situation, characterised by a high level of public indebtedness, this sector imposed conditions on the PT even before it took public office. In the second stage, Lula and his new economic team applied economic orthodoxy with greater conservatism than during the Cardoso years and negotiated the appointment of key positions in the economic team with representatives of the financial establishment. Finally, the third stage took place after the economy had stabilised, which was once the Lula government had proved its fiscal discipline credentials, and when the PT in public office gained some margins for manoeuvre. While still a strategic actor, the financial establishment was no longer playing the role of a "veto player" and the Lula administration was able to deal with this actor from a stronger position. The favourable international context during this period allowed the government to accumulate significant foreign reserves and therefore it became less dependent on the mood of the financial sector.

THE FIRST STAGE: ANTICIPATING REACTIONS FROM THE FINANCIAL ESTABLISHMENT

By the time Lula assumed the presidency, fears of a radical government that would directly antagonise business interests had been largely dissipated. During the 2002 presidential campaign, Lula did not face major opposition in the business world. In fact, he received support from various industrialists, and some 500 of its representatives endorsed his campaign.[4] Even large rural producers in the agro-business industry, some of them sceptical of Lula's historical positions on land reform, supported his candidacy.[5] A good indicator of the extent to which the PT candidate had approached business interests in 2002 is the fact that Lula received massive private donations, which allowed him to outspend all other candidates, including his main competitor, José Serra (PSDB).[6] The nomination of José Alencar, a businessman from the textile sector, as the vice-presidential candidate was an important message that signalled Lula's intention to forge an alliance with the industrial sector. Many of his alliances with these groups were maintained in office, when the new president incorporated outstanding personalities from the Brazilian establishment, such as Luiz Fernando Furlan, a representative of the agro-alimentary sector who became the Minister for Development, Foreign Trade and Industry, and Roberto Rodrigues, president of the Brazilian Association of Agri-Business, who became Minister for Agriculture.

These alliances were partly possible because since the 1994 presidential campaign, Lula had made a clear distinction between businessmen who invest in productive activities as opposed to those who speculate (Mendes 2004:48–9). Nevertheless, Lula had always assumed a critical approach towards the "financial elite", "the bankers" or the "international speculators", whom he still portrayed in very negative terms in the 1998 presidential campaign (Mendes 2004:61). In his fourth attempt to become president, Lula and his inner circle adopted a different language as part of their elite-centred approach. However, many of the PT historical positions towards dominant strategic actors such as the financial establishment were still influential. The resolution that party delegates passed in the 12th National Conference, held in December 2001, was grounded on the idea that certain "ruptures" with the existing order were "necessary" in order to construct a new economic model away from neoliberalism.[7] The document was openly hostile towards the financial establishment. In one of its passages, for instance, delegates warned that "the big rentiers and speculators" would be "*directly affected* by the redistributive policies [of the new government]", they would "not benefit from the new social contract" and would even be "penalised".[8] Although the PT no longer favoured a debt moratorium (as it had done in previous years), the document did establish that the agreements Brazil had made with the IMF needed to be "denounced" and the international debt should be "audited" before payment continued.[9] The establishment of mechanisms to control capital inflows, including a Tobin tax over speculative revenues, was also contemplated.[10]

The previous chapter showed how the elite-centred governability strategy that Lula advanced during the campaign departed in several aspects from the counter-hegemonic tradition that oriented the positions of the PT at the time. In no other area was Lula's departure from the PT position so evident as in the economy. In his electoral manifesto, and more clearly in his "Letter to the Brazilian People", the candidate made evident his differences with the PT, emphasising that his government would not employ capital controls, and would respect existing contracts, pay the external debt as planned and maintain important elements of Cardoso's macro-economic policy.[11] This switch in Lula's discourse and strategy was part of an anticipated governability strategy. I argue that it took place because Lula's inner circle understood that the relationship with the financial sector was essential for maintaining macro-economic stability in the context of an economy largely dependent on foreign capital.

In 2002 Brazil had reached one of the highest levels of public indebtedness in recent years, above the psychological threshold of the 50 percent GDP ratio; it had faced the contagion of the Asian and Russian crisis, accumulated successive current account deficits and faced several speculative attacks.[12] This put the PT in a particularly vulnerable position *vis-à-vis* financial capital. The *Plano Real* (Real Plan) implemented by Fernando Henrique Cardoso in July 1994 had successfully brought inflation under control, through a series of conservative fiscal and monetary policies that restricted public expenditure and raised interest rates. Many of these measures, which were celebrated by the financial establishment, had been bitterly criticised by both Lula and the PT. Nevertheless, Lula and his inner circle in particular had also learned that the Brazilian electorate valued economic stability, particularly given the traumatic experience of hyper-inflation during the 1980s and early 1990s (Barbosa 2008:213). Singer, a PT intellectual quoted in earlier chapters, acknowledges that "the Real [stabilisation plan] won over the popular electorate", particularly the poorest sectors directly affected by hyper-inflation in the past (Singer 2009:97). Party leaders in Lula's inner circle had understood that underestimating this plan, as Lula did during the 1994 presidential election, proved to have a negative electoral impact. This was particularly the case because during the campaign the PT criticised the Real Plan, but did not offer a feasible alternative (Amaral 2003:122). Eventually, despite the fact that Lula was the frontrunner in that election, his failure to "appreciate the popular appeal of the Real stabilisation plan" made it easy for Cardoso to present his main rival as "a threat to the new economic order" (Panizza 2004:472).

In Lula's 2002 electoral strategy, the importance of economic stability was not in question. At this stage, however, Lula's team was not driven solely by electoral concerns. The intention was to calm down the markets, having perceived that if the economic situation deteriorated it would be "hard to govern" (Arbix 06/11/08).[13] Glauco Arbix (06/11/08), who advised Lula's campaign, revealed that in several meetings with his advisors Lula stressed that under high inflation "the entire Brazilian people" would turn against his government and the legitimacy of the new administration would be jeopardised. For these reasons, leaders within Lula's entourage realised that an economic crisis would create severe difficulties not only for the economy, but also for the maintenance of social and political stability in the country.[14] During our interview, Dirceu (07/01/09) went as far as saying that "if the economic crisis [the confidence crisis generated in 2002] had deepened, Lula would not have lasted even one year in power" (see epigraph, page v).

For Lula's inner circle it became clear that accommodating the interests of the financial sector was key to securing economic governability. They perceived that the financial establishment, as a dominant strategic actor, was potentially capable of undermining the country's macro-economic indices, either by means of capital flight, or by launching speculative attacks on the Real or by simply downgrading Brazil's bonds in credit-rating agencies. For these reasons, governability in Lula's economic team meant *trust*.[15] "Confidence" was regarded as an essential element "when dealing with the large capital owners", as Bernardo Appy, the Deputy Minister of Finance during the first Lula administration, pointed out (08/04/09). "The risk of not creating confidence among the markets is too high", he stated, because "a crisis of confidence can result in losing control over inflation, exchange rates and all the macro-economic indicators" (Appy 08/04/09). Another senior official in the Ministry of Finance, Gilson Bittencourt, put it in these terms: "Governability is trust because if you have a financial sector saying that the government is bankrupt; it can eventually generate a state of bankruptcy, even if this was not actually true" (Bittencourt 20/10/10).

As part of a strategy to make his candidacy more palatable to the financial sector, Lula distanced himself from traditional PT economists who had given him advice, and brought supporters of conservative economic positions into his team. As someone who was usually advised by traditional PT economists, Lula could not easily generate trust in the financial establishment. His main economic advisors at the time were strongly emphatic about the need to promote the internal market, but were not particularly concerned with macro-economic objectives.[16] Nelson Barbosa, the Secretary for Economic Policy under the second Lula administration, argues that these economists did not seem to have a viable strategy for providing the assurances that the financial sector needed. These economists, he explains, "had a development model in mind, but not a macro-economy stabilisation plan to balance the external accounts. Their proposal was [only] radicalisation and confrontation" (20/07/09).

Dealing with Uncertainty

The uncertainty of foreign investors became crystal clear during the 2002 presidential election. When the surveys showed that José Serra, the candidate of the governing PSDB and main guarantor of the continuity of the Real Plan, was unlikely to win the election, the financial markets launched a new speculative attack over the Real. The Brazilian currency depreciated from being equivalent to US$2.31 in January 2002 to US$3.89 in September that year, one month before the election. During the course of a year there was a capital flight of more than US$19 billion, while the country's risk increased from 963 points to 1,636 (Barbosa and Pereira 2010:1–2). In contrast, during the Russian crisis the index did not reach 1,100 points (Campello 2007:2).

Scholars show that it was the prospect of a Lula government, rather than the overall situation of the Brazilian economy, that caused the greatest financial turbulence during that year.[17] Despite their concerns about indebtedness and the high deficit, foreign investors had expressed positive views about the prospects of the Brazilian economy and even considered the country as an example of a "successful emerging economy" (Campello 2012:8). Although Brazil had faced a speculative attack after the 1998 Russian financial crisis and eventually devalued in 1999 (Santiso 2004:4), the economy had been slowly recovering. Shortly after the Argentinian financial crisis in December 2001, the markets praised Brazil's "sound economic conditions", which had not suffered from contagion (Campello 2012:8). In March, even the President of the Central Bank, Armínio Fraga, was elected "Man of the Year" by *Latin Finance Magazine*, and was later referred to by *Newsweek* as "the nerd who saved Brazil" (in Campello 2012:8–9).

All of this changed when international investors realised that their preferred candidate was not going to win the presidential election, as authors have assessed.[18] Given the pro-debt moratorium position that the PT had historically adopted and Brazil's low level of reserves, "the markets" became sceptical about the future Brazilian government's ability and Lula's willingness to pay its debts (Campello and Zucco 2008:21–4). In the weeks that followed, investment banks such as Santander, Merrill Lynch and ABN-AMRO started to publish negative financial reports in which they publicised the contents of PT documents, and all of a sudden Morgan Stanley downgraded Brazilian bonds.[19] In May that year, five months before the election, BCP Securities published a report by a financial analyst, entitled "Da Lula Monster", which described how "a sense of panic" had emerged among economic agents.[20] One month later, George Soros declared in an interview: "Brazil is condemned to elect José Serra or to sink into chaos as soon as an eventual Lula administration begins".[21] In *The Accidental President of Brazil*, Cardoso's autobiography, the former president recalls that the possibility of a Lula presidency in 2002 simply "terrified investors just as much as it had before" in his previous attempts to win the presidency (Cardoso 2006:273–4).

The "Letter to the Brazilian People", presented in June 2002, was insufficient to placate fears. According to Campello (2012:10), who interviewed several representatives of the financial sector, "the markets broadly ignored the document" which was not even mentioned in the influential financial reports by the Economist Intelligence Unit. In July, one month after the publication of the letter, Standard and Poor's downgraded Brazilian sovereign bonds, allegedly based on concerns about rising public debt and heightened market concerns about political uncertainties.

The speculation on the Real only stopped one month before the election, in September 2002, when the IMF approved a new US$30 billion loan to Brazil to be paid out by the end of the following year, while the World Bank announced its intention to lend the country US$7 billion (Campello 2007:25). All four major candidates for president—most crucially Lula— were called as signatories (Cardoso 2006:273–4). The IMF imposed its conditions: The new president would honour the agreement's targets for a budget surplus of 3.75 percent (dedicated to repaying the debt). Once the agreement was signed, the Fund declared that Brazil was "on a solid long-term policy trend which strongly deserves the support of the international community" (Cardoso 2006:274–5). The massive rescue package was not aimed solely at restoring confidence among foreign investors. It also had the clear purpose of "binding the incoming administration to maintaining the status quo in economic policies", as Campello (2007:25) argues. Nelson Barbosa, a PT economist who became the Secretary for Economic Policy in the second Lula administration, wrote that the intention of the investors was very clear: They were trying to "veto pre-emptively any possible heterodox economic action" that Lula might eventually take after being elected (Barbosa 2008:193–4).

THE SECOND STAGE: REINFORCING CARDOSO'S ECONOMIC ORTHODOXY

Despite the efforts made during the electoral year, the macro-economic instability remained fragile and the uncertainty had not been dispelled by the time Lula assumed the presidency. During his first year in office, Lula diverted most of his political capital to gaining the confidence and support of the financial sector. This sector was regarded as a problem in his inner circle, yet was also perceived as part of the solution to the governability dilemma. To a certain extent, maintaining a good relationship with such a prominent strategic actor was like buying health insurance. Partially, it was seen as helpful to secure not only economic but also political and social dimensions of governability. The strategy was two-fold: On the one hand, it could position the new president better with respect to the Brazilian conservative establishment, which was opposed to him for reasons of class, ideology and history (despite the alliances with some segments of the business community) and, on the other hand, it could help to reduce potential confrontations with those who represented its interests in Congress, where the PT was particularly weak.

Lula anticipated that many of his policies would be criticised by his allies in the PT socio-political field, mainly within the party Left, but he also knew that his own faction would support him and that his allies in civil society would not mobilise against them. Singer (2009:97–8) argues that by handling the economy "with the prudence of a housewife" (an expression that Lula frequently used in public speeches), the PT administration could also establish a connection with the poorest sectors who are particularly vulnerable to hyper-inflation. Lula and his team were aware that, without macro-economic stability (and low inflation in particular), its cash transfer programmes would have no significant impact on alleviating extreme poverty (Arbix 06/11/08).

As mentioned in Chapter 5, some party and social leaders in the PT field had imagined that the "Letter to the Brazilian People" was only a tactical electoral strategy to reduce economic instability in the context of the presidential election and avoid antagonising the establishment. They were surprised, however, when Lula re-endorsed the commitments made in the letter and fiscal orthodoxy became one of the main hallmarks of his government. To begin with, the president formed a conservative economic team which his government partly negotiated with both the national and the international markets. The appointment of Henrique Mireilles, a former president of the BankBoston and member of Cardoso's PSDB, as head of the Central Bank was a key decision. As Minister of Finance Lula appointed Antonio Palocci, a PT member and one of Lula's closest political allies, who had cultivated fluid relationships with the private sector during the previous years and with bankers during the campaign (Carneiro 14/04/09). As a former mayor of Ribeirão Preto (1993–1996/2001–2002), a medium-sized Brazilian city in the state of São Paulo, Palocci became widely known as "a deficit hawk" and a "strict fiscal conservative" (Kaufman 2011:108, 109).

Within the Finance Ministry, Palocci formed a team of "good technicians with a modern vision of the economy", as he personally called the technocrats he appointed to the most important jobs, when referring to them later in his memoirs (Palocci 2007:57). Palocci also placed, in two key positions, fiscally conservative economists who did not endorse PT economic positions and who even had open disagreements with the party in the past (Palocci 2007:55).[22] Interestingly, various PSDB members or sympathisers from that party, who had relations with the financial establishment, also worked for the Ministry. Notwithstanding the wide powers that Brazilian executives have to appoint officials at the first and second levels of the administration, very few *petistas* received jobs during the first period. Having a "technical team" was perceived as essential in order to provide the confidence that the financial sector required, as Bernardo Appy, Deputy Minister of Finance at the time, asserted during our interview (08/04/09).

As an initial measure, the Central Bank increased interest rates from 25 to 26.5 percent in February 2003, reaching the highest levels in the region (Kaufman 2011:109), as part of a strategy to achieve a "fast disinflation" (Barbosa 2008:212). In order to send a "clear message" to the financial sector about the strength of its commitment to fiscal orthodoxy, the Lula government established and eventually reached a 4.25 percent primary surplus goal (Barbosa and Pereira 2010:3), far above the 3.75 required by the IMF in the agreements signed before the presidential election.[23] In order to succeed in reaching this target, the federal government had to reduce public investment from 1.1 percent of the GDP to 0.3 percent in its first year (Barbosa and Pereira 2010:3), and to limit the possibilities of substantial minimum wage increases that had been promised during the campaign, at least until the final years of the first administration.

During that first year, the government also promoted two important reforms in Congress that were aimed in great part at creating a "market-friendly" environment. In April, it passed a reform that cleared the way for Central Bank autonomy, a decision that was widely celebrated on Wall Street, and which helped to set the value of the Brazilian bonds at the levels prior to early 2002 (Santiso 2004:32). In August, it passed another reform, which modified the pension funds system (in similar terms to those previously proposed by Cardoso, and which the PT had opposed in the past) and tore down some of the rights acquired by the workers in the public sector. This reform, which alienated PT supporters (see further in Chapter 9), was emphatically pushed by the Lula government, which argued that it would help to solve the public deficit and free up funds for the government's social programmes (Pereira, Power and Raile 2011:43).[24]

Eventually, despite the success in reducing inflation, which even in the first year went down from 12.3 percent to 9.3 percent, eventually attaining 5.7 percent in 2005, the economy officially entered a "technical recession", with two consecutive terms of no growth (Barbosa and Pereira 2010:3). In the years that followed, notwithstanding the fact that Brazilian exports started to increase significantly, economic growth was mediocre and during the whole term the GDP only increased an average of 2.9 percent (Figueiras and Gonçalves 2007:69). This was higher than the 2.3 percent of the two presidential terms of Cardoso, but far below the 4.9 percent world average during the same period (Figueiras and Gonçalves 2007:74). The consequences were visible in the growing unemployment rates, which reached 18.81 percent in 2004 and 17.02 in 2005.[25]

The financial sector was one of the main winners during Lula's first administration. "The high real interest rates", as Barbosa wrote, "meant high net interest payments by the Brazilian government to the rich" (Barbosa 2008:195). Economists estimate that 80 percent of the public debt in the country is in the hands of some 20,000 people who receive the lion's share of US$120 billion annual payments of the public debt. This is 10 times more than the US$6–9 billion distributed to 11 million beneficiaries of the cash transfer programme *Bolsa Família*.[26] The earnings of the three largest banks in the country, which control almost 80 percent of the financial market, increased almost five-fold between the time of Cardoso and Lula's first term in office (Duarte and Alvarez 2010).

Numerous analyses emphasise the similarities between the macroeconomic policies of the Cardoso and the Lula administrations.[27] In fact, a number of left-wing public intellectuals in Brazil rated the Lula administration as "a third term of President Cardoso" or even as " 'leftism' without a Leftist project".[28] I contend that the PT did not make an ideological shift towards neoliberal positions, despite the fact that influential figures in the economic team assumed positions of that nature, and others experienced what seems to be an ideological conversion. Some groups in Lula's first economic team did adopt what I characterise as *a discourse of economic governability* in which the macro-economic policy decisions adopted were seen as essential for the adequate functioning of the economy. One of them could be Bernardo Appy, who defines himself as a "technician with a modern vision of the economy" and a "non-active PT member" (08/04/09). Appy emphatically argued during our interview that "having low inflation, a manageable public debt, fiscal stability and balance in the external accounts does not mean having a particular ideology". In his view, these elements are "the minimum necessary to have *an economy that works properly and a government capable of ruling*" (Appy 08/04/09, my emphasis).[29]

These types of discourses, however, are not dominant in the PT and its field. Lula's economic policy was in fact criticised both by social allies and by most of the factions in central office. In 2005, for instance, when the party held internal elections six out of seven candidates running for party president seriously condemned the macro-economic policy of the previous years. Even the candidate who represented Lula's faction, "Building a New Brazil", requested that some of its most orthodox aspects, such as inflation targets, be relaxed and public investment be increased.[30] Among 70 interviewees, 63 percent of them expressed criticisms of the economic policy. 40 percent of the economic policy in general and 23 percent of the monetary policy in particular. Even within Lula's faction, 55 percent of the interviewees criticised the economic policy.[31]

THE THIRD STAGE: ACQUIRING MARGINS FOR MANOEUVRE

By 2005 the economic governability challenge had changed. Under favourable international conditions, the government was able to accumulate significant foreign reserves. These reserves increased from US$37.8 billion in 2002 to US$54.4 billion in 2005, when Brazil reached the level of reserves it had prior to the Asian crisis in 1997, and reduced public debt to 37 percent of the GDP (Filgueiras and Gonçalves 2007:105–8), far below the 50 percent threshold when Lula first took office. As a result, the Lula government's dependence on the moods of the financial sector and its vulnerability to capital flight was greatly reduced. The international circumstances contributed a great deal because Brazil, like other countries in South America, benefited from a boom in commodity prices for most of its exports, which according to some estimations grew almost 80 percent between 2003 and 2006 (Filgueiras and Gonçalves 2007:105). These economic conditions, which were initiated in 2003 and remained until the 2008 financial crisis, "eased the constraints associated with dependence on volatile flows of external capital" in several countries, including Brazil (Kaufman 2011:110).

In this context, the Lula administration continued accumulating foreign reserves until it reached the considerable level of US$207 billion by the end of 2008. According to PT economists, the accumulation of these reserves put the government in a stronger position to face eventual speculation against the Real and even helped to prevent another exchange rate crisis like the one that took place during the second Cardoso administration.[32] In 2005, the Lula government repaid its total debt to the IMF. JP Morgan eventually reassessed the Brazilian country risk, bringing it down from 1,800 points in 2002 to 397 points in 2005 and further down to 259 in the following year. On average, the first Lula administration received a better rating (507 points) than the eight years of the Cardoso administration (888 points).

Brazil eventually received "investment grading" from important credit rating agencies such as Moody's and Standard & Poor's. For Lula's economic team, the investment grading was "the cherry on the cake"; the culmination of a process of building relations with the financial sector as well as an explicit recognition that the government had been able to build confidence and gain the support of the financial establishment, as members of Lula's economic team acknowledge.[33] By the time Lula ran for the reelection in 2006, he was no longer seen as a "monster", but as an icon of Latin America's "responsible left", one that according to *The Economist* (08/08/06), "pursues the twin goals of growth and equality within the confines of a responsible economic policy", as it expressed two months before the election. Lula's reelection in 2006 did not produce any kind of reaction in financial markets (Campello 2012:15). It would be hard to expect something different, given the depth of the fiscal adjustment undertaken during the first three years of the Lula administration, the nature of its "market-friendly" reforms, and also the significant profits that investment banks made under his administration.

Having achieved the support of the financial sector, and using the opportunities that the commodity boom provided to relax the macro-economic discipline (Kaufman 2011:110), the PT government decided to make some changes. In March 2006, Guido Mantega, leading a prodevelopmentalist team with neo-Keynesian positions, headed the Ministry of Finance and those with some of the most neoliberal positions lost their influence within the government. Primary surplus targets were reduced in order to free up public expenditure and the administration started to invest significantly in large infrastructure projects. The minimum wage began to increase and continued increasing over the years, while cash transfer programmes such as *Bolsa Família* reached a larger number of beneficiaries. In the years that followed, the Central Bank gradually brought interest rates down, eventually reaching 11.25 percent.[34] This was still high, but significantly lower than the 26.5 percent they had reached in early 2003. To foster economic growth, in January 2007 Lula launched the Growth Acceleration Programme (PAC), a public–private multimillion-Real infrastructure initiative that targeted more than R$500 billion (around US$250 billion) for the construction of roads, ports, railways, waterways, sanitation, electricity, housing, urban transport and energy supplies. The launching of this programme was largely celebrated in the party. In its Third National Congress in 2007, the PT celebrated the PAC as one capable of "overcoming economic conservatism" by "placing the state in the role of a growth inducer".[35]

However, important aspects of economic policy did not change: The fiscal balance was maintained, and the government still gave a special treatment to the financial sector. Notwithstanding the importance of *Bolsa Família*, the expenditure that this programme represented in 2006 was only the equivalent of 2 percent of the interest rates that the Brazilian government paid on its debt the previous year (Zucco 2006:15). Yet Lula and his inner circle may have realised eventually that the international economic context and the margins of manoeuvre that it gave allowed them to simultaneously carry out a propoor policy agenda and maintain the financial markets on their side. Indeed, the favourable economic context made possible a socio-economic and political arrangement from which those at the top and those at the bottom of the social scale could benefit (Barbosa 2008). Eventually, both groups managed to expand their income under Lula.[36]

CONCLUSION

I have argued in this chapter that the economic orthodoxy that characterised the first years of the PT in national public office was more of a pragmatic strategy to secure governability, understood in its elite-centred perspective, and less of an ideological shift towards neoliberalism in the PT. The analytical approach used in the previous pages aimed to explain how initial economic policy decisions were largely shaped by a strategy to accommodate the interests of dominant strategic actors with sufficient power to generate an economic crisis. It was this assessment, made within Lula's inner circle, which mainly motivated the continuation of Cardoso's macro-economic policy, and even its initial reinforcement in the first years of the Lula administration. This does not mean, however, that the PT was immune to ideological conversion. I have explained that some groups promoted a conservative discourse of economic governability in which certain policies were perceived as key to the "good functioning" of the economy and the state. I argued, however, that these types of views were neither dominant in the PT field, nor the main driving force in the adoption of a conservative economic policy.

The previous pages have shown how governability strategies can be fashioned even before parties occupy public office, during electoral periods, encouraging transformations in the discourses and strategies of political parties or in some groups within parties. In the PT case, it is clear that such transformations mainly affected Lula's inner circle and other defenders of the elite-centred strategy. In retrospect, it seems that the Lula administration exaggerated its economic orthodoxy by going beyond the commitments made with the IMF during the election or by maintaining restrictive measures long after the economy had stabilised. What strikes one as a great paradox is that a progressive party in office not only has to maintain a macro-economic policy that it has long opposed, but also that it has to exaggerate some of its elements even further than a previous conservative government. One may ask whether that is the price that the Left needs to pay in order to prove its fiscal discipline credentials and gain the confidence of international markets. The defenders of the social counter-hegemonic strategy, which proposed alternatives in the political realm, did not seem to have an answer to such a challenge in the economic sphere.

7 Participation without Counter-Hegemony

There is a certain consensus among scholars, public intellectuals in Brazil and representatives of civil society that the Lula administration was not particularly innovative in promoting meaningful and broad-based participatory processes, especially when compared to PT sub-national government experiences.[1] The Lula administration, however, did make some important efforts to include civil society and listen to its representatives. Nevertheless, participation as a political agenda at the national level was embedded in a larger and more complex political game than existing studies have acknowledged. In this chapter, I contend that participation during the Lula years was caught between electoral politics and governability strategies, which shaped both the implementation and scope of participatory initiatives.

The existing literature has failed to observe that during the first year of the Lula administration, some party groups in public office favoured a social counter-hegemonic governability strategy in which participatory democracy, a founding characteristic of the PT ideology embedded in its "genetic model", would play a central role in key policy arenas such as poverty reduction and hunger eradication, as well as the planning and budgeting processes. By examining these contentious areas, this chapter aims to explore how and why participation lost momentum at the national level, as influential leaders, mainly within Lula's inner circle, allowed the elite-centred perspective of governability to prevail. By concentrating most of their energies on reaching agreements with dominant strategic actors and forming a stable alliance in Congress, the PT at the national level relegated the participation agenda to the sidelines. Unlike local government experiences, participation was not at the centre of government action and had no role in the most important policy arenas, particularly those that Lula's inner circle regarded as strategic. As scholars argue, participation was also limited in scope because no structures with meaningful decision-making power were created.[2] Elements of this sort, present in many PT local government experiences, were among the key features with which the party promoted the counter-hegemonic strategies that were central to its progressive agenda.

Different studies have found that electoral pressures can frustrate the scope of participatory experiences at the local level.[3] Adding to the existing evidence, this chapter shows how at the national level the PT administration was reluctant to share power with civil society in two of its most important policy arenas: its main social programme, *Bolsa Família* (Family Grant), and its largest infrastructure investment plan, the *Programa de Aceleracão do Crecimento* (Growth Acceleration Programme, PAC).[4] In both cases, the need to produce quick results in order to maximise vote- and office-seeking strategies hindered attempts to promote participation. Rather, Lula and his inner circle opted for policies which would score immediate marks with the poorest sectors or impact on public opinion. In these strategic areas, participation was seen as an obstacle to efficient and effective government action. The "hard nucleus" of the party in government eventually decided that the implementation of its strategic policies would be more effective if they were centrally planned, under managerial and technocratic rationales that prioritised state action over the engagement of civil society. In addition to this, I will argue that the characteristics of Lula's leadership—the way in which he came to be regarded as the representative of the poor and the excluded—made participatory instruments less necessary, in the minds of several party leaders and social activists. Lula was, after all, "one of them".

This chapter therefore tells two stories: first, how and why the attempts to promote participation in the first year of the Lula administration fell by the wayside; and second, the profound transition at the national level from participatory budgeting to the technocratic Growth Acceleration Programme. After a first section in which I briefly argue that the Lula administration did not made significant innovations in terms of participation, I examine, in the second section, participation in the social policy arena, and look at a trajectory that started with the *Fome Zero* (Zero Hunger) programme in 2002 and concluded with the establishment of the conditional cash transfer programme *Bolsa Família*. I focus in particular on the creation of participatory management committees, initially established as a mechanism of citizen control over *Fome Zero*, and look at the reasons behind their early dismantlement when *Bolsa Família* was created. In the third section I trace the paradigmatic change by which the PT in public office, after first casting aside its political commitment to democratise the national budget through participatory budgeting, surrendered to the technocratic rationale guiding the Growth Acceleration Programme. I also look at the way in which the government engaged in a consultative process to set long-term government priorities for the first term and explain the reasons for its discontinuation when PAC emerged.

PARTICIPATION DEPRIVED OF INNOVATION

Some scholars and social activists recognise that the Lula government made important efforts to include civil society, by listening to its representatives and their claims.[5] Most studies on participation during the Lula administration, however, tend to be critical. Baiocchi and Checa (2007:413) argue, for instance, that the most distinctive element of the national PT administration was not its "economic pragmatism" and transition to the ideological centre, but what they called "the abandonment" of the party's "creative forms of empowered popular participation". Others highlight the absence of innovation in participatory institutions and their lack of meaningful influence.[6] In the PT, particularly within the party Left, many leaders were frustrated with the lack of progress by the Lula government in promoting meaningful participation. In interviews with 93 party leaders, I asked whether they believed the Lula administration made progress in this area, and 33 percent stated that the government made no progress and 22 that it only made relative progress (usually when compared to previous governments). Of the eight members in the faction Left Articulation (AE) interviewed, 6 of them (75 percent) held this opinion, as well as 60 percent of the 20 leaders from "Message to the Party" (MP). Only in Lula's centrist faction, "Building a New Brazil" (CNB), did a significant number of leaders make a positive assessment of the participatory mechanisms during the administration (63 percent of the 38 interviewees).

The PT administration did create several institutions of participatory governance, expanding significantly the number of sectoral policy councils and national conferences.[7] During the course of two terms, the Lula government created 13 councils and held 73 national conferences, which, according to official figures, "mobilised" more than 5 million people at the municipal, local and national level.[8] A government-sponsored study on the role of national conferences shows how civil society organisations were able to define several policy agendas in fields ranging from oral health, sports, youth and adolescents to others like minority rights, social assistance and the environment, which seem to have influenced new legislation (Pogrebinschi 2010:53–82). However, according to observers, participatory initiatives were more impressive for their quantity rather than their quality.[9] These schemes, not particularly new, were part of the decentralised participatory system created after the enactment of the new Constitution in 1988, as explained in Chapter 3.

Despite officials flagging up these initiatives as evidence of their commitment to participatory democracy, and some scholars presenting them as "true democratic policies" that represented Lula's "participatory method of government" (Pogrebinschi 2011:5), national conferences and sectoral policy councils were part of the same effort which had oriented participatory policies in Brazil over the two previous decades. Undoubtedly, many of these institutions were important conquests of Brazilian civil society. These institutions did contribute to state democratisation and some of them gave voice to previously excluded minority groups.[10] However, councils and conferences also present a number of limitations.[11] These structures, as Shankland (2010:49) notes, are not "elements of a radical alternative". When Lula assumed office, they were already part of "the country's democratic fabric" (Shankland 2010:49). By putting these institutions and processes at the centre of its participatory agenda, the Lula administration failed to meet the high standards of citizens' engagement promoted by the PT. Most important, it ruled out the possibility of implementing a social counter-hegemonic governability strategy of the kind implemented in cities such as Porto Alegre.

Although Lula's inner circle and the dominant sector of the PT did not contemplate a radical counter-mobilisation strategy in 2002, many analysts did expect that the party in government would rely on broad-based participatory mechanisms to mitigate, at least in part, its minority status in the legislative branch, while appealing at alternative sources of legitimacy. Participatory instruments, however, did not play this role at the national level. In contrast to several PT sub-national experiences, where participation helped to circumvent or neutralise opposition in the legislative branch,[12] no participatory instrument served this purpose at the national level. For instance, in the overall legislation enacted between 1998 and 2009, only 7.2 percent was convergent with the deliberations of national conferences (Pogrebinschi 2011:18). This is very different from processes such as the Participatory Budget, in which the annual budget was almost unchanged by legislators when it reached the floor for approval, as Chapter 4 explains.

Some PT members in central and public office did try to craft and implement alternative counter-hegemonic participatory models, but with limited success. In its first year, the government launched two important initiatives that were eventually discontinued. First, there was the capillary participatory system of management committees for the Zero Hunger programme. These committees constituted a form of delegated power that would give civil society and ordinary citizens a fundamental role in managing Lula's most important social policy at the time. Second, a consultative mechanism to define government priorities and long-term investments was established. In the following sections I examine these experiments and the reasons for their lack of success.

Fome Zero Management Committees: A Short-Lived Experiment in "Citizen Power"[13]

The *Fome Zero* management committees, shaped during the first year of the Lula administration, represent one of the most significant attempts of the PT government to create an alternative mechanism of "citizen power" beyond the existing decentralised participatory system previously established in Brazil.[14] It is interesting to note that for some of the leaders who were involved in this initiative, the management committees could have eventually led into "the federal version of the PT's Participatory Budget" (Betto 2007:428). The proposed structure was intended to give society a majority of seats on the committees and decision-making authority to both manage and control Lula's *Fome Zero*. Although those who led this adventure were eventually defeated, their story shows how electoral politics, an elite-centred perspective of governability and the nature of Lula's leadership shaped and limited participation during his administration.

In the months leading up to the 2002 presidential election, the Citizenship Institute, a think tank created by Lula after the 1998 election, discussed with experts and civil society organisations a food security programme, *Fome Zero*, which established a comprehensive set of 25 policies to address extreme poverty, hunger and malnutrition.[15] From the outset, the project was expected to attract massive popular support and confer a leading role on civil society. Before the *Fome Zero* was officially launched in October 2001, Lula and his group discussed it with several NGOs, social movements, trade union confederations and academic experts.[16] Having established that hunger eradication and poverty alleviation would be a top priority, one of Lula's first decisions as president was to create a new Ministry of Food Security and Hunger Eradication, responsible, among other things, for promoting social participation around the *Fome Zero* programme. In addition, Lula appointed two special advisors attached to the presidential office and gave them responsibilities to create a mobilisation support network—the Liberation Theology priest, Frei Betto, and one of the founders of the World Social Forum, Oded Grajew. These decisions signalled the intention of the new administration to give civil society a key role in one of the most publicised programmes of the new government.

From the beginning, *Fome Zero* generated intense polemics and was at the centre of media attention. Government officials lacked a unified vision on how to implement the programme and differed in their views on the role that civil society should play at the local level. Three main groups influenced the debate—I call them the *autonomists*, the *civil society watchdogs* and the *municipalists*. The positions of these three groups were influenced by the two main governability perspectives that were present in the PT at the time. The autonomists and the civil society watchdogs to a lesser extent were on the counter-hegemonic side, while the municipalists were more influenced by elite-centred strategies. The autonomists were the group led by Frei Betto, who expected civil society to play the most significant role in the programme, both in selecting beneficiaries at the local level and in exercising social oversight. For this group, who wanted civil society to act in a self-organising fashion, the success of the programme depended on a massive mobilisation.

The group of civil society watchdogs was based within the Ministry of Food Security and had the main responsibility for the operation of *Fome Zero*. They distrusted municipal governments because of their well-known corrupt and clientelistic practices.[17] In order to avoid them, they intended to put in place a strong mechanism of social oversight over municipalities. This group shared some of the aims of the autonomists but was less driven by mobilisation and more interested in efficiency and transparency. Both of these groups were counter-hegemonic in the sense that they distrusted the local political elites and wanted to oppose them or at least establish a counterbalance to their practices. However, whereas the autonomists defended a hard counter-hegemonic strategy, the civil society watchdogs had a softer counter-hegemonic approach.

At the other end, with an elite-centred influence, was the group of the municipalists,[18] who demanded a greater role for state institutions at the local level and was sceptical of giving civil society major responsibilities in the execution of a public programme. This group was concerned with accommodating the interests of local political elites. Given the fact that the PT had only elected 186 out of 5,565 municipalities and that many mayors control *deputados* at the national level, accommodating the interests of the mayors by *giving* them a role in Lula's main government programme was part of a strategy to form alliances with other parties and eventually secure a parliamentary base of support. The three groups established a political dispute during the first two years of the Lula administration, with autonomists and civil society watchdogs more or less united on one side and municipalists on the other. As I will show, it was the municipalists who eventually prevailed.

One of the initial components of *Fome Zero* was the implementation of a cash transfer programme by which a smartcard (the *cartão alimentação*) was distributed to the poorest families and topped up on a monthly basis for them to purchase food. In order to put the programme in place, the government needed to create a registry of potential beneficiaries and update information gathered by the previous administration. Because such a task had been performed by municipal governments in the past (often based on electoral considerations), officials in the Ministry for Food Security did not trust the existing lists of beneficiaries and sought to compile new ones or revise the existing ones without the involvement of the municipalities. These officials wanted to prevent both corrupt practices and the electoral use of the programme. In their view, these problems could be avoided by transferring resources directly from the federal government to a bank account which only the beneficiaries could access. However, if the mayors were able to manipulate the selection processes the risks of misallocation would be much higher.

By establishing *Fome Zero* management committees, those within the Ministry of Food Security who were advocating for a civil society watchdog role sought to put in place a local level social oversight institution, which would also become the programme's "operational arm" (Balsadi, Del Grossi and Takagi 2004:83). Unlike the constitutionally mandated sectoral policy councils, in which civil society and government are equally represented, officials in the ministry decided that these spaces should be controlled by two-thirds of citizens or representatives of civil society organisations and only one-third of local government officials. The committees were responsible for finding inconsistencies within the list of beneficiaries; they could suggest the inclusion of new families and eventually demand the exclusion of those who no longer required benefits. These tasks were particularly important in the Northeast, the poorest and most unequal region in Brazil, where local institutions are weak and practices of corruption and clientelism particularly widespread. In order to avoid such problems, the ministry decided that the money would only be handed to those municipalities in which management committees had been formed. This decision was not free from controversy,

Participation without Counter-Hegemony 123

as bureaucrats and party officials, many of them municipalists, claimed it would slow down the implementation of the programme.

The expected role of the committees, however, was even more ambitious for the autonomists. In particular, this group considered that the committees would help the programme evolve from the initial phase, mostly based on cash transfer distribution, to one capable of implementing deep structural changes. In May 2003, in the first interview with Frei Betto, he explained how his team envisaged committees playing a role in the creation of a "social inclusion network" to tackle the "structural causes" of hunger, poverty and malnourishment (Gordillo and Gómez 2005:156–7). Following the principles of the Ecclesiastical Base Communities, the autonomists saw the committees as having a strong component of "citizens' education" (Gordillo and Gómez 2005:155) and expected them to play a political role. During the first year of the Lula government, members of these committees received training to "elaborate local development plans", "stimulate discussions about problems in the communities" and even to promote "public actions among civil society" (Balsadi, Del Grossi and Takagi 2004:84). Did the autonomists have a counter-hegemonic strategy in mind? Did they intend to create a parallel structure to the local powers? Some party and social leaders suggest this was probably the case. Requesting anonymity, a representative of civil society offered this interpretation:

> Frei Betto wanted to implement a model inspired by the Cuban Committees for the Defence of the Revolution or the Bolivarian circles in Venezuela, organised in each neighbourhood within each municipality. *He wanted to create a base of power opposed to the representative power of Brazilian municipalities.* Following this approach, decisions for social policy would cease to be made by local politicians and would be handled instead by popular organisations. (my emphasis)

A representative of the municipalists who advised Lula at the time, Miriam Belchior, made this assessment:

> Behind the creation of those committees was a soviet-type approach that wanted to decide everything about everything (. . .) The model was too rigid and could easily have been manipulated by certain groups without allowing the participation of other sectors. In certain places, for instance, the Catholic Church could have dominated those spaces entirely for its own purposes. (Belchior 06/07/09)

Former officials from the Ministry of Food Security counted 2,285 committees officially formed during the first year of the Lula administration, and claimed that the process mobilised 20,000 volunteers all over the country (Balsadi, Del Grossi and Takagi 2004:85).[19] In his memoirs, Frei Betto described public assemblies with more than 300 participants and up to 1,000 in more than 560 municipalities, with considerable activity in the Northeast (Betto 2007:107). Despite the lack of formal evaluation, the limited available evidence suggests that an incipient but strong mechanism of social oversight was slowly emerging. Former officials of the Ministry for Food Security argue that, due to the action of the volunteers who participated in the management committees, many causes of wrongdoings were exposed.[20] The question arises, therefore, as to why the administration abruptly decided to abort these efforts despite the apparent achievements

Bolsa Família: Leaving Participation Aside

The electoral logic can generate obstacles to participation and can shape the scope of participatory mechanisms. A governing party that wants to win elections and remain in office will not always be willing to share power with civil society or lose control over policies which might have strong electoral impacts. Electoral pressures started to dominate the food security policy agenda towards the end of the first year of the Lula administration. This altered the nature of Lula's main social policy, which adopted the new brand of *Bolsa Família*, becoming a key platform for Lula's reelection in 2006. The literature identifies more generally the electoral consequences of *Bolsa Família*.[21] Here I look more specifically at its implications for participation in the programme.

The original form in which *Fome Zero* was conceived changed significantly towards the end of 2003, when Lula's inner circle perceived that its most important social policy innovation was not showing results as rapidly as the electoral cycle required. The PT faced important municipal elections in 2004 and needed to consolidate itself in power to be ready for Lula's reelection in 2006. Soon, following World Bank prescriptions, the government decided to unify a series of federal government cash transfer programmes created during previous administrations with the *cartão alimentação* that the Lula government created in 2003. The result of this unification was *Bolsa Família*. Along with this change, the administration decided that the recently created Ministry for Food Security and Hunger Eradication would be abolished, and its functions subsumed into a new Ministry for Social Development. To take charge of this new area, Lula appointed Patrus Ananias, a former mayor of Belo Horizonte, who came to represent the interest and views of *the municipalists*. Lula was anxious to see the programme functioning at full speed and set his new minister a tight deadline: to reach around 11 million beneficiary families before the presidential election. As the Lula administration had only reached 3.5 million families with its *cartão alimentação*, the challenge to Ananias and his team was considerable.

A radical modification in the composition and attributes of the committees accompanied these changes. Lula eventually decided that the municipal government, rather than civil society, should assume the main role in the implementation of the programme at the local level. Most of the management committees' functions were transferred to the municipalities, including expanding the lists of beneficiaries of *Bolsa Família*, acquiring a critical political tool as a result. The committees formally remained as institutions for social oversight of the new programme; however, their role was weakened in great part because the number of civil society representatives was reduced. As with most sectoral policy councils in Brazil, from then on they had an equal number of government and civil society representatives. To make matters worse, mayors were given the freedom to determine which type of social oversight mechanisms they wished to put in place in their municipalities.[22]

Ananias prioritised the relationships with municipal governments over civil society, in spite of the fact that he was an activist in the progressive Church and even promoted a Participatory Budget when he was mayor. In December 2004, Frei Betto decided to leave the government, possibly because he realised that his agenda would not move forward. In the following years, the *Bolsa Família* programme spread around the country, with civil society playing only a marginal role. The committees created during the first year were not formally abolished, but only some of them remained active. Despite the overwhelming call by the 2004 National Conference on Food Security to maintain committees controlled by civil society (Consea 2004, in Takagi 2006:115), the government ignored this appeal. Those who favoured this decision argue that control by civil society was not necessarily a guarantee that politically biased decisions or wrongdoings would not take place. "We cannot think that the state is evil and society is full of saints", claimed Ananias (16/07/09). "It is very childish to say that civil society is free of all bad things and the government is inherently evil", was the argument of Adriana Aranha (07/07/09), his chief of staff. A civil servant in the Ministry for Social Development also made this point: "Who guarantees that civil society organisations do not have political objectives and would not develop a list of beneficiaries based on political criteria?"

Existing scholarly evidence shows that participation in *Bolsa Família* was weak. Hevia (2009), who conducted comparative studies on social oversight institutions in different cash transfer programmes in Latin America, found that the way in which *Bolsa Família* operates does not allow space for civil society, nor does it contemplate forms by which beneficiaries can engage in the programme and hold authorities to account. Even some of the main civil servants and party leaders directly involved in this programme recognised that the role of civil society was marginal.[23] Their most common justification was the pressures which they faced to massively expand the number of beneficiaries and the speed with which they had to put *Bolsa Família* in place.[24] Those leading the implementation of the cash transfer programme emphasised the importance of a government-led programme, rather than one in which civil society would act as a mediator. This was justified as being part of the state's responsibilities to guarantee basic rights, as explained by Ananias:

> We are interested in social participation, but in our view the responsibility for securing rights rests with the state (. . .) Hunger cannot wait.

> Immediate and energetic action is needed, therefore state action (. . .) As a citizen and as a Christian I believe in mobilisation and social organisation, but when you assume a public job you have to work with deadlines and goals, and respond effectively to the demands and needs of the people. (Ananias 16/07/09, my emphasis)

This emphasis on state action was also present in the discourse of the Secretary for Food Security, Crispim Moreira:

> Our emphasis is on the state and its capacity to manage a massive social policy on a legal and institutional basis. You need the state to manage a R$22 billion budget to spend on a programme like this. Fully institutionalised structures with procedures set in decrees and laws are necessary. This is our view and this has been our task. . . . *We are not in charge of the "ministry of the popular power* [the people power]".[25] Can you imagine what that would be like? (. . .) *Bolsa Família* is a rights-based programme. All Brazilians with a low income have a right to benefit from it. Period. There is a right to a minimum income. You don't need to engage in a political struggle, to be entitled to a right. (. . .) The committees no longer decide whose names are included in the registry because the criteria are set in law. (Moreira 03/04/09, my emphasis)

It is interesting to note how according to these views, efficiency and effectiveness are synonymous with "state actions", rather than being attributes of civil society. Such a stance contrasts with the social counter-hegemonic governability strategy promoted by the PT in a number of municipalities. More in tune with the elite-centred approach that emphasises the role of the state over civil society, participation at the national level was regarded as something that can generate obstacles rather than facilitate solutions. It would be hard to disagree with the view that fundamental rights should be guaranteed by the state. Yet participation in *Bolsa Família* was not weak because the government wanted to emphasise the role of the state as the main guarantor of the right to food or a minimum income. If the management committees were ignored or left aside, it was mostly because the administration wanted to retain control over a social policy that was a key plank of the PT's electoral strategy.

Electoral pressures eventually determined the characteristics and pace of implementation of *Bolsa Família*. Clarice dos Santos, an activist of the MST who worked for INCRA, put it bluntly: "*Bolsa Família* responded to the most immediate political need to re-elect Lula". In her view, "organising the people or promoting participatory mechanisms would have taken more time and effort" (Santos 07/05/09). It is clear that the president wanted to see results much earlier. The strategy proved electorally successful when Lula won the 2006 presidential election with more than 60 percent of the vote against rival Geraldo Alckmin, after the *Bolsa Família* programme reached 51.4 million beneficiaries. As a number of studies have shown, the extension of

Lula's social programmes, especially transfer schemes that distribute income to the lower rungs of the social pyramid, produced "excellent results in bolstering Lula's popularity" (Barros Silva, de Souza Braga et al. 2010:131).[26]

Governability also played a significant role in removing meaningful participatory mechanisms from Lula's main social policy. Not only did the counter-hegemonic characteristics of the management committees cause suspicion among the defenders of the elite-centred perspective, but the administration also needed to accommodate the interests of those opposition parties who became allies in Congress and who wanted to have a role in *Bolsa Família*. This was suggested by Frei Betto in his memoirs, where he explained how granting more power to the municipal governments was part of a strategy of the Lula government to broaden its political alliances before the 2004 municipal elections (Betto 2007:249).

FROM THE PARTICIPATORY BUDGETING PROMISE TO THE PAC'S TECHNOCRATIC RATIONALE

The trajectory of the PT participatory agenda at the national level is paradoxical. Not only did the party fail to use participatory instruments in the planning and budgeting processes at the national level as promised, but it also adopted a technocratic rationale in which decisions on its most important infrastructure programme, the Growth Acceleration Programme (PAC), were mostly made by experts and bureaucrats. In order to show this trajectory, I start with the promises made to include Participatory Budget (PB) at the national level, which were quickly left aside; and I then move on to explore how Lula's inner circle failed to promote a meaningful debate on democratising the budgeting process once in office. Possibly as a palliative remedy, the administration organised a national consultation process to legitimise its plan, the *Plano Plurianual: "Um Brasil para Todos"* ["Pluriannual Plan: 'One Brazil for All'"] 2004–2007. Although this process was regarded by civil society organisations as a first step towards democratising the planning process, it went no further after the Lula administration launched the PAC. Both the governability dilemma and electoral motivations shaped this trajectory, I will argue in this section, by forcing participation to take a back seat to what was perceived by Lula's inner circle as a more pressing issue: economic and political governability. However, even when the economy and national politics stabilised, participation in the planning process was not introduced, as the administration concentrated on infrastructure projects, motivated by electoral concerns and the interests of dominant strategic actors.

Leaving the Participatory Budget Behind

When Lula assumed office, participatory budgeting mechanisms had already spread across several municipalities (see Chapter 4), with some particularly successful cases. At the state level, however, the experience was limited to one single case in which PB lasted for a whole government term—the Olívio Dutra administration in Rio Grande do Sul (1999–2002).[27] From its Second National Congress in 1999 onwards, the PT envisaged scaling up participatory budgeting mechanisms from the local level to the national sphere.[28] The idea of a federal PB was revisited by the party in its Third National Congress in 2001,[29] and was incorporated into the first pages of Lula's electoral manifesto in 2002.[30]

Given the enormous size of the Brazilian territory and its population, a federal PB was obviously not an easy promise to deliver. Yet the intention was never to automatically implement this instrument at the national sphere, but to adapt it to the Brazilian federal structure, as it was made explicit in the 2001 and 2002 documents.[31] In any case, this was rather complicated because a wide range of actors influenced the deliberation of the public budget at the federal level. Whereas in the municipal sphere, a mayor may only face opposition from one institutional actor, namely the legislative assembly, national presidents face various intermediate levels, such as mayors and state governments. Some PT officials claim that a federal PB could only work with the support of city mayors and state governors (Alves 03/12/08), which is probably the case given the influence they have over the National Congress, particularly governors. Despite the difficulties, it was reasonable to expect, considering the history of the PT and the commitments made, that a creative mechanism to democratise the federal public budget would eventually be discussed. This was not the case, however, as those with influence kept it off the table.

Party leaders have mixed opinions on the extent to which PB would be feasible beyond the municipal sphere. Leaders of the party Left, particularly those who participated in the Dutra administration in Rio Grande do Sul, think that PB has potential at the state level,[32] while many in Lula's inner circle disagree.[33] Luiz Dulci, who was the main authority responsible for the promotion of participatory mechanisms, argued that the municipal model based on assemblies and citizens' individual participation, had practically failed at the state level, and therefore was even less feasible in the national sphere (Dulci 10/12/08). During the interviews conducted for this study, it emerged that most of the leftist groups within the PT supported the creation of a federal PB, while leaders in Lula's faction were reluctant or sceptical. I asked 70 party leaders whether they thought a federal PB was a good idea. Within Lula's faction, "Building a New Brazil" (CNB), only 35 percent said they did think so, while among the "Message to the Party" (MP), which includes several leaders who played key roles in PT administrations in Rio Grande do Sul, 88 percent were in favour.

Despite the scepticism within Lula's faction and among his inner circle, PB was included in the electoral manifesto in 2002, possibly because it was not easy to leave aside a banner that was so strongly identified with the PT. What mainly stands out, however, is that there was no discussion about scaling up PB or even on alternatives to democratise the formulation of the annual budget. Neither the party in central office, nor the party in government, discussed the question. Only an isolated group within Socialist Democracy (DS), arguably the most enthusiastic promoter of participation within the party, formally proposed a federal PB based on a synthesis of previous municipal and state experiences and the incorporation of new technologies.[34] For Ubiratan de Souza, who was in charge of the implementation of PB in Rio Grande do Sul, a federal PB was promising because it would have a considerably greater impact than in the sub-national sphere (19/12/08). The proposal, however, did not reach government circles. According to Pedro Pontual, an associate of the Polis Institute, the main resistance to the discussion came from Lula's economic team, who dismissed PB as a "mere form of assembly-ism" (Pontual 17/10/08).[35]

High-ranking party leaders in government acknowledged that initiatives to democratise the budget were relegated because more important political issues took priority.[36] The way in which priorities were established clearly followed the elite-centred strategy. As José Dirceu explained:

> It was a choice. If the government had decided to promote more participation or more mobilisation, it could certainly have achieved better results. However, when the PT took office, the priority was to solve the economic crisis, take hold of the state apparatus and achieve a majority in the Legislature. ... You cannot do everything at the same time. You have to know what your priorities are. (Dirceu 07/01/09)

Interestingly, even Tarso Genro, one of the main champions of participatory budgeting as Mayor of Porto Alegre (1993–1997/2000–2001) put forward a similar argument. In his view, the democratisation of the public budget was not promoted at the federal level, because the administration had "urgent matters to solve". His explanation is that when the PT took office in 2003, "we had a country in bankruptcy; high inflation, stratospheric interest rates, unfavourable trade balance and lack of foreign reserves" (Genro 31/04/09). Clearly, within the elite-centred governability strategy that the Lula administration adopted, macro-economic stability and the formation of a stable parliamentary alliance determined the order of priorities in a wide range of areas, including participation.

Participation by Consultation:[37] Lula's First Pluriannual Plan

The Lula administration found a way to incorporate the demands for democratisation in the planning process by promoting a national consultation to define the Pluriannual Plan (2004–2007). The Pluriannual Plan in Brazil is a legal instrument by which the federal executive, with congressional approval, establishes its priorities for a whole government term, specifying the general objectives, the main programmes to be implemented and the specific goals.[38] Activists who took part in the consultation and scholars wrote that the process lacked meaningful influence, and was mostly government-controlled.[39] Here, I suggest that the way in which this process was organised was part of a governability strategy to include a wide range of strategic actors for governability and at the same time create a sense of social ownership to legitimise Lula's government. The outcome of this process was eventually influenced by the same governability dilemma that affected different policy arenas of the Lula administration.

The consultation over the Pluriannual Plan was organised by the General Secretariat of the Presidency and the Ministry for Planning, and supported at the local level by civil society organisations. The process did not attempt to reach ordinary citizens because carrying out such a task, as one of its main organisers explained, would have taken "entire football fields" (Dulci 10/12/08). It was an inclusive process, however, because a wide range of organisations participated, ranging from members of rural and urban workers' organisations, to business associations and religious congregations, to gender groups, gay rights movements and academic organisations. According to official figures, 2,170 organisations participated. Between May and June 2003, a series of one-day public hearings took place in each of the 26 state capitals and the Federal District, totalling 4,700 participants from all over the country.[40] A 700-page document was eventually presented to the president in a public ceremony and two weeks later, the Pluriannual Plan 2004–2007 was sent to Congress for approval.

Observers and participants had many complaints about the process. They argued that the government had the final say in the selection of participants,[41] and set and controlled the agenda as well as the modalities of the hearings.[42] Although the presidency reported that the consultation resulted in various alterations of the government's first draft (Dulci 2003:20–2), participants from civil society did not have a similar impression. After the whole process was concluded, 33 social networks and forums—which included ABONG and Inter-Redes, among others—contended that the participatory process of consultation was not adequately incorporated into the final version of the plan. According to Inter-Redes, the government only included secondary issues that could help to improve the main strategic orientations that inspired the PPA, but nothing capable of changing the logic of its policies.[43]

The final version was severely modified (Baiocchi and Checa 2007:420), not only by the executive, but also by the legislative branch. Unlike PB at the local level, where the budget acquired sufficient legitimacy and robustness to be endorsed by the legislative branch, when the Pluriannual Plan went to Congress the opinions of civil society were ignored by federal legislators. The elite-centred governability strategy that led the PT government to become a partner with dominant strategic actors conditioned and limited the scope of the participatory process. The final document sought to accommodate the interests of particularly powerful groups. The plan, as authors suggest, was largely subordinated to macro-economic objectives[44] which were part of the strategy by which the Lula administration sought to accommodate the interests of the financial sector and secure its support. Baiocchi and Checa (2007:420) argue that the final government plan "mystified 'technical decisions' such as interest rates or budgetary priorities as the executive realm of government technocrats".

Despite the fact that a government plan had never been discussed in such a participatory fashion, key figures in Lula's economic team could not escape the idea that certain economic decisions should be exempt from participation, particularly when they play an important role to secure economic or political governability. When I asked the Deputy Minister for Finance, Bernardo Appy, why some people argue that participation did not influence the economic arena during the Lula administration, he answered:

> I don't know what they mean exactly by participation. We are dealing with technical problems here. A macro-economy is either balanced or unbalanced. When you deal with economic issues you handle things that are not clear to the general public. They wouldn't know how to manage interest rates in order to keep inflation down or how to balance external accounts. It is difficult to have direct participation in these sorts of things. (Appy 08/04/09)

Despite the criticisms, the consultation over the 2004–2007 Pluriannual Plan was not considered a bad starting point. Both government officials and civil society representatives argued at the time that it represented a step towards democratising the planning process. Some even emphasised that it was the first time that a government development plan had been opened to social input.[45] For some, it even held up the prospect of creating a participatory process on national investment priorities (Baiocchi and Checa 2007). Many others expected that Lula's second term would see an improved consultation, but this was not the case. Although Lula campaigned for reelection in 2007 on a commitment to "expand and deepen" this experience,[46] his government did not fulfil this promise. No consultation on the second Pluriannual Plan (2008–2011) ever took place. The official argument for this is that the second plan would incorporate resolutions and recommendations from sectoral policy councils and national conferences in order to profit from the existing instruments.[47] Nonetheless, the second plan only incorporated the inputs from these institutions in very exceptional cases. Neither the first nor the second Pluriannual Plan incorporated these resolutions, as a former advisor to the presidency acknowledged (Toni 02/04/09).

By the beginning of his second term, Lula was more secure in power and no longer needed to promote a consultative process to create a sense of social ownership and legitimacy for his government plan. The president had gained the confidence of strategic actors outside the PT and his policies proved palatable to the business and financial sectors. The economy was already growing above 4 percent, and the effects of the government's social policy had produced visible effects, reducing extreme poverty from

17 to 40 percent between 2003 and 2005 (Soares and Herculano 2010:47). After August 2006, Lula's approval rating started to recover from the 2005 corruption scandals and climbed even higher than it had been at the beginning of Lula's first term, reaching 61.2 percent in October 2007 and 66.8 in February 2008 (CNT/Sensus 2007, in Barros, Souza Braga et al. 2010:131). For his second term, early on, Lula had a developmentalist plan to promote economic growth, based on large infrastructure projects through public–private partnerships. Such a plan was presented as ready-made and did not require consultations of any kind.

PAC: The Urgency of Economic Growth and the Technocratic Rationale

The incipient participatory innovations that the Lula administration promoted in its first Pluriannual Plan vanished with the emergence of the Growth Acceleration Programme (PAC), launched in 2007. As a top priority of his second term, the whole state machinery concentrated on the promotion of large-scale infrastructure public works in areas such as energy, highways, railways, airports, urbanisation, housing and sanitation. The programme had no specific participatory mechanism attached and mostly assumed a technocratic rationale in which, as I advanced in Chapter 1, the "common good" seemed to be objectively identified by a group of experts based on their knowledge and their capacity to "get things done". Electoral considerations, coupled with the need to secure governability and the nature of Lula's leadership, largely explained this lack of participation.

Lula's second term started with the investment projects "ready and organised", as a civil servant from the Ministry of Planning explained (Almeida 03/04/09). PAC mostly functioned within a managerial approach in which the government established a set of centrally monitored goals and created mechanisms to secure the allocation of massive resources during the time of economic bonanza. Determined to make "a big step forward in Brazilian infrastructure projects" (Belchior 06/07/09), the Lula administration did not want any obstacles that could delay completion of the works. In many cases (as civil servants explained), rather than starting new projects, the administration preferred to finish those underway.[48] This was a reasonable approach, but there was also an electoral motivation behind it: By including projects started in previous administrations, the government could take the credit for their completion and make the PAC seem much more robust and ambitious in the eyes of public opinion.

Government officials found it difficult to reconcile the organisational approach that led to the creation of the PAC with the initial participatory arrangements discussed in the previous section. The administration wanted to promote economic growth and time was precious. Many officials argue that the urgency to launch the PAC was one of the reasons why no participatory process was put in place.[49] A civil servant in the Ministry for Planning argued, for instance, that it could take between two and three years to discuss such a complex programme in a participatory fashion (Almeida 03/04/09). In any case, the emphasis of the programme, as other government sources acknowledged, was mostly on "efficiency and competence".[50] Miriam Belchior, one of the main PAC strategists, recounted the following:

> The PAC was conceived after the 2006 presidential election as a result of the president's obsession with guaranteeing economic growth during his second term in office. In fact, the programme was designed in three months, between October 2006 and January 2007, when the new term officially started (. . .). This programme represented a vision of how to make the country grow. *It was innovative in terms of management, but not in terms of participation.* There was no consultation: not even the governors were consulted, still less the mayors (. . .). I think that the programme could have been more participatory, but the president decided to get things done quickly. (Belchior 06/07/09, my emphasis)

There is no evidence that the administration contemplated alternative ways of discussing the contents of the PAC in a participatory fashion, during the entire second term. Even high-ranking government officials acknowledge the lack of participatory mechanisms within this important programme.[51] The idea that participatory processes take time and can generate delays, which often precludes politicians from promoting meaningful participation (Teixeira and Tatagiba 2005), was a commonly held view among many of the PT leaders at the national level. Like *Bolsa Família*, the PAC became immersed in the electoral strategy of both Lula and the PT. Monitored from the Civil House of the Presidency (the equivalent of a ministry of the interior), the programme became part of the strategy to promote the candidacy of Dilma Rousseff, the Minister of the Civil House who was appointed in 2005 and Lula's hand-picked candidate for president in 2011. Clearly, the PT in government and Lula's inner circle wanted not only to inaugurate public works at high speed, but also to publicise them on a grand scale.

The governability strategy adopted by the PT did not generate incentives to promote participation around the PAC. To a large extent, the government negotiated the allocation of resources for infrastructure projects with powerful strategic actors such as state governors and big construction companies, with little or no input from civil society. This strategy might have helped to secure congressional support, because PAC resources were largely distributed among state governors from allied parties. Since big construction companies became the main beneficiaries of PAC projects,[52] the PT could receive crucial support from the private sector. In fact, many of the companies who benefited became important funders of the PT and its allies in Congress and gave generous support to Dilma's presidential campaign in 2010.[53]

Interestingly, a number of civil society organisations and minority groups which the PT sought to represent from the time of its creation, such as environmentalists or indigenous movements, actively opposed the construction of large infrastructure projects. Many of these projects have a strong environmental and social impact, such as the transposition of the River São Francisco; the construction of the BR 38 (an 87-km highway from Manaus to Porto Velho which crosses one of the best-preserved areas of the Amazon) or the building of the Belo Monte hydroelectric dam, which may dry up 100 kilometres of the River Xingú in the Legal Amazon.[54] Lula and his administration strongly defended these projects.[55] Now that the president had learnt "what needs to be done in order to make the country grow", as he claimed towards the end of his first term, he dismissed the groups that opposed large infrastructure projects as "obstacles to Brazil's development".[56]

The administration did not put in place a participatory process around the PAC, not even a merely token one. Possibly this was because there were no major incentives for doing so. In his second term in office, Lula not only became the most popular president since Getúlio Vargas and Juscelino Kubitschek, but he also came to be regarded among many in Brazil and the PT as the representative of the poor and the excluded. In April 2007, for instance, a survey study on Lula's performance ratings by level of family income showed how Lula enjoyed his best rates of approval among those earning up to 1 minimum wage (81.4%) and from 1 to 5 minimum wages (66%) (CNT/Sensus 2007, in Barros Silva, de Souza Braga et al. 2010:131).[57] Party members recognise that Lula's leadership style and his direct and unmediated relationship with the poor was another reason why the participatory agenda did not acquire significant dynamism during those years.[58] One of Lula's presidential advisors, Oded Grajew, argued that because there was "a strong assumption that with Lula as President everything would be solved", promoting participation too seriously would have meant "questioning his legitimacy" as a leader (Wainwright and Branford 2005:38).

CONCLUSION

In this chapter I have shown how electoral pressures and the elite-centred governability strategy adopted by the PT in national executive public office limited the scope and depth of the participatory mechanisms put in place during the first year of the Lula administration. It is not easy to determine which of these two factors played the most important role. The trajectory from a national PB promise to the PAC, with its technocratic rationale, shows that the need to accommodate the interests of dominant strategic actors for governability precluded party leaders from discussing a meaningful process to democratise the public budget and frustrated the first consultation to define the priorities of the Lula administration. However, electoral pressures also played a role in making the government opt for policies capable of generating immediate impact and a larger electoral appeal, particularly among the poorest, as was the case of the *Bolsa Família* programme.

Within this context, participation was regarded as something that could slow down the implementation of the most important government policies.

The adoption of a conservative, elite-centred governability strategy, however, might have been a more powerful reason. Ultimately, as Chapter 4 showed, electoral pressures were also influential at the local level, but many PT administrations found ways to promote participation and simultaneously perform successfully in elections. It is not evident that participatory policies could have rendered similar electoral dividends at the national level (at least not in the short run), given the time that participatory processes may take to consolidate. It is clear, however, that the strong suspicion with which the defenders of an elite-centred strategy regarded counter-hegemonic participatory institutions, such as the *Fome Zero* management committees, was a strong deterrent to any possible attempts at innovation. Ultimately, the governability strategy adopted by Lula's inner circle became a suprarationale that shaped the substance, character and scope of participatory initiatives and limited its progressive potential at the national level.

A secondary factor contemplated in this chapter was the nature of Lula's leadership, and how it drove energies away from participatory processes. Lula's leadership had important implications for the transformative project of the PT because the party in public office would no longer rely on the input of civil society as much as on those who had been elected and who would govern in its name and in the name of the whole society. All these issues had important implications for the PT's transformative project because the Workers' Party during the Lula administration seemed to leave aside one of the most powerful and original ideas that inspired its creation: the need to organise the poor and transform society as a whole, without seeking state power as the only source of transformation.

8 Securing Social Governability
Dealing with Allies in Civil Society

The prevalent idea in the literature is that political parties move away from their allies in civil society when they enter government. The experience of the PT in public office shows that this is not always the case. Rather than a movement away from civil society, I argue, it is *the nature of the relationship* which mainly changes when a party shifts from opposition to government. Similar to the sub-national executive experiences of the PT analysed earlier, the Lula administration developed fluid relations with groups in civil society, and maintained close ties with them. However, the PT's form of engagement with its allies in the socio-political field suffered several transformations when the party took possession of a large part of the state machinery. Reward-based linkages, mainly established through the distribution of jobs and state subsidies, acquired greater relevance, very often shaped by interpersonal linkages between party and social leaders in the PT field. The change of scale from municipal to national public office exacerbated some of these trends, which were already visible at the local level. In addition, Lula's strong leadership over the PT socio-political field came to play an unprecedented role.

In this chapter I argue that these bases for the party's engagement with civil society organisations—the strong leadership exercised by Lula over the PT field, the distribution of jobs in the state apparatus, the allocation of massive state subsidies and the existence of interpersonal linkages between party and societal leaders—all contributed to secure governability by appeasing sources of opposition or by providing a greater sense of legitimacy among civil society. By accommodating the interests of the PT social base in government, the party in public office managed to secure support from an important sector of civil society and maintain contestation at low or manageable levels. However, the PT in national public office did not only distribute selective incentives, such as jobs or state subsidies. As far as it could, it also provided collective incentives by seeking to promote common agendas with its social allies. In this study I do not rely on the common assumption, present among students of the PT, party intellectuals, and even leaders in the PT socio-political field, that the distribution of jobs among social leaders automatically results in their "co-optation",[1] as some have suggested in the case of the Lula administration.² Moreover, I do not assume that state funding necessarily generates domination, subordination or control, features that some scholars have found through their research.³ My work argues for a more nuanced understanding of party–civil society relationships in the PT case, by showing the mixed evidence from the two terms of the Lula administration. That is, one in which both reward-based and programmatic linkages played important roles. These two types of linkages do not exist in pure form and are not always easy to disentangle. Because of their different natures, I analyse them in separate chapters, exploring reward-based linkages in the current chapter and programmatic linkages in the next one.

When looking at the relationship between the Lula administration and civil society organisations, this book concentrates mainly on one side of this relationship—the party in public office. My attempt is not to elaborate on the behaviour of the different social groups in the PT field, but only to analyse common tendencies in the type of linkages that the party in the national executive established with some of the most influential organisations in the PT field such as CUT; the Landless Rural Workers' Movement (MST); the National Confederation of Agricultural Workers (CONTAG); or the Housing Movement. Given the complex diversity of Brazilian civil society, my findings do not necessarily apply to all organisations in the same way. The account that I offer here only constitutes the first seeds of a more ambitious research agenda on the relationship that progressive parties in government establish towards their allies in civil society. In the case of the Lula administration, there has been no in-depth study that has explored them extensively.⁴ The existing case studies, focused on specific organisations,⁵ have tended to neglect the perspective of the party in public office and how these relationships were shaped by the governability strategy.

The current chapter is divided in five sections. The first section frames the debate of social governability. Section 2 characterises the Lula administration as a government of permanent negotiation with civil society organisations. Section 3 studies the nature of Lula's leadership and the way it shaped the relationship between the party in public office and civil society organisations in the PT field. Section 4 looks at the two main types of reward-based linkages established between the party in public office and its social allies, namely job distribution and allocation of state subsidies. The final section explores the interpersonal linkages as elements by which the party in public office, deliberately or not, limited disruptive forms of collective action and kept contestation at low or manageable levels.

THE ENDS AND THE MEANS OF SOCIAL GOVERNABILITY

The literature on party–movement relations suggests that parties in government tend to prefer "more standardized" and "non-threatening forms of collective action" (Hipsher 1998:157) and are likely to seek to reduce the "potential disruptive effects" of social movement activity (Meyer 2007:126). Some parties in public office might mobilise their own social bases to support specific policies, create a counter-hegemonic power with which they can confront dominant strategic actors, or even require assistance from social organisations to defend themselves from political attacks. Nevertheless, parties in power will discourage collective action against their own policies. The PT has been no different in this sense. During my interviews with PT leaders, a city councillor with historical ties to social organisations put it bluntly: "A government that is questioned every day becomes too unstable and compromises its own project", he said. "No government can cope with a situation in which it is permanently attacked" (Camilo 16/11/10). This approach, it is interesting to see, was internalised by some of the PT allies in civil society. Two members of CONTAG, for instance, made the following point:

> When you are in opposition you are not responsible for governability. Your actions are done in order to erode the existing government. When the government that you helped to elect is in power you maintain pressure with responsibility. You try not to break the governance process, you need to be careful not to support the accusations that the Right [wing] is making about your allies and you have to constantly measure your reactions without giving force to the opposition. This is something that limits you". (Borba and Cleia 03/04/08)

Parties in public office are not likely to promote mobilisation processes that might escape their control. In the PT case, given the difficulties that democratically elected left-wing parties had faced in the past when dealing with their allies in civil society, the need to avoid a mobilisation process that could go out of control was a particularly relevant aspect. As in other aspects that I examine in this book, the Chilean case under Salvador Allende (1970–1973) was revealing, in spite of the different historical circumstances. One of the main sources of political instability in that country, as Winn (1986:6–7) notices, was a "revolution from below" in which a group of actors with "relative autonomy" took the revolutionary process into "their own hands". As Winn (1986:6) persuasively explains, it was the radical mass mobilisation of certain groups in a highly polarised context that forced Allende to modify his original "carefully controlled and phased strategy for socialism from above", leading to an unmanageable confrontation with dominant strategic actors which eventually resulted in the 1973 military coup.

The reality in Brazil in 2003 was different from 1970s Chile in several aspects. No revolutionary socialist programme was on the PT agenda, no nationalisation of industries was contemplated and no movement represented "a serious challenge to the political system", as Campello and Zucco (2008:7) observed. However, the Chilean experience did suggest that over-radicalised or too undisciplined societal groups are never good allies. This concern was clearly seen in the PT national administration from the outset. Not coincidentally, what Lula mainly asked his supporters for in his inaugural speech on 1 January 2003 was "patience", while he made an appeal to "keep our many legitimate social concerns under control so that they can be addressed at the right pace and in the right moment".[6] Allende's failure had been a warning about the potential risks of lacking a clear "hierarchy of command" and possibly showed how one of the main obstacles to securing social governability derived, to quote Winn (1986:7, 141) again, from the existence of different "centres of authority" competing for ascendancy and leadership. In Lula's Brazil such a risk was avoided because a clear leadership managed to modulate the tactics and the strategies. It was the party in government, and Lula in particular, who set the pace and the modalities of the process.

Parties use a wide range of strategies to promote more "routinized and predictable" forms of mobilisation (Meyer 2007:126) and to limit their potentially disruptive effects. Some governments simply repress mobilisation, while others try to integrate social organisations into established political channels, as the experience of postdemocratic Brazil confirms (see Chapter 3). In the case of the Lula government, there is a consensus among scholars, PT members and social leaders that, unlike Cardoso, Lula's government did not resort to repressive practices.[7] Rather, the administration put in place an unprecedented "open-doors" policy towards civil society organisations, allowing dialogue and negotiation to become common practice. In this regard, social leaders noticed the difference between the Cardoso and Lula administrations. Arthur Henrique, elected as CUT leader in 2006, recalls that "[W]e were coming from the experience of a government that did not listen to us, did not receive us and called the police to solve trade union problems". In his view, "Lula changed all this radically", as many negotiation spaces were opened to them in matters such as minimum wage, small-scale agriculture or education (Henrique 15/04/09).

Brazilian political scientists such as Wanderley Guilherme dos Santos and Leonardo Avritzer have emphasised that the Lula administration was the first since 1964 in which no one lost their lives for mobilising against the federal government.[8] Even in the case of the MST, one of the most radical organisations in the PT field, the fact that the organisation increased the number of occupations of land and public buildings from the first year of the Lula administration did not result in the violent clashes with national security forces that had been so common in previous years (Hochstetler 2004:13).[9] This supports the idea that the PT in national public office was able to manage social conflict successfully, not least by accommodating the interests of key strategic actors in civil society in a way that limited disruptive actions.

From the very start, Lula incorporated social organisations into various institutionalised and noninstitutionalised mechanisms. These mechanisms included institutions of participatory governance such as sectoral policy councils and national conferences, as explained in the previous chapter. A practice of negotiation with a wide array of social organisations was the hallmark of the PT national administration. Many of these negotiations took place in formally established or newly created *ad hoc* institutional mechanisms, while many others happened spontaneously in private and noninstitutional settings. The presidential palace of Planalto was symbolically opened to the visits of social leaders, who were not regular guests in the past and who came to meet senior officials (and sometimes the president himself) more frequently. The different forms of engagement by which the party in public office related to civil society organisations—the nature of Lula's leadership, reward-based linkages, interpersonal linkages, as well as the willingness to honour certain programmatic linkages—facilitated compromise, and discouraged more radical or potentially disruptive forms of collective action, particularly among those groups or actors who still contemplated them within their repertoires.

LULA'S LEADERSHIP AND THE POWER OF A SYMBOLIC IDENTITY

Hochstetler (2004:10) suggests that the most significant addition to the PT's procedural repertoire at the national level was the "heavy use" it made of Lula "as an individual and as the representative of national government" in its dealings with civil society organisations. Here I argue that Lula's strong leadership was largely based on the symbolic identification that certain groups had towards his personal background.[10] This had an impact on the government's capacity to secure social governability, despite the fact that this intention was not necessarily explicit.

Lula's strong leadership historically represented a unifying authority among the different factions of the party and he exercised an informal leadership among other segments of the PT field, most notably union leaders, who strongly identified themselves with his trajectory. From the beginning of Lula's first term, the government relied heavily on his personal history as a northeasterner born into poverty, on his legacy as a former trade union leader and on his moral authority among civil society organisations and PT allies. Lula was well aware of this. In a famous documentary recorded during the 2002 electoral campaign, *Entreatos*, he could be heard informally speaking with his colleagues describing himself as "the only politician in Brazil of a national stature", and emphasising: "I have come this far because I have a movement supporting me: a major portion of the Catholic Church backs me, a major portion of the students, the PT, CUT (...) No Brazilian political leader ever had the constituency I have" (Moreira 2004).

For many in the PT socio-political field, "Lula was turned into an icon, and idol, a symbol of our desires for transformation" (Rangel 08/04/09), as an MST leader self-critically recalls. These elements influenced the interaction between the administration and civil society organisations and were often exploited by the former to gather political support for its policies and reforms, and to diminish sources of opposition and antigovernment reactions. In June 2003, Lula attended CUT's Eighth National Congress and used his authority and persuasive power as a leader and as head of state to support his governability strategy among CUT unionists. The labour congress took place at a time when the Lula administration had put in place a macro-economic policy that frustrated the aspirations of progressive social organisations. It also happened shortly after the government had introduced a bill to reform the social security pension system that equated the rights of public sector unions to those of the private sector.[11] Part of a second generation of reforms prescribed by the World Bank and promoted by financial institutions worldwide,[12] the bill was in great part an attempt to accommodate the interests of the financial establishment, a key element of Lula's governability strategy.

The reform of the social security pension system directly affected the interests of the public sector trade unions, most of them affiliated to CUT, and the largest constituency of this organisation.[13] At this critical moment, Lula addressed the CUT audience and emphasised his strong identification with the *Central*. In his speech, he presented himself as CUT's founding father and spoke to its members in a paternal fashion, as someone who knows what is best for the audience and best for the country. Between jokes, the president told unionists that they were all members of a common family[14] and he explained the need for certain policies and reforms. Nevertheless, Lula also made promises. He told them: "this *companheiro metalúrgico* from the North-east and from Pernambuco, who arrived at the Presidency of the Republic because of you and your responsibility, will not forget his historical commitments".[15] He received a standing ovation. Yet the president also received boos from a group of radical union leaders who opposed the controversial aspects of the government policies. The master of improvisation, Lula told the dissidents: "You know that I do not mind boos. To me boos are as important as applauses. Some people used to boo me because I intended to create the PT. Some people even booed me because I wanted to create CUT . . . .".[16]

During his first months in office, Lula held several meetings with representatives of the labour, indigenous, antipoverty, religious and women's movements, giving their agendas prominence, praising "their work" and expressing "sympathy for their aims", while simultaneously asking for support and, no less important, for their "patience" (Hochstetler 2004:10). In many of these meetings, as in most of his speeches, Lula reminded his audience of his humble origins and proudly spoke of his social background.[17] Initially, the president also relied on this personal leadership to relate to the MST, to appease that organisation and buy time. Lula and his inner circle were reluctant to conduct the type of land reform that the movement demanded—that is, one characterised by massive expropriations of unproductive land. Once in office, the government prevaricated for several months, arguing that it had to put the house in order (Bradford 2009:530). Only after the MST had initiated a national campaign of land occupations did Lula receive a delegation of members from the movement's National Directorate. During the meeting, the president assured his visitors that land reform was a "measure of justice", and he promised a "peaceful",[18] but nonetheless "massive land reform" (Betto 2007:148). For a brief moment the cameras registered that the president wore a red MST cap, with the inscription "Land reform: For a Brazil without *latifundio*". Lula's words and actions seemed to seduce the attendants. Clearly excited, the intellectual guide and most visible figure of the MST, Jõao Pedro Stédile, told the press: "Land reform is like a football match and the government plays on our side. We will beat the landowners 5–0".[19] In the next chapter I will show how and why land reform eventually made little progress during the Lula years.

CUT and other union leaders were particularly influenced by Lula's leadership. For them, the election of a former metalworker had a "strong symbolic character" and it was seen as the "culmination of a historical process", as CUT's president from 2006 emphasised during my interview with him (Henrique 15/04/09). This symbolic character was so important that among certain union leaders the president benefited from unquestioning support. One of them was CUT's Vice President, José Antonio Lópes Feijóo, who belongs to the ABC Metalworker's Trade Union, the same one in which Lula initiated his trajectory as a union leader. Lópes Feijóo went as far as saying: "Even if the government had performed very poorly, it still would have been [an] incredibly important [government] because we were able to elect a president as a result of 30 years of struggle" (Lopes Feijóo 16/12/09). His words show the tremendous importance which Lula's leadership had, that the president could sometimes count on something close to a blank cheque for support.

Lula's informal leadership, coupled with the strong influence the PT always had over CUT, was used to orientate the succession of the *Central's* presidency, during its Eighth Congress in 2003. Since 1999, the labour peak organisation had been led by João Felício, head of the schoolteachers' union, whose leadership was strongly associated with the public sector workers, more combative than unions associated with the private sector at the time. The party in government and its supporters opposed his reelection as CUT president, most likely because his union base was reluctant to support the reform of the pension fund system, which mainly affected Felício's union base. CUT had a tradition of reelecting its presidents, but this time they opted for a candidate supported by Lula, Luiz Marinho.[20] Marinho was hand-picked by President Lula and benefited from his endorsement.[21] Given the inclination of Lula and his government to engage in negotiations with civil society organisations, CUT members who supported Marinho argued that his experience as a skilful negotiator made him the most suitable candidate for the job (Lopes Feijóo 16/12/09).[22] Those who supported Felício, in contrast, claim that the former schoolteacher intended to adopt a more critical and independent position towards the government (Celestino 16/12/09).

Under Marinho's leadership, CUT intended to mediate between its grassroots and the government without taking sides. In the reform of the pension fund system, for instance, the organisation did not give full support to public sector unions, despite the importance of this category within CUT. In principle, the *Central* did not oppose the reform as a whole, but tried to negotiate with the administration in order to soften some of its most sensitive aspects.[23] Public sector unions, however, took a hard line, formally requesting that the bill be withdrawn from Congress and eventually voting for a general strike.[24] CUT leadership was initially reluctant to support the strike and refused to sign a petition requesting the bill's withdrawal.[25] Eventually, the *Central* had no option but to support the strike, although it never organised any strong resistance against the government's proposal (Galvão 2007:4). The reform was passed in Congress without major changes.[26]

Lula da Silva did not assert an incontestable leadership among social organisations of a "cult of personality" type. However, the combination between his leadership over the PT socio-political field and his role as chief of the executive branch and head of state promoted asymmetrical relationships that were reinforced by other types of linkages, as I will show. This leadership did not necessarily act as an element of control, but it did help to diminish or neutralise potential sources of opposition in civil society and to reduce the scope of contentious forms of collective action. The strategy did not necessarily have the same effects in different segments of the PT field, either because not all social groups shared the same type of historical identity with Lula's persona or because not all of them did as well under his administration. Lula's leadership was more "effective" among union leaders, particularly among labour confederations in the industrial sector, in which he started his career as a social activist. The case of the MST is interesting because despite the fact that the national leadership eventually criticised the economic policy adopted and the slow pace on land reform, it avoided criticisms of the government as a whole, and even less of Lula. Possibly this was because the president had become increasingly popular among the MST grassroots and the inhabitants of the settlements had benefited from pro-poor government policies that were clearly associated with his leadership. MST leaders were well aware of this (Rangel 08/04/09; Santos 07/05/09). The way in which Lula's leadership affected specific segments in civil society, however, needs further research.

REWARD-BASED LINKAGES I: HANDING OUT JOBS

The distribution of jobs among several social activists and trade union leaders in government had several important implications.[27] Not only did it become a form of inclusion, but it also helped to secure social governability as I argue in this section. The PT in national executive public office put in place a recruitment practice similar to the one used by the party in its local administrations, as Hochstetler (2004:11) already noticed. There was a significant change of scale, however, given the fact that in Brazil the executive branch has discretionary power to recruit up to 47,000 bureaucrats within line ministries, government agencies and state foundations (Souza 2009b). At the highest levels, several positions were occupied by leaders of social organisations, cadres strongly associated with them, or former leaders who had made political careers within the PT.[28] A survey study on the social composition of the Brazilian state apparatus since the administration of José Sarney shows the extent to which the Lula government modified the profile of the government elite. Among the highest officials of the first Lula administration, from directorate level upwards,[29] the survey showed that 46 percent belonged to a social movement, 42.8 percent were members of a trade union, while 10.6 percent participated in the leadership of a labour peak confederation (Souza 2009a:43–4).

Leaders from many organisations in the PT field were invited to participate in government on a sector-specific basis in which the distribution of quotas became standard practice. Among others, many leaders of the Housing Movement, or intellectuals identified with their demands, were appointed to the newly created Ministry of Cities;[30] associates of the National Confederation of Agricultural Workers (CONTAG) occupied several positions in the Ministry of Rural Development,[31] while MST negotiated positions in INCRA and its offices in several states, in spite of the fact that most MST leaders deny an involvement in the administrative apparatus.[32] One of these appointees, a key interviewee for this study, was Clarice dos Santos, who developed her political career simultaneously in the MST and the PT in the state of Rio Grande do Sul. In 2005 she received support from the MST to become Director of the National Programme for Education and Land Reform (PRONERA) at INCRA.

Unlike most organisations, CUT-affiliated trade union leaders or former leaders were rewarded with jobs throughout the administrative apparatus. In his first administration, Lula appointed 12 union leaders as ministers—about one-third of the cabinet positions (Souza 2009b). Between 2003 and 2007, the Ministry of Labour was consecutively occupied by three members of CUT: in 2003, by Jacques Wagner, from the oil sector trade union; between 2004 and 2005 by Ricardo Berzoini, a leader of the bank sector trade union who remained active until the late 1990s, and finally, by Luiz Marinho.[33] Union leaders or former union members also occupied between 50 and 60 senior positions at the level of Secretaries and thousands of second- and third-level jobs.[34] Neither President Vargas nor João Goulart appointed so many trade unionists when in power.

Some observers have pointed this out in negative terms, by making a criticism of co-optation.[35] Nevertheless, it is undeniable that the incorporation of leaders of a popular origin who did not have meaningful access to the administration in the past had great importance in terms of both social inclusion and representation. The number of trade union leaders who participated in the Lula administration is impressive if one considers that the union membership rate in Brazil is only 14.5 percent and, during the Lula administration only 5 percent of the high-ranking officials were part of a business organisation (Souza 2009b, 2009a). The inclusion of social activists and trade union leaders in government, as Chapter 3 mentions, was regarded as a natural phenomenon by many interviewees.[36] João Felício (28/10/08), for instance, argued that during the Cardoso administration parties such as the PSDB or the DEM appointed businessmen to public office. In his view, "there is nothing wrong in the PT appointing members of its own social base".

This recruitment strategy, however, did have consequences for civil society organisations in the PT field. The labour peak organisation, in particular, had difficulties in maintaining its independence to criticise and put pressure on the government, particularly during Lula's first years in office, as many of its members acknowledged.[37] Members of CUT's Secretariat wondered whether this situation created "an identity crisis" in which "even those cadres who were not properly in the administration considered themselves as being *the government*" (Celestino 16/12/09, my emphasis). "People were very confused about what was the government, what was the party and what was the union", CUT's president, Arthur Henrique, recalls. Nonetheless, other social leaders argued that, despite the fact that having some of their members in government created constraints, it also gave them the capacity to make direct demands on their colleagues who were occupying administrative jobs and to hold them more accountable.[38]

Having their cadres in government had a mixed effect for PT social allies. In some situations, civil society organisations were successful in using government spaces to promote their own agendas. Union leaders in the Ministry of Labour, for instance, were able to promote minimum wage increases that benefited various categories of workers (see Chapter 9). Likewise, housing activists in the Ministry of Cities articulated various demands that had been on their agendas for several years. The creation of a ministry capable of articulating housing issues, as it occurred, was in itself one of these demands (Rodrigues 12/12/08). In other cases, however, former social leaders promoted policies or reforms that were opposed by the organisations in which they used to participate or by certain groups within these organisations. The case of CUT offers two examples. Ricardo Berzoini, as Minister for Social Security, promoted the reform of the pension fund's system, while Luiz Marinho, as Minister for Labour, promoted legislation that limited the right to strike among public sector workers, opposed by the labour peak organisation. This suggests that a process of co-optation may have taken place. Further research conducted on a case-specific basis needs to be done, however, in order to understand to what extent the distribution of jobs favoured co-optation. In this study, where the main focus is on the party side of the relationship, it was not possible to achieve that task.

REWARD-BASED LINKAGES II: STATE SUBSIDIES

The Lula administration allocated massive state subsidies to civil society organisations.[39] Here I argue that the government's willingness to distribute an unprecedented amount of resources helped to secure social governability, by engaging these groups in intensive negotiations with the state or collaborative efforts with the government rather than promoting disruptive forms of collective actions. Civil society organisations in the PT field tactically used these resources, sometimes to benefit their constituencies and maintain the support of their grassroots, sometimes to solve practical needs and secure their own material survival. This had some negative consequences, however, because organisations in the PT field concentrated most of their time in specific negotiations to obtain concrete benefits from their allies in public office that did not necessarily change the rules of the game but drove energies away from substantive policy discussions.

The massive allocation of state resources to civil society organisations, a hallmark of the Lula administration at a time of economic bonanza, included both the distribution of particularistic benefits to specific groups, and the distribution of resources to benefit their constituencies in more general ways.[40] The government provided generous funding to civil society organisations from the start,[41] probably more than any previous Brazilian administration. Reliable figures are not available, in great part because state funding to social groups has historically lacked transparency in Brazil.[42] According to press sources, in 2003 alone, civil society organisations received R$1.3 billion (US$433,333) from the federal government,[43] although this figure was not disaggregated.

The administration used very different strategies to allocate public resources among different types of social organisations, not only including those in the PT socio-political field.[44] Large sums were transferred to rural cooperatives and NGOs associated with the MST to provide technical assistance, training courses or the like. This policy was initiated by previous administrations during the 1990s, as I explained in Chapter 3, but was taken much further by the Lula administration. An inquiry carried out by the NGO *Contas Abertas* (Open Accounts) found that between 2003 and 2009 the government provided R$152 million to 43 cooperatives.[45] According to the mass media, usually biased against the MST, the main leaders of these organisations were associated with the Landless Movement,[46] although its leaders have persistently denied it.[47]

An indirect type of subsidy derived from the expansion of rural credit for small-scale farmers managed by the Ministry of Rural Development, which benefited the members of many rural organisations such as CONTAG, the Movement of Small Farmers (MPA) or the MST. The National Programme for the Invigoration of Family Agriculture (PRONAF) alone expanded from R$2.4 billion in 2001/2002 to R$13 billion in 2008 (Branford 2010:424). The expansion of this programme was important in promoting small-scale agriculture and alleviating poverty. However, it also promoted a reward-based linkage. Although the resources of PRONAF were directly channelled to its beneficiaries, it is known for instance that the MST charges its members a portion (usually 3–5 percent) of the credit they receive from the government (Harnecker 2003). For these types of reasons observers argue that PRONAF became an important source of funding for organisations such as the MST because it eventually provided "the means to command further occupations" (Mueller and Mueller 2006:29).

There is no substantive evidence that social organisations ceased to mobilise because they received state resources. By and large, civil society organisations experienced different phases in their positions towards the Lula administration.[48] Some organisations even scaled up some forms of protest, calculating that there was a government willing to negotiate with them and an opportunity to advance their goals.[49] By allocating unprecedented state resources, however, the government encouraged more moderate mobilisation strategies and modified the way in which many organisations related to the executive branch. CONTAG, for instance, maintained its two most important national campaigns, the annual *Grito da Terra* (Cry of the Land), in which thousands of small rural farmers annually demonstrated against the government, and the *Marcha das Margaridas*, which gathered women farmers from all over the country. Notwithstanding, these forms of collective action lost their antigovernment rhetoric and became occasions on which leaders of the main rural federations in CONTAG negotiated resources with politicians in different ministries (Schmidt 03/12/09). Important demands were fulfilled in these negotiations, such as the credit for small farmers (Santos 03/07/09), which expanded even beyond the original expectations.

The MST also experienced the effects of state subsidies, despite the fact that the organisation continued promoting land occupations. This chapter cannot capture in detail the complexities of the relationship between this organisation and the Lula government. Suffice it to mention that during most of the first year the movement generally supported the government, but gradually became less enthusiastic, presumably due to the lack of progress in land reform and the conservative economic policy.[50] By the time Lula started his second term, the leadership of the MST had adopted a more incendiary rhetoric to the extent of arguing that land reform could only take place under Socialism (Martines 07/07/09). Despite this, the allocation of massive state resources shaped the relationship with the government and kept confrontations at a manageable level. To a great extent, this was also because the organisation became more dependent than ever before on state resources for its own survival. Paul Singer, who was Secretary of Fair Trade during the Lula administration, put it bluntly: "the MST cannot break [its relationships] with the administration because 500,000 people depend on credit from the Ministry of Rural Development" (16/04/09).

The criticisms of the MST towards the Lula administration were always carefully weighted. The Landless Rural Workers' Movement behaved pragmatically, as a party member in Porto Alegre said, "knowing to what extent they could criticise" (Fisher 15/12/08). When discussing the effects of public funding on the organisation, Clarice dos Santos (07/05/09) argued that the MST hardly ever criticised Lula. It condemned certain figures in government, such as the Minister for Agriculture or the President of the Central Bank, or it spoke against certain policies, but not against the administration as a whole, even less against the president. In 2005, for instance, when it was clear that land reform was not making progress, the MST leadership organised a large protest to show strength and apply pressure. During these events, Stédile made it clear that "the march [was] not against the Brazilian government, but for agrarian reform and change in economic policy" (Baiocchi and Checa 2007:422).

Clarice dos Santos, Director of the National Programme for Education and Land Reform, a programme which expanded its budget from R$13 to R$70 billion (US$ 6.3 to 34.41 billion) during the Lula administration, acknowledged that, in a context in which land reform was not making much progress, the resources that the MST obtained during the Lula administration were pragmatically used to keep the organisation alive and helped to deliver what she defined as "concrete benefits to its followers". In her view, credit, technical assistance and other policies that benefited the settlements are not only "necessary", but they also "help to acknowledge the role played by the MST and maintain its social base" (Santos 07/05/09). Santos pondered during our interview that the MST "could not survive just by having a radical strategy". Some leaders of the MST, such as Gilmar Mauro, from its National Coordination, argue that state subsidies had a domesticating effect. "The head thinks where the feet stand", he emphasised (17/04/09). Clarice dos Santos (07/05/09) also acknowledged that "the amount of public resources [that the movement received] did diminish anti-government reactions". However, she also argued that these resources benefited small farmers. In her view, "this is a contradiction, with positive and negative effects". Other leaders in both the movement and the PT consider the allocation of state resources to be a "natural" phenomenon, even a measure of redistributive justice, in a country where lobby groups in the business sector have received high subsidies and fiscal exemptions for many years.[51]

The policies of the Lula administration made civil society organisations in the PT field even more dependent on state resources than during the years of the postdemocratic transition. This led them to gravitate more towards the state to obtain benefits and satisfy practical interests. According to some interpretations, the massive state resources that these organisations received under Lula took them further away from both their own grassroots and society in general. A city councillor in the northeastern state of Paraíba complained that "social movements today spend most of their energies in the relationship with the government and very little in society. They no longer form popular assemblies or promote any initiative that invites civil society to participate in larger public discussions" (Camilo 16/11/10).

The relationship between the party in public office and its allies in civil society became more instrumental from both sides and less programmatic in content. Rather than discussing policies, programmes or projects, it was mostly about bargaining for resources. Manoel dos Santos, president of CONTAG, complains for instance that rural organisations never came to discuss a "development project for the rural world" capable of "articulating consistent actions to promote land reform and develop the existing land settlements". In his opinion, the Lula administration was only different from previous governments in this regard because it allocated a large amount of resources in the rural areas. However, "the main problem for small scale agriculture is in the planning, management and execution of policies". CONTAG's president regrets: "Sadly, we never discussed [with this government] the agricultural model that we wanted to implement" (Santos 03/07/09).

INTERPERSONAL LINKAGES: COMPLICITY AND MUTUAL UNDERSTANDING

Interpersonal linkages establish an unmediated and informal interaction between party and social leaders based on their personal connections, as I explained in Chapter 1. Just as they did at the local level, interpersonal linkages played an important role in relating the PT in public office with its social bases in the field. These linkages were in most cases simultaneously direct and interpersonal because they entailed a frequent and unmediated interaction between social leaders and high-ranking government officials (some of them social leaders themselves), largely based on friendship or connections forged along the years. By activating these types of linkages, social organisations could lobby the administration and bargain with it in order to obtain public goods or shape certain policies. In doing so, they were not inventing a particularly new form of interaction between society and the state. The popular organisations of the PT field simply incorporated a strategy that the elites have long used—not only in Brazil—to obtain advantages from the authorities.

Interpersonal linkages were a double weapon. On the one hand, they facilitated formal and informal negotiations at the federal level and gave social organisations further access to the state. Important officials revealed that the meetings between high-ranking officials and social leaders were constant, despite not being always publicly announced.[52] With the MST, for instance, the government had very frequent interaction, despite the fact that negotiations did not always take place in institutionalised spaces. Among others, Lula's second Minister for Rural Development, Guilherme Cassel (04/12/08) acknowledged that his office had a "direct interlocution" with this movement. On the other hand, interpersonal linkages promoted relationships that were not always transparent, participatory or democratic.

Social activists argue that important decisions were taken "at the highest levels" based on the "proximity of personal relationships" between the main social leaders and high-ranking government officials (Borba and Cleia 03/04/08). In many cases the grassroots were not consulted and knew little about the agreements made. Interpersonal linkages, which worked in two ways, created complicity, expectations of mutual understanding and acceptance of the logic under which the government had to operate. The president of CUT, Arthur Henrique, argued that one of the problems during the first two years of the Lula administration was that "those who were in government, because we were friends, thought that we had to understand their difficulties and help them solve the most immediate issues" (Henrique 15/04/09). In addition, the fact that social leaders had their acquaintances or allies in the administration made them more prone to offering each other political support and less inclined to public criticism, that according to some could give "more power to the right"[53].

Interpersonal linkages helped to "persuade" some of the closest PT allies in civil society to internalise concerns with governability, to which social leaders were not directly exposed. It was often as a result of private talks that leaders understood that they had to "measure" their actions, maintain what they called "pressure with responsibility" (Borba and Cleia 03/04/08) and avoid positions that could "support the opposition" or undermine the government.[54] To a certain extent, these linkages were also helpful in promoting discipline. Leaders mentioned anonymously, for instance, how they received "gentle phone calls" from their allies in government, which included appeals for moderation whenever they conducted actions that could be considered radical (anonymous source). Many social leaders realised that their position as members of the PT field created limitations, but there was also a trade-off, knowing that they had a privileged relationship with the administration that was advantageous in terms of giving them access to the state. Two members of CONTAG reflected as follows:

> [Having your allies in office is always a limitation] However, if you need to demand something from those government figures that you have appointed in government or from those leaders with whom you have had a partnership for a long time, your demands are even stronger because they are your allies. If they don't react properly to your criticism they can have serious problems. Precisely because you have had such a strong partnership, you also have the freedom to make personal criticisms. (Borba and Cleia 03/04/08)

Interpersonal linkages had two more important consequences: First, they brought civil society organisations closer to the party in public office and made them less interested in the party in central office, thus weakening programmatic linkages within the party structure. PT members who led *setoriais*, spaces in which PT members who took part in certain movements discussed and promoted public policies, explained during our interviews how these institutions, in which social leaders had a more enthusiastic participation in the past, lost dynamism as bodies of policy formulation. Many social leaders, occupied as they were with their relations with the administration, ceased to attend meetings or sent leaders of secondary importance (Gonçalves and Guareto 02/12/08).

Second, interpersonal linkages, as in previous PT local government experiences, diverted energies away from participatory democracy, as it made party leaders in public office and social actors lose interest in institutions of participatory governance, as previous chapters show. In some cases, these institutions were not regarded as particularly necessary, given that leaders could obtain benefits, either particularistic or general, through their interpersonal relationships. In the rural sector, for instance, no participatory institution was created to deliberate over land reform related issues during the Lula administration. According to an advisor to the Minister for Rural Development, who spoke anonymously, this was not because the administration was reluctant to institutionalise such a mechanism, but because no actor posed such a demand. This absence, however, did not concern PT members in the ministry either. After all, as the same advisor said, "we are dealing with people with whom we have shared political activism all our lives".

CONCLUSION

I have looked at four elements that helped the Lula administration to secure social governability: the strong leadership exercised by Lula over the PT field; the distribution of jobs in the state apparatus; the allocation of massive state subsidies; and the existence of interpersonal linkages between party and social leaders. There is another factor, however, that contributed to social governability and which I analyse in the next chapter: the willingness of the party in public office to maintain its programmatic linkages with its allies in civil society (conditioned by the balance of forces among strategic actors). The combination of all these features managed to produce a certain arrangement that allowed the PT in public office to maintain the political support of its social base, generated a reasonable level of social stability, maintained disruptive collective actions at manageable levels and decreased the level of criticisms against the administration.

In this work I have not relied on the general assumption that reward-based linkages necessarily generate relationships of subordination, control or co-optation. This approach was useful because it allowed a more nuanced understanding of the complexities of the relationships between the party in public office and its social allies. During the Lula years, many of these allies made a trade-off which had positive and negative consequences. Working in government, for instance, helped some leaders to promote their agendas, but it generated constraints and often made them lose capacity to make criticisms; receiving massive resources helped to improve the lives of small farmers and the practical needs of their organisations, but made them gravitate almost entirely around the state, and be less concerned in modifying rules and the status quo; exploiting personal connections sometimes helped to redistribute public goods and shape certain policies, but promoted relationships that were not always participatory and democratic.

Authors have argued that, by depending on the state for jobs or subsidies, social organisations become organisationally weak and narrow their activities to very specific concerns (Middlebrook 1995), while in their discretionary logic they promote a detachment from broader programmatic interests (Roberts 2002). Further research needs to be done to find if this is what occurred during the Lula years. As far as the PT is concerned, however, the increasing predominance of reward-based linkages is regrettable because it was often at the expense of programmatic linkages or undermining the scope of institutions of participatory governance. These were some of the elements that made the PT a qualitatively different political party and challenged the predominant way by which the Brazilian state and parties in Latin America have historically related to civil society organisations and citizens at large.

9 Accomplishments within the Balance of Forces

The PT in the federal government was willing to deliver on its main campaign pledges and maintain programmatic linkages with its most important social allies. These allies and their grassroots did manage to obtain gains under the Lula administration. Nevertheless, I argue in this chapter that the capacity of the party to deliver and maintain these linkages largely depended on the balance of forces among the most relevant strategic actors for governability on any given issue and their relative power. The PT in national executive public office established bargains in order to balance the interests of its allies in civil society *vis-á-vis* dominant strategic actors. In doing so, however, the party had to perform in a way which would not damage the relationships with the dominant strategic actors and put at risk its elite-centred governability strategy.

Party leaders in public office and their social allies maintained a dialectic process characterised by convergence and divergence of goals and interests. Social leaders eventually understood that in the Lula government a wide range of groups, classes and ideologies were represented, constantly trying to promote their views and advance their interests. In their bargains with the administration, civil society organisations in the PT field obtained different results. In the following pages I study three scenarios which resulted in different outcomes for civil society, and which I label—following the perceptions of some of their leaders—as "limited progress", "relative victories" and "substantial achievements".[1] Land reform is an example of a limited progress experienced by organisations such as the MST; the trade union reform illustrates the case of a relative victory for the trade unions in the PT field, while the rise of the minimum wage exemplifies a substantial achievement.

The objectives of civil society organisations had a limited progress when the interests of powerful strategic actors were at stake, and such actors articulated significant pressure to protect their interests. Relative victories took place when a wide range of strategic actors negotiated in more or less equal terms, but did not manage to reach consensus after long negotiations. Finally, substantive achievements were possible when certain decisions did not face a strong and articulated opposition among the dominant strategic actors, but also when the government had greater margins for manoeuvring.

This chapter is divided in three sections, each looking at the main scenarios described above. Section 1 analyses the minimum wage increases, considered a major achievement of the Lula administration, and studies the conditions under which they became possible. Section 2 explores land reform as a case of limited progress in which strategic actors such as landowners and the agribusiness sector used their veto power, reinforced by conservative parties representing their interests in the National Congress. Finally, Section 3 looks at the labour and trade union reforms in which, despite multiple negotiations among a wide range of groups, the lack of consensus resulted in only relative victories for PT allies.

THE MINIMUM WAGE: A SUBSTANTIAL ACHIEVEMENT

One of the main achievements that workers and labour organisations obtained during the Lula administration was the increase in the value of the minimum wage, which eventually allowed a cumulative 50 percent rise above inflation during two government terms. This significant achievement was possible due to the confluence of five different factors: (i) parties represented in the National Congress, even opposition parties, mostly supported the wage increases (sometimes pushing them even further to seek electoral rewards); (ii) business groups, despite being reluctant, did not articulate significant pressure against these; (iii) a favourable economic context made it possible after the initial constraints; (iv) the presidency *had sufficient* political will; and (v) the *centrais sindicais* mobilised and negotiated with the government (although this was not the main driving force).

In 2003, when the PT assumed the national executive, the minimum wage was only R$240 a month (US$76.92), and had severely lost its real value during the previous years.[2] Bearing this in mind, Lula had clearly pledged during the presidential campaign that his government would double the purchasing power of the minimum wage in four years. The value of the minimum wage in Brazil is established annually in the federal budget that the executive sends to Congress for approval. Since it is tied to social security benefits and other government programmes and salaries, it tends to have an effect on public accounts and, according to some interpretations, also on inflation. Concerned with maintaining budgetary balance, the Ministry of Finance has usually been reluctant to see high increases and tends to push for moderate ones when negotiations take place every year. In contrast, political parties in Congress, especially the opposition, have intended to amend the executive's proposal by seeking to move the values upward in order to obtain electoral dividends.

The Lula administration modified the internal way in which previous governments had discussed the minimum wage, mostly among technocrats in the Ministry of Finance, and came to bargain more directly with the *centrais sindicais* in the Ministry of Labour and the Presidency.[3] The gains that workers obtained from these negotiations, however, were not alien to dynamics of governability, and were largely subject to the political agenda of the administration. Increases with real effects on purchasing power only materialised after 2005, once the government had gained the confidence of the financial sector and fears of instability had dissipated, as I advanced in Chapter 6. During the first two years, rises were mediocre in real terms. In April 2003, despite increasing by 40 *Reais* (see Table 9.1), this only represented a 1.23-percent real gain above inflation; in 2004, the increase was even lower (1.19 percent).

CUT and leaders from other *centrais*, such as *Forza Sindical*, the second largest in Brazil, expressed their understanding of the initial adjustments[4] and even publicly acknowledged that the minimum wage "could not be hugely increased from one year to the next" (Lisboa 21/10/10).[5] In December 2004, labour peak organisations, encouraged by CUT, timidly started to mobilise for increases by organising a national march in which some 3,000 union members walked to the Palace of Planalto. In the following year, the minimum wage increased for the first time in a more meaningful way (8.23 percent above inflation). Marches were also organised during the next two years, gathering, according to CUT (2011), 15,000 participants in November 2005 and 20,000 in December 2006. Eventually, in 2007, labour organisations and government representatives agreed to a formula by which the minimum wage would be adjusted year on year, until 2023, taking into account inflation and the GDP growth.

There is no evidence that mobilisation played a key role in the negotiations that led to raise the value of the minimum wage. However, given the

Table 9.1 Minimum Wage Adjustments (2003–2010)

Period	Monthly Value R$	Monthly Value US$	Nominal Growth	Inflation	Real Growth
April 2002	200	86.21			
April 2003	240	76.92	20.0	18.54	1.23
May 2003	260	83.87	8.33	7.06	1.19
May 2005	300	122.45	15.38	6.61	8.23
April 2006	350	164.37	16.67	3.21	13.04
April 2007	380	187.01	8.57	3.30	5.10
March 2008	415	240.20	9.21	4.98	4.03
Feb 2009	465	201.52	12.05	5.92	5.79
Jan 2010	510	291.31	9.68	3.45	6.02
Total			155	65.93	53.67

Source: Adapted by the author, based on DIEESE (2008:3); Magalhães and Araújo (2010:2).

reluctance of conservative sectors in government, such as the Central Bank or the Ministry of Finance, the business sector, bankers or rural producers,[6] party and social leaders considered that, by marching, they could "show strength" in the face of public opinion, as one staff member of CUT argued (Campos 16/12/09). In any case, the actors who opposed the minimum wage increases did not articulate a particularly strong opposition and did not find many supporters in Congress, where few legislators wanted to appear against the expansion of the minimum wage. Despite organising public demonstrations, CUT never engaged in an active confrontation over this issue (Magalhães 20/10/10). A mid-ranking official in the Presidency, who preferred to speak anonymously, argued that CUT did not play a decisive role in the increases. In his view, the "political and the ideological choice made by the government" together with the "presidential commitment" were the main driving forces. In his view, the increasing value of the minimum wage that took place was mostly part of a government strategy to promote economic growth that took shape during the second term.

CUT, as the main social base of the PT, was not a particularly dynamic actor capable of playing a decisive role in pushing for progressive transformations during the Lula administration. Testimonies gathered among both government officials at different levels and CUT members show that not only was the role of the party in public office far more important, but also that the party in government set the pace and the modalities in which progressive transformation could take place. It is interesting to note, for instance, how only *"when the possibility arose"*, and not before, "the *centrais* went to the streets to demand a rise in the minimum wage" (Lisboa 21/10/10, my emphasis). Certainly, mobilisation might have been instigated by sectors in government, as the following anecdote anonymously told by a high-ranking official suggests:

> When we were negotiating the minimum wage, the economic area of the government met considerable resistance against any adjustment on top of inflation. The Ministry of Finance was arguing that increasing the minimum wage would add pressure to the pension system and consequently to the national public accounts. Our position was different: we thought that increasing it would have a positive effect on the internal market and bring other benefits . . . anyway, I spoke to the *centrais sindicais* and told them: 'this is only going to happen if you march'. When Palocci [the Minister for Finance] realised that we had spoken to them, he came and asked us to avoid the march by finding a middle way solution. Obviously, he knew that with the prospect of a march he would have to adopt a more flexible position.

The minimum wage probably constituted one of the few cases in which PT leaders in government encouraged a proactive mobilisation. It was one of the cases in which the party in public office used its social base to show strength *vis-à-vis* the dominant strategic actors in order to promote its progressive agenda. However, this strategy was not intended to alter the balance of forces in Congress and did not do so, at least in any significant way. Mobilisation was mostly used to show strength among some sceptics who resisted the hikes within the government itself. Cândido Vaccarezza (21/10/10), a former unionist who was Leader of the Lula Government in the Chamber of Deputies, reflects that, after all, "it was not difficult" to achieve minimum wage increases because "the fiscal balance allowed it, many sectors were interested and even right-wing parties supported it". "In these negotiations", Vaccarezza concluded, "We stretched the string, but we never breached the limits".

LAND REFORM: THE VETO POWER OF DOMINANT STRATEGIC ACTORS

Several scholars have argued that land reform, mainly understood as expropriation for redistribution, made little progress during the Lula administration.[7] The assessment of the MST is that land reform under Lula did not go deeper or any faster than during Cardoso's term and that the land structure in the country was not significantly altered (Santos 07/05/09). Here I show how the veto power of the dominant strategic actors created obstacles to obtaining meaningful gains in a policy area embraced by the PT since its creation and which constituted the basis of a strong programmatic linkage with the MST and other organisations. These linkages were weakened during the 1990s, as a result of the electoral strategy adopted by the PT (see Chapter 3). The strategy to achieve political and economic governability weakened these linkages even further once Lula assumed national executive public office.

Despite the fact that Lula softened his discourse on land reform during the 1990s, his electoral manifesto in 2002 still incorporated a pledge to conduct a land reform capable of altering the highly unequal land structure in the country.[8] This objective was formally endorsed when the administration adopted the Second National Plan on Land Reform.[9] In the quota logic promoted by his administration, Lula invited Plínio de Arruda Sampãio, an MST sympathiser and member of the PT Left, to coordinate the drafting of this plan in negotiations between government representatives and rural organisations. The document emphasised that state expropriation of unproductive properties would be one of the main strategies for the redistribution of land. After long discussions it was established that before the end of the first Lula administration, 400,000 families would receive new land, while another 500,000 squatter families would be granted legal rights to their plots, and 130,000 would receive credit to purchase land (INCRA 2004).

Although the expropriation of unproductive rural property on the grounds of wider social interests is contemplated in the Brazilian Constitution,[10] in order to expropriate a vast amount the government needed to modify the land productivity indices, which set the legal criteria under which a property can be considered unproductive, and thus subject to expropriation. These indices, which dated back to 1975, reflected the realities of another period and made it difficult to justify mass expropriations. Because the indices take no account of massive leaps in productivity and Brazil's newfound status as an agricultural superpower, they artificially restricted the supply of land available for redistribution (Meszaros 2010:580). The Second National Plan on Land Reform, therefore, established that the indices would be updated, a measure that did not necessarily require congressional approval. Despite the fact that the government had the power to do so by decree, it never updated these indices.

From the outset, Lula and his inner circle regarded land reform as a divisive issue that could generate political and economic instability; a source of problems, in short. Even before the election, Lula knew that powerful interests were clearly against land expropriation and acknowledged the implications that a massive land reform would have for his governability strategy. On the one hand, Lula and his closest advisors on rural issues considered the importance of the agribusiness sector as a source of macro-economic stability. On the other hand, this group expected that strong opposition against land reform would most likely come from the National Congress, in which the lobby groups of landowners have played a key role for several years.[11]

By the time Lula assumed the presidency, the agribusiness sector[12] represented more than 20 percent of Brazilian GDP (Teixeira 2009:25) and played a key role in achieving a primary surplus and a favourable trade balance. These objectives were part of the core commitments that Lula made to the financial sector in his "Letter to the Brazilian People", as mentioned in earlier chapters. Given that the economy was in a critical situation, members of Lula's inner circle considered from the beginning that the public accounts would be heavily dependent on the performance of the agribusiness. Gerson Teixeira, a PT parliamentary advisor on rural issues who participated in drafting the party's rural programme, recalls that for these reasons Lula's advisors did not want to do "anything" that could "upset" such an important sector (Teixeira 07/04/09). These estimations were confirmed already in the first year, when the exports of agribusiness reached US$25.8 billion, US$1 billion more than the total trade balance (US$24.8 billion in one year). Without this successful performance, Brazil's trade balance would have been in the red. It was clear to the government that the agribusiness sector was "an essential element to balance the public finances" (Russo 01/12/08), a key element of Lula's economic governability strategy.

The other important factor that Lula's inner circle could not ignore was the great strength of landowners and the agribusiness sector in the National Congress. Indeed, the *Bancada Ruralista* (or rural caucus) constitutes one of the strongest lobby groups in the National Congress, consisting in those years of around 200 deputies from various political parties (mainly PFL, PMDB, PSDB, PP and PR). These legislators were either landowners themselves, members of the agricultural business chambers, such as the ultraconservative

Brazilian Agriculture and Livestock Confederation (CNA), or parliamentarians directly associated with their interests.[13] Through the years, this powerful strategic actor has systematically opposed land reform and it has been so determined to block attempts to conduct land expropriation that it even rejected a constitutional amendment bill (PEC 438/2001) that would facilitate the expropriation of land in rural properties in which slave labour still takes place. Margarida Teixeira (2009), who conducted an investigation on the *Bancada Ruralista*, shows that the influence of this group on the parliamentary agenda in rural issues often exceeds the power of the executive branch, usually preponderant in most legislative agendas. According to Gerson Teixeira (07/04/09), members of Lula's inner circle argued before the election that embracing land reform decisively could generate an "uprising from the rural caucus in Parliament" and stimulate a "conservative political reaction against the future government".

Testimonies gathered for this study reflect that from the outset Lula himself considered land reform politically unviable and even counter-productive. Being a politician who "doesn't like conflict", as many party leaders describe him[14] the hopes for land reform were probably truncated from the beginning. Nevertheless, the Lula administration could not simply leave off the agenda a discourse that was mapped in the PT "genetic model" and still had many adherents within the PT field.[15] Furthermore, the government could not leave this agenda on the side because the MST, one of its most important historical allies, was capable of disruptive practices. In the years prior to Lula's arrival in power, for instance, this organisation had increasingly started to invade government offices, blocking roads and promoting other actions that not only aimed at forcing land expropriation, but also, among other objectives, to ensure its share in the fight for scarce public resources (Mueller and Mueller 2006). The MST was not a threat to political stability as a whole, but its importance could not be underestimated.[16] For that reason, Lula acted as "an administrator of balances between contradictory interests" (Russo 01/12/08).

As in other areas, his government aimed at accommodating strategic actors however antagonistic and polarised their views were. One of the main strategies of the Lula administration to accommodate the different actors in the rural world was the distribution of jobs and state resources, as Chapter 8 explains. Both the agribusiness sector and organisations that claimed to represent the rural poor benefited from these strategies, to a great extent in proportion to their respective economic and political power. Initially, Lula accommodated the agribusiness group in the Ministry of Agriculture (the president of the Brazilian Association of Agribusiness, Roberto Rodrigues, was installed as Minister) and delivered Rural Development, which deals with small-scale family agriculture, to members of rural organisations. However, because the latter were weakly represented in Congress no minister was appointed among its ranks. The distribution of state resources followed a similar power logic. Commercial agriculture benefited from debt renegotiations and abundant financing at generous terms, increasing its credit from R$18 billion in 2002 (US$7.5 billion) to R$65 billion in 2009 (US$38.23 billion) (Guimarães 2009:17). In lower proportions, rural organisations such as CONTAG or the MST benefited from the expansion of credit for small farmers. As the previous chapter mentions, PRONAF increased its resources to more than 300 percent.

Eventually, the goals of the Second National Plan on Land Reform were not met. Studies confirm that the performance of the two Lula administrations on land reform was not very different from that of the Cardoso government.[17] After the 2005 political crisis, when the formation of a stable legislative majority became one of the main priorities of the Lula administration, it was more evident than ever that promoting a meaningful land reform would generate serious obstacles to the formation of legislative alliances. By choosing conservative parties such as the PMDB and the PP as its main allies in Congress, the PT was in a rather uncomfortable position, since more than 60 percent of all the deputies in Lula's parliamentary base of support (Teixeira 2009:61) were members of the rural caucus mentioned earlier.[18] It is not difficult to understand why, in his second term in office, Lula became "more reluctant to expropriate land" (Santos 03/07/09). Although the government was not particularly committed to a massive land reform, the rural caucus made matters worse by blocking all attempts to promote measures that could have resulted in further land expropriation and putting great pressure on the Minister for Agriculture not to sign the decree to update the productivity indices, as the Second National Plan contemplated.

THE LABOUR AND TRADE UNION REFORMS: RELATIVE VICTORIES

Studies show that trade unions did not acquire greater autonomy and strength under the Lula administration, neither did workers expand their rights significantly under the PT government.[19] The scope of both the labour and trade union reforms, I clarify in this section, were largely shaped by the need to accommodate the interests of a wide range of strategic actors in the capital/labour axis. These reforms were areas in which the administration, anticipating that the National Congress would not easily reach consensus, promoted negotiations with a wide range of strategic actors and convened not only those representing antagonistic interests, irreconcilable in some cases, but also groups opposed to the very spirit of the reforms that the government wanted to put in place. The strategy gave limited results and, in some aspects, resulted in a zero sum game. Because consensus among these actors proved uneasy, the gains for labour organisations in the PT field were relatively small.

During his presidential campaign, Lula promised a broad reform of labour and trade union legislation. Such reform aimed at promoting "truly modern labour legislation" and at constituting "free, autonomous, representative and independent trade unions".[20] Debates around these reforms were intended to find "an acceptable balance between flexibility and rights", by incorporating some aspects of the "discourse of flexibility" (Hall 2009:138), internationally demanded by the business sector, while avoiding other elements more damaging to workers' interests.[21] In that context, the government sought to secure "the existence of representative and democratic trade unions" with sufficient strength to face employers successfully in future collective bargaining processes (Hall 2009:158). Defending the old principles that gave birth to the "new unionism" in the late 1970s, and which constituted an important programmatic linkage between CUT and the PT, the Lula administration intended to modify some of the most corporatist elements that remained untouched since 1943, when President Vargas enforced the so-called Consolidation of the Labour Laws (*Consolidação das Leis do Trabalho*, CLT). Essential elements of this corporatist system, as labour specialists have emphasised, are the state recognition as a precondition for the existence of trade unions; the principle of *unicidade* (or single-union system), which allows only one union per category in a specific sector; the restrictions faced by grassroots unions to freely organise in the shop floor; and the union tax, which obliges all workers, either union members or not, to pay a contribution in proportion to their salaries.[22] The government's proposal intended to tackle all of these elements.

High-ranking officials in the Lula administration, aware of the difficulty in passing a reform in Congress, attempted to reach consensus among strategic actors before sending a bill to the legislative chambers. In doing so, however, they opted to listen to all the major labour peak confederations. CUT, despite being the largest and most representative, only reached one-third of the Brazilian working population and less than a half of those belonging to a *central sindical*.[23] More important, the government estimated that the interests of both capital and labour should be brought to the bargaining table. The administration created a tripartite National Labour Forum (FNT), in which three different sectors were formally represented in equal numbers—the administration, the unions and the business sector. Seventy-two members were appointed: one-third of representatives from the administration; one-third of members from the sectoral chambers of trade, industry, agriculture, finance and transport; and one-third of members from the six *centrais*.[24] Among the latter, half of the membership came from CUT and *Força Sindical*, the largest labour peak organisations in the country.

CUT's General Secretary, Quintino Severo (15/12/09), said that most of the demands of this labour organisation were not incorporated in the final project. Reaching a compromise on labour issues among strategic actors proved very difficult. Most business representatives were reluctant to agree to important government proposals endorsed by the *centrais* such as lifting the ban on the prohibition of union activities on the shop floor,[25] the proposed reduction in the working week without effects on the salary (Campos 16/12/09), or the adoption of the ILO Convention 158 that impedes the termination of employment without a valid reason (Campos 16/12/09). Nevertheless, compromise also proved difficult, because many of the labour organisations represented in the FNT supported key elements of the corporatist legislation, particularly those aspects that were essential to their own material survival, such as the *unicidade sindical* and the union tax (Hall 2009:158). As a result, the agreements that were eventually reached maintained many elements from the old model.[26]

The broad labour reform that Lula promised in 2002 fell off the agenda after the 2005 political crisis, which established other political priorities such as maintaining a stable base of support in Congress and put the government into a "defensive position", as Hall (2009:160–1) explains. To a great extent, the logic of Lula's elite-centred governability strategy impeded the debate from being brought back. Initially, this was because CUT, which had largely internalised the constraints of the balance of forces and was seeking to protect the government, refrained from applying additional pressure, according to its own version of events, in order to avoid destabilisation. Indeed, some union leaders interpreted this at a time in which conservative parties were promoting Lula's impeachment, as a pressure from CUT which could have been "politically manipulated by the right" (Nespolo 16/12/08). After the crisis, however, the labour agenda did not return. Eventually, as part of the efforts to secure a reliable majority in Congress, Lula sacked the Labour Minister, Luiz Marinho, a member of CUT who was a more enthusiastic supporter of the reform, and appointed Carlos Lupi, head of the Partido Democrático Trabalhista, who could guarantee the support of 18 deputies in Congress. Eventually, Lupi declared in March 2007 that his party was the "heir of Getúlio Vargas" and he had no intention of ever changing the Consolidation of the Labour Laws "unless workers want to" (Hall 2009:161). This is another evidence of how the need to secure a parliamentary base of support compromised programmatic linkages during the Lula administration.

It was not until 2008 that the government was able to promote a mini-reform of the trade union legislation in Congress. One of the most important outcomes was the long-denied formal recognition of the *centrais* as legal bargaining agents, a status that was given to those capable of affiliating more than 100 unions. CUT leaders interviewed for this study claim that this recognition, which the PT had promised during the 2002 electoral campaign and for which their organisation had long campaigned, strengthened their capacity to participate in negotiations with national institutions (Nespolo 16/12/08; Severo 15/12/09). According to Marcos de Verlaine, a member of the *Departamento Intersindical de Assessoria Parlamentar* (DIAP), a lobby group of trade unions in Congress, the recognition of the *centrais sindicais* allowed the "trade union movement" to promote its own agenda in Congress after many years in which it had been virtually absent (Verlaine 18/10/10).[27] Despite these achievements, no major gains were obtained in expanding labour rights or in modifying Brazil's corporative system.

CONCLUSION

In this chapter I have shown how programmatic linkages between the PT in public office and its allies in civil society were largely shaped by the elite-centred governability strategy of the Lula administration. By emphasising the importance of accommodating dominant strategic actors I do not intend to argue that this is the only reason why certain programmatic linkages might be dissolved or maintained when parties are in office. Indeed, there are reasons to presume that Lula and his inner circle were much more committed in the second term to increasing the minimum wage, as part of a strategy to foster economic growth and alleviate poverty, than they were to land reform as a development project. In fact, many in the Lula administration considered that rather than distributing more land, the government had to improve living conditions within the existing settlements and secure their productivity.[28] Furthermore, the huge productivity of agribusiness in Brazil in recent years—especially with the rise in commodity prices and exports to China—would make land reform a tremendously expensive strategy. Even left-leaning agricultural economists tend to support this view in today's Brazil. In any case, there is no doubt that the balance of forces among strategic actors does play a significant role in determining *what* a party delivers to its social allies in public office, as well as *how* and *when*.

This chapter has also shown that governability strategies have consequences for the relationships progressive parties establish with its allies in civil society. Indeed, the constraints seem greater when these parties assume elite-centred strategies that are aimed at accommodating the interests of dominant strategic actors. This is not only because parties need to secure a majority in Congress. The cases studied in the previous pages show that having such a majority was not the only issue at stake, however important. If the administration did not promote some of its progressive agendas more seriously, it was also because it did not want to undermine its relationship with the dominant strategic actors in general. Land reform, for instance, did not necessarily require a majority in Congress, as an executive decree could have been used to alter the productivity indices and expropriate more land. Nevertheless, this would have meant confronting the agribusiness, landowners and conservative parties, thereby undermining political, economic and social governability.

By and large, civil society organisations were not able to alter the balance of forces in any meaningful way and social mobilisation did not play an important role in promoting progressive transformations under the Lula administration. As I have shown, whenever significant changes took place the initiative of the party in government was by far the main driving force. Under the PT administration it was the party in public office, and Lula in particular, the one establishing the main tactics and strategies. In this regard, another comparison with the Allende experience in Chile can be made. Unlike Chile's "revolution from below" (Winn 1986:6), explained in the previous chapter, a clearer hierarchy of command, as well as a sense of strong leadership and direction existed in the PT and its socio-political field. The relationship between the party and its social allies seemed closer, but not identical, to what Winn (1986:140) interprets as Allende's original project: one in which the masses would provide political and social support "when called on", but otherwise "await patiently the advances and benefits of the revolution from above" (Winn 1986:140).

Final Remarks

In these final passages I review the most important arguments made throughout this book and examine some of its implications for the debates on progressive parties in government. I look at the recent experience of the PT and the Lula administration and include a brief comment on the new administration inaugurated by Dilma Rousseff in January 2011. The following pages also establish some contrasts between the PT and other left-wing or left-of-centre parties in Latin America, as well as in other countries in which progressive parties have experienced emblematic transformations such as South Africa. Rather than making a comparative analysis and presenting evidence from other cases, my intention is to briefly highlight some of the differences between the PT's trajectory and that of other parties on the Left, based on the way in which they have been presented in academic studies. Analysing the lessons learnt from the PT experience, I offer a reflection on the main characteristics that should be embraced by political parties in order to promote progressive agendas.

This book has brought a new perspective to the study of progressive parties and the transformations they experience in executive public office, by bringing the notion of governability to the party literature. I have shown how the governability dilemma—the need to reconcile conflicting interests and accommodate strategic actors—affects the capacity of parties in public office to deliver on their campaign pledges and it is a powerful reason why progressive parties alter their strategies and discourses when they enter the executive. My account has not rejected other important explanations of party change, particularly the way in which electoral competition shapes parties' political behaviour. I have shown, however, that there is a specific rationale that shapes the behaviour of parties in public office and goes far beyond the electoral dimension.

Interestingly, as well as being a neglected issue in the party literature, governability has been downplayed by the Left. Many of its related issues have been appropriated by the Right, which tends to capitalise on concerns with public order, social stability, the crime and security agendas or the efficient and effective functioning of state institutions. Rooted in the Huntingtonian tradition, the governability discourse is conservative in its origin and some of its motivations, as I mention in Chapter 1. Yet the attributes of governability are relevant to citizens of Latin America, a region in which state institutions have proved to have a limited capacity and where recurrent episodes of political and economic crisis have taken place. These are sensitive issues which might also have electoral consequences for progressive parties, related as they are to the capacity of any political party in government to perform its basic functions and to deliver on its campaign pledges. Ultimately, if progressive parties have an interest in creating conditions to govern and remain in power, they need to solve the governability dilemma in one way or another.

When looking at the three main governability dimensions analysed in this study—the political, the economic and the social—the role that public resources played in accommodating the interests of strategic actors under Lula stands out. The administration distributed a vast amount of resources among different groups, ranging from political allies represented in Congress to civil society organisations, from large infrastructure companies to the influential financial establishment. While political parties benefited from pork-barrelling, social allies received state subsidies, infrastructure companies were granted ambitious projects in the Growth Acceleration Programme (PAC), and the financial sector profited from high interest rates. These resources were available not only because the Brazilian state has a heavy tax burden by Latin American standards,[1] but also because of the international economic context. As mentioned in Chapter 6, the economic bonanza which benefited Brazil and other South American countries between 2003 and 2008 allowed the PT government a margin for manoeuvre to simultaneously accommodate the interests of the powerful financial establishment and, eventually, to loosen public spending and benefit other groups.

In this book I have shown that progressive parties in public office, like any other party in the executive, have to face the governability dilemma. Yet progressive parties such as the PT—with a mass-based origin and multiple ramifications in civil society—also have the opportunity to solve this dilemma differently, by promoting the mobilisation of their own social bases, by strengthening civil society or by effectively articulating collective actors with governing institutions in participatory mechanisms, which also help to manage social conflict. The PT at the sub-national level did all of this creatively. The introduction of the Participatory Budget, in particular, contributed to improving efficiency and transparency in the delivery of public services and at the same time helped to accommodate the interests of strategic actors and neutralise the power of a conservative opposition in the legislative branch. Given the limited number of cases studied in this work, it is not possible to claim that such strategies were successfully adopted by most PT sub-national governments. Nevertheless, even if not all of them secured the achievements of Porto Alegre, it is undeniable that the party as a whole gave great value to this experience, which was a source of inspiration for its national project.

At first sight, the adoption of an elite-centred governability strategy under Lula can be seen as a corollary of the transition from the local to the national sphere. In 2003 the PT was occupying the executive branch for the first time, as one of the first democratically elected left-wing parties in Latin America since Allende. In such a context, the most influential leaders within Lula's inner circle preferred to act guardedly and cautiously. The majority of those who occupied positions in the Lula administration only had municipal government experience, and only a few had worked for the limited number of PT state governments. At the national level the political landscape was more complex and the party had to deal with more powerful strategic actors. With many of these actors, PT leaders had had little or no relationship in the past, as it occurred with the financial establishment, the largest business groups or state governors who are influential in the National Congress. Even with political parties, which the party leaders did liaise with in the municipal sphere, the relationship was more complicated because the party system is usually more fragmented at the national level.

Nevertheless, I have shown that the transition from the sub-national to the national sphere is not the only reason for the weakening of a social counter-hegemonic strategy and the strengthening of an elite-centred one. As Chapter 4 explains, before Lula became president, elite-centred strategies were already part of the PT governability repertoire in large cities such as São Paulo. One cannot but speculate as to whether the PT and the Lula administration acted too cautiously or, as Hunter (2011) thinks, more pragmatically than needed given the favourable economic situation it enjoyed and the availability of public resources. If resolving the governability dilemma is facilitated when public resources are more abundant, the PT was eventually less constrained because the commodity boom provided greater margins for manoeuvre. Lula also enjoyed high approval ratings, which enhanced his personal leverage in the second term.

I have argued that one of the reasons why the PT in government ruled out a social counter-hegemonic governability strategy was the fear of political and social instability within Lula's inner circle. What some observers and leaders in the party Left characterised as "Lula's aversion to conflict" might have also played a role. This conflict-averse stance possibly resulted from Lula's recognition and acceptance of a political culture which is in itself "inimical to conflict", as the Brazilian anthropologist Roberto DaMatta (1991:139) has persuasively argued.[2] Perhaps, Lula's position against conflict was not just part of a strategy to become palatable to dominant strategic actors. It was also a strategy that might have spoken to the perceptions of the unorganised poor, those who voted for him en masse in 2006 and then for his hand-picked successor, Dilma Rousseff, who was elected in 2010 by 56 percent of the vote in a run-off, under the legend "For Brazil to keep on changing (*Para o Brasil Seguir Mudando*)". There is some evidence that this electorate had conservative positions. Singer (2009:87) found, for instance, that in 1989 an important segment of what he calls the *sub-proletariat* in

Brazil opposed strike actions, tended to favour "order", rejected instability, were particularly afraid of inflation and even showed hostility towards strikes.

The way in which conflict is managed has profound implications for the transformative potential of progressive politics and it is something that the Left needs to reflect upon. There is little doubt that Lula's personal characteristics as a leader, coupled with the abundance of public resources, contributed a great deal to solving the PT's governability dilemma in national executive public office. During his two terms in office, Lula and his closest team, many of them products of the trade union tradition like him, proved to have a formidable capacity to reach agreements with a wide range of sectors by seating the most relevant actors (especially labour, business groups and politicians) round bargaining tables and hammering deals with them. These deals, however, were often made backdoors rather than in the more open participatory spaces that helped a number of PT administrations to solve disputes over public resources. Lula's strategy may well have prevented or efficiently solved a number of conflicts. One wonders, however, whether this type of conflict management may compromise transformative politics.

In any case, a political project is not inherently progressive because it confronts dominant strategic actors directly, and even less so because it adopts an incendiary rhetoric that demonises economic elites or opposition parties, such as the one employed by Chávez in Venezuela or, to a lesser extent, Morales in Bolivia. Different from both, Lula's bargaining style and the PT participatory agenda, which seeks to institutionalise conflict management, the strategy of some of these leaders—including others in the Andean region—[3] seems to be to intensify conflict largely by means of rhetoric. Nevertheless, the high "level of conflictivity" attributed to some of these leaders (Jácome 2011:324) would be hard to find in Lula's Brazil. This is not merely a matter of personal taste or political ideology, neither is it a set of differences that one can explain within the discourse of the "two lefts" in Latin America (Castañeda 2006),[4] in my view reductionist, Manichean and with little explanatory power. Many of the countries that adopted confrontational approaches against dominant strategic actors such as conservative parties, oligarchies or business groups experienced a collapse of their political systems which generally weakened the power of traditional elites and political parties.[5] In Venezuela, as Hellinger (2005:27-8) explains, the collapse of the Punto Fijo party system and seven decades of "oil-based rentier politics" left the country with a "weak traditional oligarchy". The situation was very different in Brazil, where the power of economic and political elites remained very strong; the economy was highly dependent on international investors and the political system was more consolidated.[6] Lula had to negotiate with dominant strategic actors from a position of relative weakness in comparison to some of his South American counterparts. He would probably have lost more than he could win by adopting a position of open conflict against them.

A progressive political project does not necessarily have to exclude or sideline dominant strategic actors. As Hellinger (2005:28) shows, even the Chávez administration has negotiated with a number of sectors of international and national capital, such as the oil and construction industries or the banking sector. Progressive politics do require, however, an extra-institutional element and a critical mobilisation of society capable of giving the Left more power to negotiate with the political and economic elites. This can eventually help to alter the balance of forces in order to make possible the redistributive policies and reforms that dominant strategic actors tend to oppose. For this reason the political parties' capacity to promote meaningful social change largely depends on their willingness to encourage mobilisation and participatory democracy, as well as on the relationships they establish with progressive collective actors, as a number of scholars in the progressive side of the debate have argued.[7]

It is still not clear, however, whether counter-hegemonic governability strategies with these characteristics, which have been successful at the sub-national level, can have similar effects in the national sphere. In Latin America, Bolivia and Venezuela are two of the countries which have seen these counter-hegemonic strategies put in place. In the former case, this was the strategy that Morales used in order to pass important reforms, such as the extension of agrarian reform, the establishment of a pension that citizens receive monthly from the revenue of hydrocarbons, and the constitutional referendum. In some of these occasions, according to Córdova (2011:165), social movement activists surrounded Congress "in order to prevent certain senators from entering, so that their substitutes, from MAS, could establish the necessary quorum, thereby ensuring the legitimacy of the sessions". In other cases, however, this strategy has generated what Mayorga (2009:114) calls "a catastrophic deadlock", resulting in a "no win" situation.

The results in Venezuela and Bolivia, where progressive parties have different characteristics than the PT, are controversial and in some cases the price has been high. At the risk of overgeneralization, one can say that the strategies that the leftist leaders in these countries have implemented tend to rely more on state power than on civil society. In the Venezuelan case, for instance, scholars have noted that the state-led transformations have often inhibited, rather than facilitated, efforts to construct participatory democracy.[8] In this sense, the governability strategies are not properly social counter-hegemonic along the lines defined in Chapter 1. In some cases these leaders have deployed strong forms of *personalismo* which concentrate power in the executive branch and rely heavily on the use of presidential decrees,[9] reproducing one of the vices of progressive parties in Latin America. In the case of the Movement to Socialism in Bolivia, some authors have criticised the counter-hegemonic governability strategies adopted, on the grounds that the Morales administration transformed social organisations into "instruments of violent mobilizations, and even into *de facto* troops for political coercion" and "intimidation" (Larson et al. 2008:7).[10]

Some of these Latin American leaders have sought to advance participatory democracy (or "protagonist democracy" in the case of Chávez) in opposition to formal representative democracy or even in detriment to the latter.[11] This stands in stark contrast with both sub-national and national PT administrations, which regard participatory and representative democracy as complementary. In the *chavista* discourse liberal democracy tends to be regarded as a "false democracy" or a "democracy of the elites".[12] This approach, in my view, does not contribute to deepening democracy in Latin America. Notwithstanding that certain strategic actors have advantages in the current formal representative institutions, as I acknowledge in Chapter 1, it is also in the interests of the disadvantaged to strengthen and change these institutions, as it is to promote broad social participation. Rather than regarding formal representative democracy and participatory democracy as antagonistic projects, progressive agendas should combine the two and find creative ways by which they can reinforce each other.

It is also my view that a progressive agenda cannot exclusively derive from political parties in control of state institutions, nor from the concentration of power in personalistic or charismatic leaders. Such an agenda will neither exclusively result from the mobilisation of civil society, in which some authors have placed their hopes as "the only available or most important domain for organizing cultural and political contestation" (Escobar, Dagnino and Alvarez 1998:48). Rather, progressive agendas can be implemented when parties—arguably in a better position to formulate policies and aggregate social interests—establish linkages with a mobilised civil society and promote further engagement by citizens. As scholars have pointed out, it is by establishing programmatic linkages based on common goals that progressive parties can help integrate (the often narrow) demands of civil society organisations into a more global political project and increase the transformative potential of their actions.[13] Such an objective can be compromised, however, when reward-based linkages become predominant, as occurred in the PT case, because rather than encouraging collective solutions, they mainly provide benefits to specific groups, offering individual and particularistic advantages.[14]

Lula and the PT did change Brazil, in profound ways and for the better. Certainly, they did not do it in many of the ways in which the party and its socio-political field had envisaged, particularly because civil society was not regarded by the most important players in public office as essential for the mission and success of the party in government and no significant efforts to "organise the people" were seen. Despite this gap, state–society relationships improved, if only for the inclusive approach of the Lula administration towards social movements, the greater deployment of dialogue and negotiation and the absence of repression. Despite the fact that many perceive Lula's record in promoting participatory democracy as mediocre, it would be hard to argue that PT administrations do not listen to civil society organisations. The Brazilian Workers' Party has not become like the African National Congress

(ANC), which also promoted participatory agendas in the past, but once in government adopted a "dirigiste" style of politics, came to exercise a "direct political control of civil society" and "almost completely neutralized or sidelined social movements", as Patrick Heller (2001:13, 155) maintains.

The PT has not adopted an "autocratic strategy of transformation that is by definition hostile to participatory local development" as the ANC apparently did (Heller 2001:155).[15] The Workers' Party in Brazil has by no means degenerated in such a way. In this book I have provided some evidence that this is because of the characteristics of its "genetic model". The ANC was different from the PT in its origins because it was always "more of a political organization than a social movement" and because its formal structures operated in a clandestine fashion, mainly from abroad and "independently of domestic struggles" (Heller 2001:156). The PT's "genetic model", in contrast, was one of strong involvement in a network of grassroots civil society organisations; the strong linkages that were established between party and social leaders could not be so quickly dissolved and the participatory ideology that evolved from this relationship has played a very important role since the party's formation.

A question arises as to whether the PT has definitively buried those features from which a progressive agenda could emerge. The answer seems to be that it has not necessarily done so. In Chapter 7, I argued that one of the reasons why the participatory agenda was left aside under the Lula administration was the fact that Lula came to be regarded as the incarnation of the poor and the excluded. Under a different administration in which no leader plays such a charismatic role, some elements of the participatory agenda might be revitalised at least for the sake of building social legitimacy. In January 2011, after assuming public office, Dilma Rousseff appointed two figures in the Presidential Office who during our interviews criticised the poor record of participation under Lula and said that a lot more could had been done: Gilberto Carvalho (10/04/09), as General-Secretary of the Presidency, and Pedro Pontual (17/10/08), a social activist as well as an enthusiastic promoter of participatory mechanisms appointed to the newly formed Department of Social Participation.

As one of their first steps, these officials have engaged a number of representatives from civil society organisations in discussions over the establishment of a National System of Social Participation. This system was devised as a regulatory framework to institutionalise state–society relations and articulate participatory institutions at all three levels of the federation. Its promoters have expressed their desires to strengthen and deepen participatory mechanisms, grant them with more power to make binding decisions and, perhaps more important, broaden participation towards strategic areas such as infrastructure, macro-economic policy and the public budget.[16] The initiative, however, mainly involves sectoral policy councils and national conferences, which have several limitations, as Chapter 7 explains. Little mention has been made of a national PB, a topic that is no longer present in party conference resolutions. In any case, given the overwhelming emphasis with which the PT has embraced the elite-centred strategy, it would not be sensible to expect that the initiatives promoted by these officials, enthusiastic of participatory democracy, could be the basis of an alternative governability, that is, one in which participation and mobilisation could be deployed to alter the balance of forces within state institutions.

The Dilma administration has been characterised by continuity and very limited innovation, as scholars have observed (Von Bülow and Lassance 2012). At the time of writing there is no indication that the elite-centred strategy could be altered, particularly because the political scenario that led the PT and the Lula government to adopt it is firmly in place and the party is not seeking to change the rules of the game. If anything, the new presidency might reinvigorate this strategy that has allowed Rousseff to enjoy a solid majority in the legislative branch and pass more than 70 percent of the initiatives it presented in the first years. This is higher than Cardoso and Lula, notwithstanding the fact that the current Congress is even more fragmented.[17] During the election, PT power brokers actively worked to form a majority by gathering 10 parties in the electoral coalition,[18] many more than Lula in 2002 and 2006, and a record high in Brazilian history. By making Michel Temer, a member of the PMDB, the vice presidential candidate, the PT strengthened its alliance with this party. Once in office—and having learnt the lessons of coalition presidentialism—Dilma formed a coalition government with seven parties in which only 12 ministerial portfolios out of 38 were distributed among PT members. The PMDB, second in the Chamber of Deputies after the PT, received 5 ministers. Leaders of another six parties were granted one cabinet seat each,[19] while a number of allies were appointed for lower-rank positions and state-owned enterprises, some of which control huge budgets.

In spite of its benefits, the elite-centred governability strategy has clear limits. Dilma has not promoted an ambitious reform agenda, notwithstanding the fact that she has enjoyed a more comfortable position in Congress than previous administrations (Von Bülow and Lassance 2012). The third PT government in the history of Brazil has not engaged in any significant effort to pass the long-awaited political reform to which both Rousseff and the PT commited themselves,[20] neither has it promoted the tax reform or the democratisation of the mass media supported by the party. Furthermore, the PT is paying high costs for the types of alliances that it has formed with opportunistic parties. Only in its first 13 months in office, Rousseff lost eight ministers, seven of them under accusations of corruption and intense attacks by the media. Ministers from five allied parties have been forced to step down,[21] including one PT member. The vice president has also been under fire.

The strategy to secure economic governability also seems to follow the elite-centred script. During Dilma's first two years macro-economic stability has become a priority once again. The expenditure and growing inflation of the last period of Lula´s government, albeit moderate, generated some concerns. Upon assuming office, Rousseff announced a new adjustment, with the aim of reaching a primary surplus of 2.9% of the GDP. This adjustment did not reach the proportions of 2003, but the government did cut R$50 billion (US$24.5 billion) from the public budget in its first year; the Central Bank increased Brazilian interest rates (which are still one of the highest in the world), and only promoted meagre minimum wage hikes. In the international context, however, Brazil still benefits from the commodity boom, which has allowed the Central Bank to continue accumulating foreign reserves, reaching the impressive amount of US$378.688 million in October 2012 (Banco Central 2012).

Rousseff also engaged in a complex negotiation to pass a controversial constitutional amendment known as *Desvinculação de Receitas da União*, by which the administration would be entitled to freely spend 20 percent of the federal budget (the equivalent of R$62 billion, US$30.4 billion in 2012) to maintain a high primary surplus, pay interest rates or reallocate resources in the event of a confidence crisis. Through this reform the government managed to secure margins for manoeuvre and, presumably, was better prepared to face the effects of the international financial crisis. A number of parliamentarians initially opposed, but the constitutional amendment eventually passed by 364 votes in the Lower House. Not surprisingly, press resources revealed that the government built support for this reform by negotiating the allocation of massive parliamentary earmarks within its allies' constituencies. The administration also bargained with new appointments in the bureaucratic structure, including the head of the National Oil Agency.[22]

Once again, with the metric of the elite-centred strategists, the PT is facing the governability dilemma with relative success. Dilma's approval rating was above 70 percent in its first year—higher than Cardoso and Lula in the same period—and remains high. In its first electoral test, the 2012 municipal election, the PT gained an extra 71 mayors only in the first round. The fact that, short before the election, the Supreme Court condemned Dirceu, Genoino and Delúbio Soares under charges of passive corruption during the first Lula administration did not seem to have any significant effect.

One final note. This book has mainly looked at the transformations of the PT in public office. The assessment on the changes studied in the previous pages should examine in more detail the way in which Brazilian civil society changed for the good and for the bad during this period. In this study I have made the case that the PT has not abandoned its social allies after it penetrated state institutions. Rather, the party penetrated those institutions with its social allies. When Perry Anderson compares Roosevelt's social reforms, introduced under "pressure from below" with those of Lula, in which "no comparable industrial militancy either sustained or challenged" his administration (2011), this British leftist intellectual is making a comparison with a historical period in which organised labour had become a very influential force. That was not the case when Lula assumed the presidency in 2003. If the PT at the national level has relied on state power, rather than on civil society, as the main source of transformation, it is not only because the government and the hegemonic faction of the PT has so decided. The reason might also be that civil society is not prepared to play the role envisioned by those who formed the progressive socio-political field in the late 1970s.

Bangkok, 15 October 2012

Notes

NOTES TO THE INTRODUCTION

1. Kupchan 2011; Onis 2008:77; Roett 2010:66.
2. Baiocchi and Checa 2007; Oliveira 2006b, 2006a; Ricci 2008; Tavaloro and Tavaloro 2007.
3. Barros, De Carvalho and Franco 2006; Loualt 2011; Singer 2009; World Bank 2010.
4. During the two Lula administrations the Gini coefficient went down from 0.59 in 2003 to 0.518 in 2009 (IBGE 2010). It is important to note, however, that measures of inequality in Brazil are generally unreliable because they do not consider those at the top (the super rich) and they ignore "capital appreciation and concealment of financial gains at the summit of society" (Anderson 2011:7). In fact, there is evidence that the income of the richest sectors increased during the period. In Brazil, the population is classified into five income categories (from A for the richest to E for the poorest). Between 2003 and 2009, the wealthiest categories (A and B) went from 10.7 percent to 15.6 percent (Loualt 2011:3–5). Despite the fact that Brazil saw the highest reduction of income inequality, the richest 10 percent of the population still receive 50 percent of the national income, which makes it one of the 10 most inegalitarian countries in the world.
5. Departamento Sindical de Estatísticas e Estudos Socioeconômicos 2008:3; Magalhães and Araújo 2010:2.
6. Heller 2001; Mainwaring 1995; Roberts 2002, 1998.
7. Abers 1996; Avritzer 2009; Baiocchi 2003a; Bittar 1992; Bittar 2003.
8. Keck 1992; Sader and Silverstein 1991:3.
9. Coligação Lula Presidente 2002a:16–17.
10. Coligação Lula Presidente 2002b:13; 2002a:21–2.
11. See Amann and Baer 2006; Amaral, Kingstone and Krieckhaus 2010; Filgueiras and Gonçalves 2007; Hunter 2010:147 and Loualt 2011.
12. See Boito 2005:60; Branford 2009; Carter 2010; Ondetti 2006; Sauer 2008 and Vergara-Camus 2009.
13. See Baiocchi and Checa 2007; Couto 2009; Feres 2010; Grzybowski 2004; Hochstetler 2010; Hunter 2011:318–20; 2010; Leite 2008; Moroni 2009; Ricci 2008, 2007a and Samuels 2008.
14. Hipsher 1998:157; Meyer 2007:126.
15. Block 1977; Lindblom 1977 and Offe 1984.
16. Campello 2008, 2007; Martínez and Santiso 2003; Santiso 2004.
17. Amorim 1994; Figueiredo and Limongi 2000; Raile, Pereira and Power 2010.
18. Camou 2001, 2000; Coppedge 2001, 1994; Winn 1986.

19. Abranches 1988; Amorim 1994; Figueiredo and Limongi 2000.
20. Amaral 2010a, 2010b, 2010c, 2010b, 2003; Hunter 2011, 2010, 2007; Martins 1997; Miguel 2006; Nylen 1997b; Ribeiro 2008, 2007, 2003; Samuels 2004.
21. Camou 2001, 2000, 1993; Coppedge 2001, 1994; Mayorga and Córdova 2007; Santos 1991; Tomassini 1993a.
22. Civil society is seen in this study as "a part of society distinct from states and markets formed for the purpose of advancing common interests and facilitating collective action" (Edwards 2004:vii). I use the terms *civil society* and *civil society organisations* interchangeably. My definition includes groups such as trade unions, nongovernmental organisations and social movements.
23. Maguire 1995; Schwartz 2005; Taylor 1993:134.
24. Haugsgjerd 2010:86; Przeworski and Sprague 1986; Taylor 1993.
25. Baiocchi and Checa 2007; Handlin and Collier 2011; Oliveira 2006b, 2006a; Ribeiro 2008; Ricci 2008, 2007b.
26. See, among others, Aylott 2003; Cayrol and Jaffré 1980; Deschouwer 2008; Haugsgjerd 2010; Ignazi, Farrell and Romele 2005; Kitschelt 2000; Lawson 1980; Lawson and Merkl 1988; Merkl 2005; Poguntke 2002; Roberts 2002; Schwartz 2005.
27. This term has no direct relationship with the broader concepts of political and social fields used by Pierre Bourdieu.
28. See Belloni and Beller 1976; Bettcher 2005; Hine 1982; Katz and Mair 1993; Rose 1964; Sartori 1976; Von Beyme 1985 and Zariski 1960.
29. Amaral 2010b:Ch.5; Bueno 1995; Freire 2002; Ozaí 1998; Ozaí 1996; Petit 1992.
30. Hunter 2010:127–8; Ribeiro 2010:120–3.
31. The *party Left* is an expressions used within the PT field to refer to the more ideologically oriented factions, which I also use in this work. Conversely, the *party Right* is the term used to label the more moderate or pragmatic factions.
32. Forty-eight interviewees identified themselves with the CNB, 23 with MP and 11 with AE. Of the remainder, 13 interviewees belonged to other factions and 23 declared themselves to be independent.
33. I offered all my interviewees the opportunity to speak anonymously if that was their wish, or to turn off the recording machine at specific moments. Although the great majority agreed to speak openly, I have indicated those cases in which I quote an anonymous source. I have cited interviews with the complete dates on which they were conducted and have included an Appendix (II) with the interviewees' most important biographical features.
34. Amaral 2010a, 2010b; Mair 2001; Reif, Caryrol and Niedermayer 1980; Rohrshneider 1994.
35. Leôncio Martins (1997:311) warns us that the radical content of some PT documents has much to do with the fact that they are "influenced and sometimes drawn up by the small left-wing groups" which are "very strong in internal conferences or meetings", but not among the congressional representatives or "the more prestigious elected leaders".

NOTES TO CHAPTER 1

1. The importance of electoral competition has been emphasised in several studies of parties, from Social Democratic parties in Western Europe (Kitschelt 1994; Sainsbury 1980; Wilson 1994), to right-wing extremists parties such as the French National Front and the Austrian Freedom party (Merkl and

Weinberg 2003). In Latin America, despite the existence of fewer studies on the subject, scholars have also looked at the ways in which parties to the left of centre have shifted their goals in order to achieve electoral majorities (Armony 2007; Cameron 2007; Castañeda 2006; Cleary 2006; Motta 2006; Panizza 2005). For conservative parties see Loaeza 2003; Magaloni and Moreno 2003.
2. Haugsgjerd 2010:98–1; Olsen, Koss and Hough 2010.
3. Although this notion is hardly ever used among Anglo Saxon scholars today, the word *governability* was first introduced in the mid-1970s by Samuel Huntington, Jozi Watanuki and Michel Crozier (1975) in their report to the Trilateral Commission, a private foundation created by David Rockefeller and a number of politicians and businessmen from the United States, Japan and Europe. This report advanced the argument that the expansion of democracy in developed countries had overloaded the political system with demands that their governments were not capable of satisfying.
4. See among others Alcántara 1994; Arbós and Giner 1993; Camou 2000; Mayorga and Córdova 2007.
5. See, for instance, Claus Offe's (1990) piece on the "rebirth of the conservative theories of crisis" in which he criticises how such theories regard the problem of governability and conceptualise it as a result of the overloaded social expectations. Such expectations would be responsible for the increasing social polarisation.
6. See among others Garretón 1994.
7. Camou 2001; Coppedge 1994; Dos Santos 1991.
8. See among others Block 1977; Lindblom 1977; and Offe 1984.
9. This conceptualisation is partly inspired on the work of Camou (2001:51–3; 2000), who distinguishes two "paradigms" of governability in Latin American political debates, the "conventional" and the "unconventional", as well as on the notion of "progressive governability" in the writings of Suárez (2002:3–5).
10. These views are also referred in the literature as "elite democracy" (Cohen and Arato 1992) or "democratic elitism" (Avritzer 2002).
11. I borrow from Gramsci's notion of "counter-hegemonic power" as one capable of promoting new understandings and practices capable of challenging dominant ideas and norms (Gramsci 1971:57–8).
12. In this work mobilised actions mostly refer to forms of protests or other attempts to have an influence which are mainly organised outside the formal political institutions (Woldsfeld 1998:23, in Kubik 1998). By participation, in contrast, I understand more institutionalised processes by which civil society organisations and citizens in general might have a say in public affairs or share decision-making power with governments. The underlying assumption of this study is that participation can be used as part of a counter-hegemonic strategy by which the popular sectors, whose power is limited within democratic representative institutions, can acquire greater influence.
13. Mayorga and Córdova 2007; Prats 2001; Tomassini 1993a, 1993b.
14. See, among others, Curzio 1998; Foweraker, Landman and Harvey 2003 and Prats 2001.
15. Heller 2009; Heller 2003; Hipsher 1998; Klandermans, Roefs and Johan 1998; Roberts 1998; Sinwell 2011.
16. The notion of an interpersonal linkage is inspired by the work of Patrick Heller (2003), who develops it in his study on the civics in post-transitional South Africa (Heller 2003:167), although not in great detail.

NOTES TO CHAPTER 2

1. See Abers 1996; Assis 1992; Bueno 1995; Burgos 1994; Davies 1997; Fernandes 1989a, 1989b; Ferreira 2008; García 2000; Guidry 2003; Harnecker 1994; Keck 1992; Martins 1997; Meneguello 1989; Moraes and Fortes 2008; Nunes 2003; Nylen 1997b; Ozaí 1996; Petit 1992; Ribeiro 1987; Sader 1986; Sader and Silverstein 1991; Tadeu 2002.
2. Keck 1992; Martins 1997.
3. Keck 1992; Sader and Silverstein 1991.
4. Keck 1992; Miguel 2006; Sader and Silverstein 1991.
5. Getúlio Vargas was president between 1930 and 1945. He first came into power through a military coup in 1930 and was a dictator for 15 years. Between 1951 and 1954 he became president once again, but in a democratic election. He promoted nationalism, industrialisation and social welfare, as well as a corporatist labour legislation which has remained in place until the present.
6. Between 1990 and 1991, for instance, when the first survey studies on the composition of the party delegations in national meetings and congresses were conducted, around 80 percent of the delegates who joined the PT in the early 1980s said that they had participated in a social organisation before joining the party (Marques 1993: 218). Another survey conducted during the same period showed that only 25 percent of the party delegates had participated in a political party when they joined the PT (Tadeu 2002:228).
7. Meneguello 1989:36; Sader and Silverstein 1991.
8. Meneguello 1989:33–4; Ribeiro 2008:61.
9. See Davies 1997; Guidry 2003; Keck 1992 and Martins 1997. It is not clear which group had more presence within the PT structure at the time of the party's creation. However, a survey study conducted among party delegates who attended the First National Congress in 1991 shows that leaders with a trade union background made up the largest group in the years of the party formation, accounting for 40.6 percent. However, other organisations, labelled under the general category of "popular movements" (not disaggregated in the survey) accounted for 53.4 percent and religious groups represented 34.4 percent (interviewees were allowed to identify themselves with more than one option) (Tadeu 2002:226).
10. Another reason for this separation was that the establishment of formal relationships between parties and unions was prohibited by Article 521 of the labour code (Keck 1992:167).
11. These types of mechanisms were used by the PRI in Mexico (Foweraker 1990; Middlebrook 1995), the Peronists in Argentina (Levitsky 2001) or, with different implications, by various European labour and social democratic parties (Alderman and Carter1994; Allern, Haugsjerd and Christiansen 2007), most notably the British Labour Party (Minkin 1991).
12. For a reference on movements parties see Gunther and Diamond 2001; Kitschelt 2006; Poguntke 2001.
13. In particular, this has been the case of the "left libertarian parties", a certain type of movement party which Kitschelt (1989:3) defines as parties spawned by diverse coalitions of social movements and seeking not only redistribution, but also "a change in the form and substance of politics to construct more participatory democracies".
14. Elvander 1972; Sänkiaho 1984.
15. For empirical accounts on how these umbrella groups interacted before the formation of the PT see Doimo 1995 and Sader 1998.

16. For a characterisation of the corporatist model under Vargas see Collier and Collier (1991:169–95).
17. According to some estimations, the number of CEBs in Brazil reached around 80,000, involving 2 million people (Novaes 1987:219–26, in Houtzager 2000:84).
18. Despite the lack of a precise definition of socialism (particularly in terms of the role of the state in promoting economic redistribution or in the ownership of the means of production), most groups in the PT were critical of the model of "real socialism" and rejected the insurrectional route to power, understanding it as a frontal attack on the state apparatus. Their intention was not to overthrow the existing state, nor to create a state-led society. The mainstream position considered from the beginning that democracy (a broad notion of it) and socialism should be blended into a form of "democratic socialism" with which most factions identified (Sader and Silverstein 1991:107).
19. *Articulaçao dos113* was later known simply as *Articulação* (Articulation). Over the years it became larger in size and changed its name to *Campo Majoritário* (Majority Camp). In 2005 it was relabelled as *Construindo um Novo Brasil* (Building a New Brazil).
20. Keck 1992; Skidmore 1989; Stepan 1989.
21. Unlike other military regimes in Latin America, the military authorities in Brazil did not abolish Congress and elections. However, they only allowed the existence of two parties: the *Aliança de Renovação Nacional* (ARENA), the pro-regime party, and the *Movimento Democrático Brasileiro* (MDB), the officially sanctioned opposition party. During the 1970s, however, the military authorities realised that this compulsory two-party system tended to consolidate the opposition in one single bloc, which would be more difficult to defeat in elections. By facilitating the creation of multiple parties among the opposition, the government sought a "divide and conquer" strategy in order to fragment the opposition. Eventually, seven new party labels were created, of which five eventually survived: the *Partido Democrático Social* (PDS), ARENA's new name; the *Partido do Movimento Democrático Brasileiro* (PMDB), successor of the MDB; the *Partido Democrático Trabalhista* (PDT), led by Leonel Brizola; the conservative *Partido da Frente Liberal* (PFL); the *Partido Popular* (PP), a conservative opposition party led by bankers; the *Partido Trabalhista Brasileiro* (PTB) and the PT (Keck 1992:26; Skidmore 1989:22).
22. The basic MST strategy consisted of moving a cluster of families onto government-owned or unproductive private land (which according to the Constitution should be subject to expropriation). By occupying farms, the movement put pressure until land titles were given. Although the movement officially adopted a position in favour of pacific means, many of its actions were portrayed by the media as violent. Movement leaders claimed, however, that most of the violence was perpetrated against the MST by the hired guards of landowners and the military police.
23. Bueno 1995; Compans 1993; Couto and Baia 2006; Keck 1992.
24. In 1982 the PT won two municipal governments, Diadema and Santa Quitéria do Maranhão.
25. During the constitutional debates, several civil society organisations, many of them from the PT field, put together the Pro-Popular Participation Plenary, a cross-sectoral coalition which mobilised to favour citizen participation in both the Constitution-writing process and the Constitution itself (Hochstetler 1997:9).
26. PT 1998:70–1, in Bianchi and Braga 2005:1749.

27. In the PT foundation ceremony, Lula emphasised: "It's time to finish with the ideological routines and self-indulgence of those who sit at home reading Marx and Lenin. It's time to move forward from theory to practice. The Workers' Party is not the result of any theory, but of twenty-four hours of practice" (Sader and Silverstein 1991:50).
28. In a similar perspective, Elvino Bohn Gass, a PT congressman in the state of Rio Grande do Sul, the state in which the MST was created, argues that the connection between the two organisations was so strong that every time a member of the landless movement organised an occupation, the Right accused the PT of being "behind it". "And we always responded: 'No, the PT is in front of it'" [tr. "O PT não está por trás, o PT está na frente"] (Bohn Gass 19/12/08).
29. A survey conducted during the Third National Congress of CUT in 1988 revealed that 91 percent of the delegates interviewed declared themselves to be PT sympathisers (Martins 1990:80).
30. During the 1989 election, MST members, despite proclamations of political autonomy and lack of official ties with parties, decisively mobilised for Lula. More than 40,000 MST supporters attended campaign rallies organised by the PT (Branford 2010:409–15).
31. Keck 1992:23; Sader and Silverstein 1991:85.
32. Bittar 1992:9, in Hunter 2010:81.
33. In order to maintain strong linkages with civil society, the PT mandated in its first statutes that candidates should have a history of activism, either in unions or within social movements. Although leaders could not simultaneously act in executive bodies or directorates, cadres permanently alternated from one sphere to another, particularly in the case of the labour unions (Keck 1992:Ch.7).
34. The meaning of participation was somewhat ambiguous at the outset of the Brazilian democratic transition, as in the PT field. By and large, it was a concept used by activists who perceived themselves as excluded from the political system. As Assis (1992:11) argues, their call for social participation was also a call for political recognition. Demands for participation had various connotations—from a direct relationship between population and government to a criticism of the representative system (Assis 1992:Ch.2).
35. Assis 1992; Compans 1993; Moraes 2001.

NOTES TO CHAPTER 3

1. Amaral 2010b; Hunter 2007; Miguel 2006; Nylen 1997b; Ribeiro 2008; Samuels 2004; Singer 2009.
2. Hunter 2010; Ribeiro 2008; Samuels 2004.
3. Haugsgjerd 2010:86; Maguire 1995; Przeworski and Sprague 1986; Schwartz 2005; Taylor 1993:134.
4. Katz and Mair 1995:13; Kirchheimer 1966:193–9.
5. Baiocchi and Checa 2007; Handlin and Collier 2011; Oliveira 2006b, 2006a; Ribeiro 2008; Ricci 2008, 2007b.
6. See among others Padgett and Paterson 1991; Przeworski 1985; Przeworski and Sprague 1986.
7. Carter 2006; Vergara-Camus 2009:21.
8. Alvarez 1994b:170–1, in Hipsher 1998:167; Macaulay 2004:105–8; 2003.
9. Alvarez 1997; Avritzer 2009; Cardoso 1992; Euzeneia 2011; Feltran 2007; Friedman and Hochstetler 2002; Gohn 1997; Hipsher 1998; Hochstetler 1997; Scherer 2007.

10. Avritzer 2009; Gohn 2000; Melo and Rezende 2004.
11. The decentralised participatory system that exists in Brazil mainly consists of a set of councils and conferences that follow the same hierarchy as the federation; they are organised at the municipal, state and national levels, and largely mirror the government's sectoral organisation (Shankland 2010:48). Almost every ministry has a specific council and almost every municipality possesses at least one type of council, in many cases because their creation is a legal requirement for the distribution of federal resources. Councils and conferences are difficult to characterise as a group. Some are constituted by appointed members, while others allow civil society organisations to select their own candidates to these bodies (Friedman and Hochstetler 2002:27). Some have the power to make binding decisions, while others have only consultative power.
12. See Carneiro 2006; Dagnino 2005; Demier 2003; Galvão 2004; Hochstetler 1997; Navarro 2006.
13. CUT, for instance, managed the resources of the Workers' Assistance Fund (or *Fundo de Amparo ao Trabalhador*, FAT), a mechanism initially created by the 1988 Constitution as an unemployment security scheme. With these resources, the organisation promoted the creation of job agencies and put in place programs of professional requalification and productivity promotion, among other initiatives (Galvão 2004:232–2). FAT resources grew significantly during the 1990s. By 2003, around 70 percent of the funding received by CUT depended on this single mechanism (Demier 2003:17).
14. As Navarro (2006:165) explains, the MST did not receive state resources directly. It deployed a wide range of rural cooperatives whose leaders were closely linked to the organisation.
15. *Folha de S. Paulo* 09/03/97, in Hochstetler 1997:13.
16. See Galvão (2007), Riethof (2004) and Rodrigues (1994). Between 1989 and 1999, unemployment in Brazil leapt from 1.8 to 7.6 million. The unemployment rate increased from 3 to 9.6 percent of the economically active population. Four out of five jobs created during the 1990s were in the informal sector (Oliveira 2006a:11).
17. Given the threat of unemployment, the number of strikes decreased considerably during the 1990s: while more than 1 million workers participated in strike actions in 1987, only 115,000 workers were involved in these types of activities in the 1990s.
18. One of the main promoters of this strategy was Vicente Paulo da Silva, known as Vicentinho, who eventually chaired CUT between 1994 and 2000. Under his leadership, the organisation promoted a number of sector-specific negotiations in which agreements between trade unions, employers and the government to maintain jobs in the sector in exchange for production increases and tax reductions were reached (Galvão 2004:231). Vicentinho was a skilful negotiator who played an important role in driving the organisation towards moderation. His trajectory as trade union leader speaks for itself. As leader of the Metalworkers' Trade Union of São Bernardo and Diadema, Vicentinho actively engaged in negotiation strategies with both the private sector and the government. In 1991, for instance, he led a delegation that travelled to the United States to convince the Ford company not to close down a motor factory situated in the ABC region of São Paulo (Singer 1996). In March 1992, when the crisis dramatically affected the automobile sector, he participated in a sectoral chamber negotiation as a result of which the workers agreed to reduce their incomes, while the car industry reduced its prices and made a commitment guaranteeing that no job would be lost (Rodrigues 1994).

19. Hunter 2010; Singer 2009; Núñez 18/12/08.
20. One of the main party intellectuals within Lula's faction, Marco Aurélio García, made the following remarks during a meeting in 1995 in which the PT discussed its relationship with civil society organisations: "The social movements that gave birth to our party are not archaeological monuments that can be now revisited (. . .). Many of them defend sector-specific interests and cannot elaborate broader policies. . . . [Furthermore], their representations have severe organisational limitations. Most of the trade unions do not reach even half of their professional categories, and neighbourhood associations gather very few people. Almost everywhere the organisations and its directions no longer represent their own social bases and just talk to themselves" (*Partido dos Trabalhadores* 1995:11–2, 30–1).
21. Azevedo 1991a, in Macaulay and Burton 2003:136.
22. Interestingly, the lower strata were more prone to supporting repression than the middle classes or the upper middle classes were. It was reported that 41.6 percent of voters earning less than twice the minimum wage favoured the use of troops to stop strike action, as against 8.6 percent of those earning more than 20 times the minimum wage (USP, Cedec, Datafolha 1990, in Singer 2009:87).
23. Kirchheimer 1966; Przeworski 1985; Przeworski and Sprague 1986
24. See among others Amaral 2003; Mendes 2004.
25. Cardozo 04/12/08; Santos 07/05/09; Felício 28/10/08; Menezes 26/07/09.
26. Américo 11/11/08; Cardozo 04/12/08; Ferro 02/07/09; Núñez 18/12/08.
27. Beze 03/07/09; Campos 03/07/09.
28. Sauer 2008:14, Teixeira 07/04/09.
29. *Partido dos Trabalhadores* 1995:17.
30. Hunter 2010:88; see also García 2000, 2008; Oliveira 2006b.
31. Among the rest, 17 percent picked "suggestions by the party" as the main criterion, while 4.2 indicated recommendation by a certain faction in the party (Figueira 2005:84).
32. Eduardo Jorge, an important leader of the Health Movement, became Secretary for Health; Teresa Tijolo, linked to the Transport movements, acted as Secretary for Transport and Ermínia Maricato, an architect with strong ties to the Housing Movement, became head of the Secretariat for Housing.
33. Likewise, members of the Slums-Dwellers' Defence Movement (*Movimento de Defensa do Favelado*, MDF) discussed policy decisions and also participated in its implementation (Feltran 2007).
34. Other party leaders, however, consider that distributing jobs to social leaders constitutes a "reasonable" and "absolutely natural" (Bemerguy 20/07/09 and Lacerda 22/07/09) political practice. If conservative parties like the PFL appoint businessmen when they assume government positions, one of my interviewees claimed, why cannot the PT bring "the workers" (Lacerda 22/07/09)? Appointing social leaders to government or state positions has positive effects, according to Senival Moura, a City Councillor in São Paulo, because "it provides shortcuts" between social organisations and the authorities and "facilitates negotiations" between the two (Moura 07/11/09).
35. Lima 2005; see also Macaulay and Burton 2003:146–9.
36. Several social leaders and members of the party Left criticised the extent to which the PT prioritised electoral politics at the expense of social mobilisation. Benedito Barbosa, a leader of the Housing Movement in São Paulo, bitterly complained during our interview that the party had become "a machine to contest elections" and that, in pursing such an objective, "it can run over whatever steps in its way" (Barbosa 02/12/08). Tarson Núñez, who

was a member of the faction Socialist Democracy, considers that the party eventually became "trapped in electoral logic". "We are involved in electoral processes almost every year", he explains. "When we are not working for a local election, we are involved in a state election; when we are not participating in a federal contest, we are operating an internal election to renew our executive bodies". According to this cadre, 90 percent of the energies of a PT activist today are "spent in achieving or reproducing existing power structures" (Núñez 18/12/08).

37. During the Third National Congress, held in 2007, for instance, party delegates noted that their "dialogue with social and popular movements [had] lost significant vigour" (*Partido dos Trabalhadores* 2007:3) and they regarded the increasing distance from the party's social roots as one of the reasons for the political crisis that the PT experienced in 2005, which had involved serious allegations of corruption (see Chapter 5).

38. The *Fundação Perseu Abramo* conducted survey studies in four consecutive party meetings which show the extent to which party delegates claim to "participate" in social organisations. The percentages were high in each survey (70 percent in 1997, 69 percent in 2001, 72 percent in 2006 and 71 percent in 2007) (Amaral 2010b:93). In my view, these data have a limited usefulness, not only because they do not say anything about the nature of that participation, but also because in the PT, leaders are expected to participate in a civil society organisation. Their answers, therefore, might be biased.

39. Based on this data, Amaral (2010b:91) found that states with the highest percentage of party delegates who perform in public office do not necessarily correlate to states with the lowest level of participation in civil society organisations.

40. The survey was conducted among 47 PT congressional representatives elected for the 1999–2002 term (80 percent of all PT representatives were interviewed).

41. Fier 03/12/08; Lopes 03/12/08; Preto 02/12/08; Suplicy 07/04/09.

42. This diagnosis was made by a large number of social leaders or activists interviewed for this study; in CUT: Celestino (16/12/09), Henrique (15/04/09) and Lisboa (21/10/10); in CONTAG: Campos (03/07/09), Santos (03/07/09) and Beze (03/07/09); in the Housing Movement: Fernandes de Oliveira (07/04/09), Gonzales (11/11/08) and Gomes (13/11/08). Within the PT this information was confirmed by Renato Simões (04/11/08), PT Secretary for Popular Movements; José Dirceu (07/01/09), former PT president; and Valter Pomar (30/09/08), leader of Left Articulation. Unfortunately, there are no statistical data on the number of PT members and sympathisers within specific organisations vis-à-vis other parties.

43. It is interesting to note that both Frateschi and Piai criticised civil society organisations in the field during our interviews. Such criticisms were not, however, detrimental to their views on the importance of civil society organisation for the PT's identity.

44. A study on the role of social movements during the Suplicy administration in São Paulo showed that many social leaders who worked with the government (or for the government) had an identity conflict: They felt themselves to be members of a social organisation, members of the party and, if not members of the government, at least its defenders (Teixeira and Tatagiba 2005).

45. Kowarick and Singer 1997:40; Teixeira and Tatagiba 2005:91–2.

46. Teixeira and Tatagiba (2005) show, in study on social movements during the Suplicy administration in São Paulo, how these types of strategies were

widely used by social leaders to obtain benefits from their allies in government. Several activists interviewed for that study considered that, if certain officials were "sensitive" to their demands and they could easily have access to them, it was reasonable to make use of their connections, especially when other options were not as effective (Teixeira and Tatagiba 2005:91–3).

NOTES TO CHAPTER 4

1. Abers 1996; Baiocchi 2003a; Macaulay 1996; Nylen 2000, 1997b, 1997a; Schneider and Goldfrank 2002; Sousa 2002.
2. The main source of local tax revenue for state governments became the Tax over the Circulation of Goods and Services (*Imposto sobre Circulação de Mercadorias e Serviços*, ICMS). Municipalities levied the Property Tax on Urban Land and Homeownership (*Imposto sobre a Propriedade Predial e Territorial Urbana*, IPTU). See Baiocchi (2003b, 2003a); Rodrigues (2006); Souza (2005).
3. Alfonso and Araújo 2008:38, in Souza 2005:110.
4. Baiocchi 2003b:10; Ramos 2004:113.
5. For a comprehensive overview of the different participatory instruments created after the 1988 Constitution see Avritzer 2009.
6. Carvalho 1998; Ramos 2004:307.
7. Couto 2000; Hunter 2010; Macaulay 1996; Schneider and Goldfrank 2002.
8. There is no strong evidence that this was always the case. By and large, there are no sufficient studies confirming that participation in PT administrations or in other cases has had significant redistributive effects. Only some academic works provide empirical evidence in this regard (Gaventa 2006, in Baiocchi, Heller and Chaudhuri 2006; Gaventa and Barrett 2010; Marquetti 2003; Navarro 1998).
9. Assis 1992; Kowarick and Singer 1997; Melo 2007:11; Macaulay and Burton 2003; Macaulay 1996; Oliveira 2008.
10. Couto, who has written about the two PT administrations in São Paulo, argues that the ability of the Suplicy government to avoid intraparty conflicts of the kind experienced by her PT predecessor was one of the reasons for her "greater success" (Couto 2003:87–8). Unlike the earliest PT administrations, Suplicy managed to form a majority in the City Assembly and simultaneously have PT representatives on her side.
11. *Folha de S. Paulo* 04/04/00.
12. Carneiro 2006:93; Teixeira 2005:52; Whitaker 2008:11.
13. Macaulay 1996:218; Singer 1996.
14. In December 1990 the Instituto Toledo & Associados conducted a survey, requested by the City Hall, which reflected that 65.3 percent of the interviewees supported the government proposal, notwithstanding the fact that 82.4 percent knew that it involved increasing the IPTU (Singer 1996:146).
15. This lack of experience was fully acknowledged by Flavio Koutzii (12/06/11), Home Affairs Secretary during the Dutra administration, during our interview.
16. *Folha de S. Paulo* 30/09/02.
17. *Folha de S. Paulo* 30/09/02.
18. The second round in municipal election in Brazil, which takes place when no candidate reaches more than 50 percent of the valid votes, was formally instituted in 1992 for municipalities with more than 200,000 voters. Before this reform, PT candidates were able to become mayors with simple majorities, as occurred in Diadema and São Paulo in the early 1980s.

19. In contrast to the number of studies on executive–legislative relationships at the national level, few studies have explored the municipal sphere (Castro 1998; Gurgel 2009; Lopes 2000; Santos 2001) or the state level (Abrucio 1998; Avelar and Cintra 2007; Limas and Ricci 2010; Nunes 2009; Pereira, Power and Raile 2011).
20. Gurgel 2009:111; Lopes 2000:305.
21. Gurgel 2009:111; Nunes 2009:65.
22. In 1997, for instance, Lula told an interviewer: "The Brazilian parliament works as a stock market. The truth is that respectable, serious and ideologically committed people are the minority there. Unfortunately, our Congress is a business bureau (tr. *um balcão de negócios*). Every time there is an important vote taking place, you can see what happens: the president has to see how much is necessary to get the votes he needs" (*Veja* 13/05/09).
23. This section draws heavily on Couto 1995; Kowarick and Singer 1997 and Macaulay 1996.
24. Only one representative of the PCB was appointed in a rather marginal position: Director of the Funerary Services (Couto 1995).
25. Despite the fact that social organisations did mobilise to support the elected government, it is not possible to determine if it was the pressure from these organisations that determined the vote of the city councillors. The support that the mayor received from a wide range of sectors might have also been an important factor. According to Erundina's press office, more than 500 relevant public figures endorsed the mayor in a supra-party meeting and signed a petition against the impeachment. The list of supporters included senators from the PMDB and the PSDB, members of the Federation of Industries from the State of São Paulo (FIESP) and 37 representatives of the business sector (Assesoria de Imprensa do Gabinete da Prefeita Luiza Erundina 1992). Many of the signatories opposed the impeachment because they saw it as an illegitimate move against a democratically elected government.
26. Compans 1993; Couto 1995; Kowarick and Singer 1997; Macaulay 1996.
27. Kowarick and Singer (1997:35) argue that participatory initiatives not only were confronted with the need to give rapid and efficient results, but initiatives to promote participation soon resulted in "paralysing, long and rhetorical assemblies that never came to an end". Other scholars argue that the government lacked sufficient interest, creating no adequate administrative structure to support a participatory process (Pires 2006:26–9), and the demands were constantly over the budget capacity (Couto 1995).
28. It is not the intention of this chapter to explain in any detail the way in which Participatory Budget worked in Porto Alegre, an issue widely studied in the literature. Among others see Abers 2000; Avritzer 2002; Baiocchi 2005; Fung and Wright 2003; Navarro 2005, 2003, 1998; Sousa 1998; Wampler and Avritzer 2004.
29. Abers 1996; Baiocchi 2003b; Moraes 2001.
30. The participants would meet in open, public assemblies to establish budgetary priorities in a process of negotiation and deliberation organised in two stages: a participatory stage, in which participation is direct, and a representative stage, in which participation takes place through the election of delegates and/or councillors (for more details see Avritzer 2009:Ch.5).
31. Fedozi 2000; Marquetti 2003; Melo 2007; Navarro 2005; Sousa 1998:447.
32. In addition to this, the government managed to update a number of tariffs on municipal services and made surveillance of tax and tariff payments more effective (Sousa 1998:477).

33. Expenditure control, combined with a municipal fiscal reform, and larger federal and state transfers allowed by the 1988 Constitution allowed the PT government in Porto Alegre to increase investment percentage of the budget to 10 percent in 1990, 16.3 percent in 1991 and 17 percent in 1992 (Sousa 1998:477).
34. See also Doctor 2007; Pinto 2004; Ramos 2004:262–6.
35. According to some observers, given the budgeting technique traditional in Brazil, the legislative branch has always played a marginal role in formulation. Because the budget is not required to indicate concrete works to be carried out, the executive at all three levels of government has always had "ample leeway in budget execution" (Sousa 1998:502).
36. Fedozi 1997; Ramos 2004:262.
37. Núñez 18/12/08; Pestana 17/12/08.
38. In 1994, according to municipal data, a total of 1,011 people attended the second round of the thematic PB plenaries: 11.5 percent were from the trade union movement, 14.3 percent business interests, 20 percent community movements, 35 percent other institutions of civil society and state, 14.4 percent individuals without organisational affiliation, and only 0.7 percent representatives of political parties (Sousa 1998:480).
39. Cidade 1999, in Ramos 2004:242.
40. In 1999, for instance, 56 percent of those who participated in PB assemblies earned less than four minimum wages and only 21 percent received more than eight (Cidade 1999; in Ramos 2004:305). In 1999 a minimum wage in Brazil was approximately US$100.
41. Major national scandals were taking place while the PT in Porto Alegre was creating Participatory Budget. The most important corruption allegations forced the impeachment of President Fernando Collor in 1992. Mobilisations and huge street demonstrations took place throughout the country. Like other scholars, Hunter argues that the wave of popular optimism about eliminating corruption certainly benefited the PT administration (Hunter 2010:97). See also Abers 2003; Schneider and Goldfrank 2002:202.
42. According to Abers (2003), support from construction companies might also account for PT governments' ability to put pressure on the city assemblies to approve property tax increases.
43. Abers 2003; Filomena 2006; Hahn 2002; Sousa 1998:464.
44. *Correio do Povo* 30/10/00.
45. The improvement in the electoral performance of the PT even allowed the party to become less marginal in the City Assembly. From only 11 seats between 1989 and 1992 (Table 4.1), it counted on 14 councillors in 1996 (13 from PT, 1 from PPS) (Sousa 1998:502).
46. Goldfrank and Schneider 2003; Schneider and Goldfrank 2002.
47. *Correio do Povo* 30/10/2000.
48. Rizek 2003, in Avritzer 2006:623; Pires 2006:14–5.
49. Among the cities that had adopted PB by 2003, 73 were governed by the PT and 33 by other left-wing parties (Rizek 2003, in Pires 2006:15).
50. In Bello Horizonte the percentage of resources related to investment that were discussed in PB assemblies was 50 (Hernández 2005:40); in São Paulo, between 62 and 63 percent (Hernández 2005:40); in Belém, between 30 and 40 percent (Ramos 2004:251). In Medianeira, Paraná, it was 100 percent—one of the few cases like Porto Alegre (Ramos 2004:251).
51. Hernández 2005:40; Ramos 2004:251.
52. Hunter 2010:Ch.4; Ottman 2009.
53. During our interview, she explained the reasons why the party first selected her as a candidate: "Many citizens in São Paulo who did not approve of the PT

did approve of me (...) They would look at me and offer me a smile. Instead, I would talk to them about Lula and the PT. I was known among women, and the middle classes liked me because I did not come from the working class". During our interview, Suplicy praised her own lack of a specific ideology. When I questioned her over this particular point she joked: "I'm going to imitate Lula when he said that he was a metal worker and not a Socialist ... well, I am a Psychologist!" (laughs). Later she became more serious, adding: "I am motivated by social justice. If I joined the PT it was to combat injustices. I don't care if that is Socialism, Democratic Socialism or Social Democracy. I don't need a label for my commitment" (Suplicy 09/01/09).

54. Suplicy included in her administration members of two traditional PT allies (PCdoB and PSB), technocrats who did not belong to any political party and even government officials who had participated in the administration of President José Sarney (1985–1990).
55. These parties were the PL, PMDB, PDT, PTB, PSB, PPS and PCdoB.
56. Meneguello 2003, in Ottman 2009:73; Teixeira and Tatagiba 2005.
57. Activists from the Housing Movement interviewed by Carneiro report that even when their organisations explicitly offered party leaders in public office in São Paulo demonstrations outside the Chamber in order to promote specific reforms in both their interests, such as higher budget allocations for popular housing or other social services, the administration refused this option (Carneiro 2006:116).
58. One indication of the low priority that the Suplicy administration accorded to the PB process as a whole is the fact that the mayor never chaired its most important meetings, as it used to occur in Porto Alegre. I asked Rui Falcão, Home Affairs Secretary at the time, why the mayor failed to appear at those gatherings. He answered that "the mayor had to take care of the whole city" (Falcão 11/12/08). This answer suggests that PB was not relevant to the government and it was regarded as a sector-specific, marginal initiative.
59. Houtzager 2008; Houtzager and Dowbor 2010.
60. The municipal administration estimates that 34,000 people participated in the first budgeting experience in 2001, then 55,000 and 80,000 in the subsequent two years (Lavalle, Acharya and Houtzager 2005:953). According to the Participatory Budget Coordination (COP) in São Paulo, between 2001 and 2004, a total of 250,000 people participated in 1,680 assemblies (Pires 2006:49).
61. Tr: *"isso é uma bagunça"*.
62. Donato 12/11/08; Falcão 11/12/08; Piai 05/11/08; Suplicy 09/01/09.
63. Belchior 06/07/09; Dulci 10/12/08.
64. For an account of Participatory Budget in the state of Rio Grande do Sul see Schneider and Goldfrank 2002; Goldfrank and Schneider 2003, 2006 and Feres 2002.
65. Núñez 18/12/08; Pestana 17/12/08; Sousa 19/12/08.

NOTES TO CHAPTER 5

1. Hunter 2010:136–40; Miguel 2006; Panizza 2004; Samuels 2004:1000.
2. Amorim 2007; Grijó 2007; Pereira, Power and Raile 2011; Power 2009; Renno 2009; Santos and Grijó 2010.
3. Abranches 1988; Amorim 1994; Figueiredo and Limongi 2000.
4. Amorim 2007; Pereira, Power and Raile 2011; Power 2009.
5. Heller 2009; Hipsher 1998; Kriesi and Koopmans 1995; Roberts 1998.

6. Other presidents from left-wing or left-of-centre parties in Latin America who were Lula's contemporaries had significant congressional support. For instance, Hugo Chávez conquered 44.3 percent of the Upper Chamber in 2000 and 68.3 percent in 2005; Evo Morales controlled 55.3 percent of the Lower House when first elected in 2005; Michelle Bachelet had 53.3 percent in 2006; Tabaré Vázquez 52.5 percent in 2004, while Nestor Kirchner eventually reached 51.5 percent in 2003. For an overview of parliamentary bases of support among Latin American presidents, see Jiménez (2007).
7. Coligação Lula Presidente 2002a:1, 2, 25, 31, 39.
8. Coligação Lula Presidente 2002a:22–3, see Chapter 9.
9. Coligação Lula Presidente 2002a:2.
10. Partido dos Trabalhadores 2004:345.
11. Partido dos Trabalhadores 2004:345.
12. Lula's government programme presented in 2001 was mostly drafted by members of his faction, *Campo Majoritário*. Only two representatives of the party Left participated in the *ad hoc* committee, composed of 22 members. Interviews conducted for this study among members of Lula's inner circle confirmed that certain documents used in the campaign, most notably the "Letter to the Brazilian People", were elaborated by very small groups in Lula's entourage (anonymous source).
13. Partido dos Trabalhadores 2004:598.
14. Partido dos Trabalhadores 2004:598.
15. Coligação Lula Presidente 2002a:2.
16. PT 1991:46–7, in Burgos 1994:122–5.
17. Partido dos Trabalhadores 2004:346.
18. An anonymous interviewee said that Lula was personally disturbed when he read this document and was convinced that its message was not a platform on which he could win the election.
19. Allende lacked a majority in Congress and failed to form a coalition with the Christian Democrats despite the fact that he was elected with their votes in the Electoral College. In 1970 Allende's Unidad Popular only received 36 percent in the ballots.
20. According to Ribeiro (2008:117), many of the PT members in the PT National Directorate were reluctant to appoint Alencar. However, Lula exerted enormous pressure, even threatening to withdraw his own candidacy.
21. See also Hunter 2010:136–40; Miguel 2006:132; Samuels 2004:1000.
22. Hunter 2010:138–9; Miguel 2006; Panizza 2004:467.
23. Partido dos Trabalhadores 2004:1421–31.
24. Contrary to the participatory and democratic tradition of the PT, in which everything was always discussed until consensus was reached, it is revealing that the discussion of the "Letter to the Brazilian People" only took place within Lula's inner circle and became a *fait acompli* shortly afterwards. One of the most visible leaders of the faction Socialist Democracy stated: "The letter was imposed on the party. Despite the fact that it was accepted by the National Directorate, it was presented in public by Lula one week before. When we received it we were told that we had to approve it because it had already been presented to the public" (Soriano, 31/10/08).
25. Partido dos Trabalhadores 2004:1428–31.
26. Already in the first round, Lula obtained 46.52 percent of the vote, well above his closest rival, José Serra, who received 23.27 percent of the votes.
27. These parties were the Workers' Democratic Party (PDT), the Brazilian Labour Party (PTB), the Liberal Party (PL), the Brazilian Socialist Party (PSB),

the Socialist Popular Party (PPS), the Communist Party of Brazil (PCdoB), the Green Party (PV) and the National Mobilisation Party (PMN).
28. Certain leaders in Lula's group supported a strategy of this type. Shortly after winning the first round of the 2002 presidential election, for instance, when it was evident that the PT would be in a marginal position in Congress, Frei Betto, a close friend of Lula and later his advisor in the presidency, wrote: "If Lula is actually elected [in the second round] the conditions for governability will only be possible with a permanent mobilisation of society" (Betto 2007:29). These observations were written in Frei Betto's personal diary, which was eventually published as a book after he left the government, disillusioned.
29. Gonzales 11/11/08; Rangel 08/04/09; Rodrigues 12/12/08; Santos 07/05/09.
30. These answers were obtained after asking 92 party members in different factions if mobilisation could be used to put pressure on the legislative branch as part of an alternative strategy to secure governability (see Appendix III for further details).
31. Cury 02/12/08; Dirceu 07/01/09; Pereira 04/04/09.
32. Some in Lula's inner circle and his faction in the party also justified their opposition to a strategy of counter-mobilisation for reasons of principle. For many, putting pressure on parliament would be incompatible with the rules and spirit of formal representative democracy. José López Feijóo, a trade union leader from the metalworkers' sector with a strong relationship with Lula, went as far as indicating that "Brazil would be close to a dictatorship if we pretended to subordinate the legislative or judiciary branches by strengthening the Executive *vis-á-vis* the Legislative through mass mobilisation" (Lopez Feijóo 16/12/09). Clara Ant, Lula's Deputy Chief of Staff, explained that such an option "would lead us to destroy everything we have done to consolidate Brazilian democracy" (Ant 26/11/08 and 03/12/08).
33. The *Movimento al Socialismo* (MAS), for instance, which lacked a majority in the Senate when Morales was first elected in 2005, combined the use of institutional channels and street demonstrations to approve several laws, such as the extension of agrarian reform; a pension that senior citizens receive monthly from the revenue from hydrocarbons or the referendums related to the approval of a Constitution project (Córdova 2011:165; Larson et al. 2008:5).
34. Santos 07/05/09; Preto 02/12/08; Rodrigues 12/12/08.
35. Lula's Chief of Staff, Gilberto Carvalho, known for his proximity to many of these organisations, made the following point: "I am not sure whether the type of mobilisations that we have achieved in Brazil would be sufficient to support and put pressures on Congress (. . .) [as] in a structured representative democracy like ours it is not reasonable to expect that the people will remain permanently mobilised on the streets (. . .). There are no social organisations capable of constantly coming to Brasilia to put pressure on Congress. Those episodes only take place in specific historical moments. It would be idealistic to expect the opposite" (Carvalho 10/04/09). Marco Aurélio García, one of the most important party intellectuals within Lula's faction, and his special advisor, argued: "I think there is a wrong assessment about the state of social movements in Brazil. The movements in 2002 were very different from what we had in the 1980s. Ten years of neo-liberalism had an extremely demoralising effect upon them. Therefore, we should not expect these organisations to have a potential that they do not have, nor that their actions could have an impact capable of generating changes in the Brazilian political system. I would like to affirm the opposite, but unfortunately it is not possible" (García 10/04/09).

36. Lopes 03/12/08; Rodrigues 13/11/08.
37. Amorim 1994; Figueiredo and Limongi 2001; Power 2009:26.
38. Alston and Mueller 2006:90; Pereira, Power and Raile 2011:37–9.
39. See among others Avelar and Cintra 2007:74; Cheibub, Figueiredo and Limongi 2009; Samuels 2000.
40. Amorim 2007; Couto and Baia 2006; Pereira, Power and Raile 2011; Raile, Pereira and Power 2010.
41. Pereira, Power and Raille (2011:48) found that, during its first year in office, when the government had to pass important reforms, about 89 percent of the pork disbursed in 2003 went to noncoalition parties, with about 34 percent of the total going to parties in the opposition governed by PSDB or PFL. See also Amorim (2007) and Power (2009).
42. These rivalries largely stemmed from the personal animosity between Cardoso and Lula (anonymous source), but also because these two parties had their main electoral bases in the state of São Paulo. I gathered testimonies from Dirceu and Cardoso in this regard. According to Dirceu (07/01/09), "different world views and visions about the role of the state" have made an alliance between these two parties unviable. Cardoso (07/04/10) gave another answer: "Essentially, it has been a question of power: who has control. Ideological differences are only a justification. When Lula won the presidency in 2002 I was expecting a more flexible attitude towards us. However, his party and Lula himself decided that we were the electoral enemy".
43. Couto and Baia 2006; Pereira, Power and Raile 2011:45–6.
44. The Chief of the Civil House of the Presidency is the equivalent to a Home Office Minister for all the domestic functions of the national government to which other ministers in government report.
45. When I asked Dirceu how governability was understood within the "hard nucleus" of the party in government, he considered five main elements: First, that it was necessary to avoid "paralysing conflicts" between the party in office and the party bureaucracy which damaged the party at the municipal and state levels. Second, it was assumed that the formation of legislative alliances was inevitable in order to pass bills in Congress that were of interest to the executive, given the fact that the PT lacked a majority in Congress. Third, it was important to secure the support of the PT social base, mainly as part of a social governability strategy. Fourth, as part of the wide range of interests that the party needed to accommodate, the business sector was particularly important. Last, the macro-economic stability had to be maintained (see main epigraph).
46. The other parties in the coalition were the PSB, PDT, PL, PPS, PCdoB and PV.
47. Amorim 2007; Grijó 2007; Pereira, Power and Raile 2011; Power 2009; Renno 2009; Santos and Grijó 2010.
48. *Folha de S. Paulo* 28/09/05.
49. *Folha de S. Paulo* 07/08/05, 17/08/05.
50. Coordenação dos Movimentos Sociais 2006:57.
51. Coordenação dos Movimentos Sociais 2006:58.
52. *Folha de S. Paulo* 26/08/05.
53. *Folha de S. Paulo* 07/08/05.
54. *Folha de S. Paulo* 16/08/05.
55. Taso Jeraissati, president of the PSDB, acknowledged later during an interview that despite the fact that they knew that legal grounds for an impeachment did exist, the opposition desisted because of the strong popular support for Lula (*Veja* 16/11/05). See also *Folha de S. Paulo* 22/07/05.

56. Dirceu 07/01/09; Dulci 10/12/08.
57. De Oliveira 07/04/09; Moroni 07/10/09.
58. Opposition parties considered that they had a good chance of winning the 2006 presidential election, calculating that the magnitude of the scandal would severely damage Lula's image and his attempt to be reelected.
59. *Folha de S. Paulo* 03/11/05.
60. *O Estado de S. Paulo* 10/10/12.
61. See Chapters 3, 8 and 9 to find more on party–civil society relationships.
62. In his second government, Lula only appointed 18 ministers from the PT. The PMDB, which was now the first minority in Congress (with 89 representatives), received six cabinet positions: Mines and Energy, Defence, Agriculture, Communications, National Integration and Health. Nine other parties were also brought into the government.
63. *Jornal do Senado* 04/10/10.
64. In the slang of Brazilian politics, someone on the far left is considered a "Shiite".
65. *Folha de S. Paulo* 22/10/09.
66. The parties supporting the government were PT, PMDB, PL, PRB, PCdoB, PSB, PP, PR (Party of the Republic), PTB, PV, PDT, PAN and PSC (Christian Social Party). The opposition consisted of four parties: PSDB, DEM (former PFL), PPS and PSOL.
67. *Folha de S. Paulo* 30/04/03.
68. Tr. *Contribuição Social sobre as Grandes Fortunas*.
69. The government even lost an existing tax collected from operations in the banking system, the Provisional Contribution over Financial Movements (CMPF), which was intended for use on social programmes, when 16 out of 20 senators from the PMDB voted against the government. This caused a R$40 billion (some US$22 billion) budgetary hole in funds that the government had promised to allocate to social policies and infrastructure projects (Amorim and Coelho 2008:88).
70. *Folha de S. Paulo* 26/05/09. The governability strategy had other implications for the PT progressive agenda that I analyse in Chapter 9, in areas such as land reform.
71. Partido dos Trabalhadores 2007:28.
72. Rosetto 24/06/09; Pomar 08/04/09.
73. As Chapter 4 explains, in Brazilian politics, a *physiological* relationship is one in which politicians support government initiatives in exchange for favours, with no programmatic or ideological coherence.
74. Partido dos Trabalhadores 2007:49:107.

NOTES TO CHAPTER 6

1. Antunes 2006; Oliveira 2006b; Paula 2005; Tavaloro and Tavaloro 2007, Stédile 06/09/07; Simões 04/11/08; Tavares, Sader et al. 2004.
2. Campello 2012, 2008, 2007; Campello and Zucco 2008.
3. Amann and Baer 2006; Arestis and Saad Filho 2007; Barbosa 2008; Barbosa and Pereira 2010; Filgueiras and Gonçalves 2007; Martínez and Santiso 2003; Santiso 2006, 2004; Wiesner 2008.
4. *Milenio Diario* 10/10/02.
5. One of them, Antonio Russo, second in the hierarchy of the Brazilian Association of Beef Industry Exports, announced that the sector would be "surprised by Lula" (Mendes 2004:88). Another representative of agro-business,

José Carlos Burilai, argued that Lula was a candidate capable of bringing "peace to the countryside" (Mendes 2004: 89).
6. The records of the Superior Electoral Court show that the PT candidate spent nearly R$40 million (US$16 million) compared to Serra's R$35 million (US$14 million). However, journalists have suggested that Lula raised R$200 million (US$80 million) in off-the-books donations (Attuch 2006:16, in Goldfrank and Wampler 2008:246). In the 1994 and 1998 presidential campaigns the PT declared contributions that were almost twenty-fold smaller than the PSDB (Samuels 2001:31).
7. Partido dos Trabalhadores 2004:598.
8. Partido dos Trabalhadores 2004:613, my emphasis.
9. Partido dos Trabalhadores 2004:593.
10. Partido dos Trabalhadores 2004:579.
11. Coligação Lula Presidente 2002a:11; Partido dos Trabalhadores 2004:1428–31.
12. Kaufman 2011:107; Santiso 2004:4.
13. A similar remark was made by Marco Aurélio García, Lula's special advisor for International Affairs, when he explained in an interview that only by resolving the "macro-economic imbalances" would the PT be able to govern. Otherwise it would fall into a catastrophic scenario in which "inflation would soon increase to 10 percent per month, then 20 percent, and then we would be forced down the same tragic path of hyper-inflation that the Brazilian economy has taken in the past" (interview with Marco Aurélio García, in Wainwright and Branford 2005:28).
14. Almeida 03/04/09; Teixeira 2005.
15. Appy 08/04/09; Bittencourt 20/10/10; Palocci 2007.
16. Arbix 06/11/08; Barbosa 20/07/09.
17. Campello and Zucco 2008:21; Martínez and Santiso 2003.
18. Campello and Zucco 2008:22; Santiso 2004.
19. Goldfrank and Wampler 2008:259; Santiso 2004:18.
20. Molano 2002, in Santiso 2004:259.
21. *Folha de São Paulo* 08/06/02, in Barbosa 2008:194.
22. Joaquim Levy and Marcos Lisboa were appointed as Secretary to the Treasury and Secretary for Economic Policy, respectively. Ricardo Carneiro, one of the traditional PT economists, affirms that some of the most important positions in the Ministry of Finance resulted from recommendations made by the International Monetary Fund, while the Central Bank was "completely handed over" to the banking sector (Carneiro 14/04/09).
23. Higher primary surplus goals were reached in the two subsequent years. It was 4.59 percent in 2004 and 4.83 percent in 2005.
24. To highlight the connections between the economic and the political dimensions of governability, it is interesting to note that these two reforms received ample legislative support in the Lower House, including from opposition parties such as the PFL and the PSDB. The reform that cleared the way for the autonomy of the Central Bank received 442 votes, while the pension reform was passed with 357 votes.
25. DIEESE 2006, in Magalhães 2010.
26. Anderson 2011:5; Singer 2010:2.
27. Amann and Baer 2006; Amaral, Kingstone and Krieckhaus 2010; Filgueiras and Gonçalves 2007.
28. "Leftism without a Leftist Project" is the title of an article published by Tavaloro and Tavaloro (2007).
29. In his autobiography, Palocci (2007:37) expressed a similar view, when he wrote that fiscal balance should be "a normal commitment of any respectable

government which does not want to go through an easy populist adventure in order to face its economic problems".
30. *Folha de S. Paulo* 17/09/05.
31. That is, 24 percent of them criticised the economic policy as a whole, and 31 percent the monetary policy. In Left Articulation and the centre-left faction "Message to the Party", criticisms against the economic policy were expressed by 86 and 77 percent of the interviewees, respectively (see Appendix III for further details).
32. Magalhães 20/10/10; Barbosa and Pereira 2010.
33. Agustín 20/10/10; Barbosa and Pereira de Souza 2010:29; Bittencourt 20/10/10.
34. *Exame* 21/07/10.
35. Partido dos Trabalhadores 2007:16.
36. Barros, de Carvalho and Franco (2006:123) found that between only 2003 and 2006 the income of the poorest 10 percent increased seven-fold, mainly due to *Bolsa Família* and the minimum wage increases. In contrast, they claim that the income of the richest 10 percent of the population increased by 1.1 percent per capita. However, as anticipated in the introduction to this book, Brazil does not have reliable statistics on the income of the wealthiest sectors. In the case of the financial sector, studies suggest that between 2005 and 2008, this sector made the highest profits in its history (Barbosa and Pereira 2010:18–19).

NOTES TO CHAPTER 7

1. Baiocchi and Checa 2007; Couto 2009; Feres 2010; Grzybowski 2004; Hochstetler and Friedman 2008; Hunter 2010; Leite 2008; Moroni 2009; Ricci 2008; 2007a; Samuels 2008.
2. Couto 2009; Leite 2008:Ch.4; Moroni 2009.
3. See among others Houtzager 2008; Houtzager and Dowbor 2010; Schönleitner 2006.
4. According to a presidential advisor, PAC and *Bolsa Família* were two of the areas that President Lula himself regarded as "strategic" for his government (Belchior 06/07/09).
5. See Hochstetler 2010; Pogrebinschi 2011; Pogrebinschi and Santos 2010; Teixeira 2005.
6. Couto 2009; Moroni 2009.
7. Leite 2008:Ch.4; Pogrebinschi and Santos 2010:75.
8. Presidência da República 2010:7.
9. Grzybowski 2004; Leite 2008; Moroni 2009.
10. Pogrebinschi 2011:9; Shankland and Cornwall 2008.
11. Councils and conferences are varied and widespread throughout Brazil, and it is not possible to generalise. However, the literature shows that these institutions have limited capacity to exercise influence, either because they lack formal decision-making power or simply because they depend on the will of high-ranking officials to put in place their recommendations (Couto 2009). Others claim that councils and conferences have many political limitations because budgetary decisions are hardly ever discussed within them and they never touch upon key issues such as the macro-economic policy (Teixeira 2005). For other studies on sectoral policy councils and national conferences see Arretche 2003; Caccia 2005; Coelho, Araújo and Cifuentes 2002; Silva and Marques 2004.

12. Couto 2009; Doctor 2007; Pinto 2004; Ramos 2004:262–6; Schneider and Goldfrank 2002; Sousa 2002.
13. In this chapter I draw on the conceptual framework of Sherry Arnstein (1969) and her "ladder of participation". According to this author, a superior form of citizen power takes place when citizens are granted delegated power by which they acquire "dominant decision-making authority over a particular plan or programme". Such a form of power takes place through institutions in which citizens have a clear majority of seats and "genuine specified powers" (Arnstein 1969:11).
14. Only a handful of academic studies analyse the creation of the Zero Hunger committees, most of them written by actors who were involved in the process (see Balsadi, Del Grossi and Takagi 2004; Takagi 2006). There are also written memoirs which touch upon this subject (see Betto 2007; Poletto 2005).
15. The initiative, which targeted 9.3 million families earning less than US$1 per day, half of whom were in the impoverished Northeast, aimed at combining "emergency policies" of social assistance, such as income transfer programmes or popular restaurants, with others seeking the promotion of structural change such as income redistribution, job creation or land reform (Instituto Cidadania 2001).
16. Instituto Cidadania 2001:5.
17. Officials contemplated information from the National Audit Office (TCU), which show that as much as 70 percent of the municipal governments in Brazil have corruption problems (quoted in Betto 2007:444).
18. This characterisation was made by Takagi (2006:163–4) in her doctoral thesis on the implementation of the food security policy during the Lula administration.
19. The estimates are subject to different interpretations. Another official who worked for the Ministry for Food Security, requesting anonymity, acknowledged that there were no more than 1,500 committees that actually functioned. *The municipalists* made even lower estimates. Adriana Aranha, Chief of Staff to the Minister for Social Development, maintained that only 500 committees worked in reality (07/07/09).
20. An academic study conducted in three states of Northeast Brazil between July and August 2003 showed that, despite operational problems in many committees, not only were they promoting transparency and accountability, but they were also helpful in reaching the most needy within their municipalities, in making the beneficiaries spend the money on food and in achieving other objectives of the programme (Ortega 2003, in Takagi 2006). Even the National Court of Audit (TCU) praised the committees for being important elements in preventing corrupt practices (TCU 2004, in Betto 2007:117).
21. Bohn 2011; Hunter and Power 2007; Licio, Rennó and Castro 2009; Zucco 2006.
22. In May 2005, the ministry decided that mayors could opt, on a case-specific basis, for their preferred type of social oversight structure. All that was required was that in order to adhere to the programme, municipalities needed to put in place some kind of social oversight mechanism. They had to follow a set of loose guidelines (such as intersectoriality and equal representation of civil society and government officials), but they were free to decide, for instance, who would belong to the committees and how long each member would hold their position (Ministério de Desenvolvimento Social e Combate a Fome 2005).
23. Ananias 16/07/09; Mesquita 02/07/09; Aranha 07/07/09.
24. Aranha 07/07/09; Menezes 26/07/09; Mesquita 02/07/09.

25. Tr: "*Nos não encabeçamos a secretaria do poder popular*". The interviewee was possibly using an irony about the names that some ministries receive in Venezuela, such as Minister of the Popular Power for Labour or Ministry of the Popular Power for Communal Economy.
26. See also Bohn 2011; Hunter and Power 2007; Licio, Rennó and Castro 2009; Zucco 2006.
27. In contrast to the vast amount of literature that explores participatory budgeting mechanisms at the municipal level, particularly in Porto Alegre (see Chapter 4 for references), only a few studies look at PB at the state level during the government of Olívio Dutra (Feres 2005, 2002; Oliveira 2004; Schneider and Goldfrank 2002). These studies usually point out that at the state level, participatory budgeting proved feasible, but worked differently from municipal PBs, particularly because they drew more on organised groups and less on the participation of ordinary citizens, and also on fewer assemblies (see Chapter 5).
28. Partido dos Trabalhadores 2004:692–717.
29. Partido dos Trabalhadores 2004:1657.
30. Coligação Lula Presidente 2002a:3.
31. Coligação Lula Presidente 2002a:3; Partido dos Trabalhadores 2004:1657.
32. Agustín 20/10/10; Rosetto 24/06/09; Sousa 19/12/08.
33. Belchior 06/07/09; Dirceu 07/01/09; Dulci 10/12/08.
34. The suggestion of this group in Socialist Democracy was to launch a federal participatory budget that would guarantee broad-based participation and grant decision-making power to both civil society organisations and citizens. Participation would take place in public assemblies organised by groups in civil society within all Brazilian municipalities, and priorities would be systematised by using software (Democracia Socialista 2003; Souza 2003).
35. Critical voices inside the PT suggested that a federal PB was not possible simply because "the government refused to share power with the people" (Zimmerman 03/12/08) or lacked interest in the idea (Sousa 19/12/08). The former Deputy Governor of Rio Grande do Sul and Minister for Rural Development during the first Lula administration, Miguel Rosetto, argues that the administration made "a conservative choice " (Rosetto 24/07/09).
36. Ananias 16/07/09; Dirceu 07/01/09; Genro 31/04/09.
37. Following Arnstein's (1969) conceptual framework on participation, *participation by consultation* is understood in this section as a process in which people's opinions are taken into account through mechanisms such as attitude surveys, neighbourhood meetings or public hearings. In most cases, authors argue, this type of participation does not concede any share in decision making and it offers no assurance that citizens' concerns and ideas will be taken into account (Arnstein 1969; Pretty 1995).
38. The Pluriannual Plan is put together by the Ministry of Planning, based on the inputs of the different departments, and it must be completed before the end of the first year of a new government. In theory, this document must be taken into account when the public budget is formulated every year, although in practice, this is not usually the case. For this reason, the importance of this instrument is limited.
39. Delgado and Limonic 2004:18; Feres 2010; IBASE 2005; Moroni 2009; Ricci 2007a.
40. Dulci 2003:20; Ministério do Planejamento 2003.
41. A peculiar selection process was used to select the list of participatns: civil society organisations were allowed to suggest names, but the General-Secretary of the Presidency made the final decision following criteria that was not transparent (Moroni 2009; Ricci 2008).

42. Delgado and Limonic 2004; Moroni 2009; Ricci 2008.
43. Inter-Redes 2004, in Moroni 2009:19–20.
44. Delgado and Limonic 2004; Inter-Redes 2004.
45. Delgado and Limonic 2004; Dulci 2003; Ministério do Planejamento 2003; Toni 2006.
46. Coligação a Força do Povo 2006:26.
47. Presidência da República 2007.
48. Almeida 03/04/09; Schmidt 03/12/09.
49. Almeida 03/04/09; Belchior 06/07/09; Dulci 10/12/08.
50. Belchior 06/07/09; Schmidt 03/12/09.
51. Almeida 03/04/09; Belchior 06/07/09; Dulci 10/12/08.
52. According to the NGO *Contas Abertas* (Open Accounts), most of the PAC was concentrated on three large infrastructure companies when it was first launched in 2007 (*Diario do Nordeste* 27/06/08).
53. Press reports based on information from the National Audit Office showed that the PT received the largest donations from among PAC contractors during the first electoral round of the 2010 presidential election. The party received R$70.5 billion (approximately US$41.47 billion). The PT National Directorate alone obtained R$18.7 billion (some US$11 billion) (*O Estado de S. Paulo* 13/11/10a; 13/11/10b). Approximately 25 percent of all donations that Dilma received came from PAC beneficiaries such as Camargo Corrêa, OAS and Queiróz Galvão (*O Estado de S. Paulo* 13/11/10b).
54. Carneiro and Braga 2009:14; Carvalho 2006.
55. *El Comercio* 08/02/12; *Peripecias* 29/11/06.
56. *Peripecias* 29/11/06.
57. Among voters earning from 5 to 10 minimum wages, Lula's approval rating was 59.5%; from 10 to 20 it was 52.5%, and above 20 minimum wages it was 50% (CNT/Sensus 2007, in Barros, Souza and Cabral 2010:131).
58. Soriano 31/10/08; Tatto 12/11/08.

NOTES TO CHAPTER 8

1. If co-optation is understood as a process by which an individual or a group leaves its concerns aside or "sells out", as the term is most commonly understood, this research did not find strong evidence, at least not in a way that can be generalised to the whole spectrum of civil society organisations in the PT field.
2. Barbosa 02/12/08; Moroni 07/10/09; Escobar 2008:Ch.3; Galvão 2007; García 2008; Oliveira 2006b; Ricci 2007b.
3. Collier and Collier 1979; Lavalle, Acharya and Houtzager 2005; Middlebrook 1995; Roberts 2002.
4. A book chapter written by Hochstetler (2010) is a valuable first approximation, but it only covers the first few years of the Lula administration and more emphasis is given to civil society organisations than to the party.
5. In the case of CUT, several studies examine its behaviour during the two Lula administrations (Alvarenga 2008; Druck 2006; Galvão 2007; Reiner and Melleiro 2007), while only a few explore the relationship between CUT and the Lula administration from the party side (Escobar 2008; García 2008:Ch.3; Leyendeker 2004). Something similar has occurred with studies on the Landless Rural Workers' Movement during the Lula administration (Branford 2010; Meszaros 2010; Sauer 2008; Vergara-Camus 2009).
6. *Folha de S. Paulo* 01/01/03.

7. Avritzer 13/06/10; Belchior 06/07/09; Hochstetler and Friedman 2008; Sauer 2008.
8. Avritzer 13/06/09; *Carta Capital* 20/01/11.
9. It is worth noting, however, that incidents of rural violence involving assassinations, despite not involving national security forces, are still common in many Brazilian states (Ministério de Desenvolvimento Agrario 2008).
10. Despite Lula's strong charisma, I do not use the term *charismatic linkage* used by other authors (Kitschelt, Mansfeldova and Markowski 1999:47) to characterise these relationships. This is because, by definition, these types of linkages are established between a leader and unorganised groups and lack "significant mediations" (Madsen and Snow 1991:5).
11. The reform of the social security pension system, which both CUT and the PT had opposed during the Cardoso administration, also allowed the creation of private funds and deprived public sector workers of previously gained benefits, such as fiscal exceptions among state workers' pensions or the so-called *aposentadoria integral* (the right to obtain a pension based on the highest salary earned and the number of years worked, rather than on a fixed retirement age). This reform was meant to tackle the fiscal deficit and change a system that was considered extremely costly.
12. Escobar 2008; Galvão 2007; Sader 2005.
13. In 2003, when CUT's Eighth National Congress took place, 40 percent of its delegates represented unions in the public sector. In contrast, the industrial sector only represented 16 percent of the organisation (*Folha de S. Paulo* 02/05/04).
14. "(. . .) Every time I participate in a CUT Congress", he began by saying, "I feel as if I was at home talking to my wife and my sons, I feel as if I was in my house among *companheiros*" (*Estado de S. Paulo* 04/06/03).
15. *Estado de S. Paulo* 04/06/03.
16. *Estado de S. Paulo* 04/06/03.
17. This practice, which resembled those of charismatic leaders, was not used in order to present himself as a messianic agent of "massive social change" (Ansell and Fish 1999:288). Instead, he assumed a more "representational role" similar to a "quasi-charismatic" phenomenon which, according to Ansell and Fish, takes place in parties with strong internal ideological divisions, such as the PT, in which the leader of the triumphant group emerges as a quasi-charismatic figure.
18. *Folha de S. Paulo* 03/06/03a.
19. *Folha de S. Paulo* 03/06/03a.
20. Luiz Marinho was the leader of the ABC Metalworkers' Trade Union, in which Lula began his career as a social activist. Marinho was elected president of CUT in June 2003 with 1,950 votes: by 74.6 percent of all the delegates (*Folha de S. Paulo* 08/06/03a).
21. This information was published in press reports (*Correio Braziliense* 29/01/03; in Leyendeker 2004: LXXVII; *Folha de S. Paulo* 08/06/03), is supported by some Brazilian scholars and was corroborated by members of CUT's National Executive Commission interviewed for this study (Celestino 16/12/09; Galvão 2007; Morães 16/12/09; Moroni 07/07/09; Oliveira 2006a). CUT leaders from the Metalworkers' sector who supported Marinho's candidacy, however, deny Lula's involvement in the process, arguing that the organisation had always been "autonomous" from governments (Lopes Feijóo 16/12/09; Severo 15/12/09).
22. Marinho epitomised the so-called propositive trade unionism, which emerged during the 1990s, promoting bargaining processes with both the business sector and the government (Galvão 2004:238), as explained in Chapter 3.

23. *Folha de S. Paulo* 18/07/03; Galvão 2007:3–4.
24. *Folha de S. Paulo* 17/06/03, 27/06/03.
25. *Folha de S. Paulo* 11/06/03, 17/06/03. The reform of the pension funds system was not the only occasion in which CUT failed to support strike actions of a particular CUT affiliated sector. In 2004, the organisation made "all possible attempts" to avoid a strike decided by the public sector bank workers, most likely because it could affect the municipal elections that were to take place that same year (García 2008:144). In 2006 something similar happened in the context of the 2006 presidential election (Galvão 2007:4).
26. *Folha de S. Paulo* 06/08/03a.
27. With the exception of Hochstetler (2010), who explores this issue, the inclusion of social activists in government and its implications, remain largely unexplored and are virtually absent in studies on the MST.
28. It is not always easy to draw a clear line between those who are still social leaders or active members of a social organisation although they have mostly followed political careers.
29. In the Brazilian public administration the highest levels are the upper-level directions (or *Direções de Asesoramento Superiores*, DAS), level 5 and 6; and the special posts (or *Cargos de Natureza Especial*, NES).
30. At least 10 leaders of the Housing Movement became government officials in the first Lula administration, according to Evaniza Rodrigues (12/12/08), a member of the executive committee of the National Union of Popular Housing (UNMP) who became Under Secretary of Urban Policy.
31. CONTAG negotiated the appointment of at least three important Secretaries in the Ministry of Rural Development: Technical Assistance, Rural Credit and Territorial Reorganisation (Bradford 2009).
32. MST leaders offer different versions about their involvement in government. In general, its main leaders tend to deny that they negotiated positions in the Lula administration. João Pedro Stédile said: "The MST and the social movements have no participation in the government whatsoever. On the contrary, we behave with total autonomy. The only difference is that today we have more friends occupying public office, people who might pick up a phone call from us, which did not happen before" (Stédile 06/09/07). Alexandre Rangel made a more nuanced point: "Officially, the MST did not appoint anyone in the federal government. The movement was consulted on certain occasions, but that's different. We have resisted making such kinds of appointments, which CONTAG does, because we want to remain independent" (Rangel 08/04/09). In contrast, when I asked Clarice dos Santos whether the appointment of many cadres to INCRA "who sympathise with the MST" was part of negotiation with the government, she gave a straightforward answer: "Yes, I was never involved in those talks, but I know they took place. All social movements made these sorts of negotiations" (Santos 07/05/09).
33. Marinho had no previous experience in public office or in the party bureaucracy. After leading CUT for two years, he came to government in 2005 to become the Minister for Labour. Two years later, Lula appointed him as Minister for Social Security.
34. *Jornal do Brasil* 15/09/03, in Hochstetler 2004:11.
35. Barbosa 02/12/08; Galvão 2007; García 2008; Moroni 07/07/09; Oliveira 2006a; Ricci 2007b.
36. Bemerguy 20/07/09; Felício 28/10/08; Lacerda 22/07/09.
37. Celestino 16/12/09; Henrique 15/04/09; Nespolo 16/12/08.
38. Members of CONTAG offered the example of Eugênio Peixoto, an activist from their organisation who was appointed in Lula's first term as Secretary of

Territorial Reorganisation in the Ministry of Rural Development. CONTAG associates considered that his work had been unsatisfactory and asked Lula for a replacement (Borba and Cleia 03/04/08).

39. The allocation of state resources to civil society organisations and its implications during the Lula administration are understudied. While students of the PT paid little attention to this issue, case studies on specific organisations, most notably the MST (Branford 2010; Meszaros 2010; Sauer 2008; Vergara-Camus 2009) have failed to address this important issue.

40. It is not always easy to draw a line between general and particularistic benefits, in part because they sometimes overlap. While some state subsidies are the bases of reward-based linkages, others might have more programmatic features.

41. Hochstetler 2010:48; Soriano 04/11/08.

42. Heck 01/04/09; Moroni 07/07/09; Soriano 31/10/08.

43. *O Globo* 03/05/04, in Hochstetler 2010:48.

44. State-owned companies, for instance, were an important source of funding. Press reports show that the area of Communications in Petrobras, the state-owned oil company, had a R$1-billion (US$491,617) annual budget that it could manage with considerable autonomy. Part of these funds may have benefited social organisations, among other actors (*Estado de S. Paulo* 31/05/09).

45. *Folha de S. Paulo* 27/02/09, 29/03/09.

46. *Veja* 02/09/06; *Folha de S. Paulo* 27/02/09, 29/03/09.

47. MST leaders such as João Pedro Stédile persistently denied that the organisation used any kind of state resources to conduct land occupations (*Jornal do Brasil* 20/10/09). Other leaders even deny that the movement receives state resources. According to one of them, "only entities or technicians linked to the movement receive money from the government" (Martines 07/07/09).

48. The MST shifted from an initial moment in which it characterised the government as an "ally" (Gordillo and Gómez 2005:214), to one in which it considered that the administration as a whole was not necessarily on its side, and came to criticise specific sectors, policies and institutions. CUT leaders, although they never ceased to regard the government as their ally, after the second term realised that they had to put a certain amount of pressure on the administration and made some criticisms, in part to avoid alienating their own social base (Campos 16/12/09; Celestino 16/12/09; Henrique 15/04/09).

49. During the Lula administration, for instance, the average of land occupations was 1.2 per day, above the 0.7 percent of occupations during the two Cardoso administrations. According to the Ministry of Rural Development, the total number of land occupations conducted by all rural organisations in the country was relatively low during the final two years of the Cardoso administration: 158 in 2001 and 103 in the electoral year of 2002. In 2003 and 2004, however, they escalated to 222 and 327, respectively. It is considered that the MST was responsible for more than 50 percent of all these occupations (Ministério de Desenvolvimento Agrario 2008:2). Among the unions, particularly from 2007 when the economy started to grow, the number of strikes which had reached very low levels in the late 1990s (only 50 strikes took place in 1998 and 46 in 1999), reached 316 in 2007 and 411 in 2008 (DIEESE 2008:3; 2007:4; Riethof 2004:39). Certain categories in CUT such as the bank sector workers, the electricity sector and, in general, public sector unions, conducted strikes every year (Henrique 15/04/09).

50. Hochstetler 2004, 2010; Branford 2010.

51. Ferro 02/07/09; Stédile, interviewed by *Jornal do Brasil* 20/10/09.
52. Ananias 16/07/09; Cassel 04/12/08; Singer 02/07/09.
53. Santos 07/05/09; Henrique 15/04/09.
54. Borba and Cleia 03/04/08; Lopes Feijóo 16/12/09.

NOTES TO CHAPTER 9

1. These labels capture the views of a number of social leaders expressed during the interviews. In CUT: Lisboa 21/10/10; Morães 16/12/09 and Severo 15/12/09. In the MST: Martines 07/07/09; Rangel 08/04/09 and Stédile 06/09/07. In CONTAG: Beze 03/07/09; Borba and Cleia 03/04/08.
2. According to DIEESE, between 1995 and 1998 the minimum wage decreased its real value by 2.40 percent (*Folha de S. Paulo* 30/04/06). Although from 2000 the second Cardoso administration increased the minimum wage above the inflation, the adjustments were never sufficient to recuperate its pre-1995 levels (Magalhães and Araújo 2010:3).
3. Dulci 10/12/08; Severo 15/12/09.
4. *Folha de S. Paulo* 01/04/03.
5. According to the *Departamento Intersindical de Estatística e Estudos Sócio-Econômicos* (DIEESE), the minimum wage at the time had to be R$1,399 a month (US$451) in order to cover the basic needs of a family with four members; in other words, to cover food, housing, health, education, transport, hygiene, clothing, leisure and social security (*Folha de S. Paulo* 01/04/03).
6. Lisboa 21/10/10; *Folha de S. Paulo* 21/12/06.
7. Boito 2005:60; Carter 2010; Ondetti 2006; Sauer 2008; Vergara-Camus 2009.
8. Coligação Lula Presidente 2002a:21–2.
9. The First National Plan on Land Reform was issued by the Sarney administration in 1985.
10. According to Articles 184 and 185 of the Brazilian Constitution, the Union has powers to expropriate on account of social interest, for purposes of agrarian reform, any rural property which is not performing its social function, except when it comes to productive land (National Constituent Assembly 1988).
11. Arruda Sampãio 11/12/08; Borba and Cleia 03/04/08; Russo 01/12/08; Teixeira 07/04/09.
12. Strictly speaking, any exchange of agricultural merchandise would fall into the category of agribusiness, whether practised by small farmers or large rural enterprises. Among Brazilian landless workers, however, the term is rhetorically usually used to define a specific way of organising rural activities which usually involves large properties, and a high degree of specialisation dedicated to satisfying the demands of external markets, monoculture, the use of pesticides and high technology.
13. It is estimated that 73 percent of the members in the rural caucus own rural property, while 45 percent of them have between 100 and 1,000 hectares of land (Teixeira 2009:74).
14. Pereira 04/04/09; Pomar 30/09/08 and 08/04/09; Rodrigues 13/11/08; Soriano 31/10/08.
15. Even in 2007, during the Third PT National Congress, the party dedicated several pages of its final resolution to reaffirming its commitment to land reform (Partido dos Trabalhadores 2007:55–2) The large majority of party leaders interviewed for this study (79 percent) still consider land reform a relevant matter. I gathered the opinion of 78 party leaders from different

factions. Even within Lula's faction (CNB), 62 percent of them still regard land reform as a relevant topic. Within Left Articulation, the cause has 100 percent of adherents (see Appendix III for details).
16. Perhaps for that reason Lula might have said in a private conversation that "land reform is important because we have the MST". This was mentioned by a high-ranking official who requested anonymity.
17. According to Ondetti (2008:527), between 2003 and 2006 Lula only granted land to 228,098 families, for an average of 57,025 per year. This figure is somewhat higher than Cardoso's overall average of 51,326, but lower than his first term average of 66,968. Most land used for settlement under the PT administration was either public or unclaimed. Land expropriation, the main instrument contemplated in the Second National Plan on Land Reform, was relatively rare. Certainly, only 8.4 percent of the land distributed between 2003 and 2006 was obtained in this manner. The situation did not change much during the second Lula administration. During both the first and second terms, the largest part of the land distributed was state-owned or purchased (Carter 2010; *O Globo* 05/07/10).
18. Among two of the most important PT allies in Congress, the PMDB and the PP, 55 percent and 45 percent of its deputies, respectively, were members of the rural caucus (Teixeira 2009:61).
19. Druck 2006; Galvão 2007; Hall 2009; Martins 2005.
20. Coligação Lula Presidente 2002a:22–3.
21. One of the first decisions adopted by Lula in defence of labour rights was to withdraw from Congress a bill proposed by the Cardoso administration to modify Article 7 of the Constitution and Article 618 of the Consolidation of Labour Laws (CLT), by which it was established that "what is negotiated should prevail over what is legislated", meaning that guarantees in labour law would be subject to bargaining between workers and employers (Hall 2009:155; Nespolo 16/12/08; Reiner and Melleiro 2007). Given the fact that many unions in Brazil are small and might not be able to defend workers effectively, critics point out that such a measure could undermine workers' rights, particularly in the context of an economic crisis.
22. Boito 1991; Galvão 2007; Hall 2009; Perondi 2010.
23. In 2003 CUT represented 3,352 affiliated unions and 22 million workers (*Folha de S. Paulo* 03/06/03b). Surveys conducted in 2001 showed that CUT accounted for 32 percent of the total number of Brazilian workers (unionised and nonunionised) and 48 percent of those who belong to a labour peak organisation. *Forza Sindical*, the second largest *central*, had 6,120,759 workers (20.52 percent), *Social Democracia Sindical* represented 2,376,778 members (15.54 percent), while the rest were distributed among 14 other organisations (IBGE 2002, in Santos 2007:294–5).
24. The National Labour Forum was formed by 72 members: 21 from each category and 9 representatives of cooperatives and other forms of work. The block of the labour peak organisations was formed by CUT (6), *Forza Sindical* (5), CGT (3), SDS (2), CGTB (2), CAT (2) and CNTI (1). The block of the business sector incorporated members of the different chambers, including Agriculture (CNA), Industry (CNI), Transport (CNT), Trade (CNC) and Finance (CFN) who were represented in more or less equal proportions (Perondi 2010:60; Rozentino 2007:58–1).
25. Nespolo 16/12/08; Perondi 2010:65.
26. The *unicidade* was formally abolished on paper, but plurality is still restricted, as some unions are now able to maintain exclusive representation in their areas, provided that they can enrol 20 percent of the workers and meet

other criteria (Galvão 2007:11; Hall 2009:159). The union tax was formally abolished, but unions were allowed to create other compulsory contributions. Scholars observe that the final proposal of the FNT created new forms of state control over the unions, mainly through a newly established National Council on Labour Relations, whose members will be appointed by the Ministry of Labour among workers, business and government representatives. This body will have powers to register or legalise trade unions and *centrais sindicais*, or even to dissolve the existing ones, following certain rules (Druck 2006:334; Galvão 2007:10–1).

27. A research conducted in 2007 by Luiz Alberto dos Santos as part of a PhD thesis on the practice of lobbying in Brazil shows that, despite their historical weaknesses and limited resources to influence decision-making processes, during the Lula administration the *centrais sindicais* became one of the groups with the greatest capacity to represent their interests in Congress, coming only after government officials and business groups (Santos 2007:417–8).

28. These types of arguments were made by Cassel (04/12/08), Minister of Rural Development; Carvalho (10/04/09), Lula's Chief of Staff, or José Genoino, former PT President (08/12/08). The latter argued: "Land reform is not so important today as it was in the past. The main question now is to invest in the small rural properties, in family agriculture and in cooperatives".

NOTES TO FINAL REMARKS

1. In 2010 the tax burden in Brazil reached 33.5 percent of the country's GDP. This is far above that of countries such as Mexico (19.82), Chile (21.28), Ecuador (15.58) or Bolivia (20.13) (*Tribunal de Contas da União* 2009:2).
2. In this influential work, *Carnival, Rogues and Heroes*, DaMatta (1991:140) explains that in a society "heavily oriented toward the universal and the cordial", conflict is seen as a "failure" or as a "crisis" that would entail "efforts to change the whole web of relationships implied in the social structure".
3. See Tanaka and Jácome 2011.
4. Castañeda (2006:28) argues that there are two lefts in Latin America: one that is "open-minded and modern", and the other one is "closed-minded and stridently populist". In his view, whereas the former "respects democracy", the latter is "irresponsible and abusive"; while the first operates within an orthodox market framework, the second is "statist"; while one seeks "good relations with the United States", the other taunts the United States and seeks confrontation.
5. See among others Arditi 2007; Cleary 2006; Luna 2010; Luna and Filgueira 2009.
6. During the interviews conducted for this study, members of Lula's entourage observed that in countries such as Bolivia and Venezuela, the opposition does not always respect formal institutions. In their view, this is not necessarily the case of "the factual power" of the Brazilian establishment, which is more prone to respect the rules of representative democracy and act within institutional mechanisms (Ant 26/11/08, 03/12/08; Dirceu 07/01/09).
7. See, among others, Chalmers, Vilas and Hite 1997; Chávez 2004; Fung and Wright 2003; Gaventa and McGee 2010; Goldfrank 2004; Heller 2001; Huber, Rueschemayer, and Stephens 1997; Laclau and Mouffe 2001; Mouffe 1992; Osterman 2002; Roberts 1998; Stolowicz 2004.
8. Wilpert 2007:58; Ellner 2008:183; Fernandes 2010:85; Goldfrank 2011; López Maya and Lander 2011.

9. Kohl 2010:113; Mayorga 2011:21.
10. These authors fail to mention, however, that such practices have also been deployed by the conservative opposition in Bolivia, a country in which, often, neither the Right nor the Left is willing to be bound by institutional politics and the rule of law.
11. In the case of Venezuela, a number of scholars contend that the populist mobilization of the Chávez regime has undermined democratic norms (McCoy 2004; Castañeda and Morales 2008; Sanchez Uribarri 2008; Hawkins 2010; Corrales and Penfold 2011).
12. French 2008:13; Hellinger 2005:9.
13. Roberts 1998; Stolowicz 2004.
14. Kitschelt 2000; Roberts 2002.
15. See also Bond 2004; Glaser 1997; Sinwell 2011.
16. Presidência da República, Secretaria Geral. 2011:17.
17. In 2010, 22 parties were elected against 19 in 2002 and 21 in 2006 (Limongi and Cortez 2010:32).
18. The parties in Dilma's coalition were PT, PMDB, PCdoB, PR, PDT, PRB, PSC, PCB, PTC, PTN.
19. These parties were RN, PR, PDT, PP, PCdoB and PSB.
20. Dilma made a commitment with political reform in her manifesto for election in 2010 (Coligação Para o Brasil Seguir Mudando 2010:9), and the party endorsed it, once again, in its Fourth National Congress in 2011 (Partido dos Trabalhadores 2011:20–4).
21. These parties are PMDB, PR, PCdoB, PDT and PP.
22. *Folha de S. Paulo* 21/12/11.

References

Abers, Rebecca. 1996. From Ideas to Practice: The Partido dos Trabalhadores and Participatory Governance in Brazil. *Latin American Perspectives* 23 (4):35–54.
———. 2000. *Inventing Local Democracy: Grassroots Politics in Brazil*. London: Lynne Rienner.
———. 2003. Reflections on What Makes Empowered Participatory Governance Happen. In *Deepening Democracy*, edited by A. Fung and E.O. Wright, pp. 200–207. London: Verso.
Abranches, Sérgio. 1988. Presidencialismo de coalizão: O dilema institucional brasileiro. *Dados* 31 (1):5–33.
Abrucio, Luiz Fernando. 1998. *Os barões da Federação: os governadores e a redemocratização brasileira*. São Paulo: Editora Hucitec.
Alcántara, Manuel. 1994. *Gobernabilidad, crisis y cambio: Elementos para el estudio de la gobernabilidad de los sistemas políticos en épocas de crisis y cambio*. Mexico, D.F.: Fondo de Cultura Económica.
Alderman, Keith, and Neil Carter. 1994. The Labour Party and the Trade Unions: Loosening the Ties. *Parliamentary Affairs* 47:321–337.
Allern, Elin, Juul Haugsjerd and Flemming Christiansen. 2007. Social Democrats and Trade Unions in Scandinavia: The Decline and Persistence of Institutional Relationships. *European Journal of Political Research* 46:607–635.
Alston, Lee, and Bernardo Mueller. 2006. Pork for Policy: Executive and Legislative Exchange in Brazil. *Journal of Law, Economics, and Organization* 22 (1):87–114.
Alvarenga, Mateus. 2008. A CUT e a reforma sindical do Fórum Nacional do Trabalho: Posições e divergências, Master's thesis. Faculdade de Filosofia e Ciências, Universidade Estadual Paulista, Marília.
Alvarez, Sonia 1997. Reweaving the Fabric of Collective Action: Social Movements and Challenges to "Actually Existing Democracy" in Brazil. In *Between Resistance and Revolution: Cultural Politics and Social Protest*, edited by R. Fox and O. Starn, pp. 83–117. New Brunswick, NJ: Rutgers University Press.
Amann, Edmund, and Werner Baer. 2006. Economic Orthodoxy versus Social Development? The Dilemmas Facing Brazil's Labour Government. *Oxford Development Studies* 34 (2):219–241.
Amaral, Aline, Peter Kingstone and Jonathan Krieckhaus. 2010. The Limits of Economic Reform in Brazil. In *Democratic Brazil Revisited*, edited by P. Kingstone and T. Power, pp. 145–146. Pittsburgh: Pittsburg University Press.
Amaral, Oswaldo. 2003. *A Estrela nao é mais vermelha: As mudancas do programa petista nos anos 90*. São Paulo: Garçoni.
———. 2010a. Adaptação e resistência: o PT no Governo Lula entre 2003 e 2008. *Revista Brasileira de Ciência Política* 4:105–134.

———. 2010b. As transformações na organização do Partido dos Trabalhadores entre 1995 e 2009, PhD thesis. Instituto de Filosofia e Ciências Humanas, Universidade Estadual de Campinas, Campinas.

———. 2010c. Adaptação e resistência: o PT no Governo Lula entre 2003 e 2008. *Revista Brasileira de Ciência Política* 4:105–134.

Ames, Barry. 2000. *The Deadlock of Democracy in Brazil*. Ann Arbor: University of Michigan Press.

Amorim, Octavio. 1994. Formação de Gabinetes Ministeriais no Brasil: Coalizão versus Cooptação. *Nova Economia* 4:9–34.

———. 2007. Algumas Conseqüências Políticas de Lula: Novos Padrões de Formação e Recrutamento Ministerial, Controle de Agenda e Produção Legislativa. In *Instituições Representativas no Brasil: Balanço e Reformas*, edited by J. Nicolau and T. Power, pp. 55–73. Belo Horizonte: Editora UFMG.

Amorim, Octavio, and Carlos Federico Coelho. 2008. Brasil en el 2007: el desencuentro entre la economía y la política. *Revista de Ciencia Política* 28 (1):81–102.

Anderson, Perry. 2011. Lula's Brazil. *London Review of Books* 33 (7):3–12, http://www.lrb.co.uk/v33/n07/perry-anderson/lulas-brazil, accessed 17/06/12.

Ansell, Christopher, and Steven Fish. 1999. The Art of Being Indispensable: Noncharismatic Personalism in Contemporary Political Parties. *Comparative Political Studies* 32:283–312.

Antunes, Ricardo. 2006. *Uma Esquerda Fora do Lugar: O Governo Lula e os Descaminhos do PT*. São Paulo: Autores Associados.

Arbós, Xavier, and Salvador Giner. 1993. *La Gobernabilidad: Ciudadanía y democracia en la encrucijada mundial*. Madrid: Siglo Veintiuno de España Editores.

Arditi, Benjamin. 2007. Four Arguments about the Latin American Left(s). Paper presented at *Left Turns? Progressive Parties, Insurgent Movements, and Policy Alternatives in Latin America*. Peter Wall Institute for Advanced Studies, University of British Columbia, Vancouver, Canada, 25–27 May.

Arestis, Philip, and Alfredo Saad Filho. 2007. *Political Economy of Brazil: Recent Economic Performance*. London: Palgrave Macmillan.

Armony, Victor. 2007. The "Civic Left" and the Demand for Social Citizenship. Paper presented at *Left Turns? Progressive Parties, Insurgent Movements, and Policy Alternatives in Latin America*. Peter Wall Institute for Advanced Studies, University of British Columbia, Vancouver, Canada, 25–27 May.

Arnstein, Sherry. 1969. A Ladder of Citizen Participation. *Journal of the American Institute of Planners* 35 (4):216–224.

Arretche, Marta. 2003. Financiamento Federal e Gestão Local das políticas Sociais: O Difícil Equilíbrio entre Regulação, Responsabilidade e Autonomia. *Ciência & Saúde Coletiva* 8 (2): 331–345.

Assesoria de Imprensa do Gabinete da Prefeita Luiza Erundina. 1992. *Erundina, uma razão*. São Paulo: MPM/LINTAS.

Assis, Julio. 1992. *O dilema da participação popular: A etnografia de um caso*. São Paulo: Marco Zero.

Astudillo, Javier. 2001. Without Unions, but Socialist: The Spanish Socialist Party and Its Divorce from Its Union Confederation (1982–96). *Politics & Society* 29:273–296.

Avelar, Lucia, and Antonio Cintra. 2007. *Sistema político brasileiro: uma introdução*. São Paulo: UNESP.

Avritzer, Leonardo. 2002. *Democracy and the Public Sphere in Latin America*. Princeton, NJ: Princeton University Press.

———. 2006. New Public Spheres in Brazil: Local Democracy and Deliberative Politics. *International Journal of Urban and Regional Research* 30 (3):623–637.

———. 2009. *Participatory Institutions in Democratic Brazil*. Washington, DC: Woodrow Wilson Center Press, Johns Hopkins University Press.

Aylott, Nicholas. 2003. Linkage and Political Exchange in Mass Parties: A Swedish Case Study. Paper presented at the *XIVth Political Studies Association annual conference*. Leicester, 3–4 May.
Baeza-Rodríguez, Cecilia. 2008. Los discursos públicos sobre la gobernabilidad en Chile como relatos de acción pública: un enfoque cognitivista sobre la importación de ideas. Paper presented at the *Coloquio Internacional GRESCH: ¿Chile de país modelado a país modelo?* Santiago de Chile, 5–6 September.
Baiocchi, Gianpaolo. 2003a. *Radicals in Power: The Workers' Party (PT) and Experiments with Urban Democracy in Brazil*. London: Zed Books.
———. 2003b. Decentralization as Opportunity Structure: Inequality and Innovation in Brazil. In *Decentralization and Local Governance in Developing Countries: A Comparative Perspective*, edited by P. Bardhan and D. Mukerjee, pp. 53–80. Cambridge, MA: MIT Press.
———. 2005. *Militants and Citizens: The Politics of Participatory Democracy in Porto Alegre*. Standord, CA: Standford University Press.
Baiocchi, Gianpaolo, and Sofia Checa. 2007. The Brazilian Workers' Party: From Local Practices to National Power. *Journal of Labor Society* 10 (4):411–430.
Baiocchi, Gianpaolo, Patrick Heller and Shubham Chaudhuri. 2006. Evaluating Empowerment: Participatory Budgeting in Brazilian Municipalities. In *Empowerment in Practice: From Analysis to Implementation*, edited by R. Alsop, B. Frost and J. Holland. Washington, DC: World Bank.
Baldez, Lisa. 2003. Women's Movements and Democratic Transition in Chile, Brazil, East Germany and Poland. *Comparative Politics* 35 (3):253–272.
Balsadi, Octavio, Mauro Del Grossi and Maya Takagi. 2004. O Programa Cartão Alimentação (PCA) em Números: Balanço de sua Implementação e Contribuições para as Políticas Sociais. *Cadernos do CEAM* 44 (14):81–97.
Banco Central, Reservas Internacionais: Liquidez Internacional, http://www.bcb.gov.br/?RP20121005, accessed 10/10/12.
Barbosa, Nelson. 2008. An Unusual Economic Arrangement: The Brazilian Economy during the First Lula Administration. *International Journal of Politics, Culture and Society* 19 (3–4):193–215.
Barbosa, Nelson, and José Antonio Pereira. 2010. A inflexão do Governo Lula: Política economica, crescimento e distribuicão de renda, http://marx21.com/2010/04/19/a-inflexao-do-governo-lula-politica-economica-crescimento-e-distribuicao-de-renda/, accessed 10/09/11.
Barros, Pedro, José Carlos Souza Braga and Vera Lúcia Cabral. 2010. Lula's Administration at a Crossroads: The Difficult Combination of Stability and Development in Brazil. In *Leftist Governments in Latin America: Success and Shortcomings*, edited by K. Weyland, R. Madrid and W. Hunter, pp. 124–139. Cambridge: Cambridge University Press.
Barros, Ricardo, Mirela de Carvalho and Samuel Franco. 2006. Uma análise das principais causas da queda recente na desigualdade de renda brasileira. *Revista Economica* 8 (1):117–147.
Belloni, Frank, and Dennis Beller. 1976. The Study of Party Factions as Competitive Political Organizations. *Western Political Quarterly* 29 (4):531–549.
Berman, Sheri. 1998. *The Social Democratic Moment: Ideas and Politics in the Making of Interwar Europe*. Cambridge, MA: Harvard University Press.
Bettcher, Kim. 2005. Factions of Interest in Japan and Italy: The Organizational and Motivational Dimensions of Factionalism. *Party Politics* 11 (3):339–358.
Betto, Frei. 2007. *Calendário do Poder*. Rio de Janeiro: Rocco.
Bianchi, Alvaro, and Ruy Braga. 2005. Brazil: The Lula Government and Financial Globalization. *Social Forces* 83 (4):1745–1762.
Bittar, Jorge. 1992. *O modo petista de governar*. São Paulo: Fundação Perseu Abramo.

Bittar, Jorge. (Ed.). 2003. *Governos estaduais: Desafio e Avaços*. São Paulo: Fundação Perseu Abramo.
Block, Fred. 1977. The Ruling Class Does Not Rule: Notes on the Marxist Theory of the State. *Socialist Revolution* 33:6–28.
Bohn, Simone. 2011. Social Policy and Vote in Brazil: *Bolsa Família* and the Shifts in Lula's Electoral Base. *Latin American Research Review* 46 (1):54–79.
Boito, Armando. 1991. *O sindicalismo do estado no Brasil*. São Paulo: Hucitec.
Boito, Armando Jr. 2005. A burgesia no Governo Lula. *Crítica Marxista* 21:52–76.
Bond, Patrick. 2004. *Resurgent South African Civil Society: The Case of Johannesburg—and the Challenge of Globalisation (of People) and Deglobalisation (of Capital)*. Durban: Centre for Civil Society, pp. 1–32.
Branford, Sue. 2010. Lidando com governos: o MST e as administrações de Cardoso e Lula. In *Combatendo a Desigualdade Social: O MST e a Reforma Agrária no Brasil*, edited by M. Carter, pp. 409–432. São Paulo: Editora da UNESP.
Branford, Sue, and Bernardo Kucinski. 1995. *Brazil: Carnival of the Oppressed—Lula and the Brazilian Workers' Party*. Nottingham: Russel Press.
Bueno, Clovis. 1995. *A estrela partido ao meio: Antiguidades do pensamento petista*. São Paulo: Estrelinhas.
Burgos, Raúl. 1994. As peripécias de Gramsci: entre Gulliver e o Pequeno Polegar, PhD thesis. Instituto de Filosofia e Ciências Humanas, Universidade Estadual de Campinas, Campinas.
Caccia, Bava. 2005. Democracia e participação. In *Os sentidos da democracia e da participação*, edited by A. C. Teixeira. São Paulo: Instituto Polis.
Cameron, Maxwell. 2007. Latin America's Left Turns: Parties, Populism and Social Movements in the Post-Neoliberal Era. Paper presented at *Left Turns? Political Parties, Insurgent Movements, and Policy Alternatives in Latin America*. Peter Wall Institute for Advanced Studies, University of British Columbia, Vancouver, Canada, 27–25 May.
Camou, Antonio. 1993. Gobernabilidad y democracia en México. Avatares de una transición incierta. *Nueva Sociedad* 128:102–119.
———. 2000. La múltiple (in) gobernabilidad: elementos para un análisis conceptual. *Revista Mexicana de Sociología* 62 (4):159–199.
———. 2001. *Los desafíos de la gobernabilidad*. Mexico, D.F.: Plaza y Valdés.
Campello, Daniela. 2007. Do Markets Vote? A Systematic Analysis of Portfolio Investors Responses to National Elections. Paper presented at the LBJ School of Public Policy, University of Texas, Austin, 14 October.
———. 2008. Between Votes and Capital: Democracy and the Internationalization of Financial Markets in the Developing World, PhD thesis. Department of Political Science, University of California, Los Angeles.
———. 2012. What Is Left of the Brazilian Left? Paper presented at the workshop *The PT from Lula to Dilma: Explaining Change in the Brazilian Workers' Party*. Mansfield College, Oxford, 27 January.
Campello, Daniela, and Cesar Zucco. 2008. A esquerda em um país democrático, globalizado e desigual: Uma analise do Brasil de Lula, http://fas-polisci.rutgers.edu/zucco/, accessed 09/09/11.
Cardoso, Fernando Henrique. 2006. *The Accidental President of Brazil*. New York: PublicAffairs.
Cardoso, Ruth. 1992. Popular Movements in the Context of the Consolidation of Democracy in Brazil. In *The Making of Social Movements in Latin America: Identity, Strategy and Democracy*, edited by A. Escobar and S. Alvarez, pp. 291–302. Oxford: Westview Press.
Carneiro, Arnaldo, and Oswaldo Braga. 2009. *Atlas of Pressures and Threats to Indigenous Lands in the Brazilian Amazon*. São Paulo: Socioenvironmental Institute.

Carneiro, Gustavo. 2006. Uma concessão ao passado: Trajetórias da união dos movimentos de moradia de São Paulo, Master's thesis. Departamento de Sociologia, Universidade de São Paulo, São Paulo.
Carter, Miguel. 2006. O Movimento dos Trabalhadores Rurais Sem-Terra (MST) e a Democracia No Brasil. *Agrária* 4:124–164.
———. 2010. The Landless Rural Workers' Movement and Democracy in Brazil. *Latin American Research Review* (Special Issue):186–217.
Carvalho, Georgina. 2006. Environmental Resistance and the Politics of Energy Development in the Brazilian Amazon. *Journal of Environment & Development* 15 (3):245–268.
Carvalho, Maria do Carmo. 1998. Participação social no Brasil hoje, pp. 27–41. In *Pólis Papers* 2, São Paulo: Instituto Polis.
Castañeda, Jorge. 2006. Latin America's Left Turn. *Foreign Affairs* 85 (3):28–43.
Castañeda, Jorge, and Morales, M. (Eds.). 2008. *Leftovers: Tales of the Latin American Left*, New York: Routledge.
Castro, Regis de. (Ed.). 1998. *Processo de governo no município e no estado: Uma análise a partir de São Paulo*. São Paulo: Edusp.
Cayrol, Roland, and Jérome Jaffré. 1980. Party Linkages in France: Socialist Leaders, Followers, and Voters, pp. 27–46. In *Political Parties and Linkage*, edited by Kay Lawson. New Haven, CT: Yale University Press.
Central Única dos Trabalhadores (CUT) '. 2011. Cronología de Lutas, http://www.cut.org.br/institucional/68/cronologia-de-lutas, accessed 19/09/11.
Chalmers, Douglas, Carlos Vilas and Katherine Hite. (Eds.). 1997. *The New Politics of Inequality in Latin America: Rethinking Participation and Representation*. Oxford: Oxford University Press.
Chávez, Daniel. 2004. Local Left Politics in a Democratising Region. In *The Left in the City: Participatory Local Governments in Latin America*, edited by D. Chávez and B. Goldfrank, pp. 7–24. London: Latin America Bureau, Transnational Institute.
Cheibub, José Antonio, Argelina Figueiredo and Fernando Limongi. 2009. Political Parties and Governors as Determinants of Legislative Behavior in Brazil's Chamber of Deputies, 1988–2006. *Latin American Politics and Society* 51 (1):1–30.
Cleary, Matthew. 2006. A "left turn in Latin America"*"?: Explaining the Left's Resurgence. *Journal of Democracy* 17 (4):35–49.
Coelho, Vera Shattan, Ilza Araújo and Mariana Cifuentes. 2002. Deliberative fora and the democratisation of social policies in Brazil. *Institute of Development Studies Bulletin* 33 (2):1–16.
Cohen, Jean, and Andrew Arato. 1992. *Civil Society and Political Theory*. Cambridge, MA: MIT Press.
Coligação a Força do Povo. 2006. *Programa de Governo 2007–2010*: PT, PCdoB, PRB.
Coligação Lula Presidente. 2002a. *Programa de Governo 2002*: PT, PTB, PCdoB, PL.
———. 2002b. *Vida Digna no Campo: Desenvolvimento Rural, Política Agrícola, Agrária e de Segurança Alimentar: Programa de Governo 2002*: PT, PCdoB, PL, PMN, PCB.
Coligação Para o Brasil Seguir Mudando. 2010. *Os 13 compromissos programáticos de Dilma Rousseff para debate na sociedade brasileira*: PT, PMDB, PCdoB, PR, PDT, PRB, PSC, PCB, PTC, PTN.
Collier, Ruth, and David Collier. 1979. Inducements versus Constraints: Disaggregating "Corporatism". *American Political Science Review* 73 (4):967–986.
———. 1991. *Shaping the Political Arena: Critical Junctures, the Labor Movement, and Regime Dynamics in Latin America*. Princeton, NJ: Princeton University Press.

Collier, Ruth, and Samuel Handlin. (Eds.). 2009. *Reorganizing Popular Politics: Participation and the Interest Regime in Latin America*. University Park: Pennsylvania State University Press.
Compans, Rosemary. 1993. *Conselhos populares: Trajetória de um debate*, Master's thesis. Instituto de Pesquisa e Planejamento Urbano, Universidade Federal de Rio de Janeiro.
Coordenação dos Movimentos Sociais. 2006. Carta ao Povo Brasileiro. In *Leituras da Crise: Diálogos sobre o PT, a democracia e o socialismo*, edited by M. Chaui, L. Boff and J. P. Stédile. São Paulo: Editora Fundação Perseu Abramo.
Coppedge, Michael. 1994. Instituciones y Gobernabilidad democrática en América Latina. *Revista Síntesis* 22.
———. 2001. Instituciones y gobernabilidad democrática en América Latina. In *Los desafios de la gobernabilidad*, edited by A. Camou, pp. 211–240. Mexico, D.F.: Plaza y Valdés.
Córdova, Eduardo. 2011. Social Movements in Bolivia: Collective Action and Democracy in Times of Change (1990–2009). In *Challenges to Democratic Governance: Political and Institutional Reforms and Social Movements in the Andean Region*, edited by M. Tanaka and F. Jácome, pp. 147–182. Ottawa: Canada's International Development Research Centre.
Corrales, Javier, and Michael Penfold. 2011. *Dragon in the Tropics*. Washington, DC: Brookings Institution Press.
Couto, Cláudio. 1995. *O desafio de ser governo: O PT na prefeitura de São Paulo (1989–1992)*. São Paulo: Paz e Terra.
———. 2000. Desafios para um governo de esquerda. *Lutas Sociais* 5:169–173.
———. 2003. The Second Time Around: Marta Suplicy's PT Administration in São Paulo. In *Radicals in Power*, edited by G. Baiocchi, pp. 79–90. London: Zed Books.
———. 2009. La participación irrelevante: Una evaluación del gobierno de Lula. In *La nueva izquierda en América Latina: Derechos humanos, participación política y sociedad civil*, edited by C. Arnson and A. Armony, pp. 247–270. Washington, DC: Woodrow Wilson International Center for Scholars.
Couto, Cláudio, and Paulo Baia. 2006. Lula Administration: The Limits of Change. Paper presented at the *XXX International Congress of the Latin American Studies Association*. San Juan, Puerto Rico, 23–26 May.
Curzio, Leonardo. 1998. La gobernabilidad en el México contemporáneo. *Afers Internacionals* 40–41:187–215.
Da Silva, Lula. 1995. Como construir o futuro do PT. In *O PT e os Movimentos Sociais, Seminário 1995*, edited by Secretaria Nacional de Movimentos Populares, Agrária e Sindical, 118–122. São Paulo: Partido dos Trabalhadores.
Dagnino, Evelina. 2005. Meanings of Citizenship in Latin America. In *IDS Working Paper 258*. Brighton: Institute of Development Studies.
DaMatta, Roberto. 1991. *Carnivals, Rogues, and Heroes: An Interpretation of the Brazilian Dilemma*. Notre Dame, IN: University of Notre Dame Press.
Davies, Diane. 1997. New Social Movements, Old Party Structures: Discursive Organizational Transformations in Mexican and Brazilian Politics. In *Politics, Social Change and Economic Restructuring in Latin America*, edited by W. Smith and R. Korzeniewicz. Boulder, pp. 154–159. CO: North/South Centre Press.
Delgado, Nelson, and Flávio Limonic. 2004. Reflexões preliminares sobre espaços públicos de participação no governo Lula. In *MAPAS, Relatório do Projeto*. Rio de Janeiro: Instituto Brasileiro de Análises Sociais e Econômicas.
Demier, Felipe 2003. *As transformações do PT e os rumos da esquerda no Brasil*. Rio de Janeiro: Bom Texto.
Democracia Socialista. 2003. Resoluçoes, VII Conferencia Nacional da Democracia Socialista. Jornal Em Tempo.

Departamento Intersindical de Estatística e Estudos Sócio-Econômicos (DIEESE). 2007. Balanço das Greves em 2007. Departamento Sindical de Estatísticas e Estudos Socioeconômicos.

———. 2008. Balanço das Greves em 2008. Departamento Sindical de Estatísticas e Estudos Socioeconômicos.

Deschouwer, Kris. 2008. Comparing Newly Governing Parties. In *New Parties in Government: In Power for the First Time*, edited by K. Deschouwer, pp. 1–16. New York: Routledge.

Dirceu, José. 1999. Governos locais e regionais e a luta política nacional. In *Governo e cidadania: Balanços e reflexões sobre o modo petista de governar*, edited by I. Magalhães, L. Barreto and V. Trevas, pp.18–25. São Paulo: Editora Fundação Perseu Abramo.

Doctor, Mahrukh. 2007. Lula's Development Council: Neo-Corporatism and Policy Reform in Brazil. *Latin American Perspectives* 34 (6):131–148.

Doimo, Ana Maria. 1995. *A vez e a voz do popular: movimentos sociais e participação política no Brasil pós-70*. Rio de Janeiro: Relume-Dumará.

Downs, Anthony. 1965. *An Economic Theory of Democracy*. New York: Harper.

Druck, Graça. 2006. Os sindicatos, os movimentos sociais e o governo Lula: Cooptação e resistência. *Observatório Social de América Latina* VI (19):329–339.

Duarte, Patricia, and Regina Alvarez. 2010. A exuberância do setor financeiro: bancos quintuplicam seus ganhos na era Lula, http://outrapolitica.wordpress.com, accessed 22/09/11.

Dulci, Luiz. 2003. O PPA e a participação social no novo governo, estenographic version of the conference delivered by Luiz Dulci on 9/10/03, Presidencia da República, Brasília, http://www.planalto.gov.br/casacivil/foruns/, accessed 10/10/08.

Duverger, Maurice. 1959. *Political Parties: Their Organization and Activity in the Modern State*. London: Methuen & Co.

Edwards, Michael. 2004. *Civil Society*. Cambridge: Polity Press.

Ellner, Steve. 2008. *Rethinking Venezuelan Politics*. Boulder, CO: Lynne Reiner.

Elvander, N. 1972. Democracy and Large Organizations. In *Politics in the Post-Welfare State: Responses to the New Individualism*, edited by D. Hancock and G. Sjoberg. New York: Columbia University Press.

Escobar, Arturo, Evelina Dagnino and Sonia Alvarez. 1998. *Cultures of Politics and Politics of Cultures*. Boulder, CO: Westview Press.

Escobar, Merilyn. 2008. Sob o signo do "novo sindicalismo": das mudanças de identidade e de estratégia, na trajetória do PT e da CUT, à consolidação do populismo sindical no Governo Lula, Master's thesis. Ciências sociais, Pontifícia Universidade Catolica de São Paulo, São Paulo.

Euzeneia, Carlos. 2011. Movimentos Sociais: Revisitando a Participação e a Institucionalização. *Lua Nova* 84:353–364.

Fedozi, Luciano. 1997. Orçamento Participativo: reflexões sobre a experiência de Porto Alegre. Porto Alegre: Tomo Editorial.

———. 2000. Orçamento Participativo e esfera pública: Elementos para um debate conceitual. In *Por uma nova esfera pública: a experiência do orçamento participativo*, edited by N. Fisher and J. Moll. Petrópolis: Voces.

Feltran, Gabriel. 2007. Vinte anos depois: A construção democrática brasileira vista da periferia de São Paulo. *Lua Nova* 72:83–114.

Feres, Cláudia. 2002. Do conflito jurídico ao consenso democrático: uma versão da implementacão do OP-RS. In *A inovação democrática no Brasil*, edited by Z. Navarro and L. Avritzer, pp. 240–273. São Paulo: Cortez.

———. 2005. O Estado em Movimento: Complexidade Social e Participação Política no Rio Grande do Sul, PhD thesis. Faculdade de Filosofia e Ciências Humanas, Universidade Federal de Minas Gerais, Belo Horizonte.

———. 2010. Estado e organizações da sociedade civil no Brasil contemporâneo: construindo uma sinergia positiva. *Revista de Sociologia e Politica* 18 (36):187–204.
Fernandes, Florestan. 1989a. *Pensamento e ação: O PT e os rumos do socialismo*. São Paulo: Brasiliense.
———. 1989b. *O PT en movimento*. São Paulo: Cortez.
Fernandes, Sujatha. 2010. *Who Can Stop the Drums? Urban Social Movements in Chávez's Venezuela*. Durham, NC: Duke University Press.
Ferreira, Jacquelin. 2008. O Partido dos Trabalhadores e os Núcleos de Base, Master's thesis. Faculdade de Filosofia e Ciências, Universidade Estadual Paulista, Marília.
Figueira, Paulo Roberto. 2005. *O PT e o dilema da representacão política*. São Paulo: FGV Editora.
Figueiredo, Argelina, and Fernando Limongi. 2000. Presidential Power, Legislative Organization, and Party Behavior in Brazil. *Comparative Politics* 32 (2):151–170.
———. 2001. *Executivo e Legislativo na nova ordem constitucional*. Rio de Janeiro: Editora FGV.
Filgueiras, Luiz, and Reinaldo Gonçalves. 2007. *A economia política do Governo Lula*. São Paulo: Contraponto.
Filomena, César Luciano. 2006. O agonismo nas relações do partido, dos espaços públicos da sociedade civil e do sistema administrativo estatal: A experiência da administração popular em Porto Alegre, Master's thesis, Faculdade de Filosofia e Ciências Humanas, Pontifícia Universidade Católica do Rio Grande do Sul, Porto Alegre.
Fiorilo, Paulo. 2006. A relação entre executivo e legislativo no governo petista de Marta Suplicy: 2001–2004, Master's thesis. Ciências sociais, Pontificia Universidade Catolica de São Paulo, São Paulo.
Foweraker, Joe. 1990. Popular Movements and Political Change in Mexico. In *Popular Movements and Political Change in Mexico*, edited by J. Foweraker and A. Craig, pp. 3–22. London: Lynne Rienner.
Foweraker, Joe, Todd Landman and Neil Harvey. 2003. *Governing Latin America*. Cambridge: Polity Press.
Fox Piven, Frances. 1991. *Labor Parties in Postindustrial Societies*. Cambridge: Polity Press.
Frankland, Gene. 1995. Germany: The Rise, Fall and Recovery of Die Grünen. In *The Green Challenge: The Development of Green Parties in Europe*, edited by D. Richardson and C. Rootes, pp. 17–33. London: Routledge.
Freire, Alan. 2002. O PT e a Unidade Partidária como Problema. *Revista de Ciencias Sociais* 45 (1):39–76.
French, John. 2008. Understanding the Politics of Latin America's Plural Lefts (Chávez/Lula): Social Democracy, Populism and Convergence on the Path to a Post-Neoliberal World, Working Paper 355. Kellog Institute.
Friedman, Elisabeth, and Kathryn Hochstetler. 2002. Assesing the Third Transition in Latin American Democratization: Representational Regimes and Civil Society in Argentina and Brazil. *Comparative Politics* 35 (1):21–42.
Fung, Archon, and Erik Wright. 2003. *Deepening Democracy: Institutional Innovations in Empowered Participatory Governance*. London: Verso Press.
Galvão, Andréia. 2004. La CUT en la encruzijada: Impactos del neoliberalismo sobre el movimiento sindical combativo. *Revista Venezolana de Economía y Ciencias Sociales* 10 (1):219–239.
———. 2007. Syndicalisme et politique: la reconfiguration du mouvement syndical brésilien sous le gouvernement Lula. In *Congrès Marx International V—Section Sociologie*. Paris: Sorbonne et Nanterre.

García, Cyro. 2000. Partido dos Trabalhadores: Rompendo com a lógica da diferença, PhD thesis. Instituto de Ciências Humanas e Filosofia, Universidade Federal Fluminense, Niterói.
———. 2008. Partido dos Trabalhadores: Da ruptura da lógica da diferença á sustentação da ordem, Instituto de Ciências Humanas e Filosofia, Universidade Federal Fluminense, Niterói.
Garretón, Manuel Antonio. 1994. Redefinición de gobernabilidad y cambio político. *Síntesis: Revista Documental de Ciencias Sociales Iberoamericanas* 22:53–60.
Gaventa, John. 2006. Perspectives on Participation and Citizenship. In *Participatory Citizenship*, edited by R. Mohanty and R. Tandon. New Delhi: Sage Books.
Gaventa, John, and Gregory Barrett. 2010. So What Difference Does It Make? Mapping the Outcomes of Citizen Engagement, IDS Working Paper 347. Brighton: Institute of Development Studies.
Gaventa, John, and Rosemary McGee. (Eds.). 2010. *Citizen Action and National Policy Reform: Making Change Happen.* London: Zed Books.
Glaser, Daryl 1997. South Africa and the Limits of Civil Society. *Journal of Southern African Studies* 23 (1):5–25.
Gohn, Maria da Glória. 1991. *Movimentos sociais e lutas pela moradia.* São Paulo: Edições Loyola.
———. 1997. *Teorias dos movimentos sociais.* São Paulo: Edições Loyola.
———. 2000. Os Conselhos de Educação e a Reforma do Estado. In *Conselhos gestores de políticas públicas*, edited by M. Carmo and A. C. Teixeira. São Paulo: Polis.
Goldfrank, Benjamin. 2004. Conclusion: The End of Politics or a New Beginning for the Left? In *The Left in the City: Participatory Local Governments in Latin America*, edited by D. Chávez and B. Goldfrank, pp. 193–212. London: Latin America Bureau, Transnational Institute.
———. 2011. The Left and Participatory Democracy. In *The Resurgence of the Latin American Left*, edited by Steven Levitsky and Kenneth M. Roberts, pp. 162–183. Baltimore: Johns Hopkins University Press.
Goldfrank, Benjamin, and Aaron Schneider. 2003. Restraining the Revolution or Deepening Democracy? The Workers' Party in Rio Grande do Sul. In *Radicals in Power: The Workers' Party and Experiments in Urban Democracy in Brazil*, edited by G. Baiocchi, pp. 27–52. London: Zed Books.
Goldfrank, Benjamin, and Aaron Schneider. 2006. Competitive Institution Building: The PT and Participatory Budgeting in Rio Grande do Sul. *Latin American Politics & Society* 48 (3):1–31.
Goldfrank, Benjamin, and Brian Wampler. 2008. From Petista Way to Brazilian Way: How the PT Changes in the Road. *Revista Debates* 2 (2):245–271.
Gordillo, Gustavo, and Hernán Gómez. 2005. *Conversaciones sobre el Hambre: Brasil y el derecho a la alimentación.* México, D.F.: CEDRSSA.
Gramsci, Antonio. 1971. *Selections from the Prison Notebooks.* New York: International.
Grijó, Márcio. 2007. Taxa de Sucesso Legislativo do Executivo no Processo Bicameral: Comparando os Governos FHC e Lula (1995–2006). Paper presented at the *6° Encontro da Associação Brasileira de Ciencia Politica.* Universidade Estadual de Campinas, 29 July-1 August.
Grzybowski, Cândido. 2004. Cidadania Encurralada. In *Proyecto MAPAS, Relatório do Projeto.* Rio de Janeiro: Instituto Brasileiro de Análises Sociais e Econômicas.
Guidry, John. 2003. Not Just Another Labor Party: The Workers' Party and Democracy in Brazil. *Labor Studies Jornal* 28 (1):83–108.
Guimarães, Marcelo Fernandes. 2009. Políticas Públicas para a Agropecuária. In *47 Congresso Sober.* Porto Alegre.

Gunther, Richard, and Larry Diamond. 2001. Types and Functions of Parties. In *Political Parties and Democracy*, edited by L. Diamond and R. Gunther, pp. 3–39. Baltimore: Johns Hopkins University Press.

Gurgel, Elder. 2009. Teoria da separação dos poderes: A literatura atual da ciência política e sua aplicação aos níveis subnacionais de governo eis subnacionais de governo. In *O Sistema Político Brasileiro:Continuidade ou Reforma?*, edited by J. P. Saraiva and G. Dos Santos, pp. 93–122. Rondônia: Editora da Universidade Federal de Rondônia.

Hahn, Lígia Helena. 2002. Possibilidades e limites da democracia deliberativa: a experiencia do orçamento participativo de Porto Alegre, PhD thesis. Facultade de Filosofia e Ciencias Humanas, Universidade Estadual de Campinas, Campinas.

Hall, Michael. 2009. The Labour Policies of the Lula Government. In *Brazil under Lula*, edited by J. Love and W. Baer, pp. 151–165. New York: Palgrave Macmillan.

Handlin, Samuel, and Ruth Collier. 2011. The Diversity of Left Party Linkages and Competitive Advantages. In *The Resurgence of the Latin American Left*, edited by K. Roberts and S, pp. 139–161. Levitsky. Baltimore: John Hopkins University Press.

Harnecker, M. 1994. *O sonho era possível: A história do Partido dos Trabalhadores narrada por seus protagonistas*. São Paulo: Casa América Livre.

Harnecker, Marta. 2003. *Landless People: Building a Social Movement*. São Paulo: Expressão Popular.

Haugsgjerd, Elin. 2010. *Political Parties and Interest Groups in Norway*. Colchester: ECPR Monograph Series.

Hawkins, Kirk. 2010. *Venezuela's Chavismo and Populism in Comparative Perspective*. New York: Oxford University Press.

Heller, P. 2009. Democratic Deepening in India and South Africa. *Journal of Asian and African Studies* 44 (123):124–149.

Heller, Patrick. 2001. Moving the State: The Politics of Democratic Decentralization in Kerala, South Africa and Porto Alegre. *Politics & Society* 29:131–163.

———. 2003. Reclaiming Democratic Spaces: Civics and Politics in Posttransition Johannesburg. In *Emerging Johannesburg: Perspectives on the Postapartheid City*, edited by R. Tomilson, R. Beauregard and L. Bremner, pp. 155–184. New York: Routledge.

Hellinger, Daniel. 2005. When "No" Means "Yes to Revolution": Electoral Politics in Bolivarian Venezuela. *Latin American Perspectives* 32 (3):8–32.

Hernández, Esther. 2005. "Tensioning Democracy": Participatory Budgeting in the Global City of São Paulo, Department of Sociology, Brown University.

Hevia, Felipe. 2009. Mecanismos de Participación Ciudadana y Control Social en los Programas de Transferencia Condicionada de Renta en México y Brasil, un análisis comparado. *Revista Crítica de Ciencias Sociales y Jurídicas* 22 (2):383–392.

Hine, David. 1982. Factionalism in West European Parties: A Framework for Analysis. *West European Politics* 5 (1):36–53.

Hipsher, Patricia. 1998. Democratic Transitions as Protest Cycles: Social Movement Dynamics in Democratizing Latin America. In *The Social Movement Society: Contentious Politics for a New Century*, edited by D. Meyer and S. Tarrow, pp. 153–172. Oxford: Rowman & Littlefield.

Hochstetler, Kathryn. 1997. Democrazing Pressures from Below? Social Movements in New Brazilian Democracy. Paper presented at the *Latin American Studies Association XX International Congress*. Guadalajara, Mexico, 17–19 April.

———. 2004. Civil society in Lula's Brazil. Working Paper Number. CBS-57-04. Centre for Brazilian Studies. University of Oxford.

———. 2006. Rethinking Presidentialism: Challenges and Presidential Falls in South America. *Comparative Politics* 38 (4):401–418.

———. 2010. Organized Civil Society in Lula's Brazil. In *Democratic Brazil Revisited*, edited by P. Kingston and T. Power, pp. 33–56. Pittsburgh: University of Pittsburgh Press.

Hochstetler, Kathryn, and Elisabeth Friedman. 2008. Can Civil Society Organizations Solve the Crisis of Partisan Representation in Latin America? *Latin American Politics and Society* 50 (2):1–32.
Houtzager, Peter. 2000. Social Movements amidst Democratic Transitions: Lessons from the Brazilian Countryside. *Journal of Development Studies* 36 (5):59–88.
———. 2001. Collective Action and Political Authority: Rural Workers, Church and State in Brazil. *Theory and Society* 30:1–45.
———. 2008. The Silent Revolution in Anti-Poverty Programmes: Minimum Income Guarantees in Brazil. *Institute of Development Studies Bulletin* 38 (6):56–63.
Houtzager, Peter, and Monika Dowbor. 2010. Social Sector Reform from the Middle: Reformist Professionals in the Metropolis of São Paulo, Brazil (1990–2008). Paper presented at the *13th Basic Income Earth Network (BIEN) Congress*, São Paulo, 30 June–2 July.
Huber, Evelyne, Dietrich Rueschemayer and John Stephens. 1997. The Paradoxes of Contemporary Democracy: Formal, Participatory, and Social Dimensions. *Comparative Politics* 29 (3):323–342.
Hunter, Wendy. 2007. The Normalization of an Anomaly: The Workers' Party in Brazil. *World Politics* (59):440–75.
———. 2010. *The Transformation of the Workers' Party in Brazil (1989–2009)*. Cambridge: Cambridge University Press.
———. 2011. The PT in Power: Shifting Policies and Patterns of Political Support. In *The Resurgence of the Latin American Left*, edited by K. Roberts and S. Levitsky, pp. 306–324. Baltimore: John Hopkins University Press.
Hunter, Wendy, and Timohy Power. 2007. Rewarding Lula: Executive Power, Social Policy and the Brazilian Election of 2006. *Latin American Politics and Society* 49 (1):1–30.
Huntington, Samuel. 1968. *Political Order in Changing Societies* New Haven, CT: Yale University Press.
Huntington, Samuel, Michel Crozier and Jozi Watanuki. 1975. *The Crisis of Democracy: Report on the Governability of Democracies to the Trilateral Commission*. New York: New York University Press.
Instituto Brasileiro de Análises Sociais e Econômicas (IBASE). 2005. Projeto MAPAS. Rio de Janeiro: IBASE.
Ignazi, Piero, David Farrell and Andrea Romele. 2005. The Prevalence of Linkage by Reward in Contemporary Parties. In *Political Parties and Political Systems*, edited by P. Ignazi, D. Farrell and A. Romele, pp. 17–35. Westport, CT: Praeger.
Instituto Nacional de Colonização e Reforma Agrária (INCRA). 2004. II Plano Nacional de Reforma Agrária: Paz, Produção e Qualidade de Vida no Meio Rural. Ministério de Desenvolvimento Agrário.
Instituto Brasileiro de Geografía e Estatística (IBGE). 2010. Pesquisa Nacional de Amostra de Domicílio (PNAD), http://ibge.gov.br/home/presidencia/noticias/noticia_visualiza.php?id_noticia=1708&id_pagina=1, accessed 15/01/11.
Instituto Cidadania. 2001. *Projecto Fome Zero: Uma Proposta de Política de Segurança Alimentar para o Brasil*. São Paulo: Instituto Cidadania.
Inter-Redes. 2004. Direitos e Política. PPA e a Construção da Participação, www.inter-redes.org.br and www.abong.org.br, accessed 01/05/07.
Jácome, Francine. 2011. Social Movements, Democracy and Reforms in the Andean Region. In *Challenges to Democratic Governance: Political and Institutional Reforms and Social Movements in the Andean Region*, edited by M. Tanaka and F. Jácome, 311–330. Ottawa: Canada's International Development Research Centre.
Jiménez, Margarita. 2007. Desempeño de los presidentes latinoamericanos sin mayorías parlamentarias. *El Cotidiano* 22 (143):92–105.
Katz, Richard, and Peter Mair. 1993. The Evolution of Party Organizations in Europe: The Three Faces of Party Organization. *American Review of Politics* 14:593–617.

———. 1995. Changing Models of Party Organization and Party Democracy: The Emergence of the Cartel Party. *Party Politics* 1(1): 5–28.
Kaufman, Robert. 2011. The Political Left, the Export Boom, and the Populist Temptation. In *The Resurgence of the Latin American Left*, edited by S. Levitsky and K. Roberts, 93–116. Baltimore: Johns Hopkins University Press.
Keck, Margaret. 1992. *The Workers' Party and Democratization in Brazil*. New Haven, CT: Yale University Press.
Kirchheimer, Otto. 1966. The Transformation of the West European Democracy. In *Political Parties and Political Development*, edited by J. W. LaPalombra, Myron Weiner, pp. 177–200. Princeton, NJ: Princeton University Press.
Kitschelt, Herbert. 1989. *The Logics of Party Formation: Ecological Politics in Belgium and West Germany*. Ithaca, NY: Cornell University Press.
———. 1994. *The Transformation of European Social Democracy*. Cambridge: Cambridge University Press.
———. 2000. Linkages between Citizens and Politicians in Democratic Politics. *Comparative Political Studies* 333:845–878.
———. 2006. The Movement Party. In *Handbook of Party Politics*, edited by R. C. Katz and W. J. Crotty, pp. 278–290. London: Sage.
Kitschelt, Herbert, Zdenka Mansfeldova and Radoslav Markowski. 1999. *Post-Communist Party Systems, Competition, Representation, and Inter-Party Cooperation*. Cambridge: Cambridge University Press.
Klandermans, Bert, Marlen Roefs and Olivier Johan. 1998. A Movement Takes Office. In *The Social Movement Society: Contentious Politics for a New Century*, edited by D. Meyer and S. Tarrow, pp. 173–194. Oxford: Rowman & Littlefield.
Kohl, Benjamin. 2010. Bolivia under Morales: A Work in Progress. *Latin American Perspectives* 37 (107):107–122.
Kowarick, Lucio, and André Singer. 1997. La experiencia del Partido dos Trabalhadores en la Alcaldía de São Paulo. *Revista de Ciencias Sociales* 15:31–42.
Kriesi, Hanspeter, and Ruud Koopmans. 1995. *The Politics of New Social Movements in Western Europe: A Comparative Analysis*. Minneapolis: University of Minnesota Press.
Kubik, Jan. 1998. Institutionalization of Protest during Democratic Consolidation in Central Europe. In *The Social Movement Society: Contentious Politics for a New Century*, edited by D. Meyer and S. Tarrow, pp. 131–152. Oxford: Rowman & Littlefield.
Kupchan, Charles. 2011. Charting a Course for Brazil's Rise. In *Charting New Directions: Brazil's Role in a Multi-Polar World*, edited by A. Cabral, E. Jurado and P. Shankar, pp. 77–81. Berlin: Foresight.
Laclau, Ernesto, and Chantal Mouffe. 2001. *Hegemony and Socialist Strategy: Towards a Radical Democratic Politics*. London: Verso.
Larson, Brooke, Raúl Madrid, René Mayorga and Jessica Varat. 2008. Bolivia: Social Movements, Populism, and Democracy. In *Democratic Governance and the 'New Left'*, 2. Washington, DC: Woodrow Wilson International Center for Scholars.
Lavalle, Adrián, Arnab Acharya and Peter Houtzager. 2005. Beyond Comparative Anecdotalism: Lessons on Civil Society and Participation from São Paulo, Brazil. *World Development* 33 (6):951–964.
Lawson, Kay. 1980. *Political Parties and Linkage*. New Haven, CT: Yale University Press.
Lawson, Kay, and Peter Merkl. 1988. *When Parties Fail: Emerging Alternative Organizations*. Princeton, NJ: Princeton University Press.
Leach, Melissa, Ian Scoones and Brian Wynne. 2005. *Science and Citizens: Globalization and the Challenge of Engagement*. London: Zed Books.

Lehmann, David. 1990. *Democracy and Development in Latin America: Economics, Politics and Religion in the Post-War Period.* Oxford: Polity Press.
Leite, Clovis Henrique. 2008. Partilha de poder decisório em procesos participativos nacionais, Master's thesis. Instituto de Ciencia Politica, University of Brasília, Brasília.
Levitsky, Steven. 2001. Organization and Labor Based Party Adaptation: The Transformation of Argentian Peronism on Comparative Perspective. *World Politics* 54:27–56.
Leyendeker, Cristiane. 2004. A relação partido/sindicato: um estudo de caso, Master's thesis. Instituto de Ciência Política, Universidade Nacional de Brasília, Brasília.
Licio, Elaine, Lucio de O. Rennó and Henrique Carlos Castro. 2009. Bolsa Família e Voto na Eleição Presidencial de 2006: em busca do elo perdido. *Opinião Pública* 15 (1):31–54.
Lievesley, Geraldine. 2006. The Latin American Left: The Difficult Relationship between Electoral Ambition and Popular Empowerment. *Contemporary Politics* 11 (1):3–18.
Lima, José de. 2005. *O PT e a CUT no anos 90: Encontros e desencontros de duas trajetórias.* São Paulo: Fortium.
Limas, Fabrício Ricardo de, and Paolo Ricci. 2010. Instituições e decisões: estudo comparativo do processo legislativo nas Assambléias Estaduais. In *7 Encontro da Associação Brasileira de Ciencia Política.* Recife, Pernambuco, 4–7 August.
Limongi, Fernando, and Rafael Cortez. 2010. "As eleições de 2010 e o quadro partidário", *Novos Estudos Cebrap* 88: 21–37.
Lindblom, Charles. 1977. *Politics and Markets: The World's Political-Economic System.* New York: Basic Books.
Loaeza, Soledad. 2003. The National Action Party (PAN): From the Fringes of the Political System to the Heart of Change. In *Christian Democracy in Latin America*, edited by S. Mainwaring and T. Scully, pp. 196–246. Stanford, CA: Stanford University Press.
Lopes, Valmir. 2000. Poder local e representação política: Estudo sobre os vereadores cumunitários e institucionais em Fortaleza. In *A produção da política em campanhas eleitoriais: eleiçoes municipais de 2000*, edited by R. Carvalho. Campinas: Pontes.
López Maya, Margarita, and Luis E. Lander. 2011. Participatory Democracy in Venezuela: Origins, Ideas, and Implementation. In *Venezuela's Bolivarian Democracy*, edited by D. Smilde and D. Hellinger, pp. 58–79. Durham, NC: Duke University Press.
Loualt, Frédéric 2011. Lula: Father of the Poor? http://www.booksandideas.net/IMG/pdf/20110411_Lula.pdf, accessed 11/02/12.
Luna, Juan Pablo. 2010. The Left Turns: Why They Happened and How They Compare. In *Latin America's Left Turns: Politics, Policies, and Trajectories of Change*, edited by M. A. Cameron and E. Hershberg, pp. 23–40. Boulder, CO: Lynne Rienner.
Luna, Juan Pablo, and Fernando Filgueira. 2009. The Left Turns as Multiple Paradigmatic Crises. *Third World Quarterly* 30 (2):371–395.
Macaulay, Fiona. 1996. "Governing for Everyone": The Workers' Party Administration in São Paulo, 1989–1992. *Bulletin of Latin American Research* 15 (2):211–229.
———. 2003. The Purple in the Rainbow: Gender Politics in the PT. In *Radicals in Power: The Workers' Party (PT) and Experiments with Urban Democracy in Brazil*, edited by G. Baiocchi, pp. 176–201. London Zed Books.
———. 2004. La política de género en el gobierno del PT. *Revista de Ciencias Sociales* 37:101–120.

Macaulay, Fiona, and Guy Burton. 2003. PT Never Again? Failure (and Success) in the PT's State Government in Espiritu Santo and the Federal District. In *Radicals in Power: The Workers´ Party and Experiments in Urban Democracy in Brazil*, edited by G. Baiocchi, pp. 131–154. London: Zed Books.

Madsen, Douglas, and Peter Snow. 1991. *The Charismatic Bond*. Cambridge, MA: Harvard University Press.

Magalhães, Luís Carlos. 2010. Política Econômica: Principais Indicadores, nota técnica. Brasília: Liderança do Partido dos Trabalhadores, Câmara dos Deputados.

Magalhães, Luís Carlos, and Carla de Araújo. 2010. Evolução do salário mínimo real no Governo Lula: principais considerações, nota técnica. Brasília: Liderança do Partido dos Trabalhadores, Câmara dos Deputados.

Magaloni, Beatriz, and Alejandro Moreno. 2003. Catching All Souls: The Partido Acción Nacional and the Politics of Religion in Mexico. In *Christian Democracy in Latin America*, edited by S. Mainwaring and T. Scully, pp. 247–274. Stanford, CA: Stanford University Press.

Maguire, Diarmuid. 1995. Opposition Movements and Opposition Parties: Equal Partners or Dependent Relations in the Struggle for Power and Reform? In *The Politics of Social Protest*, edited by C. Jenkins and B. Klandermans, pp. 99–112. London: University College London Press.

Mainwaring, Scott. 1995. *Building Democratic Institutions: Party Systems in Latin America*. Stanford, CA: Stanford University Press.

———. 1999. *Rethinking Party Systems in the Third Wave of Democratization*. Stanford, CA: Stanford University Press.

Mair, Peter. 2001. Searching for the Position of Political Actors. In *Estimating the Policy Position of Political Actors*, edited by M. Laver, pp. 10–30. New York: Routledge.

Marques, Carlos Alberto. 1993. PT: Dilemas da burocratização. *Novos Estudos CEBRAP* 35:217–237.

Marquetti, Adalmir. 2003. Participação e redistribuição: o orçamento participativo em Porto Alegre. In *A inovação democrática no Brasil: o Orçamento Participativo*, edited by L. Avritzer and Z. Navarro, pp. 129–156. São Paulo: Cortez.

Martínez, Juan, and Javier Santiso. 2003. Financial Markets and Politics: The Confidence Game in Latin American Emerging Economies. *International Political Science Review* 24 (3):363–395.

Martins, Leôncio. 1990. *CUT: os militantes e a ideologia*. Rio de Janeiro: Paz e Terra.

———. 1997. PT: A New Actor in Brazilian Politics. In *Political Culture, Social Movements and Democratic Transitions in South America in the XXth Century*, edited by F. Devoto and T. Di Tella, pp. 293–316. Milan: Fundazione Giangiacomo Feltrinelli Milano.

———. 2005. Parties, Ideology and Social Composition. *Revista Brasileira de Ciências Sociais* 17 (48): 31–47.

Mayorga, Fernando. 2011. Bolivia: The Hazardous Path of Political Reform. In *Challenges to Democratic Governance: Political and Institutional Reforms and Social Movements in the Andean Region*, edited by M. Tanaka and F. Jácome, pp. 11–38. Ottawa: Canada's International Development Research Centre.

Mayorga, Fernando, and Eduardo Córdova. 2007. Gobernabilidad y Gobernanza en América Latina. In *Working Paper Norte-Sur IP8*. Ginebra.

Mayorga, René Antonio. 2009. Sociedad civil y Estado bajo un populismo plebiscitario y autoritario. In *La Nueva Izquierda en América Latina: Derechos Humanos, Participación Política y Sociedad Civil*, edited by C. Arnson and A. Armony, pp. 106–114. Washington, DC: Woodrow Wilson International Center for Scholars.

McCoy, Jennifer. 2004. From Representative to Participatory Democracy? In *The Unraveling of Representative Democracy in Venezuela*, edited by J. McCoy and D. Myers, pp. 263–296. Baltimore: Johns Hopkins University Press.

Melo, Marcus, and Flavio Rezende. 2004. Decentralization and Governance in Brazil. In *Decentralization and Democratic Governance in Latin America*, edited by J. S. Tulchin and A. Selee, pp. 37–66. Washington, DC: Woodrow Wilson International Center for Scholars.
Melo, Wagner de. 2007. O PT, os movimentos sociais e a questão da participação: preocupações metodológicas no estudo das experiências de São Paulo e Porto Alegre, unpublished manuscript, http://www.geocities.ws/politicausp/instituicoes/grupos_interesse/ROMAO.pdf, accessed 10/09/10.
Mendes, Gabriel. 2004. De Frente Brasil Popular a Aliança Capital/Trabalho: as campanhas de Lula a Presidente de 89 a 2002, Master's thesis. Instituto Universitario de Pesquisas do Rio de Janeiro (IUPERJ), Rio de Janeiro.
Meneguello, Rachel. 1989. *PT: A formacão de um partido (1979–1982)*. São Paulo: Paz e Terra.
Merkl, Peter. 2005. Linkage, or What Else? The Place of Linkage Theory in the Study of Political Parties. In *Political Parties and Political Systems*, edited by A. Rommele, D. Farrell and P. Ignazi, 3–16. Westport, CT: Praeger.
Merkl, Peter, and Leonard Weinberg. (Eds.). 2003. *Right-Wing Extremism in the Beginning of a New Century*. London: Fran Cass.
Meszaros, George. 2010. O MST e o Estado de Direito no Brasil. In *Combatendo a Desigualdade Social: O MST e a Reforma Agrária no Brasil*, edited by M. Carter, pp. 433–470. Editora da UNESP.
Meyer, David. 2007. *The Politics of Protest: Social Movements in America*. New York: Oxford University Press.
Michels, Robert. 1998. *Political Parties—A Sociological Study of the Oligarchical Tendencies of Modern Democracy*. Piscataway, NJ: Transaction Publishers.
Middlebrook, Kevin. 1995. *The Paradox of Revolution: Labor, the State, and Authoritarianism in Mexico*. Baltimore: John Hopkins University Press.
Miguel, Luis Felipe. 2006. From Equality to Opportunity: Transformations in the Discourse of the Workers' Party in the 2002 Elections. *Latin American Perspectives* 33 (4):122–148.
Ministério de Desenvolvimento Agrario. 2008. Relatório de Ouviduria Agraria. Ouviduria Agraria.
Ministério de Desenvolvimento Social e Combate a Fome. 2005. Instrução Normativa no. 1 de mayo de 2005, www.mds.gov.br/arquivos/Instrucao . . . 09-2005_5 . . . /, accessed 04/08/09.
Ministério do Planejamento, Orçamento e Gestão. 2003. Plano Pluri Anual 2004–2007. Brasília: Secretaria de Planejamento e Investimentos Estratégicos.
Minkin, Lewis. 1991. *The Contentious Alliance: Trade Unions and the Labour Party*. Edinburgh: Edinburgh University Press.
Moraes, Lincoln. 2001. Estado e democracia no programa do PT e nos governos petistas. In *X Congresso Brasileiro de Sociologia*. Fortaleza, 3–6 September.
———. 2004. Crônica de um partido não anunciando: programa e governos do PT entre 1979–2000, Master's thesis. Instituto de Economia, Universidade Estadual de Campinas, Campinas.
Moraes, Marieta, and Alexandre Fortes. 2008. *Muitos Caminhos, Uma Estrela: Memórias de Militantes do PT*. São Paulo: Editora Fundação Perseu Abramo.
Moreira, Jõao. 2004. *Enatreatos—Lula a 30 dias do Poder*, documentary produced by Videofilmes.
Moroni, Jose Antonio. 2009. O direito a participação no Governo Lula, unpublished manuscript, http://www2.abong.org.br/final/download/3_moroni.pdf, accessed 17/06/09.
Motta, Sara. 2006. Utopias Re-Imagined: A Reply to Panizza. *Political Studies* 54:898–905.
Mouffe, Chantal. 1992. *Dimensions of Radical Democracy: Pluralism, Citizenship, Community*. London: Verso.

Mueller, Charles, and Bernardo Mueller. 2006. The Evolution of Agriculture and Land Reform in Brazil, 1960–2006. Conference in honour of Werner Baer, University of Illinois, 1–2 December.

Müller, Wolfang. 2007. Political Institutions and Linkage Strategies. In *Patrons, Clients and Policies: Patterns of Democratic Accountability and Political Competition*, edited by H. Kitschelt and S. Wilkinson, pp. 251–275. New York: Cambridge University Press.

National Constituent Assembly. 1988. Brazilian Constitution, with amendments current as of 1998, http://web.mit.edu/12.000/www/m2006/teams/willr3/const.htm, accessed 05/06/11.

Navarro, Zander. 1998. *Affirmative Democracy and Re-Distributive Development: The Case of Participatory Budgeting in Porto Alegre*. Cartagena: World Bank.

———. 2003. *Inovações democráticas no Brasil (o caso do Orçamento Participativo)*. Edited by L. Arvitzer and Z. Navarro. São Paulo: Cortez Editores.

———. 2005. Decentralization, Participation and Social Control of Public Resources: "Participatory Budgeting" in Porto Alegre (Brazil). In *Citizens in Charge: Managing Local Budgets in East Asia and Latina America*, edited by I. Licha, pp. 247–290. Washington, DC: Inter-American Development Bank.

———. 2006. "Mobilization without Emancipation": The Social Struggles of the Landless in Brazil. In *Another Production Is Possible: Beyond the Capitalist Canon*, edited by B. D. Sousa, pp. 146–178. London: Verso.

Nunes, Felipe. 2009. Governos de Coalizão e resultados de soma positiva en Minas Gerais e no Rio Grande do Sul 1999–2006, Master's thesis. Facultade de Filosofia e Ciencias Humanas, Universidade Federal de Minas Gerais, Belo Horizonte.

Nunes, Paulo Giovani. 2004. O Partido dos Trabalhadores e a Política na Paraíba: Construção e Trajetória do Partido no Estado (1980/2000), PhD thesis. Centro de Filosofia e Ciências Humanas, Universidade Federal de Pernambuco.

Nylen, William. 1995. The Workers' Party in Rural Brazil. *NACLA Report on the Americas* 24 (1):27–32.

———. 1997a. Popular Participation in Brazil's Workers' Party: Democratizing Democracy in Municipal Politics. *The Political Chronicle, the Journal of the Florida Political Science Association* 8:1–9.

———. 1997b. Contributions of the Workers' Party (PT) to the Consolidation of Democracy in Brazil. Paper presented at Latin American Studies Association Conference, Guadalajara, Mexico, 17–19 April.

———. 2000. The Making of a Loyal Opposition: The Workers' Party (PT) and the Consolidation of Democracy in Brazil. In *Democratic Brazil: Actors, Institutions, and Processes*, edited by P. Kingstone and T. Power, pp. 126–143. Pittsburgh: University of Pittsburgh Press.

———. 2003. *Participatory Democracy versus Elitist Democracy: Lessons from Brazil*. New York: Palgrave Macmillan.

Offe, Claus. 1984. *Contradictions of the Welfare State*. London: John Keane.

———. 1990. "Ingobernabilidad". Sobre el renacimiento de teorías conservadoras de la crisis. In *Política: Teoría y métodos*, edited by E. Torres-Rivas, pp. 15–37. San José: EDUCA-FLACSO.

Oliveira, Daniela. 2004. A experiência do Orçamento Participativo no Rio Grande do Sul (1999/2002), Cidade, Centro de Assessoria e Estudos Urbanos, Porto Alegre.

Oliveira, Francisco de. 2006a. O Momento Lenin. *Novos Estudos* 75 (4):23–47.

———. 2006b. Lula in the Labyrinth. *New Left Review* (42):5–22.

Oliveira, Uber de. 2008. Desempenho político-eleitoral do Partido dos Trabalhadores no Espíritu Santo, nas eleiçoes 1982–2002, Master's thesis. Centro de Ciências Humanas e Naturais, Universidade Federal do Espírito Santo, Espiritu Santo.

Olsen, Jonathan, Michael Koss and Dan Hough. 2010. *Left Parties in National Governments*. New York: Palgrave Macmillan.

Ondetti, Gabriel. 2006. Lula and Land Reform: How Much Progress? Paper presented at the Meeting of the Latin American Studies Association. San Juan, Puerto Rico, 23–26 May.

———. 2008. Up and down with the Agrarian Question: Issue-Attention and Land Reform in Contemporary Brazil. *Politics & Policy* 36 (3):510–541.

Onis, Juan de. 2008. Brazil's Big Moment: A South American Giant Wakes Up. *Foreign Affairs* 87 (6):110–122.

Osterman, Paul. 2002. *Gathering Power: The Future of Progressive Politics in America*. Boston: Beacon Press.

Ottman, Goetz. 2009. *Democracy in the Making: Municipal Reforms, Civil Society, and the Brazilian Workers' Party*. Hauppauge, NY: Nova Science.

Ozaí, Antonio. 1996. *Partido de massas e partido de quadros: a social-democracia e o PT*. São Paulo: CPV.

———. 1998. Os partidos, tendências e organizações marxistas no Brasil (1987–1994): permanências e descontinuidades, Master's thesis. Ciências Sociais, Pontifícia Universidade Católica de São Paulo.

Padgett, Stephen, and William Paterson. 1991. *History of Social Democracy in Postwar Europe*. London: Longman.

Palocci, Eduardo. 2007. *Sobre formigas e cigarras*. São Paulo: Objetiva.

Panebianco, Angelo. 1988. *Political Parties: Organization and Power*. Cambridge: Cambridge University Press.

Panizza, Francisco. 2004. "Brazil Needs to Change": Change as Iteration and Iteration of Change in Brazil's 2002 Presidential Election. *Bulletin of Latin American Research* 23 (4):465–482.

———. 2005. The Social Democratisation of the Latin American Left. *Revista Europea de Estudios Latinoamericanos y del Caribe* 79:95–103.

Partido dos Trabalhadores. 2004. *Resoluções de encontros e congressos & Programas de governo 1979–2002*, CD Rom. São Paulo: Diretório Nacional do PT: Editora Fundação Perseu Abramo.

———. 2007. 3o Congresso Nacional do PT: PT concepcão e funcionamento, http://www.fpabramo.org.br/uploads/Resolucoesdo3oCongressodoPT.pdf, accessed 10/09/11.

———.2011. Resolução Política do 4° Congresso Nacional do PT, www.pt.org.br/ . . . /resolucoes_do_4_congresso, accessed 10/10/12.

Partido dos Trabalhadores. 1995. *Caderno de Debates 3: A relação do PT com os movimentos sociais (segunda parte)*. Edited by Secretaria Nacional de Movimentos Populares, Agrária e Sindical, São Paulo: Partido dos Trabalhadores.

Paula, Jose Antonio de. 2005. *Adeus ao Desenvolvimento*. Belo Horizonte: Autentica.

Pereira, Carlos, Timothy Power and Eric Raile. 2011. Presidentialism, Coalitions and Accountability. In *Corruption and Democracy in Brazil: The Struggle for Accountability*, edited by T. Power and M. Taylor, pp. 31–55. Notre Dame, IN: University of Notre Dame Press.

Perondi, Eduardo. 2010. Conciliação e precarização: A política trabalhista do governo Lula (2003–2010), Bachelor's dissertation. Centro de Filosofia e Ciências Humanas, Universidade Federal de Santa Catarina, Florianópolis.

Petit, Pedro. 1992. Primer Congreso del PT. Alianzas, hegemonías y divergencias. *Nueva Sociedad* 121:68–77.

Pinto, Céli. 2004. Espaços deliberativos e a questão da representação. *Revista Brasileira de Ciencias Sociais* 19 (54):97–113.

Pires, Jõao Marcus. 2006. O orçamento participativo na cidade de São Paulo—confrontos e enfrentamentos no circuito do poder-, Master's thesis. Ciências sociais, Pontifícia Universidade Católica de São Paulo, São Paulo.

Pogrebinschi, Thamy. 2011. Democratic Policymaking in Brazil: Participation as Representation. Paper presented at Sixth General Conference of the European Consortium for Political Research, Reykjavik, 24–27 August.

Pogrebinschi, Thamy. (Ed.). 2010. Entre Representação e Participação: As conferências nacionais e o experimentalismo democrático brasileiro, Projeto Pensando o Direito. Ministério da Justiça, Brasil.
Poguntke, Thomas. 2001. From Nuclear Building States to Cabinet: The Career of the German Green Party. Keele European Parties Research Unit, School of Politics, International Relations and the Environment, Keele, Staffordshire.
———. 2002. Parties without Firm Social Roots? Party Organizational Linkage. Working Paper 13. Keele European Parties Research Unit, School of Politics, International Relations and the Environment, Keele, Staffordshire.
Poletto, Ivo 2005. *Brasil: Oportunidades Perdidas*. Rio de Janeiro: Garamond.
Power, Timothy. 2009. Optimism, Pessimism, and Coalitional Presidentialism: Debating the Institutional Design of Brazilian Democracy. *Bulletin of Latin American Research* 29 (1):18–33.
Prats, Joan. 2001. Gobernabilidad democrática para el desarrollo humano: Marco conceptual y analítico. *Revista Instituciones y Desarrollo* 10:103–148.
Presidência da República, Secretaria de Comunicação Social. 2010. Caderno Destaques: ações e programas do Governo Federal. Brasília: Secretaria de Comunicação Social do Governo Federal.
Presidência da República, Secretaria Geral. 2007. Elaboração do PPA-2008–2011: Particpação Social. Brasília: Secretaria Nacional de Articulação Social.
Presidência da República, Secretaria Geral. 2011. I Seminário Nacional de Participação Social. Brasília: Secretaria Nacional de Articulação Social.
Pretty, Jules. 1995. Participatory Learning for Sustainable Agriculture. *World Development* 23 (8):1247–1263.
Przeworski, Adam. 1980. Social Democracy as a Historical Phenomenon. *New Left Review* 122:27–58.
———. 1985. *Capitalism and Social Democracy*. Cambridge: Cambridge University Press.
Przeworski, Adam, and J. Sprague. 1986. *Paper Stones: A History of Electoral Socialism*. Chicago: University of Chicago Press.
Raile, Eric, Carlos Pereira and Timothy Power. 2010. The Executive Toolbox: Building Legislative Support in a Multiparty Presidential Regime. *Political Research Quarterly* XX (X):1–12.
Ramos, Denise. 2004. Democracia semidireta no Brasil pós-1988: a experiência do Orçamento Participativo, PhD thesis. Facultade de Direito, Universidade de São Paulo, São Paulo.
Reif, Karlheinz, Roland Caryrol and Oskar Niedermayer. 1980. Middle Level Elites and European Integration. *European Journal of Political Research* 8 (81):112–132.
Reiner, Radermacher, and Waldeli Melleiro. 2007. Mudanças no Cenário Sindical Brasileiro sob o Governo Lula. *Nueva Sociedad* (211):34–56.
Renno, Lúcio. 2009. Executive-Legislative Relations in Brazil: Is 2009 the First Year of the Rest of Our Lives? *Revista de Ciencia Política* 30 (2):213–230.
Ribeiro, Isabel. 1987. *Trabalho e política: As origens do Partido dos Trabalhadores*. Petrópolis: Voces.
Ribeiro, Pedro. 2003. O PT sob uma perspectiva sartoriana: de partido anti-sistema a legitimador do sistema. *Política & Sociedade* 3:45–70.
———. 2007. Las elecciones en Brasil: consolidación electoral del PT y reafirmación de la fuerza personal del presidente Lula. Paper presented at V Congreso del Consejo Europeo de Investigaciones Sociales de América Latina, Brussels, 11–14 April.
———. 2008. Dos sindicatos ao governo: a organização nacional do PT de 1980 a 2005, PhD thesis. Programa de pós-graduaçao em Ciencia Política, Centro de Educação e Ciências Humanas, Universidade Federal de São Carlos, São Paulo.

———. 2010. *Dos sindicatos ao governo: a organização nacional do PT de 1980 a 2005*. São Carlos: EdufSCar.
Ricci, Ruda. 2007a. *Plano Plurianual: sem participação no governo Lula*, www.ibase.org.br, accessed 10/10/08.
———. 2007b. Cojuntura Nacional e as Organizações Populares. *Espaço Académico* 75, http://www.espacoacademico.com.br/075/75ricci.htm, accessed 12/09/10.
———. 2008. A Crise do modelo burocrático de poder e o esquecimento dos compromissos com a gestão participativa: O governo Lula, www.cultiva.org.br, accessed 10/10/08.
Riethof, Marieke. 2002. *Responses of the Brazilian Labour Movement to Economic and Political Reforms*. Amsterdam: Rozenberg.
———. 2004. Changing Strategies of the Brazilian Labor Movement: From Opposition to Participation. *Latin American Perspectives* 31 (139):31–47.
Roberts, Kenneth. 1998. *Deepening Democracy? The Modern Left and Social Movements in Chile and Peru*. Stanford, CA: Stanford University Press.
———. 2002. Party-Society Linkages and Democratic Representation in Latin America. *Canadian Journal of Latin American and Caribbean Studies* 27 (53):9–34.
———. In progress. *Changing Course: Party Systems in Latin America's Neoliberal Era*, Cambridge: Cambridge University Press.
Rodrigues, Iram. 1994. Perspectivas do sindicalismo no Brasil: O caso da CUT. In *O Brasil no rastro da crise*, edited by E. Diniz and S. Leite, pp. 98–122. São Paulo: HUCITEC.
Rodrigues, José Roberto. 2006. Decentralization and Budget Management of Local Government in Brazil, http://www.federativo.bndes.gov.br/bf_bancos/estudos/e0001056.doc, accessed 11/06/11.
Roett, Riordan 2010. The Cautious Emergence of Brazil. In *Charting New Directions: Brazil's Role in a Multi-Polar World*, edited by A. Cabral, E. Jurado and P. Shankar, pp. 65–68. Berlin: Foresight.
Rohrshneider, Robert. 1994. How Iron Is the Iron Law of Oligarchy? *European Journal of Political Research* 25 (2):207–238.
Ros, César Augusto da. 2007. A política fundiária do governo Olívio Dutra no Rio Grande do Sul—Brasil (1999–2002): diretrizes, dinâmica política e resultados atingidos. *Revista de Estudios Rurales* 8 (15), http://redalyc.uaemex.mx/redalyc/pdf/845/84501501.pdf, accessed 10/11/08.
Rose, Richard. 1964. Parties, Factions and Tendencies in Britain. *Political Studies* XII (1):34–46.
Rozentino, Gelsom. 2007. O governo Lula, o Fórum Nacional do Trabalho e a reforma sindical. *Katál* 10:54–64.
Sader, Eder. 1998. *Quando novos personagens entraram em cena: experiências, falas e lutas dos trabalhadores da grande São Paulo (1970–1980)*. Rio de Janeiro: Paz e Terra.
Sader, Emir. 1986. *E agora PT?* São Paulo: Brasiliense.
———. 2005. Lula, PT e os movimentos sociais, www.outrobrasil.net, accessed 10/09/09.
Sader, Emir, and Ken Silverstein. 1991. *Without Fear of Being Happy: Lula, the Workers' Party and Brazil*. London: Verso.
Sainsbury, Diane. 1980. *Swedish Social Democratic Ideology and Electoral Politics (1944–1948): A Study of the Functions of Party Ideology*. Stockholm: Almqvist & Wiksell International.
Samuels, David. 2000. The Gubernatorial Coattails Effect: Federalism and Congressional Elections in Brazil. *Journal of Politics* 62 (1):240–253.
———. 2001. Money, Elections, and Democracy in Brazil. *Latin American Politics and Society* 42 (3):27–48.

———. 2004. From Socialism to Social Democracy: Party Organization and Transformation of the Workers' Party in Brazil. *Comparative Political Studies* 37 (9):999–1024.

———. 2008. Brazilian Democracy under Lula and the PT. In *Constructing Democratic Governance in Latin America* (3rd. edition), edited by J. Domínguez and M. Shifter. Baltimore: John Hopkins University Press.

Sanchez Uribarri, R. A. 2008. "Venezuela, Turning Further Left?" In *Leftovers: Tales of the Latin American Left*, edited by J. Castañeda and M. Morales, New York: Routledge.

Sänkiaho, Risto. 1984. Political Remobilization in Welfare States. In *Electoral Change in Advanced Industrial Democracies: Realignment or Dealignment?*, edited by R. Dalton, S. Flanagan and P. Allen, pp. 70–92. Princeton, NJ: Princeton University Press.

Santana, Janaína, and Lucas Rodrigues. 2009. Presidencialismo e multipartidarismo em Brasil e Chile: dois exemplos de governabilidade que contrariam as teses sobre a "combinação explosiva". Paper presented at XXIX Student Conference of the Institute of Latin American Studies Student Association, Austin, 5–7 February.

Santiso, Javier. 2004. *Wall Street and Emerging Democracies: Financial Markets and the Brazilian Presidential Elections*. Paris: American University of Paris.

———. 2006. *Latin America's Political Economy of the Possible: Beyond Good Revolutionaries and Free Marketeers*. Cambridge, MA: MIT Press.

Santos, Fabiano, ed. 2001. *O Poder Legislativo nos Estados: Diversidade e Convergência (2001)*. Rio de Janeiro: FGV Editora.

Santos, Fabiano, and Márcio Grijó. 2010. Political Institutions and Governability from FHC to Lula. In *Democratic Brazil Revisited*, edited by P. Kingstone and T. Power, pp. 57–80. Pittsburgh: University of Pittsburgh Press.

Santos, Luiz Alberto dos. 2007. Regulamentação das atividades de lobby e seu impacto sobre as relações entre políticos, burocratas e grupos de interesse no ciclo de políticas públicas: análise comparativa dos Estados Unidos e Brasil, PhD thesis. Instituto de Ciências Sociais, Centro de Pesquisa e Pós-Graduação sobre as Américas, Universidad Nacional de Brasília, Brasília.

Santos, Mario dos 1991. Gobernabilidad en la transición a la democracia en Argentina. *Revista Mexicana de Sociología* 53 (1):293–304.

Sartori, Giovanni. 1976. *Parties and Party Systems: A Framework for Analysis*. Cambridge: Cambridge University Press.

Sauer, Sergio. 2008. Rural Social Movements and Their Historical Contribution for Building Democracy in Brazil, http://www.tni.org, accessed 12/09/09.

Scherer, Ilse. 2007. Movimentos sociais no Brasil contemporâneo. *História: debates e tendências* 7 (1):9–21.

Schneider, Aaron, and Ben Goldfrank. 2002. Budgets and Ballots in Brazil: Participatory Budgeting from the City to the State. IDS Working Paper (149), Brighton: Institute of Development Studies.

Schönleitner, Günter. 2006. Between Liberal and Participatory Democracy: Tensions and Dilemmas of Leftist Politics in Brazil. *Journal of Latin American Studies* 38:35–63.

Schwartz, Mildred. 2005. Linkage Process in Party Networks. In *Political Parties and Political Systems: The Concept of Linkage Revisited*, edited by P. Ignazi, A. Romele and D. Farrell, pp. 37–56. Westport, CT: Praeger.

Selznick, Philip. 1966. *TVA and the Grass Roots: A Study in the Sociology of Formal Organization*. New York: Harper Torchbooks.

Shankland, Alexander. 2010. Speaking for the People: Representation and Health Policy in the Brazilian Amazon, Institute of Development Studies, PhD thesis. Institute of Development Studies, University of Sussex, Brighton.

Shankland, Alexander, and Andrea Cornwall. 2008. Realizing Health Rights in Brazil: The Micropolitics of Sustaining Health System Reform. In *Development Success: Statecraft in the South*, edited by A. Bebbington and W. McCourt, pp. 163–88. London: Palgrave Macmillan.
Silva, Marcelo, and Paulo Eduardo Marques. 2004. Democratização e Políticas Públicas de Desenvolvimento Rural. In *Políticas Públicas e Participação Social no Brasil Rural*, edited by S. Schneider and M. K. Silva. Porto Alegre: UFRGS.
Singer, André. 2000. *Esquerda e Direita no Eleitorado Brasileiro: A identificação nas Disputas Presidenciais de 1989 e 1994*. São Paulo: Edusp.
———. 2009. Raízes Sociáis e Ideológicas do Lulismo. *Novos Estudos* 85:83–102.
———. 2010. O lulismo e seu futuro. *Piauí* 49, http://revistapiaui.estadao.com.br/edicao-49/tribuna-livre-da-luta-de-classes/o-lulismo-e-seu-futuro, accessed 07/10/11.
Singer, Paul. 1996. *Um Governo de Esquerda para Todos: Luiza Erundina na Prefeitura de São Paulo (1989–1992)*. São Paulo: Editora Brasiliense.
Sinwell, Luke 2011. Is "Another World" Really Possible? Re-Examining Counter-Hegemonic Forces in Post-Apartheid South Africa. *Review of African Political Economy* 38 (127):61–76.
Sirianni, Carmen. 1983. Councils and Parliaments: The Problems of Dual Power and Democracy in Comparative Perspective. *Politics & Society* 12:83–122.
Skidmore, Thomas. 1989. Brazil's Slow Road to Democratization: 1974–1985. In *Democratizing Brazil: Problems of Transition and Consolidation*, edited by A. Stepan, pp. 5–42. Oxford: Oxford University Press.
Soares, Sergei, and Pedro Herculano. 2010. Os Impactos do Benefício do Programa Bolsa Família sobre a Desigualdade e a Pobreza. In *Bolsa Família 2003–2010: avanços e desafios, volume 2*, edited by J. Abrahão de Castro and L. Modesto, pp. 25–52. Brasília: Instituto de Pesquisa Econômica Aplicada.
Sousa, Boaventura de. 1998. Participatory Budgeting in Porto Alegre: Toward a Redistributive Democracy. *Politics & Society* 26 (4):461–510.
———. 2002. Orçamento Participativo em Porto Alegre: para uma democracia distributiva. In *Democratizar a Democracia*, edited by B. d. Santos. Rio de Janeiro: Civilização Brasileira.
Souza, Celina. 2005. Sistema brasileiro de governança local: inovações institucionais e sustentabilidade. In *Desenho Institucional e Participação Política: experiências no Brasil contemporâneo*, edited by C. Lubambo and D. Coelho, pp. 108–130. Petropolis: Voces.
———. 2009a. *A Elite Dirigente do Governo Lula*. Rio de Janeiro: Fundação Getulio Vargas.
———. 2009b. Os ministros da Nova República: Notas para entender a democratização do Poder Executivo. Paper presented at the *II Congresso de Gestão Pública*, Brasília, 6–7 May.
Souza, Ubiratan de. 2003. Projeto de resolucão para implantação do Orçamento participativo a nacional, unpublished manuscript.
Stepan, Alfred. 1989. *Democratic Brazil: Problems of Transition and Consolidation*. Oxford: Oxford University Press.
Stolowicz, Beatriz. 2004. The Latin American Left: Between Governability and Change. In *The Left in the City: Participatory Local Governments in Latin America*, edited by D. Chávez and B. Goldfrank, pp. 169–192. London: Latin America Bureau, Transnational Institute.
Suárez, Alejandro. 2002. Gobernabilidad: algunos enfoques, aproximaciones y debates actuales. Paper presented at the *VII Congreso Internacional del CLAD sobre Reforma del Estado y de la Administración Pública*. Lisboa, 8–11 October.
Tadeu, Benedito. 2002. *PT: a contemporaneidade possível: base social e projeto político (1980–1991)*. Porto Alegre: Editora da Universidade Federal do Rio Grande do Sul.

Takagi, Maya. 2006. A Implantação da Política de Segurança Alimentar e Nutricional no Brasil: seus limites e desafios, PhD thesis. Instituto de Economia, Universidade Estadual de Campinas, Campinas.
Tanaka, Martín, and Francine Jácome. 2011. *Challenges to Democratic Governance: Political and Institutional Reforms and Social Movements in the Andean Region*. Ottawa: Canada's International Development Research Centre.
Tavaloro, Sergio, and Lília Tavaloro. 2007. Accounting For Lula's Second-Term Electoral Victory: "Leftism" Without a Leftist Project? *Constelations* 14 (3):426–444.
Tavares, Laura, Emir Sader, Rafael Gentilli, and Cesar Benjamin. 2004. *Governo Lula: Decifrnado o Enigma*. São Paulo: Viramundo.
Taylor, Andrew. 1993. Trade unions and the politics of social democratic renewal. *West European Politics* 15 (1):133–155.
Teixeira, Ana Cláudia, ed. 2005. *Os sentidos da democracia e da participação*. Vol. 47. São Paulo: Polis.
Teixeira, Ana Cláudia, and Luciana Tatagiba. 2005. *Movimentos sociais: Os desafios da participação*. Vol. 25, *Acompanhamento e análise das politicas públicas da cidade de São Paulo* São Paulo: Instituto Polis/PUC-SP.
Teixeira, Margarida de Jesus. 2009. Bancada Ruralista: A representação do setor agropecuário na Câmara dos Deputados, monograph. Programa de Pós-Graduação do Centro de Formação, Treinamento e Aperfeiçoamento da Câmara dos Deputados, Brasília.
Tomassini, Luciano. 1993a. Estado y Gobernabilidad. In *La Reforma del Estado y las Políticas Públicas*. Santiago: Centro de Análisis de Políticas Públicas.
———. 1993b. Estado, gobernabilidad y desarrollo. Washington, DC: Banco Interamericano de Desarrollo.
Toni, Jackson de. 2006. A participação social no planejamento governamental: a experiência do governo Lula, Brasil. Paper presented at *XI Congreso Internacional del CLAD sobre la Reforma del Estado y la Administración Pública*, Guatemala, 7–10 November.
Tribunal de Contas da União. 2009. [Simplified version of the General Government Accounts of the Republic—Year 2009 Tax Burden], http://portal2.tcu.gov.br/portal/pls/portal/docs/2056554.pdf, accessed 29/03/12.
Valencia, Cristobal. 2005. Venezuela's Bolivarian Revolution: Who Are the Chavistas? *Latin American Perspectives* 32 (3):79–97.
Vergara-Camus, Leonardo. 2009. The Politics of the MST: Autonomous Rural Communities, the State, and Electoral Politics. *Latin American Perspectives* 36 (4):178–191.
Von Beyme, Klaus. 1985. *Political Parties in Western Democracies*. New York: St. Martin's Press.
Von Bülow, Marisa, and Antonio Lassance. 2012. Brasil después de lula: ¿más de lo mismo? *Revista de Ciencia Política* 32 (1): 49–64.
Wainwright, Hillary, and Sue Branford. 2005. In the Eye of the Storm: Left Wing Political Activists Discuss the Political Crisis in Brazil. Transnational Institute, http://www.tni.org/tnibook/eye-storm, accessed 15/10/10.
Wampler, Brian. 2004. Delegation, Authority, and Co-Optation: Brazil's Participatory Democracy. Paper presented at the Annual Meeting of the American Political Science Association, Chicago. 2–5 September.
———. 2007. *Participatory Budgeting in Brazil*. University Park: Pennsylvania State University Press.
Wampler, Brian, and Leonardo Avritzer. 2004. Participatory Publics: Civil Society and New Institutions. *Comparative Politics* 36 (3):291–312.
Whitaker, Narcisa. 2008. Os sem-teto do centro de São Paulo: um balanço dos anos 2001–2004, PhD thesis. Instituto de Filosofia e Ciências Humanas, Universidade Estadual de Campinas, Campinas.

Wiesner, Eduardo. 2008. Brazil: The Market Enhancing Role of Political Economy Factors. In *The Political Economy of Macroeconomic Policy Reform in Latin America: The Distributive and Institutional Context*, edited by E. Wiesner, pp. 120–135. Cheltenham: Edward Elgar.
Wilpert, Gregory. 2007. *Changing Venezuela by Taking Power*. New York: Verso.
Wilson, Frank. 1994. The Source of Party Change: The Social Democratic Parties of Britain, France, Germany and Spain. In *How Political Parties Work*, edited by K. Lawson. Westport, CT: Praeger.
Winn, Peter. 1986. *Weavers of Revolution*. Oxford: Oxford University Press.
World Bank. 2010. Lifting Families Out of Poverty in Brazil—*Bolsa Família* Program, http://web.worldbank.org, accessed 02/02/12.
Zariski, Raphael. 1960. Party Factions and Comparative Politics: Some Preliminary Observations. *Midwest Journal of Political Science* 4 (1):27–51.
Zucco, Cesar. 2006. A governabilidade num segundo governo lula. Paper presented at the *1o Encuentro de la Asociación de Ciencia Politica del Uruguay (AUCIP)*. Montevideo, 1–3 June.

Newspaper and Magazines

Carta Capital (2011), *Lula e sua herança*, Wanderley Guilherme dos Santos, 20 January.
Correio do Povo (1997), *Apuraçao confirma segundo turno*, 06 October.
Correio do Povo (1997), *Olívio eleito governador*, 27 October.
Correio do Povo (2000), *PT vence em Porto Alegre, Caxias e Pelotas e o PSDB ganha em Canoas*, 30 October.
Diario do Nordeste (2008), *Obras do PAC estão concentradas em três construtoras*, 27 June.
The Economist (2006), *Contentment and complacency: Lula is coasting towards a second term*, 08 August.
El Comercio (2012), *Indígenas piden suspender proyecto hidroeléctrico en Amazonía brasileña*, 08 February.
Exame.com (21/0710), *Copom reduz ritmo de alta dos juros*, Luiz Artur Nogueira, 21 July.
Folha de Sâo Paulo (1997), *Os números das eleiçoes no RS*, 27 October.
Folha de Sâo Paulo (2000), *Professores encerram greve de 32 dias no Rio Grande do Sul*, 04 April.
Folha de Sâo Paulo (2003), *Discurso de Lula no Congresso Nacional*, 01 January.
Folha de Sâo Paulo (2003), *PT usa reforma tributária como "âncora social"*, 03 March.
Folha de Sâo Paulo (2003), *Lula anuncia aumento do salário mínimo para 240*, Wilson Silveira, 01 April.
Folha de Sâo Paulo (2003), *Veja texto de reforma tributária que Lula entrega ao Congresso*, 30 April.
Folha de Sâo Paulo (2003a), *Lula repete promessas ao MST, mas não obtém trégua*, 03 June.
Folha de Sâo Paulo (2003b), *Em congresso, CUT debate seu papel no governo Lula*, Claudia Rolli and Fatima Fernandes, 03 June.
Folha de Sâo Paulo (2003a), *Luiz Marinho é eleito presidente da CUT*, Sandra Balbi and Vinicius Albuquerque, 08 June.
Folha de Sâo Paulo (2003b), *Para sindicalista, central manterá independência em relação a Lula*, Claudia Rolli, 08 June.
Folha de Sâo Paulo (2003), *Protesto opõe direção da CUT e servidores*, Leila Suwwan, 11 June.
Folha de Sâo Paulo (2003), *Lula e a CUT*, 17 June.
Folha de Sâo Paulo (2003), *Manifestações de servidores expõem a divisão na CUT*, 27 June.
Folha de Sâo Paulo (2003), *CUT abandona trégua e ameaça greve*, Lilian Christofoletti, 18 July.
Folha de Sâo Paulo (2003a), *Lula cede, e Câmara aprova a reforma da Previdência*, Ranier Bragon and Julia Duailibi, 06 August.

230 Newspaper and Magazines

Folha de Sâo Paulo (2003b), *Reformas de Lula podem rachar a CUT*, Marta Salomon, 06 August.
Folha de Sâo Paulo (2004), *CUT "envelhece" e se aproxima do Estado*, 02 May.
Folha de Sâo Paulo (2005), *Eventual impeachment já é debatido*, Eliane Catanhede, 22 July.
Folha de Sâo Paulo (2005), *Núcleo lulista aprova apelo às massas, mas vê exageros*, Valdo Cruz, 07 August.
Folha de Sâo Paulo (2005), *Oposição não vê clima para impeachment*, Chico de Gois and Leila Suwwan, 16 August.
Folha de Sâo Paulo (2005), *Impeachment está longe do Planalto, afirma Lula*, Luciane Constantino, 17 August.
Folha de Sâo Paulo (2005), *5.000 fazem ato pró-Lula na Bahia*, 26 August.
Folha de Sâo Paulo (2005), *Oposição lidera ato em SP contra corrupção*, Flávia Marreiro, 07 September.
Folha de São Paulo (2005), *Ataque à política econômica une candidatos à presidência do PT*, Conrado Corsalette, 17 September.
Folha de Sâo Paulo (2005), *Bornhausen nega ter criticado esquerda*, Paulo Peixoto, 28 September.
Folha de Sâo Paulo (2005), *Palocci e Bastos articulam "missão de paz" junto a dirigentes do PSDB*, Kennedy Alencar, 03 November.
Folha de São Paulo (2005), *Lula apóia Dilma e rejeita nova elevação do superávit*, Kennedy Alencar, 20 November.
Folha de São Paulo (2006), *Sob Lula, emprego cresce, mas renda cai*, Claudia Roli and Fátima Rodrigues, 30 April.
Folha de São Paulo (2006), *Para empresários, adiar pacote é melhor que frustrar expectativas*, 21 December.
Folha de São Paulo (2007), *Lula critica ambientalistas ao defender construção de usinas hidrelétricas*, 04 May.
Folha de Sâo Paulo (2008), *PT quer tributar fortunas acima de R$ 10,98 milhões*, Juliana Rocha, 03 April.
Folha de São Paulo (2009), *Repasse federal ao MST cai 25% por ano desde 2004*, 27 February.
Folha de São Paulo (2009), *MST multiplica entidades para não perder repasses federais*, 29 March.
Folha de São Paulo (2009), *Câmara adia voto em lista fechada para 2011 e tenta aprovar pontos consensuais da reforma*, 26 May.
Folha de São Paulo (2009), *Para Lula*, empresários *decepcionaram na crise*, Kennedy Alencar, 22 October.
Folha de São Paulo (2011), *Senado libera gastos da União após Dilma prometer emendas*, 21 December.
Jornal do Brasil (2009), *MST vai às ruas para garantir novos índices*, 20 October.
Jornal do Senado (2010), *Congresso inicia discussão sobre Orçamento*, 04 October.
Milenio Diario (2002), *Lula, ganador antes de serlo*, Hernán Gómez, 10 October.
O Estado de Sâo Paulo (2003), *Íntegra do discurso de Lula no Congresso da CUT*, 04 June.
O Estado de São Paulo (2009), *PT controla repasses da Petrobras para ONGs*, 31 May.
O Estado de São Paulo (2010a), *Empreiteiras com obras irregulares do PAC deram R$70,5 milhões ao PT*, 13 November.
O Estado de São Paulo (2010b), *Camargo Corrêa foi a que mais colaborou a partidos e candidatos, com R$50 milhões*, 13 November.
O Estado de São Paulo (2012), *Maioria do STF condena Dirceu por corrupção*, 10 October.
O Globo (2010), *Governo Lula desapropriou apenas 8% das terras destinadas à reforma agrária*, Evandro Éboli, 5 July.

Peripecias (2006), *Lula da Silva ataca a movimientos sociales y queda al desnudo*, 29 November.
Veja (2005), *"Fomos incompetentes": O futuro presidente do PSDB diz que "despreparo" dos tucanos fez com que denúncias graves contra o governo passassem em branco*, interview with Tasso Jereissati, Thaís Oyama, 16 November.
Veja (2006), *Por dentro do cofre do MST*, 02 September, edition 2128.
Veja (2009), *Revelações de Lula (final): "O Congresso é um balcão de negócios"*, Augusto Nunes, 13 May.

Appendix 1
Statistical Information on Interviewees

Party in public office						
Executive branch	National			Sub-national		
	Ministers	Secretaries and deputy ministers	Presidential advisors	Mayors	Secretaries	Others
	10*	18	13	7	27	13
Legislative branch	Congressional representatives		Parliamentary advisors	Members of state congress	City councillors	Advisors
	15		7	8	13	4

Party in central office			
National		Sub-national	
Executive Commission	Party presidents (including interims)	Executive Commission	Party presidents
12	6	10	6

Factions or intra-party groups				
Left Articulation (AE)	Message to the Party (MP)	Building a new Brazil (CNB)	Other factions	Independents
11	23	48	13	23

Civil society organisations**				
CUT	CONTAG	MST	Housing movement	Others
10	5	8	7	4

(*Continued*)

Non PT members	19
Civil servants with no party affiliation but identified or close to the PT	2
Civil servants with no party identification	4
Technocrats close to the PT with no party affiliation	2
Parliamentary advisors with no party affiliation	4
Members of sectoral policy councils	4
Former President of the Republic (Fernando H. Cardoso)	1

Constituency	
São Paulo	55
Rio Grande do Sul	33
Minas Gerais	5
Others	47

* Includes two names who occupied different ministerial positions each, Ricardo Berzoini and Tarso Genro.
** Refers only to active members of these organisations at the time of interviews.

Appendix 2
Biographies of Interviewees

Agustín, Arno—*Brasília, 20/10/10*. Secretary to the Treasury during the second Lula administration. Formerly Finance Secretary in Porto Alegre and Rio Grande do Sul; member of the faction *Democracia Socialista* (Socialist Democracy).

Almeida, Alfonso—*Brasília, 03/04/09* (nonrecorded interview). Secretary for Strategic Investments in the Ministry of Planning. A civil servant.

Almeida, Gerson—*Brasília, 03/04/09*. Secretary for Social Articulation at the General Secretariat of the Presidency. Was Home Affairs Secretary in Rio Grande do Sul and Secretary for the Environment.

Alves, Antonio—*Brasília, 03/12/08*. Secretary for Strategic and Participatory Management at the Ministry of Health. Was a union leader in the health sector.

Américo, José—*São Paulo, 11/11/08*. President of the PT in São Paulo. Responsible for Food Supplies and Communications in the Suplicy administration (2000–2004). One of the principal figures of *Novo Rumo* (New Direction).

Ananias, Patrus—*Brasília, 16/07/09*. Minister for Social Development and Hunger Eradication (2004–2010). Has strong links to the Catholic Church. He started his career as a lawyer, advocating for trade unions and popular movements. Was Mayor of Belo Horizonte (1993–1996).

Ant, Clara—*Brasília, 26/11/08 and 03/12/08*. Deputy Chief of Staff to the President. Part of Lula's inner circle for over three decades. Former unionist who started her political activity in the Trotskyist movement *Liberdade e Luta* (Freedom and Struggle).

Appy, Bernardo—*Brasília, 08/04/09*. Deputy Minister of Finance during the first Lula administration. He presents himself as a nonactive *petista* and a "technician".

Appendix 2

Árabe, Carlos Henrique—*São Paulo, 30/10/08*. Has occupied various executive positions within the party, but has never been elected to public office. Belongs to the faction Socialist Democracy.

Aranha, Adriana—*Brasília, 07/07/09*. Chief of Staff to the Minister for Social Development (2004–2010). A social worker who started her activism in the Catholic Church and worked on food security issues under the Patrus Ananias administration of Belo Horizonte.

Arbix, Glauco—*São Paulo, 06/11/08*. An economist who advised Lula's campaign committee in 2001. President of the Institute for Applied Economic Research (IPEA), a public research institution, during the first term.

Arruda Sampãio, Plinio de—*São Paulo, 11/12/08*. Former member of the PT Left, abandoned the party in 2006. Was largely involved in rural issues and has strong ties to the MST, many rural movements and the progressive Church.

Avritzer, Leonardo—*Rio de Janeiro 13/06/09*. A scholar who has written extensively on participatory government institutions and Brazilian civil society, former PT member.

Baccarin, Giacomo—*Interviewed by e-mail, 11/8/09*. Deputy Minister for Food Security and Hunger Eradication at the Ministry for Social Development (2003–2004) and Secretary for Food Security (2004–2005). Was Mayor of Jabotical in São Paulo, and Congressman in the São Paulo State Assembly.

Barbosa, Benedito (Dito)—*Brasília, 02/12/08*. Member of the Coordination for the National Movement for Popular Housing (UNMP). Active in the housing movement for 30 years. Has always considered himself a PT member despite lacking formal membership.

Barbosa, Guilherme—*Porto Alegre, 15/12/08*. City Councillor in Porto Alegre. Was Secretary for Sanitation and Drainage during the Dutra administration; belongs to Left Articulation.

Barbosa, Nelson—*Brasília, 20/07/09*. Secretary for Economic Policy at the Ministry of Finance during the second Lula administration. Contributed to the drafting of Lula's economic program in 2002. Claims to be "a supporter, but not a PT member".

Belchior, Miriam—*Brasília, 06/07/09*. Lula's special advisor, responsible for monitoring the Growth Acceleration Program (PAC). Very influential over strategic programmes. Worked in several positions for the government of Santo André, São Paulo, during the 1990s.

Bemerguy, Esther—*Brasília, 20/07/09*. Secretary to the Economic and Social Development Council (CDES). Occupied several positions in the municipality of Belém in the late 1980s and 1990s.

Benevides, Maria Vitoria—*São Paulo, 29/10/09*. Party intellectual, became increasingly critical of the PT after the *mensalão* scandal in 2005. Supports the group "Message to the Party".

Bertoto, Luiz Carlos—*Brasília, 01/12/08*. Worked for the National Secretariat of Transport at the Ministry of Cities. Former head of the Transport Enterprise Company in Porto Alegre and Municipal Secretary of Transport.

Berzoini, Ricardo—*São Paulo, 29/10/08*. President of the PT (2007–2010). Was twice a Minister, first for Social Security (2003), then for Labour (2004–2007). Started his political career as a union leader in the banking sector. Three times a member of Congress.

Beze, Zeke—*Brasília, 03/07/09*. Advisor to the National Confederation of Agricultural Workers (CONTAG). Has no formal affiliation to the PT, but has been close to the party since its formation.

Bittencourt, Gilson—*Brasília, 20/10/10*. Secretary for Rural Policy at the Ministry of Finance. Was a PT member between 1986 and 2001. Served for the Cardoso administration as Secretary for Family Farming.

Bohn Gass, Elvino—*Porto Alegre, 19/12/08*. Representative in the State Assembly of Rio Grande do Sul. Former president of the Rural Workers' Trade Union in his home state. Has strong ties to rural organisations; member of the faction Socialist Democracy.

Bonduki, Nabil—*São Paulo, 08/12/08*. Former city councillor in São Paulo; responsible for the popular housing sector during the Erundina administration (1989–1992).

Borba, Adriana, and Cleia, Anice (Nicinha)—*Brasília, 03/04/08 (interviewed together)*. Advisors to the National Confederation of Agricultural Workers (CONTAG). They lack formal party affiliation but define themselves as "PT activists".

Camilo, Jorge—*João Pessoa, 16/11/10*. City Councillor in the northeastern state of Paraiba. Initiated his career as a lawyer, on behalf of CUT and other organisations.

Campos, Anderson—*São Paulo, 16/12/09*. Advisor of CUT. Former leader of the National Students' Union (UNE), joined the PT in 1998; member of the faction Socialist Democracy.

Campos, Edson—*Brasília, 03/07/09*. Advisor to the National Confederation of Agricultural Workers (CONTAG). Former trade union member with ties to the banking sector; PT member since the party's foundation.

Capp, Mario—*Brasília, 20/10/10*. PT parliamentary advisor on budgetary issues, but with no party affiliation.

Cardoso, Fernando Henrique—*Ithaca, NY, 07/04/10*. President of Brazil (1995–1998/1999–2002).

Cardozo, José Eduardo Martins—*Brasília, 04/12/08*. PT General-Secretary (2007–2010) and National Congress Representative. Was Home Affairs Secretary during the Erundina administration (1989–1992). One of the main leaders of the faction *Mensagem ao Partido* (Message to the Party).

Carneiro, Ricardo—*Campinas, 14/04/09*. PT economist between 1989 and 2001. Distanced himself from the party during the 2001 presidential campaign.

Carvalho, Gilberto—*Brasília, 10/04/09*. Lula's Chief of Staff. Was Home Affairs Secretary in Santo André (São Paulo); has strong links to the progressive Church and organisations in the PT field.

Cassel, Guilherme—*Brasília, 04/12/08*. Minister of Rural Development (2006–2010). Occupied several positions in his home state, Rio Grande do Sul; belongs to the faction Socialist Democracy.

Celestino, José—*São Paulo, 16/12/09*. CUT's Secretary for Training. Represents the teachers' unions; supported João Felício against Luiz Marinho.

Cotta, Teresa—*Brasília, 02/07/09*. Civil servant with no party affiliation. Advised the *Bolsa Família* Programme at the Ministry for Social Development and witnessed internal debates over the Zero Hunger Programme management committees.

Cury, Betto—*Brasília, 02/12/08*. Under-Secretary for Social Articulation during Lula's fist term. Organised the *Plano Pluri Annual: "Um Brasil para Todos"* (Pluriannual Plan: "One Brazil for All") 2004–2007.

Daneris, Marcelo—*Porto Alegre, 15/12/08*. City councillor in Porto Alegre. Joined the PT in 1996.

Diniz Macedo, Elcione—*Brasília, 28/11/08*. Head of Institutional Development at the Ministry of Cities; Executive Coordinator of the Conference of Cities. Not a PT member.

Dirceu, José—*São Paulo, 07/01/09*. President of the PT five times (1995–2002), and Minister for the Civil House (2003–2005), a position similar to a prime minister being responsible for all domestic functions. The main political architect of the party's shift to a moderate, centre-left strategy. Started in a student movement and was later involved in a guerrilla organisation. Was exiled in Cuba, where he changed his face through plastic surgery, and came back to Brazil in the early 1970s with a different identity. Four times PT General-Secretary; three time federal deputy.

Donato, Antonio—*São Paulo, 12/11/08*. City councillor in São Paulo. Former manager of the city's local transport services in São Paulo and head of sub-municipalities during the Suplicy administration (2000–2004). Belongs to *Novo Rumo* (New Direction).

Dulci, Luiz—*Brasília, 10/12/08*. General Secretary of the Presidency (2003–2010). Was politically responsible for the relationship with civil society; the organisation of national conferences and sectoral policy councils. Former PT Vice President, General Secretary and Secretary for Organisation. Was Home Affairs Secretary in Bello Horizonte, Minas Gerais.

Dutra, Domingos—*Brasília, 02/04/09*. National Congressman and PT President in the northeastern state of Maranhão. Close to rural trade unions and landless movements. Coordinated the rural activities of the PT parliamentary group in the mid-1990s.

Erundina, Luiza—*São Paulo, 14/11/09*. First PT mayor in São Paulo (1989–1992). A social worker of humble origins, born in the northeastern state of Paraiba. Was active in popular movements during the 1980s. After being Mayor, she left the PT to join the Brazilian Socialist Party (PSB) in 1996; ran unsuccessfully for the São Paulo City Hall three more times.

Falcão, Rui—*São Paulo, 11/12/08*. Home Affairs Secretary during the Suplicy administration in São Paulo (2000–2004). Was President of the PT in the same city during the Erundina administration (1989–1992). Interim National PT President in 1994 and coordinator of Lula's second campaign. The main leader of *Novo Rumo* (New Direction), one of the most influential factions in São Paulo.

Felício, Jõao—*São Paulo, 28/10/08*. Twice President of CUT (2000–2003/2005–2006) and once General-Secretary (2003–2005). Led the São Paulo's main state education trade union. Was PT National Secretary for Trade Unions.

Fernandes de Oliveira, Donicete, and Abrão, Jose de—*São Paulo, 07/1/09 (interviewed together)*. Leaders of the National Union of Popular Housing (UNMP).

Fernandes, Francisco (Mineiro)—*Brasília, 01/04/09*. Parliamentary advisor on rural issues. Claims to be "both an MST and a PT member without any distinctions"; belongs to the faction Left Articulation.

Ferreira, Duvanir—*Brasília, 07/07/09*. Secretary for Human Resources in the Ministry of Planning. Was a trade union leader in the Health sector and a member of CUT until 2002.

Ferro, Fernando—*Brasília, 02/07/09*. National Congressman and Deputy Coordinator of the PT in the Lower Chamber. Belonged to Lula's faction, *Articulaçao*, but then joined the faction *Movimento PT* (PT Movement) in 1994.

Fier, Florisvaldo (Rosinha)—*Brasília, 03/12/08*. National Congress Representative. Has occupied various positions in the party bureaucracy in the southern state of Paraná. Belongs to the faction Socialist Democracy; close ties to the MST and other organisations.

Fiorilo, Paulo—*São Paulo, 12/11/08*. City councillor in São Paulo. Former Chief of Staff to Marta Suplicy (2000–2004) and PT president in the city (2005–2007). Belongs to the local faction *Novo Rumo* (New Direction).

Fisher, Nilton—*Porto Alegre, 15/12/08*. Former Secretary for Education in Porto Alegre. His political activism started within church-based organisations and urban social movements. Has distanced himself from the party.

Frateschi, Paulo—*São Paulo, 11/11/08*. PT Secretary for Organisation (2007–2010). Was three times president of the PT in the state of São Paulo. Former education union leader; his political career has mainly developed within the party bureaucracy.

García, Marco Aurélio—*Brasília, 10/04/09*. Lula's advisor on International Affairs and Deputy-President of the PT (2007–2010). One of the main party intellectuals within the moderate sector. Coordinated the drafting of Lula's government programmes in 1994 and 1998, and was the main campaign coordinator in 2006.

Genoino, José—*São Paulo, 08/12/08*. PT President (2002–2005). Former member of the Communist Party of Brazil (PCdoB) who was involved in the guerrilla movement of Araguaia and later imprisoned. National Congressman, reelected six times.

Genro, Tarso—*Brasília, 31/04/09*. Minister for Justice (2007–2010) and former Minister for Education (2004–2005). Mayor of Porto Alegre twice (1993–1997/ 2001–2002). Defeated in 2002 in his attempt to become governor of Rio Grande do Sul. Supports the group "Message to the Party". Interim PT President in 2005.

Gomes, Dorival—*São Paulo, 13/11/08*. Member of the housing movement in São Paulo. Works for Arselino Tatto; city councillor, since 1994; belongs to the faction PT for Mass and Struggle (PTLM).

Gonçalves, Edson, and Guareto, Renato—*Brasília, 02/12/08 (interviewed together)*. Members of the PT Transport Section.

Gonzales, Luiz (Gegê)—*São Paulo, 11/11/08*. Leader of the housing movement and Coordinator of the PT Housing and Urban Reform Section. Member of the PT National Directorate.

Hackbart, Rolf—*Brasília, 20/10/10*. President of the Institute for Colonisation and Land Reform (INCRA) during the two Lula administrations. He has maintained close relations with the MST and other rural organisations.

Heck, Selvino—*Brasília, 01/04/09*. Presidential advisor in charge of mobilising support for the Zero Hunger Programme. Started to participate in politics in church-based communities and helped to found the MST; was representative in the State Assembly of Rio Grande do Sul and party president in that state.

Henrique, Arthur—*São Paulo, 15/04/09*. President of CUT (2006–2012). Was elected after its former president, Luiz Marinho, was appointed Minister for Labour. Former CUT Secretary for Organisation (2003–2005). Union leader from the gas and electricity sectors.

Hipólito, Sonia—*Brasília, 03/04/09*. Parliamentary advisor. PT Secretary for Social Movements during the 1990s; member of the faction Left Articulation.

Kieji, Jean Uema—*Brasília, 21/10/10*. Advisor to the Presidential Office in charge of executive–legislative relationships.

Koutzii, Flavio—*Phone interview, 12/06/11*. Home Affairs Secretary in Rio Grande do Sul between (1999–2002); Representative in the State Assembly.

Lacerda, Guillermo—*Brasília, 22/07/09*. President of FUNCEF, a pension fund of the Caixa Economica Federal (one of the largest state banks in Brazil) (2003–2010). Former union leader in the banking sector and founder of CUT.

Leite, Carlos José—*Brasília, 20/10/10*. Parliamentary advisor to Cândido Vaccarezza; leader of the Lula government in the Lower House of the National Congress.

Lisboa, Antonio—*Brasília, 21/10/10*. Member of CUT's National Executive Committee. Lisboa coordinates CUT's national office in Brasília, where he liaises between the organisation and government institutions.

Lopes, Iriny—*Brasília, 03/12/08*. Three times federal deputy from Espiritu Santo. She is one of the leading figures in her faction, Left Articulation.

Lopes Feijóo, José—*São Paulo, 16/12/09*. CUT's Vice President (elected in 2009). He has also been its General-Secretary and President in the state of São Paulo. Feijóo is one of the most prominent leaders of the Metallurgic Workers' Trade Union in the ABC region (Lula's original political base of support).

Ludwig, Paulo—*Porto Alegre, 18/12/08*. Coordinator of the PT Section on Rural Issues in Porto Alegre, parliamentary advisor and a member of the faction Socialist Democracy.

Maciel, Paulo Sergio—*São Paulo, 06/11/09*. PT Secretary for Mobilisation in the city of São Paulo.

Magalhães, Inês—*Brasília, 07/07/09*. National Secretary for Popular Housing, Ministry of Cities (2003–2010). Magalhães was Secretary for Planning, Urban Development and Environment in the municipality of São Vicente (1995–1996). One of her first jobs was in the government of Luiza Erundina (1989–1992).

Magalhães, Luis Carlos—*Brasília, 20/10/10*. Parliamentary advisor to the PT in the Chamber of Deputies. A public servant with no party affiliation.

Marcon, Dionilso—*Porto Alegre, 15/12/08*. Twice local deputy in the state of Rio Grande do Sul, he was the party leader in Congress in 2002. He is an MST member who made his political career within the PT.

Martines, Evelaine—*Brasília, 07/07/09*. Member of the national coordination of the MST. She was a PT-affiliated member from 1988 to 1994, but maintained relations with the party until 2002.

Mauro, Gilmar—*São Paulo, 17/04/09*. Member of the National Coordination of the MST. He was politically active in the PT during the 1980s, but gradually distanced himself in the 1990s.

Menezes, Francisco—*Rio de Janeiro, 26/07/09*. President of the Food Security National Council during the first Lula administration; Head of the Brazilian Institute for Economic and Social Analysis (IBASE), a research-oriented NGO. Participated in the drafting of the Zero Hunger Programme.

Merss, Marinete—*Brasília, 10/12/08*. PT's Secretary for Social Mobilisation.

Mesquita, Camille—*Brasília, 02/07/09*. A civil servant with no party affiliation; worked for the Ministry for Social Development and Hunger Eradication where she was responsible for coordinating mechanisms of social oversight (*controle social*) of Bolsa Família.

Morães, Leandro—*São Paulo, 16/12/09*. CUT's advisor. Morães has participated in the PT since 1999; belongs to Left Articulation.

Morales, Carlos—*Brasília, 27/07/09*. Advisor to the Secretary of State Patrimony in the Ministry for Planning as well as Head of Urban Regulation during the first Lula term. At the local level, he was president twice of the public transport companies (Santo André, 1989–1999 and São Bernardo do Campo, 1991–1992).

Moreira, Crispim—*Brasília, 03/04/09*. Secretary for Food Security in the Ministry for Social Development. He worked for various municipal governments in the state of Minas Gerais.

Moroni, Jose Antonio—*Brasília, 07/10/09*. He is one of the top coordinators of the Brazilian Association of NGOs (ABONG), a national network of civil society organisations. Moroni left the PT in 1988 and has worked in civil society organisations ever since.

Moura, Senival—*São Paulo, 07/11/09*. City councillor in São Paulo. President of the Bus Cooperatives' Trade Union in São Paulo. He worked for the Suplicy administration (2000–2004) in the Department of Transport; belongs to one of the most influential factions in the city.

Nespolo, Claudir—*Brasília, 16/12/08*. Coordinator of the PT Section on Trade Unions in Porto Alegre; president of the Metallurgic Trade Union and member of CUT.

Netto, Orlando—*Brasília, 20/10/10*. Head of the Senate's Budget Office, a nonpartisan body that advises senators and provides information to the public on budgetary and financial issues.

Núñez, Tarson—*Porto Alegre, 18/12/08*. Parliamentary advisor. He was one of the architects of the participatory budget in Porto Alegre, where he coordinated the participatory planning cabinet.

Oliveira, Carlos Roberto de—*Brasília, 07/04/09*. Housing movement activist and member of the National Union for Popular Housing. He has been a PT member since the party's foundation.

Olivoni, Aldacir—*Porto Alegre, 18/12/08*. City councillor. Former union leader from the health sector, he joined the PT in 1996. He belongs to the faction Movimento PT.

Ortega, César—*Interviewed by e-mail, 17/11/09*. Former consultant to the Ministry for Food Security and Hunger Eradication; PT member until the mid-1980s.

Paes, Rómulo—*Brighton, 15/10/10* (nonrecorded interview). Deputy Minister for Social Development (2010). He was also Secretary for Evaluation and Information Management and Assistant Deputy Minister. He is a nonactive PT member.

Pedroso, Maria—*Brasília, 28/11/08*. Parliamentary advisor on rural issues.

Pereira, Athos—*Brasília, 04/04/09*. Coordinator of the PT group of parliamentary advisors in the Lower House.

Pereira, José Antonio—*Brasília, 18/10/10*. Advisor to the Secretary for Economic Policy in the Ministry of Finance. Public servant without party militancy.

Pereira, Solaney—*São Paulo, 19/11/08*. CUT's Secretary of Social Policy and a PT member. He belongs to the faction Left Articulation.

Pestana, Carlos—*Porto Alegre, 17/12/08*. PT General Secretary in the state of Rio Grande do Sul; belongs to the faction Socialist Democracy.

Piai, Glauco—*São Paulo, 05/11/08*. PT Secretary for Organisation in São Paulo. He started his political career within church-based organisations and was active in the health movement in Capela do Socorro (East of São Paulo). He belongs to the faction PT for Mass and Struggle (PTLM), which is very influential in São Paulo.

Pomar, Valter—*Brasília, 30/09/08 and 08/04/09*. PT Secretary for International Relations, the main leader of Left Articulation. Pomar has belonged to the PT National Directorate since 1997. In the 2007 internal elections, he launched his candidacy for president of the PT, but only managed to obtain 12 percent of the vote. He was Secretary for Culture, Sports and Leisure in Campinas (São Paulo).

Pont, Raúl—*Porto Alegre, 19/12/08*. Mayor of Porto Alegre (1997–2001). Has been a congressional representative at the local and national level. In 2005, he ran for the PT presidency. Pont is a founder of the faction Socialist Democracy and one of its main leaders.

Pontual, Pedro—*São Paulo, 17/10/08*. Member of the Polis Institute, an NGO which advocates social participation. He coordinated literacy programmes with Paulo Freire, when the latter was Secretary of Education in São Paulo (1989–1991) and was Secretary of Social Participation in Santo André (1997–2002). He belongs to the faction Socialist Democracy.

Pretto, Adão—*Brasília, 02/12/08*. Three times Representative at the National Congress. Preto is a member of both the MST and the PT.

Rabelo, Lourimar and Lopes, Flavia—*Brasília, 21/10/10 (interviewed together)*. Parliamentary advisors to the Leader of the Lula government in the Chamber of Deputies, Candido Vaccarezza. Not PT members.

Rangel, Alexandre—*Brasília, 08/04/09*. Young MST activist. Participated in the PT from 1994 to 2003 before leaving the party, disillusioned with the Lula administration. Worked for the government of Christovam Buarque in Brasília between 1996 and 1998.

Reske, Alexandra—*Brasília, 08/04/09*. Secretary for National Patrimony at the Ministry of Planning. Former Secretary for Housing in Santo André. A former Trotskyist who participated in church-based communities and supported housing movements.

Rezende, Conceição—*Brasília, 28/11/08*. Coordinator of the PT Health Section; parliamentary advisor; former Secretary for Health in the municipality of Betim (Minas Gerais). Was a union leader in the health sector.

Ribeiro, Miguel—*Brasília, 04/12/08*. Chief of Staff to the Secretary for National Patrimony at the Ministry of Planning.

Rodrigues, Evaniza—*São Paulo, 12/12/08*. Activist in the housing movement. Member of the executive committee of the National Union of Popular Housing (UNMP). Under-Secretary for Urban Policy during the first Lula administration.

Rodrigues, Julian—*São Paulo, 13/11/08*. Coordinator of the PT Sector on GLBT issues. He is a young member of Left Articulation who works for the PT executive office in São Paulo.

Rosetto, Miguel—*Rio de Janeiro, 24/06/09* (nonrecorded interview). Minister for Rural Development (2003–2006). Former Deputy Governor of Rio Grande do Sul (1998–2002). Was twice president of the Oil Industries' Trade Union (1986–1992) and occupied various executive positions in CUT, where he was active until the mid-1990s. Belongs to the faction Socialist Democracy.

Russo, Osvaldo—*Brasília, 01/12/08.* Coordinator of the PT Rural Section, parliamentary advisor, and Head of the Land Reform Brazilian Association (ABRA). Former president of INCRA with President Itamar Franco (1993—1994).

Santos, Clarice dos—*Brasília, 07/05/09.* Head of the National Educational Programme for Land Reform (PRONERA) at the National Institute for Colonisation and Land Reform (INCRA). Former Church activist, developed her political career simultaneously in the MST and the PT.

Santos, Manoel dos—*Brasília, 03/07/09.* President of the National Confederation of Agricultural Workers (1997–2009). Started his political activism in Catholic Rural Action; has belonged to the PT since its formation.

Schmidt, David—*Brasília, 03/12/09.* Advisor to the Social Articulation Secretariat in the Presidency. Was involved in the Participatory Budgeting process in Porto Alegre.

Sell, Adeli—*Porto Alegre, 15/12/08.* City councillor. Former Secretary for Production, Trade and Industry in Porto Alegre (2003–2004). First belonged to a Trotskyist faction, *O Trabalho* (The Work), until he entered *Articulaçao* (Articulation), Lula's faction, in 1983.

Selma, Rocha—*Brasília, 12/12/08.* Coordinator of the PT Section on Education, Member of the PT National Directorate and the Directorate of the party's foundation Perseu Abramo.

Severo, Quintino—*São Paulo, 15/12/09.* CUT's General Secretary (2006–2012). With a background in the metallurgic sector, he was president of CUT in the state of Rio Grande do Sul twice.

Silva, Francisco—*São Paulo, 05/11/08.* Secretary for Social Movements in the city of São Paulo. A member of the PTLM, one of the most important factions in the city.

Simões, Renato—*São Paulo, 04/11/08.* Secretary for Popular Movements (2007–2010) and three-time Representative in the State Assembly of São Paulo. Belongs to *Militância Socialista* (Socialist Activism), a small leftist faction.

Singer, André—*São Paulo, 16/04/09* (nonrecorded interview). Party intellectual, Professor of Political Science, University of São Paulo. Was part of the presidential campaign committee in 2001 and later spokesman of the Presidential office during Lula's first term. One of the main ideologues of the faction "Message to the Party".

Singer, Paul—*Brasília, 02/07/09*. Secretary for Fair Trade, with Lula (2003–2010). Former Secretary for Planning in São Paulo under the administration of Luiza Erundina (1989–1992); belongs to "Message to the Party" (MP).

Soriano, Joaquim—*São Paulo, 31/10/08*. Member of the PT National Directorate several times. Has been Party Treasurer, Secretary for Organisation, General Secretary and four times Secretary for Political Formation. He belongs to the faction Socialist Democracy.

Sousa, Ubiratan de—*Porto Alegre, 19/12/08*. Coordinated the Cabinet for the Participatory Budget, in Porto Alegre, during the administrations of Tarso Genro and Raul Pont (1993–1998). Later was secretary for Budget and Finance in Rio Grande do Sul and was in charge of scaling up PB at the state level. Belongs to the faction Socialist Democracy.

Souza, Maria Celeste—*Porto Alegre, 15/12/08*. City councillor in Porto Alegre; belongs to Democratic Left, a local faction.

Stédile, João Pedro—*São Paulo, 06/09/07*. The most visible figure of the MST and its main intellectual guide. Member of its National Directorate. Joined the PT during the party's foundation. He distanced himself from the party during Lula's first term in office, like many other MST members.

Stival, David—*Porto Alegre, 17/12/08*. President of the PT in Rio Grande do Sul (2001–2005). MST member who made his career within the PT. Participated in the first land occupations in the mid-1980s and soon afterwards started work as a PT parliamentary advisor. Belongs to Left Articulation.

Suplicy, Eduardo—*Brasília, 07/04/09*. One of the most respected parliamentarians in the PT. Was the party's first Senator, elected in 1990 and reelected three times. He claims to be a strong supporter of civil society organisations, including the MST.

Suplicy, Marta—*São Paulo, 09/01/09*. Mayor of São Paulo (2000–2004) and Minister for Tourism (2007–2008). A psychologist who was married to Eduardo Suplicy, a well-respected PT Senator. First gained public attention in a TV programme concerning sexual issues. Her political career started in 1994, when elected Representative at the National Congress. Although Suplicy claims to be independent, she draws most of her political support from the factions *Novo Rumo* (New Direction) and the *PT de Luta e de Massas* (PT Mass and Struggle).

Takagi, Maya—*Brasília, 06/07/09*. Advisor to the Presidency. Specialist on rural issues and food security; participated in the drafting of the Zero Hunger Programme at the Citizenship Institute. Later, she advised the Minister for Food Security (2003–2004).

Tatto, Arselino—*São Paulo, 12/11/08*. Five-time city councillor, he is one of nine brothers, all of them involved in politics. Arselino, Jilmar and Ênio, known as "the Tatto brothers", are the creators of PT Mass and Struggle (PTLM), a powerful intraparty group.

Teixeira, Gerson—*Brasília, 07/04/09*. Parliamentary advisor on rural issues. Worked for the PT Secretary for Rural Issues during the 2001 presidential campaign.

Teixeira, Paulo—*Brasília, 14/07/09*. National Congress Representative. Former Secretary for Housing and Urban Development during the Suplicy administration (2000–2004). Member of the PT National Directorate; supports the faction "Message to the Party".

Terribili, Alessandra—*São Paulo, 06/10/08*. Vice President of the PT in the city of São Paulo. Started her career in the National Students' Union (UNE) and entered the PT in 2001; belongs to the faction Socialist Democracy.

Todeschini, Atilio—*Porto Alegre, 16/12/08*. City councillor in Porto Alegre. Former Secretary for Sanitation and Drainage and Secretary for Public Policies in Porto Alegre.

Toni, Jackson de—*Brasília, 02/04/09*. Advisor to the Office of the Civil House of the Presidency. Has written on participatory mechanisms implemented during the Lula administration.

Vaccarezza, Cândido—*Brasília, 21/10/10*. National Congress Representative, Leader of the Lula government in the Lower House (2010). Former Secretary of Culture, Sports and Leisure in the municipality of Mauá São Paulo. Occupied several positions in the PT bureaucracy. Belonged to the public trade union sector.

Vargas, Pepe—*Brasília, 02/12/08*. National Congress Representative. Former legislator at municipal and state levels in Rio Grande do Sul; belongs to the faction Socialist Democracy.

Verlaine da Silva Pinto, Marcos and de Queiroz, Antonio Augusto—*Brasília, 18/10/10 (interviewed together)*. Members of the Departamento Intersindical de Asessoria Parlamentar (DIAPP), a think tank that promotes trade unions in Congress.

Vilela Nelsis, Luiz Felipe—*Brasília, 04/12/08*. Advisor and Chief of Staff to the Minister for Rural Development. Was PT's General Secretary in Porto Alegre and Secretary for Trade and Industry at the City Hall; a member of the faction Socialist Democracy.

Villaverde, Adão—*Porto Alegre, 19/12/08*. Congress Representative at the State Assembly of Rio Grande do Sul. Former Secretary for Planning under the state government of Olívio Dutra (1999–2002). Was president of the PT in his home state.

Welik, Walter—*Campinas, 14/04/09*. Specialist in Rural Economy, University of Campinas. Participated in the drafting of the Zero Hunger Programme at the Citizenship Institute; later advised the Ministry for Food Security and Hunger Eradication (2003–2004).

Zimmerman, Tarcisio—*Brasília, 03/12/08*. Three-time National Congressman. Former Secretary for Transport, Citizenship and Social Assistance during the administration of Olívio Dutra in Rio Grande do Sul (1999–2002); member of the faction Socialist Democracy.

Appendix 3
Answers to Semi-Structured Questions

1. Opinions on the MST

    Number of party leaders who are critical of the MST
    Question: *Are you critical of the MST?/ Do you have criticisms about the MST?*

    Table A3.1

	PT	CNB	MP	AE
Yes	52	24	9	4
No	26	7	6	6
Total	78	31	15	10

    Table A3.2

    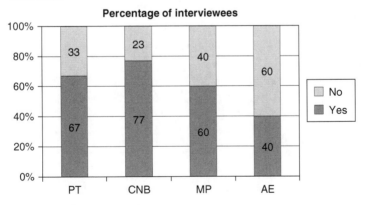

Appendix 3

2. Perceptions on Party–Civil Society Relationships

Number of party leaders who consider that the PT distanced itself from civil society

Question: *Has the PT distanced itself from civil society?*

Table A3.3

	PT	CNB	MP	AE
Yes	62	21	15	7
No	23	17	0	0
Total	85	38	15	7

Table A3.4

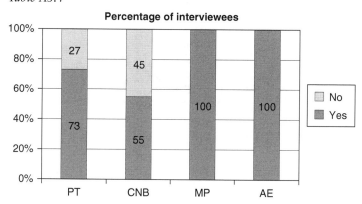

3. Support for Counter-Mobilisation Strategies

Number of party leaders who support counter-hegemonic governability strategies

Question: *Do you think that the PT could have instigated social mobilisation in order to put pressure on Congress and change the balance of forces in its favour?*

Table A3.5

	PT	CNB	MP	AE
Yes	42	8	13	9
No	38	19	4	2
Don't know	12	8	-	-
Total	92	35	17	11

Appendix 3 253

Table A3.6

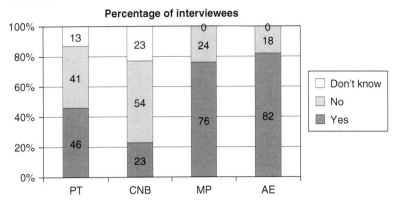

4. Opinions on Economic Policy

Number of party leaders who are in favour of the economic policy of the Lula administration

Question: *Do you agree with the economic policy of the Lula administration?*

Table A3.7

	PT	CNB	MP	AE
Yes	28	13	2	1
No	26	7	3	5
Opposed to monetary policy	16	9	4	1
Total	70	29	9	7

Table A3.8

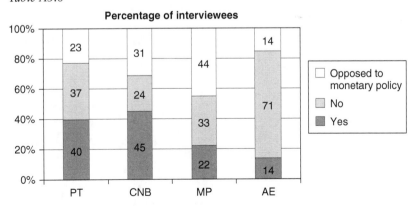

254 Appendix 3

5. Estimations of Progress on Social Participation

Number of party leaders who consider that the Lula administration made progress on participation

Question: *Do you think that participation made progress under the Lula administration?*

Table A3.9

	PT	CNB	MP	AE
Yes	42	24	5	1
No	31	4	12	6
Relative progress	20	10	3	1
Total	93	38	20	8

Table A3.10

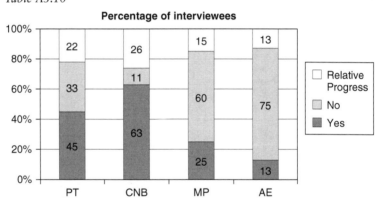

6. Support for a National Participatory Budget

Party leaders who support the establishment of a Participatory Budget at the national level

Question: *Do you support a Participatory Budget at the national level?*

Table A3.11

	PT	CNB	MP	AE
Yes	42	12	15	5
No	25	12	0	1
"It would be difficult"	3	10	2	1
Total	70	34	17	7

Table A3.12

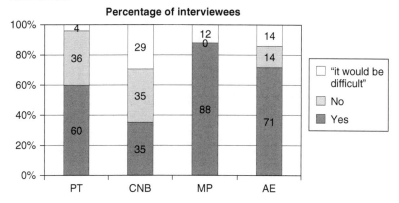

7. **Importance of Land Reform**

Party leaders who consider land reform an important matter
Question: *Is land reform still an important issue on the agenda?*

Table A3.13

	PT	CNB	MP	AE
Yes	62	18	13	10
No	16	11	12	0
Total	78	29	25	10

Table A3.14

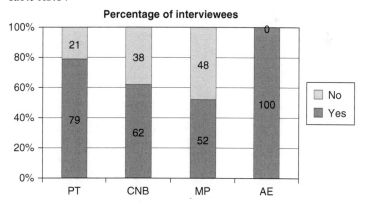

Index

alliances 14, 20, 48, 68, 69, 72, 76, 77, 80, 81, 86, 89, 96, 97, 99–100, 101, 102, 122, 129, 133, 162

Bolsa Família 111, 113, 115, 118, 124–7, 133, 134
Building a New Brazil 8, 49, 47, 55, 58, 114, 120, 128
business groups *see* dominant strategic actors

cash transfer programmes *see Bolsa Família*
church *see* progressive church
civil society 4, 5–6, 8, 17, 19, 20, 28, 29–30, 30–2, 42–59, 64, 103, 136–52, 173–4; approach towards 29–30, 35–7, 39, 47–8, 77, 78–9, 91, 92–3, 98, 111, 118, 124–5, 131, 166, 173–4; autonomy 38, 39, 46, 53, 160
coalition presidentialism 85, 95, 96, 172
Constitutional Assembly 34–5, 38, 45
CONTAG 53, 55–6, 92, 137, 138, 144, 146, 147, 150
co-optation 53–4, 136–7, 144–5, 151, 136–7, 144, 151–2
CUT 8, 17, 33, 36, 37, 46–7, 48, 54, 71, 98, 137, 139; relations with the PT and Lula administration 36, 47, 55–6, 98, 140, 141, 142–3, 144–5, 150, 154–7, 161–2

democratic transition 32–3, 34–5, 38, 41, 45–6

Dirceu, José v, 77, 93, 97, 99, 108, 129, 173
Dutra, Olívio 54, 66, 67, 68, 73–6, 80, 128

economic growth 87, 113, 115, 155, 156
economic policy 9, 10, 143, 148; attitudes towards 107, 114, 115
electoral motivations 3–4, 20, 42, 50, 60, 69, 71–2, 75, 76, 85, 90, 108, 124, 126, 132, 134–5, 157, 165, 166
electoral politics *see* electoral motivations
electoral system *see* political system
Erundina, Luiza 47–8, 52, 63–4, 65–6, 67, 69–72, 73, 76

factions 7, 17, 63–64, 78, 97, 102, 140
financial sector 90, 105–16, 131, 155, 158, 166, 167
fisiologismo see pork-barrelling

governability 3, 6, 13–23, 78, 81, 109, 155; economic 5, 20, 105–16, 131, 157, 158, 163, 166, 172; political 15, 19, 20, 61, 66–8, 68–80, 85–104, 111, 127, 157, 163, 166; social 15, 20, 21, 136–52, 163, 166
governability dilemma 4, 103, 111, 130, 165, 166, 168, 173
governability strategies 17–19, 60–81, 68–80, 86, 97, 101, 107–8, 129–30, 133, 158, 163; elite-centred 4, 18, 69, 76–80, 86, 88, 102, 116, 117, 122,

126, 127, 129, 130, 134–5, 162, 163, 167, 172, 173; social-counter hegemonic 4, 18, 41, 69–76, 77, 78, 81, 86, 88–9, 91–4, 103–4, 116, 117–35, 167, 169
Growth Acceleration Programme 115, 118, 127, 131, 132–4, 166

Housing Movement 9, 39, 47–8, 52, 53, 55–56, 57, 64, 71, 88, 137, 144

inflation 48, 106, 108, 109, 111, 112, 114, 155, 168, 172–3
interest groups *see* strategic actors for governability

labour-based parties *see* socialist parties
labour movement 28, 30, 33, 37
land reform 9, 20, 31, 37, 46, 50, 87, 106–7, 141–2, 143, 147, 148, 151, 153, 157–60, 163; *see also* trade union reform
Left Articulation 8, 49, 55, 88, 92, 94, 102
left-wing parties Latin America 87, 165, 167, 168–70
linkages *see* party linkages
Lula da Silva, Luiz Inázio 151, 157, 158, 159, 160–1, 163, 167–8, 170, 171

Majority Camp 66, 88
mensalão (big monthly payment) *see* political crisis
"Message to the Party" 8, 49, 55, 63, 88, 92, 102, 128, 129
minimum wage 153, 154–7, 163, 173
mobilisation 4, 19, 33, 34, 35–7, 38, 44, 45, 46, 69–71, 72–6, 89, 91, 94, 97–9, 103–4, 121, 123, 138, 139, 156–7, 163, 166, 169, 170
MST 8–9, 17, 21, 33, 36, 37, 44–5, 46, 48–50, 54, 55, 56, 57, 58–9, 71, 88, 99, 137, 139, 141–2, 143, 144, 146, 147–8, 149, 157, 159

national conferences 45, 62, 119–20, 131, 139, 171

PAC *see* Growth Acceleration Programme
Palocci, Antonio 66, 112, 156
parliamentary alliances *see* alliances
participation 4, 128, 30, 39–40, 45, 62, 71, 79, 104, 117–35, 139, 149, 151, 166, 168, 169, 170–1, 172; attitudes towards 30, 33, 35, 39–40, 45, 79, 88, 89, 118, 120, 125, 128, 131, 133, 169
participatory democracy *see* participation
Participatory Budget 60, 62, 71, 72–6, 79–80, 87, 120, 127–8; implementation national level 80, 120, 127–9, 130, 166, 171–2
participatory strategies 71, 73–6, 79–80
party alliances *see* alliances
party linkages 5–6, 21–3, 171; interpersonal 5, 23, 38–9, 57–8, 136, 149–51; programmatic 5, 22, 28, 37, 52, 58, 59, 136–7, 149, 150, 151, 152, 153–64, 170; reward-based 5, 22–3, 50–4, 59, 64, 136–7, 143–9, 151, 152
party-movement relationships 5–6, 21–3, 39, 43, 124, 133–4, 136–52, 170, 173–4
party socio-political field 6, 7
party system Brazil 33, 66–7, 100–1, 167
pension funds system reform 113, 141, 142–3, 145, 156
physiological relationships *see* pork barrelling
political crisis 95, 97, 99, 162, 100–3
political reform 87, 101, 172
political parties 5–6, 13; central office 7, 99; Latin America 21, 27, 29; mass-based 3, 4, 28–9, 166; public office 7, 50–4, 59, 137, 163
political system 3, 19–20, 61, 68–9, 76, 85–6, 88, 94–5
popular councils 40, 73
postdemocratic transition 43–7, 94, 148
pork-barrelling 68–9, 70, 74, 78, 95, 100, 102, 166, 173

progressive church 30–1, 33, 35, 52–3, 125, 126, 140
progressive politics 3, 18, 21–3, 165–74
PRONAF 46, 146–7
PT 1: attitude towards representative democracy 34–5, 38, 41, 43–45, 46, 47, 48, 74, 92, 96, 123, 135; formation 27–30, 31, 39; genetic model 37–40, 41, 43, 56–58, 159, 171; ideology 35; institutionalisation 39; Left 44, 49, 54–55, 56, 63, 73, 88, 92, 93, 99, 111, 128; origins 28–30; presence in rural areas 31, 36, 37; "PT way of governing" 2, 30, 40, 77, 87; socio-political field 30–2, 33, 56–8; 104, 111, 144; *see also* party-movement relationships
public sector unions 64, 142

Rousseff, Dilma 133, 165, 167–8, 171–3

sectoral policy councils 45, 62, 119–20, 122, 131, 139, 171
Socialist Democracy *see* "Message to the Party"
socialist parties 16, 17, 22, 27, 29, 30, 44, 48
social movements 20, 30–2, 33, 70, 71, 91, 98–9, 121; *see also* approach towards civil society; civil society autonomy
state-society relationships 1–2, 28, 29, 33, 39, 42–59, 45–59, 125–6, 139, 149, 152, 160–2, 170–1
state subsidies 46, 52–3, 136, 146–9, 166, 167
strategic actors for governability 15–17, 62–3, 89, 97–8, 130, 131, 153, 166, 167; dominant 16–17, 65–8, 72, 75, 77, 87–90, 96–7, 106–7, 111, 130, 131, 133, 134, 153–64, 167, 168, 169; party's socio-political field 16–17, 63–4, 153
Suplicy, Marta 52, 53, 64, 67, 68, 76–80

tax reform 2, 73–4, 87, 101, 172
technocratic view 18, 79, 118, 132
technocracy *see* technocratic view
technocratic rationales *see* technocratic view
trade union reform 37, 87, 153, 160–2